Success and Failure in Limited War

Success and Failure in Limited War

Information and Strategy in the Korean, Vietnam, Persian Gulf, and Iraq Wars

SPENCER D. BAKICH

The University of Chicago Press

CHICAGO AND LONDON

SPENCER D. BAKICH is assistant professor in the Department of Government and International Affairs at Sweet Briar College.

The University of Chicago Press, Chicago 60637
The University of Chicago Press, Ltd., London
© 2014 by The University of Chicago
All rights reserved. Published 2014.
Printed in the United States of America

23 22 21 20 19 18 17 16 15 14   1 2 3 4 5

ISBN-13: 978-0-226-10768-4 (cloth)
ISBN-13: 978-0-226-10771-4 (paper)
ISBN-13: 978-0-226-10785-1 (e-book)
DOI: 10.7208/chicago/9780226107851.001.0001

Library of Congress Cataloging-in-Publication Data
Bakich, Spencer D., author.
Success and failure in limited war : information and strategy in the Korean, Vietnam, Persian Gulf, and Iraq Wars / Spencer D. Bakich.
pages cm
Includes bibliographical references and index.
ISBN 978-0-226-10768-4 (cloth : alk. paper) — ISBN 978-0-226-10771-4 (pbk. : alk. paper) — ISBN 978-0-226-10785-1 (e-book) 1. United States—History, Military—20th century. 2. United States—History, Military—21st century. 3. Korean War, 1950–1953. 4. Vietnam War, 1961–1975. 5. Persian Gulf War, 1991. 6. Iraq War, 2003–2011. I. Title.
E745.B35 2014
355.00973—dc23
2013022422

♾ This paper meets the requirements of
ANSI/NISO Z39.48-1992 (Permanence of Paper).

Contents

Acknowledgments

No book is written in isolation; or, at least this one wasn't. The debts I have accumulated over the years are substantial, and I am grateful to have worked with, and learned from, truly talented people. The four people to whom I am most indebted are Jeff Legro, John Owen, Dale Copeland, and Mel Leffler. Each of them read multiple manuscript drafts, offered trenchant critiques, and provided me with tremendous support. I could have asked for no finer group of scholars to have worked with. Jeff, in particular, has been a model mentor and colleague of many years; he is honest, demanding, and always encouraging. Many others, of course, read parts of the manuscript and were extraordinarily gracious with their time and focus. In particular, I must thank Allen Lynch who not only read an early draft of the book but also has been a source of steadfast support over my career. Herman Schwartz, Brantly Womack, Mark Haas, Will Waldorf, Eric Cox, David Waldner, Gerard Alexander, and Sophie Richardson provided valuable critical commentary for which I am thankful. Two individuals merit special attention: Kelly Erickson and Dennis Smith. This book would not exist had it not been for their machete work on my earliest ideas and drafts; they were (and are) available at the drop of a hat to hear me out and push back hard. I have no better colleagues and friends than these two. With the exception of Mel Leffler (who is in the Department of History), I crossed paths with all of these fine people in the Department of Politics at the University of Virginia.

I have benefited from the advice and support of many of my colleagues at Sweet Briar College. Most importantly, Steve Bragaw and Padmini Coopamah have been unflagging in their enthusiasm for this project. I could have asked for no finer colleagues, and I cannot thank them enough. Kevin Honeycutt, John Ashbrook, Dan Gottlieb, Janet Steven, Dave Griffith, Claudia Chang, and Lisa Johnston have been similarly supportive. Comments and criticisms from a number of my students over the years have been quite helpful, and I am grateful to Morgan Roach, Caroline Sapp, Sarah Jones, Emily Richonne, Sarah Gray, and Nina Peck for them. Kat Alexander (currently a graduate student at Duke University) did a marvelous job compiling the index. I look forward to many years of intellectual engagement—both cooperative and combative—with her.

While working on the Persian Gulf War and Iraq War chapters, I was fortunate to have had the opportunity to participate in the George H. W. Bush and George W. Bush oral history projects at the Miller Center of Public Affairs at the University of Virginia. While there, I worked with many exceptional people, most notably Russell Riley and Barbara Perry. Barbara is among those on whom I can always count for strong words of encouragement and sage advice. I was fortunate to have been able to use the Miller Center's resources while conducting research for this book, the George H. W. Bush oral history project interviews, in particular. Sheila Blackford at the Miller Center's Scripps Library was tremendously helpful and accommodating, as were the many librarians at UVA's Alderman and Clemons libraries.

When beginning a project like this one, early encouragement can be particularly impactful. I am appreciative of the time that Steve Rosen gave me over a few lunch sessions at the Summer Workshop on the Analysis of Military Operations and Strategy (SWAMOS) in 2001. His encouragement—and the off-the-cuff reading list he gave me—came at just the right time.

Working with the University of Chicago Press has been a wonderful experience. David Pervin showed early interest in this project, and Christie Henry's editorship has been exemplary. Shenyun Wu was of tremendous assistance in all phases of the publication process. Last, but certainly not least, the two anonymous reviewers who read the manuscript in its entirety provided me a treasure of critical comments and suggestions for improvement. I was fortunate to have had the chance to work with them—whoever they are.

I received funding to present selections of this book at multiple conferences from the Faculty Grants Committee at Sweet Briar College. Sections of chapters 2 and 4 appeared in "Institutionalizing Supreme Command: Explaining Political-Military Integration in the Vietnam War, 1964-1968," *Small Wars and Insurgencies* 22 (2011): 688-711.

Finally, and by far most importantly, I owe a debt of gratitude to my family. My mother and father, Kris and Rus Bakich, and my brother, Trent, have given me nothing but pure support throughout my life. I always know they are in my corner, no matter what the situation. My mother- and father-in-law, Ann and Bob Raikes, have been wonderful in their encouragement over the years. My two boys, Aiden and Jack, are my lights; they bring joy to my life every day. Among the sweetest questions I get is, "Daddy, how is your writing coming?" (It is usually followed with, "Daddy, can I use that computer yet?") Finally, to my best friend, partner in crime, and love of my life, Kate. Without her, this book would not have been written. Who she is and what she does are a constant source of inspiration for me. How did I get so lucky? It is to her that this book is dedicated.

Abbreviations

ARVN	Army of the Republic of Vietnam, or South Vietnamese Army
CCF	Chinese Communist Forces
CENTCOM	US Central Command
CFLCC	Combined Forces Land Component Command
CIA	Central Intelligence Agency
CINC	Commander in chief
CINCFE	Commander in chief, Far East Command
CINCUNC	Commander in chief, United Nations Command
COMINT	Communications intelligence
CPA	Coalition Provisional Authority
DC	Deputies Committee
DCI	Director of Central Intelligence
DIA	Defense Intelligence Agency
DOD	Department of Defense
DOS	Department of State
DPRK	Democratic People's Republic of Korea, or North Korea
DRV	Democratic Republic of Vietnam, or North Vietnam
ESG	Executive Steering Group
FEAF	Far East Air Forces
FEC	Far East Command
FOI	Future of Iraq Project
FPDM	Foreign policy decision making
GVN	Government of South Vietnam

IC	Intelligence community
ICAPS	Interdepartmental Coordinating and Planning Staff
IDF	Israel Defense Forces
IMINT	Imagery intelligence
INR	Bureau of Intelligence and Research
IPMC	Iraq Political-Military Cell
IR	International relations
IR+R	Iraq Relief and Reconstruction
ISA	International Security Affairs
ISG	Intelligence Survey Group
JCS	Joint Chiefs of Staff
LOCs	Lines of communication
MACV	Military Assistance Command, Vietnam
MCOs	Major combat operations
NIC	National Intelligence Council
NKPA	North Korean People's Army
NLF	National Liberation Front, or Viet Cong
NSAM	National Security Action Memorandum
NSC	National Security Council
NSD	National Security Directive
NSPD	National Security Presidential Directive
NSS	National Security Strategy of the United States of America
OIR	Office of Intelligence Research
ORE	Office of Reports and Estimates
ORHA	Office of Reconstruction and Humanitarian Assistance
ORR	Office of Research and Reports
OSA	Office of Systems Analysis
OSD	Office of the Secretary of Defense
OSO	Office of Special Operations
OSP	Office of Special Plans
OSS	Office of Strategic Services
OVP	Office of the Vice President
PAVN	People's Army of Vietnam, or North Vietnamese Army
PC	Principals Committee
PCCs	Policy Coordinating Committees
PDB	President's daily brief
PDD	Presidential Decision Directive
PLA	People's Liberation Army

POL	Petroleum, oil, and lubricants
PPBS	Planning, Programming, and Budgeting System
PPS	Policy Planning Staff
PRC	People's Republic of China
PROVN	Program for the Pacification and Long-Term Development of South Vietnam
ROKA	Republic of Korea Army, or South Korean Army
RVN	Republic of Vietnam, or South Vietnam
SAC	Strategic Air Command
SCAP	Supreme commander, Allied Powers
SGCI	Special Group, Counterinsurgency
SIGINT	Signals intelligence
SIOP	Single Integrated Operational Plan
SOF	Special Operations Forces
TFIV	Task Force IV
TPFDL	Time Phased Force Deployment List
UNC	United Nations Command
USAFFE	US Army Forces, Far East
USAID	United States Agency for International Development
VC	Viet Cong, or National Liberation Front
WMD	Weapons of mass destruction

CHAPTER ONE

Information Institutions
and Strategy in War

Despite the label, limited wars are big events. These wars, fought with restraint but at a high level of intensity, are a prominent feature of international political life. Waged by democracies and nondemocracies alike, limited warfare has occurred in all types of international environments. The outcomes of these events, moreover, are of considerable consequence for the states involved and for the broader international system. Among the outcomes of the Crimean War in 1856, for example, were the substantial reductions of Russian power and influence in the system for decades.[1] The series of limited wars known collectively as the "Wars of German Unification" led to dramatic change in the balance of power in Europe by creating for the first time a powerful state in the heart of the Continent.[2] More recently, the costs and consequences of the Iraq War are substantial and widespread not only for the states in the Middle East but also for the state at the apex of a unipolar world, the United States of America.[3] Finally, limited wars are among the most strategically difficult forms of statecraft to prosecute effectively. In particular, states prefer to prosecute limited wars with restraint in order to avoid having these conflicts escalate in ways that undermine the strategic objectives sought. Compounding the problem are the multiple ways in which escalation can occur. Limited wars can scale up in terms of their intensity, can expand to include unwelcomed belligerents, or can be so prolonged that strategic resources are drained in excess. In short, the prevalence, importance, and complexity of limited warfare pose important questions for scholars and policy makers alike. Under what conditions are states able to design and execute limited war strategies that defeat the opponent and avoid escalation *simultaneously*? More generally, when and how are states able to wield power effectively in dynamic and complex international environments?

Due to its importance in international politics since 1945, the United States has found itself at limited war with great frequency. Indeed, America's wars in Korea, Vietnam, the Persian Gulf, and Iraq are among the most significant foreign policy events in the past seven decades. Despite its familiarity with this form of warfare, and notwithstanding the dramatic advantage in raw material power it possessed over each of its opponents, the United States has an uneven track record in waging limited wars. America's limited wars during the Cold War were consequential due in large part to the intensity of the competition between the United States and the Soviet Union. Amid this strategic backdrop, the United States waged war in Korea and Vietnam with the intention of securing what were perceived to be vital national interests. At the same time, American officials understood that these wars had to be controlled, either out of fear that direct superpower conflict might result, or out of the desire to avoid prolonged and costly confrontations that could undermine American security. In the Korean War, the United States failed to avoid escalation by inducing Chinese intervention in November 1950. In the Vietnam War, the United States was able to avoid repeating this fate, but the war dragged on for many years beyond the point that American officials thought desirable. In the post–Cold War era, with American power at its zenith, the United States again found itself at limited war. In both the Persian Gulf and Iraq wars, the United States held objectives that while vital were balanced by the goal of avoiding escalation. In the Persian Gulf War, the United States sought to oust Iraq from Kuwait, but in a manner that was supported by the countries in the region and the great powers in the system. In this effort, America succeeded. In the Iraq War, by contrast, the United States sought to topple the regime of Saddam Hussein and to establish a solid ground for democracy to take root. Only the first objective was secured. In the aftermath of America's conventional military victory, new belligerents joined the war in the form of an insurgency. The United States thus found itself waging war for many years past what was initially expected, at costs far exceeding what was desired.

This checkered track record deserves an explanation. Why was the United States able to succeed across the board in the Persian Gulf War but unable to defeat its opponent and avoid escalation in Korea? Why was the United States able to avoid inducing Chinese intervention in Vietnam but incapable of defeating its primary opponent in South Vietnam? Why was the United States able to achieve a decisive victory over Iraqi forces in a very short period of time only to have that success squandered with the eruption of the Sunni-based insurgency? Given America's position in the world, and the frequency of limited war in international affairs, understanding the sources of American strategic success and failure in its limited wars is of the utmost importance.

My focus in this book is on the strategic sources of America's success and failure in limited war. The extant literature on the effectiveness of strategy in war is, as one would expect, vast and impressive. For decades, scholars have explored an extensive array of potential variables, ranging across levels of analysis, which affect strategic outcomes. Factors such as the distribution of power, the nature of the political regimes of the belligerents, the interaction of military strategy and operations on the battlefield, and even the qualities of executive leadership have all been scrutinized extensively.[4] As insightful as these studies are, a gap remains in our understanding of the sources of strategic success in war. A critical factor, one that is widely seen as being important in matters of strategy, has yet to receive explicit and extensive consideration: *information*. Specifically, in this book I seek answers to two interrelated questions. First, how does information from outside the state affect leaders' abilities to design limited war strategies that are well tailored to complex and dynamic environments? Second, how does information from inside the state enable leaders to ensure that the organizations that prosecute the various aspects of limited war strategies do so in a coordinated fashion?

Such questions about the role of information in statecraft are of course not new to the study of international relations.[5] Surprisingly, however, these two questions have yet to be addressed within a single explanatory framework.[6] I take up this task in this book. In so doing, I develop an original institutional approach that examines how different governmental actors communicate and share information with one another. This approach is novel to the extent that the institutions I examine are not those that international relations (IR) theorists have widely studied. While important insights have been gained in the study of international institutions and domestic political institutions,[7] I argue that it is *information institutions* that affect the nature of strategic design and the behavior of the organizations that execute strategy in times of war.

The crux of my argument is that information institutions directly affect a state's capacity to extract and convert information to perform complex security policies. Specifically, I argue that information flow patterns within governments play a critical role in determining strategic success and failure in limited wars. Properly defined, information institutions are "interconnected communications channels for receiving information from the environment, for processing that information to serve specific objectives, and for sending internal and external messages."[8] This approach postulates that when top policy makers have access to multiple sources of information, and when national security organizations are connected to one another by dense information channels, the chances for strategic success in limited wars increase dramatically. Conversely, when top policy makers have access to very few sources of information, and when national security organizations operate in isolation from one another, the chances of overall success in limited war decrease. I argue that the information institutions have two effects on the quality of limited war strategies. First, information flow patterns affect leaders' ability to understand the complex strategic environments in which they are acting. Second, these patterns determine the degree of coordination between the military and diplomatic aspects of the limited war strategies. The "information collection and analysis" and "military and diplomatic coordination" mechanisms combine in ways that profoundly influence the ability of states to understand their environments and act effectively in them.

My aim is to provide an information-based explanation of the sources of strategic success and failure in limited war. To accomplish this, it is necessary to firmly establish the theoretical foundations on which my argument rests. On what conceptual bases do I make my claims that information institutions exist? What are the differences between individuals, organizations, and institutions? How do information flow patterns structure the relationships among relevant state-level actors? And, when are information institutions likely to exert influence over strategy design and execution?

STRATEGIC DECISION MAKING AND THE PROBLEM OF INFORMATION

In order to design and implement effective national security policies, leaders must clearly understand the Janus-faced nature of strategy, a problem identified centuries ago by the Chinese military theorist Sun Tzu, "He who knows the enemy and himself / Will never in a hundred battles be at risk."[9] In the modern context, the outcomes of strategy in war are affected by state capacities to acquire and exploit information about the enemy and the strategic situation in which a war will unfold as well as information about the organizations that implement the adopted strategy. When formulating national security policies in complex strategic environments, leaders must be able to understand in depth the nature of that environment. When acting in such environments, leaders must be able to ensure that various national security organizations work in concert and with an eye to the common objective sought. Failure in either domain, analysis or coordination, can have profoundly negative security implications for the state.

These information-based problems have not gone unnoticed by scholars, and to a considerable extent information plays a prominent role in many arguments, across all levels of analysis, on the origins and the outcomes of strategy. At the systemic level of analysis, rationalist strategic choice theory (or, bargaining theory) sees information problems as being central in all aspects of war. Bargaining theory maintains that the onset and termination of war are strongly conditioned by uncertainty about the opponents' relative power and resolve, and the revelation of information from fighting, respectively.[10] This approach underscores the importance of international communication in explaining how states interact in times of conflict, specifically, the ability and willingness of states to offer credible commitments. Bargaining theory postulates that states are best able to modify the behavior of their opponent when the signals they send are costly.[11] Further, as more information about the opponent is revealed during times of conflict, this approach holds that states will update their strategies to reflect the newly revised understanding of the strategic environment.[12]

With respect to the outcomes of strategy, bargaining theory focuses exclusive theoretical attention on endogenous information, or the information revealed once states interact on the battlefield.[13] Yet because scant theoretical attention is devoted to the role of exogenous information (to states' capacities to extract and convert information into their strategies before they interact on the battlefield) this approach cannot explain why some states are able to achieve their strategic objectives early in war while others are not, ceteris paribus. For example, in designing its air campaign against North Vietnam, the United States was able to accurately determine Chinese intentions *well before* Beijing sent anything approximating a credible or costly signal to Washington. The ability to know the conditions under which China would enter in the Vietnam War early on, before explicit signals were sent, allowed the United States to design a strategy that prevented the very real possibility of China's intervention.[14] In this case, rationalist approaches are incapable of explaining how the United States was able to reach this accurate conclusion in the absence of a credible signal.

At most, rationalist approaches recognize that information asymmetries among the belligerents play an important role in the conflict process. But the nature of a given state's uncertainty is critical. For rationalism to offer compelling causal explanations for strategic outcomes in war, information asymmetries must result strictly from private information, information the opponent holds that is truly unknowable to the state. Information that is widely available, but which goes unrecognized by the state, is not private per se. States must be able to learn from and adapt to new information. A state's inability to do so constitutes a substantial challenge to a rationalist explanation of strategic outcomes in war. As David Lake argues, rationalist approaches are blind to the domestic-level information processing failures that prevented learning (that is, rational updating) by American policy makers before and during the Iraq War. These deviations from rationality directly affected the ability of the United States to contemplate and then adequately plan for postwar occupational challenges.[15]

Ultimately, rationalist approaches offer compelling explanations of strategic outcomes in war when information asymmetries result only from private, or truly unknowable, information and when the states involved are immune from breakdowns in information processing. The problem is that these approaches lack the analytical tools to differentiate between unknowable and unrecognized information and to identify which states do and do not meet the criteria of "rationality." As Charles Glaser notes, explanations of the sources of strategic choice are essential components of the rationalist approach.[16] With respect to information, rationalist approaches are without a foundation.

At the individual level of analysis, scholars of individual and group psychology have examined numerous obstacles that prevent leaders from effectively managing large volumes of information as they make strategic decisions.[17] Building on the insights of these psychological studies, scholars in the foreign policy decision making (FPDM) school argue that the decision-making processes leaders and their advisers adopt can have a considerable impact on whether policy and strategy are adversely affected by these pathologies.[18] Importantly, studies find that not all decision-making groups devolve into dysfunction; under certain conditions, "vigilant problem solving" by decision-making groups is possible. Moreover, some of the same groups examined performed quite well in certain episodes of strategic decision making, but poorly in others.[19] Recently, Mark Schafer and Scott Crichlow confirmed these findings, concluding that "structural [that is, procedural] faults were consistently the most powerful predictor of outcomes in terms of national interest—fewer structural faults in the decision-making process apparatus lead to better national interests."[20]

Nevertheless, this approach suffers from two broad problems with respect to information processing at the highest level. First, because the information that leaders must consider when designing strategy originates from organizations outside the group, any approach that systematically excludes those organizations from analytical scrutiny can only provide incomplete explanations of how information affects the strategic decision-making process. For example, President Truman's understanding of the strategic situation in Korea was profoundly (if not completely) dependent upon information General Douglas MacArthur's UN Command provided to Washington.[21] Yet MacArthur's command and intelligence organization were riddled with information processing pathologies that even the most vigilant group of top policy makers in Washington could not have overcome. Notwithstanding the importance of the process of decision making among small groups of individuals at the apex of the state, approaches that focus narrowly on those groups cannot account for the quality of the information before leaders.

Second, because leaders do not themselves execute strategy, any approach that truncates its analysis by excluding state-level organizations will not be able to understand how new information affects strategic decision making. President George H. W. Bush and his top advisers were able to exploit a wealth of strategic information from the national security apparatus as the military and diplomatic campaigns of the Persian Gulf War unfolded.[22] How information was collected from their subordinate organizations, analyzed by policy makers, and then exploited by different state-level actors prior to and during the war was critical to its outcome. Thus a satisfactory explanation of how information affects strategic decision making and implementation requires that our analysis include the organizations that provide information and implement policy, as well as decision makers at the apex of the state.

In sum, prominent approaches at the systemic and individual levels of analysis offer incomplete explanations for how information affects strategic choice and the outcomes of strategy in war. To overcome these limitations, to better understand the role information plays in the design and execution of strategy, it is necessary to consider the role of information at the level of the state, specifically within governments. To do so, three crucial concepts must be addressed: organizations, institutions, and the distribution of information across relevant actors.

ORGANIZATIONS VERSUS INSTITUTIONS

A first cut for understanding how information affects strategic design and implementation requires a consideration of the relationship between state-level organizations and the institutions in which they are embedded. According to Helen Milner, "institutions [are] socially accepted constraints or rules that shape human interaction; in contrast . . . [organizations] are agents rather than structures."[23] To the extent that the design and implementation of national security strategy entails multiple organizations within the state providing information to top policy makers, and acting to achieve specific objectives, our focus must then be directed toward the institutional settings in which strategy originates. In other words, limited war strategies are not the products of single organizations but rather of many organizations working and communicating with one another. Recognizing this distinction between organizations and institutions is critical for two reasons. First, because my focus is on the institutional setting of strategic decision making, it is necessary to separate state-level actors from the constraints and rules in which they operate. "Separating the analysis of the underlying rules from the strategy of the players is a necessary prerequisite to building a theory of institutions."[24] Second, as Douglass North argues, the behavior of organizations is powerfully affected by the institutional setting in which they are embedded.

> The organizations that come into existence will reflect the opportunities provided by the institutional matrix. That is, if the institutional framework rewards piracy, then piratical organizations will come into existence; and if the institutional framework rewards productive activities, then organizations—firms—will come into existence to engage in productive activities.[25]

The general understanding of the relationship between institutions and organizations many institutional economists hold is, thus, causal where different forms of institutional settings generate different types of organizational behaviors.[26]

This understanding of the relationship between institutions and organizations, it must be noted, is not held by organizational theory within IR scholarship. Traditionally, organizational theory has focused on the hierarchically arranged, yet distinct, corporate entities that constitute the state or government.[27] Organizational theory views organizations as actors with their own set of preferences, modes of behavior, and worldviews. Graham Allison and other traditional organizational theorists explain foreign policy outcomes by focusing on individual organizations and then comparing observed outcomes to a rational baseline, one that is stipulated to be the ideal mode of strategic choice for the state as a whole. After decades of research, traditional organizational theory has reached startlingly pessimistic conclusions about the ability of states to behave purposively and rationally. Organizations have been found to deviate systematically from top policy makers' preferences, to act less nimbly and adaptively than is required by them, and to view the world more narrowly than leaders prefer and need.[28]

Such pessimistic conclusions result from a common assumption scholars of traditional organizational theory hold, that organizations themselves constitute the primary actors in foreign policy. In other words, traditional organizational theory largely ignores how the relationships among organizations and leaders can be differently structured, or institutionalized. Numerous studies have demonstrated that leaders have far more flexibility in conceiving, designing, and implementing security policies than traditional organizational theory suggests.[29] Leaders act through their organizations, and much of what leaders know about the world is influenced by them—sometimes detrimentally, but sometimes productively. Capturing this variation requires a theoretical lens that focuses on the rules and constraints that establish how organizations relate to each other and to top policy makers.

Furthermore, the outcomes of security policies result from international interactions. Whether military operations or diplomatic missions succeed or fail depends on the interaction between states. Yet traditional organizational theory purports to explain outcomes by focusing solely on the behavior of a single state. As Arthur Stein argues,

> By failing to incorporate any sense of international interaction, this [organizational] approach . . . fails to provide any sense that decisions and calculations come in response to, or in a context of, an ongoing relationship that constrains and shapes interests, choices, and behavior. Instead, agencies are seen as automata that employ standard operating procedures and, as a result, respond similarly to comparable situations . . . people and organizations within a nation interact with one another but are not seen as having any relationships with or any ability to calculate strategy toward other nations.[30]

The primary problem here is that according to the traditional understanding of organizations, national security agencies act solely according to internal motivations, not according to the strategic demands of national security policy. Of course, it is possible that agencies can turn inward and disregard the broader environment in which they operate.[31] It is also possible that they are highly attuned to the demands of leaders and of the international environment. In the end, traditional organizational theory cannot systematically account for this type of variation because it largely ignores the institutional setting in which state-level organizations operate.

In order to address the limitations of the traditional approach, recent contributions to organizational theory have examined the relationship between organizations and institutions directly. According to this approach, governments are not viewed as a collection of organizations that are hierarchically situated, but rather as hierarchical organizations themselves, where different functional and geographic divisions within the broader organization relate to one another in different ways.[32] Based on the pioneering work of Alfred Chandler and Oliver Williamson in the field of management studies, Alexander Cooley examined the organizational structures of hierarchies in terms of "unified" and "multidivisional" forms.[33] Generally, this approach understands institutional patterns among divisions as being determined by the particular hierarchical form of the organization. As Cooley describes, "the U-form organizes its periphery according to distinct administrative functions (such as sales, manufacturing, and finance), which require integration and coordination by the center for the whole range of products produced by the firm."[34] The U-form, which best typifies the modern centralized state, results in a particular set of institutional relationships among core executives and functional divisions. Specifically, three institutional patterns emerge in the unified organizational form. First, in terms of information flows, functional divisions (for example, the Departments of State and Defense) and core executives (for example, presidents) share a great deal of information with each other, while little to no information is shared at lower levels (directly between State and Defense). As a result of this institutional pattern, an increasing number of activities or policies that the state enacts necessarily results in information processing problems for top policy makers. Second, top policy makers tend to suffer from high "governance costs" (costs associated with ensuring coordination) over their functional divisions. Finally, this hierarchical organizational form exhibits a tendency toward "departmentalism" (the elevation of the department's operational subgoals over the overall best interest of the organization by departmental managers). As a result, the quality of strategic design is impaired by the substitution of leaders' preferences with those of subordinate divisions.[35]

The benefit of this hierarchical approach to organization theory is that, unlike the traditional variant, the institutionalized relationships among important actors (top policy makers and their subordinate departments) play a significant role in explaining strategic outcomes. At the same time, however, this approach runs into a significant empirical obstacle: within the unified form, the organizational structure best approximating modern centralized states, there has been wide variation in the institutional patterns of information flows, governance costs, and departmentalism. While much of Cooley's predicted outcomes are evident in the Truman administration's management of the Korean War, the pattern of information flows, level of governance costs, and degree of departmentalism all contradict that which Cooley's model anticipates in the Bush administration's management of the Persian Gulf War.[36] In the end, such variations cannot be explained by the deterministic logic of hierarchical organizational structures as it pertains to institutionalized relationships among top policy makers and subordinate departments.

In sum, both traditional and hierarchical organizational theories make the case that organizations as agents need to be incorporated into any explanation for the outcomes of strategy. At the same time, neither approach adequately models the relationships among top policy makers and national security organizations. The traditional approach runs into problems due to its failure to systematically examine the institutional relationships between organizations and their leaders. Hierarchical organizational theory attempts to overcome this deficiency, but errs by failing to capture the potential variation in institutional patterns that can emerge in a single organizational form. To make sense of how organizations affect strategic outcomes, we need to reconceptualize the relationship between institutions and organizations, specifically in terms of how strategy is designed and then executed. To do so, I argue, requires that we examine the different institutional settings in which leaders and national security organizations are situated.

INSTITUTIONS VERSUS INFORMATION

IR theory typically treats institutions and information as distinct and causally related entities. Neoliberal institutionalism, for example, posits that international institutions provide member states with greater amounts of information than they otherwise would be able to obtain. As a result of transparency, institutions are able to ameliorate the pernicious effects that uncertainty has on interstate relations.[37] In her study of the domestic sources of international cooperation, Milner also conceives of institutions and information as being separate variables that in combination affect the relationship between executives and legislatures. For Milner, the distinction between institutions and information is necessary and correct because her study examines the relationship between actors who have *shared policy authority*. In each of the cases considered in Milner's study, legislatures possessed ratification authority over the treaties that the executives negotiated with their foreign counterparts. Domestic political institutions determined the extent of power sharing over policy, while the distribution of information between actors influenced the efficiency of outcomes and the relative influence each branch had over policy.[38]

The relationship between institutions and information is very different, however, when a given actor has a *monopoly of policy authority*, as is the case in the design and implementation of limited war strategies. Because executives have the final word in determining how a war will be waged, authority is concentrated and not shared in a meaningful sense.[39] Moreover, while functional differences exist among national security organizations, their relative influence over strategy is ultimately a matter of executive discretion, and the extent of that influence can vary widely.[40] To explain this potential variation, theoretical attention needs to be placed on how the interactions among agents under executive authority are structured. The relative degree of influence that any agent has is ultimately determined by the distribution of information among top policy makers and their subordinate national security organizations. For example, if a given organization possesses an information advantage over the executive and its organizational counterparts, then that organization will have far greater influence in strategic decision making and implementation. The distribution of information, in turn, is conditioned by the information flow patterns that connect the relevant actors to one another. In other words, the pattern of information flow constitutes the institutional framework of relationships within the national security apparatus.[41]

Specifically, information flow patterns among leaders and national security organizations have two institutional effects. The first pertains to the processes by which preferences are aggregated and adjudicated domestically.[42] Under certain patterns, the preferences of top policy makers will guide design and execution of strategy. Under other patterns, the preferences of particular organizations will dominate and have corresponding effects on strategic design and implementation. In all cases, information flow patterns will establish whose preferences guide strategic decision making in national security policy. The second type of institutional effect information flow patterns exert concerns the ability of top policy makers to extract and convert resources from within the state,[43] in this case information from state-level organizations. Under certain information flow patterns, leaders will be able to extract and convert a substantial amount of information, while in other patterns information will go unmobilized. In the former case, leaders will be better able to design precise and coordinated policies; in the latter, leaders become increasingly beholden to their subordinates who benefit from insurmountable short-term information asymmetries. In all cases, information flow determines the degree of strategic sophistication of the state as it designs national security policies.

Information asymmetries confer power and influence on those privileged. By examining the pattern of information flows among top policy makers and their national security organizations—information institutions—we can not only arrive at a deeper understanding of how particular strategies are designed, but also of the likelihood of strategic success in limited war. Because they determine how top policy makers receive information from their national security organizations, information institutions affect both the degree of departmentalism and the governance costs involved in the design and execution of strategy. Information institutions that reduce departmentalism by enabling top policy makers to square departmental preference with information about the strategic environment will reduce the chances of policy errors excessively biased analyses cause. Further, information institutions that reduce governance costs and facilitate military and diplomatic coordination will similarly reduce the chance of policy failures due to excessive organizational parochialism. In short, the institutional relationships among top policy makers and national security organizations must be examined with an eye toward the different ways these actors share information. The pattern of information flows among them will, I argue, directly affect the extent to which the state knows its enemy and itself in limited warfare.

THE SALIENCE OF INFORMATION INSTITUTIONS

One should not conclude from the preceding analysis that domestic political institutions are irrelevant, or that the effects of information institutions will always prevail, in every domain of national security policy. To the contrary, the literature on domestic political institutions and foreign policy is vast, offering compelling perspectives and numerous examples of how domestic politics directly affects important aspects of foreign policy.[44] Domestic political institutions have been shown to have significant effects on how leaders evaluate threats from abroad,[45] the nature and content of grand strategy,[46] the efficiency of power balancing behavior,[47] and the ability of militaries to make appropriate doctrinal adjustments.[48] What is at issue, rather, is when information institutions are likely to be more salient than domestic political institutions in their influences on national security policy.

As discussed above, information institutions will prevail over other domestic institutions in their effects on national security policy when executives monopolize policy authority. Two factors determine when policy authority is monopolized and when other political bodies or branches will share it. The first is the designation to executives the authority to direct the state's national security organizations, including the armed forces. If the executive does not have the authority to direct all of the relevant national security organizations, then other political bodies will have influence on the content of the state's national security policy.[49] The second is the immediacy of the threat that the particular national security policy is designed to address. Issues such as foreign economic policy, the terms of international treaty obligations, and the allocation of budgetary resources to national security organizations are all heavily influenced by both legislatures and executives.[50] The design and execution of limited war strategy, on the other hand, is a policy domain that satisfies both criteria for monopolized policy authority, especially in modern democracies. In most cases, executives are vested with the power to make war (if not to declare it in the first place). In addition to the conduct of diplomacy, the direction of the armed forces ensures that executives possess authority over all relevant national security organizations. And because of the size and immediacy of the stakes involved, it is executives who assume responsibility for the conduct of warfare (limited, or otherwise), often with little consideration given to other political bodies.[51]

THE STAKES FOR THEORY AND POLICY

The information institution approach developed in this book has significant implications for IR theory and for policy. Because of its attention to the information extraction and conversion capacities of states, my argument enables information to be treated as a truly independent and exogenous variable. That is, information can be seen as causing strategic choice, rather than only being an endogenous element of state interaction, or simply a byproduct of power. To be sure, rationalist strategic choice theory has shown that the information states reveal in the process of interaction has important effects on state behavior in highly competitive settings.[52] Yet without a prior understanding of the capacities of states to extract and convert information, their ability to understand the international environment and use that information to design strategies prior to interaction, information cannot be understood as *directly* affecting strategic choice. Realist scholars have long shown that different capacities of resource extraction and conversion determine the relative power of states in the system.[53] In the same way, the different capacities of states to extract and convert information can be understood as determining the "strategic sophistication" of states in the system. The information institution approach provides a deeper understanding of how and when states can wield power effectively in a competitive international system.

In particular, the information institution approach can be fruitfully applied to explain outcomes that run contrary to the expectations of many realist arguments concerning the outcomes of war. In general, realism postulates that states possessing superior military power are likely to prevail in limited wars because they are better able to select when wars occur and are able to devote sufficient resources to the war effort.[54] More specifically, when a state has preponderant power, escalation pressures are more likely to be checked through intrawar deterrence.[55] Since World War II, the United States has waged numerous limited wars against much weaker opponents, yet America's record in these wars has been mixed: in both the Korean and Persian Gulf wars, the United States confronted opponents that were militarily inferior, but only in the latter war was the United States able to avoid escalation while securing its primary military objective. In short, realism runs into significant problems in dealing with variations in limited war outcomes even in cases of dramatic power asymmetry. The information institution approach goes a long way in explaining how even the most powerful of states can be hamstrung when facing substantially weaker powers.

Additionally, a focus on information institutions can better establish the bridge between the literatures on decision making and security studies. Generally, studies of foreign policy decision making seek to explain the process and content of policy choices.[56] While such a focus generates critical insights into how decisions are made, the conclusions pertaining to foreign policy outcomes are at best suggestive. Security studies tend to focus on varying degrees of uncertainty facing states, but in a way that does not fully appreciate how information processing affects strategic design and execution.[57] Given the widespread understanding in the post-9/11 era that information collection, analysis, and sharing is essential to state security, this gap is all the more surprising.[58] My argument seeks to fill this lacuna by establishing a direct connection between the process of decision making and the strategic outcomes in limited war. As discussed, existing arguments regarding the effects of national security organizations on strategy formulation and implementation are limited either by excessively pessimistic expectations or by an inability to capture the variation in institutional relationships among top policy makers and their organizations. My approach offers a productive alternative view of how governments process information and behave in strategic contexts.

Due in large part to the evident role that militaries play in strategic matters, it is not surprising that the literature on civil-military relations has been employed to explain the outcomes of strategy in war. Yet this book reveals that central arguments in the civil-military relations literature are incapable of explaining strategic outcomes in limited war. In particular, I find that the information institution approach performs better in direct tests against two prominent variants in the literature on civil-military relations: those focusing on military organizational cultures and those examining the power and preference relationships between leaders and militaries in democratic states. Both of these approaches are important alternative explanations to my argument because of the role that information plays in their explanatory frameworks.

The organizational culture approach holds that the content of warfighting philosophies of professional militaries strongly conditions the way in which states prosecute limited wars.[59] Military organizational cultures are argued to have this effect in times of war because state leaders come to see military organizations as being more salient than other types of organizations.[60] I find that in some cases (most notably Korea and in the ground campaign in Vietnam) the organizational culture approach fares well. In other cases (the air campaign in Vietnam, the Persian Gulf War, and the Iraq War), military organizational culture had little effect on the content of strategy and the manner in which those strategies were executed. Indeed, I show that the conditions under which military organizational culture influences limited war strategies are themselves determined by the particular features of the information institutions present in each case.

Studies that examine the particular nature of civil-military relations in democratic states contend that the quality of limited war strategies is greatly affected by the political-military balance of power within states, and the degree to which political-military preferences diverge.[61] A hallmark of democratic governance is political domination of military organizations. The postulated effect of political domination is fluid information flows among leaders and top military officers.[62] Further, when political-military preferences converge, strategic coordination is anticipated; when political-military preferences diverge, strategic coordination is expected to suffer. My findings show that this explanation fares poorly in most instances. Despite the constancy of political domination, information exchange between the military and civilian leadership varied widely across the cases considered here. And in some cases where political-military preferences diverged profoundly (for example, in the air campaign in Vietnam and in the Persian Gulf War), strategic coordination was nevertheless tight.

In short, neither military organizational cultures nor the political institutions of democracies explain the strategic outcomes of America's limited wars as well as the information institution approach. The primary reason for the weak performance of the civil-military relations literature is its relatively narrow analytical focus. Limited wars are complex events, entailing political, diplomatic, and military dynamics. As such, effective strategic decision making entails more than the communications between top policy makers and their military officers. Information from multiple organizational sources is essential to the overall success in limited war strategies. Because of its relatively broader analytical focus, the information institution approach is better positioned to explain the capacities of states to perform on multiple "fronts" during wartime.

My argument has at least three implications for policy. The first is that given the inherent difficulties in achieving overall success in limited wars, states should approach them with a substantial dose of caution. At minimum, this study should serve as an antidote to the pervasive optimism that has informed America's use of force in the era of unipolarity. A second implication pertains to the sources of information that leaders should avail themselves of when considering the use of force. If policy makers take one thing from this book, it is this: no national security agency should be left to starve out in the cold. Strategically important information comes from military, foreign service, and intelligence officers alike. How these individuals and their agencies relate to one another, and to their leaders, is a vital matter of statecraft. Finally, in order for states to use all of their resources effectively in statecraft (a strategy popularized by the label "smart power"), sound information institutions at the domestic level must be in place. In an era of power transitions and power diffusions, the ability of the United States to act intelligently will depend on how strategic information is managed and used in the coming decades.[63] The ability to conduct effective strategic planning in the future will turn on the extent to which interagency relationships are institutionalized. Since 2005, American national security officials have undertaken efforts to break down "information stovepipes" and have endeavored to more fully institutionalize the interagency process.[64] The information institution approach confirms the wisdom of these reform efforts by demonstrating what can happen if such reforms are allowed to languish.

THE ROAD AHEAD

Thus far, my objective has been to make the case that the outcomes of limited warfare are worthy of study, and that the pattern of information flows among top policy makers and national security organizations are likely to significantly affect how a state fares strategically in war. The task directly ahead is to make that argument explicit and to subject it to rigorous empirical tests. In the chapter that follows, I specify in detail the nature of this study's critical variables and establish the logical connections between them. Chapter 2 begins with a typology of warfare that situates limited war in between major and small wars. This discussion makes clear that the defining feature of limited wars is their inherent tendency to escalate. I then lay out the information institutional argument for the origins of strategic success and failure in limited war. The chapter concludes with discussions of the two alternative explanations drawn from the civil-military relations literature, and the nature of the methodology that drives the remainder of the study.

Chapters 3-6 provide an in-depth examination of my argument in the Korean, Vietnam, Persian Gulf, and Iraq wars. These chapters are structured in the following manner. First, I provide a brief narrative of the each war to show whether the United States succeeded or failed (or something in between) in achieving its military and diplomatic objectives. Second, I describe the pattern of information flows among top policy makers and their national security organizations prior to the outbreak of each war. Third, to test the causal logic of my argument, I process-trace American strategic decision making, paying particular attention to the quality of information collection and analysis and the degree of military-diplomatic coordination exhibited in each case of limited war. Finally, I conclude each empirical chapter by assessing the explanatory logic of the information institution approach compared to the alternative explanations. In the final chapter, I provide a summary of the conclusions of this study and discuss in greater detail the broader theoretical and policy relevant implications of the information institution approach.

CHAPTER TWO

Explaining Strategic Performance
in Limited Warfare

Understanding the sources and quality of strategic performance in limited warfare requires an explanation of how information flow patterns structure the relationships among top policy makers and national security organizations within governments. Some may object to this approach on the grounds that material power alone suffices to account for the outcomes of war, limited or otherwise. Others may object on the grounds that uncertainty is both pervasive and pernicious at the start of all wars, and that strategic success and failure can only be determined by information that is made evident in the course of fighting. These arguments are wrong in many important respects. More powerful belligerents do not always win their wars. Indeed, America's track record in limited war demonstrates this quite clearly. And, while complete and perfect information about a state's opponents is never possible in highly competitive anarchic settings, sufficient information often does exist to enable states to devise sophisticated and effective strategic approaches *ex ante*—that is, before the first shots in war are fired.

How then do information institutions influence limited war strategies? To answer this question, I will begin at the end of the causal chain, with limited warfare itself. In the first section of this chapter, I describe in detail what limited wars are (and are not), and how states approach them strategically. Next, I will describe the functions that information plays in limited war strategies. Third, I present my information institution argument by examining how information flow patterns structure the relationships among top policy makers and national security organizations, and how those institutional patterns, in turn, affect strategy. I then consider two competing explanations for strategic success and failure in limited war drawn from the literature on wartime civil-military relations. This chapter concludes with a discussion of how I evaluate my information institution argument against its competitors and the history of America at limited war.

STRATEGIC SUCCESS AND FAILURE IN LIMITED WAR

Given its importance, the subject of limited war has been the topic of much debate among international relations (IR) scholars. The result of these debates, however, has been the proliferation of murky concepts and a blurring of the essential nature of this type of war. This section seeks to clarify matters by defining limited wars more precisely. To do so, I offer a typology that distinguishes different types of wars according to their scale and scope. Further, I argue that properly understood, limited war strategy incorporates all of the components involved in the war effort, not simply the military aspect. Ultimately, the defining feature of limited war is the inherent potential of escalation. Limited war strategies seek to obtain a state's military objectives while simultaneously controlling the pressures of escalation.

A Typology of War

Interstate wars can be differentiated along two dimensions. First, the *scale* of war pertains to the intensity with which the belligerents fight and the degree of military mobilization that countries commit to the effort. Second, the *scope* of war looks at the number of belligerents that are involved (or likely to become involved) in the conflict. My intention in differentiating among interstate wars along these dimensions is to establish a concept that puts the strategic logic of limited war in stark relief. Other typologies of war are possible, of course. This one shows how limited wars differ from "major wars" and "small wars" in their inherent tendency to escalate dramatically.

In terms of their scale, major wars are conflicts fought at the highest level of intensity with states committing to full military mobilization. In terms of scope, major wars include all of the great powers in a system. Combined, the scale and scope of major wars generate existential stakes for the countries involved. As Dale Copeland argues, major wars "contain a strong possibility that one or more of the contending great powers could be eliminated as sovereign states."[1] As major wars are all-out contests fought for existential aims, the problem of escalation is not among their defining features.[2] Examples of major wars are the Napoleonic wars and the two world wars.

The scale of small wars, on the other hand, is exceptionally modest, entailing minimal mobilization commitments for the state. The scope of small wars is highly restricted because they are prosecuted to influence the policies (internal or foreign) of lesser powers in the system.[3] Small wars are waged for interests far below that which could be deemed "vital" for a great power, and as such, the chances of dramatic escalation are small. Examples of small wars include "Plan Colombia," waged jointly by the United States and the Colombian government; the American intervention in Haiti (1994); and the American intervention in Somalia (1992–93).

In between these two extremes lies limited warfare. Limited wars contain both positive and negative aspects. On the one hand, limited wars entail a substantial commitment of a state's military and diplomatic resources to the conflict, the aims of which are considered vital to the security of the state. Because of the importance of the stakes involved, and the relatively high intensity of the effort required to achieve those objectives, both actual and potential enemies will be pressured to respond to the initiating state. As a result, while these wars are waged at a high level of intensity, the initiating state will attempt to prosecute them with restraint in order to avoid undesired escalation.[4] Conceptually, limited wars embody a tension: a substantial, but restrained commitment of resources to achieve vital, but not existential objectives.[5] It is this tension that generates the inherent possibility of escalation that characterizes limited war, and which distinguishes limited wars from major and small wars.

Limited wars are a product of state interaction, one where escalation constitutes the primary challenge to the achievement of the state's ultimate objectives. As Richard Smoke argues, "limited war and escalation are co-extensive: neither is 'larger' as an idea, or encountered more frequently in reality, than the other. But *limited war* is the static term; *escalation* is the dynamic term."[6] In this view, limited wars are structured by "saliencies," or thresholds, the crossing of which constitutes an escalation of the war.[7] The challenge in waging limited war is understanding where those thresholds lie and designing limited war strategies that work within the structure of the conflict. Strategic success in limited war requires an approach that is finely tuned to achieving both the state's military objectives and to avoiding undesired escalation.

Undesired escalation in limited war can come in three forms. The vast majority of the limited war scholarship, written during the Cold War, concentrates on vertical escalation, or the intensity with which the war is waged. Cold War limited war theory was dedicated to understanding how a localized conventional war between the United States and the Soviet Union could escalate in its intensity to a situation of all-out nuclear war.[8] Scholars of horizontal escalation attempt to explain the conditions under which wars fought between or among an initial set of belligerents can expand to include additional belligerents.[9] These additional belligerents can be other states, transnational actors, or previously unmobilized elements of the target's society. A third type of escalation is that of a war's duration. In this case, the state finds itself in a position where it must continue to fight at the current level of intensity for a period of time beyond which it initially thought necessary and desirable.[10] While each of these forms of escalation is conceptually distinct, they can interact in ways that pose significant obstacles to achieving ultimate victory.

The American experience of limited warfare after the Second World War has been plagued by the problem of undesired escalation. In the Korean War, the United States attempted to "roll back" communism on the Korean Peninsula by seeking the destruction of North Korea in the fall of 1950. By widening its war aims from the restoration of the status quo ante to that of unification, the United States convinced China that its physical security was under threat, and China intervened in force. In this case, the limited war escalated horizontally, and as a result, the war dragged on far longer, cost substantially more, and ran significantly larger strategic risks than American policy makers desired. In the Vietnam War, the United States sought to preserve the viability of a noncommunist South Vietnam. Toward that end, the United States waged a ground campaign in South Vietnam and an air campaign against North Vietnam. While the air campaign ran the risk of inducing a second round of Chinese intervention, horizontal escalation was avoided. However, the United States was unable to defeat the forces hostile to the government of South Vietnam. In this case, the United States experienced durational escalation of the war.

In terms of achieving its military objectives and controlling escalation, two American limited wars of the post–Cold War era stand in marked contrast. In the Persian Gulf War, the United States sought to carefully construct the strategic environment so that the war to oust Iraq from Kuwait would not expand to include Israel and the Arab states. To achieve this, a broad coalition was constructed, political objectives were efficiently translated into military operations, and pressures to expand American war aims were kept in check. The Persian Gulf War is remarkable to the extent that American military objectives were achieved and escalation was avoided. The Iraq War proved to be far less successful. While the regime of Saddam

Hussein was toppled in short order, American actions induced horizontal escalation by generating an insurgency from within Iraq's Sunni population. Again, horizontal escalation induced durational escalation, resulting in a massive expansion of resources (both blood and treasure) committed to the conflict.

As each of these American limited wars reveals, escalation can come in different forms, and these different forms can interact. The central challenge for a state is the design of a sophisticated approach that maximizes the probability of achieving its military objectives and which minimizes the probability of escalation. A state must identify the possible escalation thresholds, design military and diplomatic strategies that accommodate those thresholds, and implement those strategies in a coordinated fashion.[11] These multiple facets and challenges typify the workings of complex systems. As Robert Jervis warns, in such situations states have little choice but to do several things at once.[12] Moreover, the ability to "get it right the first time" is essential to avoiding undesired escalation. Otherwise, a state will find itself fighting "the wrong war, in the wrong place, at the wrong time, against the wrong enemy."[13]

Strategies and Their Outcomes

Wars are fought for political purposes. Yet only in major wars can outright battlefield victory, or unconditional surrender, secure a country's political objectives. In limited wars, political objectives are secured by balancing the demands of military strategy with those of diplomatic policy, postwar occupational strategies, and the inevitable strain on domestic resources that such conflicts entail. While the burden on a state waging limited war is far less when compared to those of major wars, achieving political objectives in limited war can be just as difficult, if not more so.

Limited war strategies are thus conceived as being more than simply the ability of a state's armed forces to achieve military victory. Properly understood, limited war strategies include the "broadest planning for the conduct of war; encompassing all the policy instruments, nonmilitary as well as military; tailoring them to meet the political goals of the state; and considering how the conduct of hostilities will affect the peace to follow."[14] This definition of limited war strategy is essentially that of "grand strategy" as conceived originally by B. H. Liddell Hart, and more recently by Terry Deibel.[15] Boiled down to its essentials, limited war strategy entails three components: political objectives, military strategy, and diplomatic strategy.

The first, the political objectives, are the ends that states seek; the second and third are the means by which they are sought. As is the case with all sound strategies, these elements—ends and means—must be linked together logically and coherently.

At issue is whether the military and diplomatic strategies employed in a limited war are likely to deliver the political objectives sought, including avoiding escalation. Militarily, the concern is whether political goals have been effectively translated into military strategic objectives and missions.[16] In terms of diplomacy, states engaging in limited wars often need to conduct delicate diplomatic operations to attract allies' support, to dissuade opponents' disruption attempts, and frequently to conduct a myriad of postwar reconstruction projects. The challenge is to ensure that these policies are tailored to the overall political objectives the state seeks from the limited war. Finally, the coordination of the military and diplomatic strategies is critical to the attainment of a state's political objectives. If military and diplomatic strategies are uncoordinated, or work at cross-purposes, the state is unlikely to achieve its wartime objectives. Essential to coordination is the mutual understanding by military officers, diplomats, and intelligence officers of the numerous ways in which their own efforts can obstruct or assist the others' efforts. The notion of cooperation is important because it reflects the inherent interdependence of the military and diplomatic elements in limited war.[17] Key here is whether the political objectives of the state serve as the focal point for military-diplomatic cooperation in limited war. Ideally, the content of the military and diplomatic means employed will flow directly from the political objectives sought.

A state's strategic performance in limited warfare is the product of the interaction between the military and diplomatic strategies employed. To simplify, I posit that states can either succeed or fail in accomplishing their military and diplomatic objectives. This interaction generates four possible outcomes (displayed in table 2.1): double success, double failure, and two instances of mixed success. While similar insofar as they are "mixed cases," these last two are conceptually distinct, each resulting from a different configuration of military and diplomatic strategic success and failure.

The two clear-cut cases are relatively easy to conceive. "Double success" occurs when the state achieves its military and diplomatic objectives. Central to this outcome is the relationship between military and diplomatic strategies. Military strategy and operations are designed to achieve the specific battlefield outcomes considered necessary to obtain the state's political objectives in the war. Similarly, diplomatic policies are enacted with

TABLE 2.1. Possible outcomes of limited war strategies

	Military success	Military failure
Diplomatic success	Double Success	Mixed success 2: *Little Consolation*
Diplomatic failure	Mixed success 1: *Win the Battle, Lose the War*	Double Failure

an eye toward the construction and maintenance of favorable international and internal strategic environments. Moreover, the military and diplomatic elements work in concert. Each is sufficiently flexible to accommodate the other, if possible. If accommodation is not feasible, then strategic adaptation is attempted, aided by the mutual understanding of the interdependencies of military and diplomatic aspects of the broader war effort. The implications of double successes can be quite beneficial to the state. The principal military opponent is defeated, and through its diplomatic policies, disturbance of the broader international system is mitigated, at least in the short run.

Conversely, "double failure" results when neither the military nor diplomatic missions are accomplished. Military strategy can be ill suited to the political objectives the state seeks. For example, as the war unfolds, military objectives can expand or become increasingly ambiguous despite the stability of the political objectives that lead to war in the first place.[18] Additionally, diplomatic policies fail to construct and maintain a favorable strategic environment. This can result either because diplomats fail to abide by political objectives, or because the conduct of military missions undermines that of the diplomatic missions (that is, when military behavior convinces a third party that the state is a threat, despite the diplomatic signals sent to convey the opposite). In the case of double failure, there is a marked absence of cooperation among those responsible for the military and diplomatic elements of the war. Actors behave without consulting each other, leading to an increase in the chances of one undermining the other. The implications of double failures can be profound. These cases of limited war have the potential to dramatically weaken the state in terms of military power. And because the state was unable to construct and maintain a favorable strategic environment through its diplomatic policies, these cases of limited war can substantially disrupt the international system.[19]

The first case of mixed success, described as "win the battle, lose the war," occurs when a state is able to achieve its military objectives but fails in achieving its diplomatic aims. There are two relevant types of diplomatic failure. The first is a failure of international communication. In the extreme, a state's military victory can trigger third-party intervention. Despite the circumscribed political objectives held by the state in a limited war, third parties can come to perceive the state to be a significant threat to its territory and/or interests. In this situation, the state would have failed to accurately signal its limited objectives to third parties, failed to credibly deter undesired intervention, or both.[20] Less extreme, but still damaging, is the diplomatic failure to hold and maintain allies during the war. The inability to maintain allies can be detrimental if the state needs their financial and/or military contribution to the war effort. Additionally, the loss of allies can harm the "legitimacy" of the state's actions, diminishing the overall gains the state achieves from the war.[21] A second form of diplomatic failure can come in the postwar phase. In order for military objectives to be completely translated into political objectives, significant postwar investment is often required. Security operations are only one form of postwar investment. Other forms include political-institutional development, economic recovery, and international legitimacy efforts.[22] In all of these cases, early military victories can be squandered, or severely diminished, if diplomatic policies do not fully backstop those gains.[23] Despite these losses, the state nevertheless retains potency in military power because of its prior military victory.

The second case of mixed success, "little consolation," occurs when diplomatic objectives are achieved, but the military fails to secure its aims. There are two ways in which militaries can fail to deliver political objectives. The first, and most obvious, is an outright loss on the battlefield. In this case, the state correctly identified the specific military objectives necessary for the attainment of its political goals, yet was beaten by the opponent. The second way in which militaries can fail to deliver political objectives is to misidentify the proper battlefield objectives in the first place. In these situations militaries adopt an inappropriate strategy, misunderstand the nature of the opponent, or both. The result of either case of military strategic failure is the inability to achieve the state's political objectives. In terms of the broader impact on the international system, this case is less severe than that of double failure because through its diplomatic efforts the state has cordoned off the international system from the ongoing war.

The principal feature of limited wars is their inherent tendency to escalate. Escalation can occur along multiple dimensions, and the dimensions of escalation can interact in different ways. By focusing on the political, military, and diplomatic elements of limited war strategies, we are better able to systematically identify the primary and secondary sources of escalation in any given case of limited warfare. By linking strategic performance to escalation, moreover, my objective is to explain the dynamics of limited warfare in terms of a state's initial strategic choices. The effectiveness of those initial strategic choices, I argue, turns on how information is managed by top policy makers and their national security organizations.

INFORMATION:
THE SINEWS OF LIMITED WAR STRATEGIES

Many factors can affect the prospects of strategic success in limited war. The overall balance of military power, military strategic acumen, level of competence of the diplomatic corps, and the intelligence capacities of the state all play a role in explaining limited war outcomes. But even if a state possesses a wealth of these capacities, the task of designing precise and coordinated military and diplomatic strategies remains.[24] The precise tailoring of missions can only occur if top policy makers have an accurate understanding of the opportunities and challenges contained in the strategic environment. And effectively coordinated missions are likely to result only when political leaders possess sufficient information about the military and diplomatic activities undertaken before and during a war. No matter how well these actors perform in isolation, if their efforts are not coordinated then actions taken in one realm may undermine those in another. The sinews of limited war strategy—the threads that tie the political, military, and diplomatic aspects of the limited war effort together—are the information flow patterns linking top policy makers to their national security organizations, and those organizations to one another. In short, the information management capacities of the state have a strong bearing on the strategic outcomes of limited wars.

I argue that two information management mechanisms are critical to generating strategic success in limited wars. The first is the collection and analysis of information pertaining to the international environment. Comprehensive collection and optimal analysis are important for the design and implementation of high quality security policies. To stand any chance of success in a limited war, leaders need to know the level of threat tolerance of potential interveners, the interests and motivations of allies, and the nature of the enemy (its strengths, weaknesses, and its strategic and operational approaches).[25] The second information management mechanism pertains to coordination, the ability to link together the military and diplomatic strategies, and the organizations implementing these strategies.

Specifically, leaders need to know the military and diplomatic requirements for victory and the likely trade-offs that must be made in the pursuit of military and diplomatic objectives.[26] A state's information management capacities strongly affect its leaders' ability to clearly understanding the strategic context in which the state acts and the ability to design and execute policies that are well tailored to that context.[27] In sum, the conjunction of these two information processing mechanisms has a direct impact on strategic performance in limited warfare. How a state performs strategically is determined by its specific capacities to collect, analyze, and coordinate external and internal information.

INFORMATION INSTITUTIONS

Information institutions directly affect how information is managed as states design and implement limited war strategies. As discussed in chapter 1, information flow patterns among top policy makers and national security organizations have two institutional effects. The first is the aggregation and adjudication of strategic preferences of the relevant actors within governments. The second is information extraction and conversion, the collection and selection of essential data to provide the information that leaders employ when designing strategy and that organizations use to perform their specific missions.[28] To a certain extent, a state's information institution is amenable to intentional manipulation. Once created, however, information institutions tend to resist significant short-run change. Part of the reason for this rigidity is captured by the familiar saying, "Information is power." An individual's influence on policy is powerfully affected by the access he or she has to information about his or her own organization, and that of others' organizations. As such, political pressures will be brought to bear whenever information institution design comes under scrutiny.[29] Furthermore, we can expect leaders to be hesitant to alter information institutional relationships as war approaches. Such "alternations under threat" can breed confusion in the short run; leaders are thus more likely to go with what they know into the next crisis.[30] As a result of this stickiness, at any particular time information flow patterns and interagency relations tend to resist substantial alteration in the short run.[31]

Two features of the information institutional relationships among state-level actors deserve attention: hierarchy and division of labor. First in terms of vertical relationships, the higher an individual is in the hierarchy of the state, the more his or her information demands become diverse, externally oriented, and strategic in nature. The lower an individual is in the hierarchy, information demands become more specific, internally (or task) oriented, and operational or tactical in nature. In functional terms, as an individual moves up in the hierarchy, the more he or she adopts the role of information processor and disseminator—a coordinator of activity of those at lower levels. Moreover, as an individual moves up the hierarchy, the types of uncertainties that he or she confronts change. At lower levels, the greatest obstacle to effective performance is "task uncertainty," or the vagaries associated with completing specific jobs under internally derived constraints. At higher levels, task uncertainty is replaced with "environmental uncertainty," or the difficulties in determining how the organization's objectives are being affected by outside actors and influences.[32]

In any hierarchy, top decision makers are responsible (or are accountable) for strategic design and implementation. This is particularly the case in the context of the state, where national leaders hold ultimate power and authority. Although it is the state's leaders who must determine security policies, the information upon which decisions are based comes from lower levels in the state hierarchy. Military, diplomatic, and intelligence organizations deliver vital information to state leaders so that these leaders will have an understanding of the risks and opportunities in the international system. By necessity, these organizations will possess more information than a state's leaders require at any given time, and leaders must have a means of calling forth only strategically relevant information from them. This poses a potential problem: those most in need of strategically relevant information may not know what specific pieces of information are required at any given time, and the suppliers of that information may not know what among the abundance of data to deliver.[33]

In terms of horizontal relationships, different organizations within a state are tasked with distinct missions and, as such, have distinct information demands and processes for satisfying those demands. For example, the basic function of militaries is combat, or as Samuel Huntington observed, "The direction, operation, and control of a human organization whose primary function is the application of violence is the peculiar skill of the officer."[34] At any given time, the military confronts a discrete set of opponents on a well-delineated battlefield. While the uncertainties in combat are typically high, they are contained to that environment. The methods and procedures for dealing with the uncertainties inherent to combat are developed by the organization and are modified internally. Thus when militaries are performing their function, information from other state organs becomes less essential to the completion of their task—defeating the enemy.[35] In other words, militaries are organizations that respond to "local knowledge" and are characterized by closed circles of communication. As Arthur Stinchcombe argues, such organizations tend to develop specific subcultures that separate them from other organizations in the hierarchy, or state.[36]

While the armed forces confront unique uncertainties through internally derived standard operating procedures, diplomatic and intelligence organizations confront uncertainty of a different type and respond to it in very different ways. The sources of uncertainty for diplomats and intelligence officers are far more diffused than they are for the military. Diplomatic and intelligence organizations are tasked with a myriad of problems of different types, including but not limited to that of defeating an opponent on the battlefield. Because these uncertainties stem from a number of different sources, diplomatic and intelligence organizations depend on information from other agencies in order to fulfill their function effectively.

The key point is that the types of uncertainty and information requirements an individual confronts vary according to his or her position in the hierarchy and to the specific organization in which he or she is embedded. Not only will superiors and subordinates conflict over information supply and demand,[37] but so too will the multiple organs comprising the state. For example, the more that the military is separated from other national security organizations as a result of closed communication circles around localized informational bases, the more likely it will be that the military, diplomatic, and intelligence functions of the state will be uncoordinated. Still, national security organizations operate in an environment of bureaucratic interconnectedness. As Amy Zegart explains, national security organizations cannot and do not function in isolation, their activities and jurisdictions overlap significantly. Foreign policy bureaucracies exhibit a high degree of "asset co-specialization," where "the value of one agency's work hinges, at least in part, on the work of another." The upshot is that organizational interconnectedness frequently leads to information "holdup problems," situations where one agency imposes demands or restrictions on another agency leading to suboptimal performance.[38] When attempting to implement complex policies (such as limited war strategies), the ability of top decision makers to effectively acquire and manage information is at a premium. Only "knowledgeable" leaders can properly determine a state's objectives and effectively monitor the activities of subordinate organizations.[39]

Under what conditions will top policy makers be able to effectively adjudicate among the competing strategic preferences of their national security organizations? When are state leaders able to effectively extract and convert information possessed by their organizations to design and implement high quality limited war strategies? I argue that the probability of strategic success in limited war is highest when information institutions are "robust," when top policy makers receive information from multiple organizational sources, and when those organizations widely and routinely share information with one another. Conversely, the probability of strategic success in limited war is lowest when information institutions are "truncated," when top policy makers receive information from a single organization source, and when national security organizations withhold information from one another.

Multisourced Information Flows

The information supplied by any one organization to top policy makers will pertain primarily to that organization's function. Because state leaders and their subordinate organs are hierarchically related, the type of uncertainty to which each responds differs substantially: top policy makers must be concerned with the overall performance of the state, while particular agencies will be dedicated to their functional performance. As such, information derived from a given organization will not provide state leaders with a complete picture of the external environment. Furthermore, there is a tendency for the information supplied by any single agency to be biased. As traditional organizational theory recognizes, biased information can result from a number of causes: the functional orientation of the agency, entrenched parochialism, and competition among agencies for greater bureaucratic resources and responsibility.[40] Thus if state leaders rely too extensively on a single organization for strategic information, there is a strong possibility that decisions will be based on incomplete, inaccurate, and/or out of date information.[41] Most troubling for limited war strategies, state leaders run the risk of becoming marginalized in the decision-making process when they receive information only from a single organizational source. Under these conditions, top policy makers find themselves at a stark information disadvantage, and the empowered organization will be able to exert more influence over strategy than its nominal superiors. When information access and control descends to lower rungs of the hierarchy, the subordinate organization acquires a substantial amount of functional authority over the design and implementation of policy.[42] In such circumstances, an organization may even be able to instrumentally feed information up the ladder as a means of preserving its de facto authority over policy.

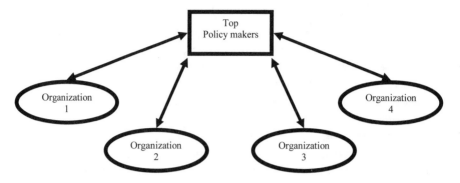

FIGURE 2.1. Multisourced information flows

A significant benefit of a robust information institution is the ability for top decision makers to obtain information from multiple organizational sources. By breaking through the bureaucratic obstacles to efficient information transmission, multisourced information flows permit top decision makers to obtain a far more complete picture of the international environment.[43] Further, multisourced information flows are a means of providing state leaders information about the coordination of their national security organizations. As the institutional economist Geoffrey Hodgson observes, institutions (and the routinized behavior they facilitate), "provide more or less reliable information regarding the likely actions of others."[44] As the number of organizations that become institutionally tethered to top policy makers increases, so too does the information pertaining to the behavior of those organizations. If, on the other hand, state leaders are forced to rely on a single organization for information, then they will likely base their decisions on a biased interpretation of the strategic environment, and further, their capacity to ensure coordination among all of the relevant agencies will be significantly diminished. Figure 2.1 illustrates this characteristic of robust information flows.

Lateral Connections

Significantly, the existence of multisourced information pathways is a resource for *leaders* to acquire a substantial amount of information from their organizations. While this is a potentially powerful tool for state leaders, it does come at a price: information overload.[45] When designing and executing complex strategies, state leaders cannot be overburdened with an excessive amount of information, and the sole reliance upon multisourced information pathways will almost certainly result in this outcome. Political psychologists have shown that the information processing capabilities of leaders is limited, and that the continuous flow of dynamic communications from multiple organizations can quickly swamp top decision makers' facilities.[46] To avoid information overload, information vetting processes must be in place at lower levels in the governmental hierarchy.[47]

Studies in the fields of institutional economics and network analysis demonstrate the power that lateral information pathways among interdependent but functionally distinct organizations can bring to bear on the problem of information overload.[48] Generally, as Elinor Ostrom notes, human information processing capabilities can be substantially improved by establishing "rules and routines" that enable individuals and organizations to view the strategic environment in similar and comprehensive ways, and that allow them to "take actions that lead to better rather than worse outcomes." Ultimately, Ostrom concludes, "humans are thereby able to compensate for—as well as replicate—cognitive processing limits by the way they organize themselves and the procedures they follow."[49] More specifically, Duncan Watts has shown that information institutions characterized by dense lateral connections among organizations have the ability to "handle large volumes of information efficiently and without overloading any *individual* processors."[50]

In this sense, a key characteristic of a robust information institution is the ability to redistribute the burden of information processing while maintaining the necessary hierarchical configuration needed to facilitate control over the broader enterprise, or state. Locally connected information pathways, or connections among subordinate agencies, allow for this critical redistribution of information processing. When functional organizations are laterally connected, the ability for top decision makers to receive properly vetted information in a timely fashion increases substantially.[51] As new information enters the information system, it can be scrutinized by a number of different individuals, each of whom will interpret that information from a different perspective.[52] While consensus on interpretation is never guaranteed, the ability to distinguish signals from noise will be enhanced through continuous debate and discussion at lower levels. Further, if the interpretation of a particular piece of information remains in dispute after this process, the ambiguity of that information may be reduced significantly, thereby allowing top decision makers to assess the situation with greater speed and accuracy.[53] An absence of these information-vetting processes places top policy makers in a precarious position. Without such procedures, leaders are likely to succumb to the cognitive and emotional

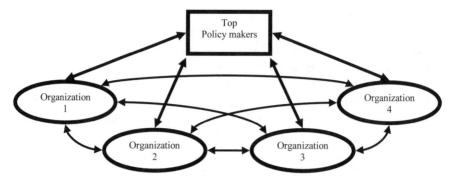

FIGURE 2.2. Lateral connections—Robust information institution

constraints that prevent individuals from conducting full information searches and performing objective and rigorous analyses.[54]

Additionally, dense lateral connections have the ability to overcome the holdup problems associated with state bureaucracies. As subordinate organizations interact, they are able to press their counterparts to provide critical information without having to force top decision makers to expend time and political capital in resolving bureaucratic disputes. In other words, coordination among subordinate agencies is significantly bolstered by the existence of dense lateral connections at lower levels.[55] As the economist Masahiko Aoki argues, pure centralized planning in highly complex and dynamic environments is strategically inefficient. Information sharing among "different task units" (state-level organizations and agencies) facilitates a greater degree of organizational coordination.[56]

A dearth of lateral connections among subordinate agencies (a phenomenon known as "stovepiping"), on the other hand, will likely lead to information overload at the top, the result of which will be faulty strategic analysis. Further, as the density of lateral connections decreases, coordination among agencies will likely decrease due the overburdening of top decision makers with excessive information. Figure 2.2 illustrates both of the characteristics of robust information institutions.

A potential objection might arise to my argument that greater lateral connections provide better information to state leaders that can facilitate coordination among national security organizations. Won't the widespread sharing of information at lower levels result in collusion against the state's leaders? There are two reasons for rejecting this skepticism. First, as more and more individuals and organizations become connected, a collective action problem emerges. To the extent that collusion can produce material gains, and to the extent that those gains must be more widely distributed, the incentive for any one individual or organization to risk detection and punishment decreases.[57]

Second, lateral connections do not completely eradicate parochialism from the system. This residual parochialism can serve as a critical "whistle-blowing" mechanism whereby state leaders can become aware of potential colluders before the damage has been done. In this sense, lateral connections facilitate a type of oversight known in principal-agency theory as fire alarms. The essence of fire alarm oversight is the ability of third parties to identify agents who are not fulfilling the principal's objectives and bring those violators to the attention of their superiors. In the context of planning for and waging limited wars, principal-agent dynamics constitute a series of dyadic relationships between top policy makers and the respective organizations within the national security apparatus. In each of these dyadic relationships, other national security organizations constitute the third parties that can make top policy makers aware of potential behavioral violations in a timely fashion.

As the density of lateral connections increases, fire alarm oversight begins to complement another oversight mechanism known as police patrols. Police patrol oversight is more centralized, active, and direct, entailing the examination of only a sample of an agent's behavior by the principal. Because police patrol oversight is more costly in terms of the principal's time and resources, it suffers from inefficiency.[58] Yet when these two oversight mechanisms are combined, principals benefit from more, and more accurate, information about the behavior of their agents. Thus by virtue of efficiency gains achieved in overseeing the actions of their subordinate national security organizations, lateral connections better enable top policy makers to ensure coordination among them. In sum, while lateral connections do not guarantee completely bias-free information transmissions and organizational coordination, the probability of error is significantly reduced. Furthermore, in conjunction with multisourced information pathways, the ability of a state to design and implement complex strategies increases dramatically when subordinate organs are laterally connected.

INFORMATION FLOWS VERSUS THE QUALITY OF INFORMATION IN STRATEGIC RISK ASSESSMENT

My central argument is that information institutions have powerful effects on the ability of leaders to accurately understand the strategic environment and to ensure that their national security organizations work in concert in the design and execution of limited war strategies. Before deriving the specific propositions related to the causal relationships between information flow patterns and the outcomes of limited wars, one important question deserves consideration. To what extent do information institutions matter when the quality of the available information is particularly poor? Put another way, "Won't a robust information institution chock full of garbage be more likely to lead to failure than a truncated system with a high-quality stovepipe?"[59] This question is important because it reveals that even under the best conditions, there is simply no guarantee that leaders will know with precision everything about the strategic environment, or that they will in every instance resolve all of their strategic challenges before a war commences. Critical information may simply not be available, and the absence of such information may hinder strategic performance. At issue is how ambiguous and/or incomplete information affects strategic decision making in robust information institutions. Based on the logic of my argument detailed in the previous sections, we can conclude that among the benefits of robust information institutions is the ability of top policy makers to base their strategic decisions on more accurate risk assessments. High quality strategic risk assessments have the effect of mitigating (though not eradicating) the problems associated with poor quality information.

Within IR theory, the dominant approach to the study of risk resides at the individual level of analysis. Scholars applying prospect theory to foreign policy decision making argue that leaders are likely to make riskier choices when they anticipate future losses to themselves or to their state. Conversely, leaders are likely to make more cautious, less risk-acceptant foreign policy choices when they anticipate future gains.[60] While this approach offers compelling explanations for how leaders decide based on their expectations of the future, it has comparatively less to say about how organizations acquire and process the information that informs leaders' expectations. Prospect theory seeks to explain the risk propensity of state leaders, and not how governments perform risk assessments per se.

Risk assessment can be characterized along four dimensions. The first is how strategic interactions are understood. Typically, strategic interactions do not occur between unitary actors, but rather by "complex sprawling organizations that break big problems down into manageable smaller ones." The process of breaking down larger problems into smaller constituent components, and then reconstituting them into national policy, increases the probability that analytical errors will be made. Once discrete problem sets are assigned to different functional organizations for evaluation, there is no guarantee that they will be efficiently and accurately integrated in the final analysis. Whether governments possess the ability to effectively integrate the separate organizations' analytical efforts will affect the quality of their risk assessments. The second is how the opponent is conceived in the analytical process. How governments understand the opponent (either as a unitary actor or as a conglomeration of organizations whose actions may or may not be well coordinated) will inevitably affect the range of potential outcomes of future interactions. The third is how states understand the nature of strategic asymmetries. Are asymmetries assumed to arise only from differences in material power, or are they seen as coming from a range of different sources? For example, opponents may employ technologies differently than the government conducting the analysis, or may adopt alternative operational schemes for employing their forces. Overall material size may or may not confer strategic benefits; recognizing and evaluating a wide range of strategic asymmetries is thus essential to rigorous risk assessments. Finally, sound risk assessment must be conducted with an eye toward whether or not an opponent will be able to effectively knit together the various components of its strategy. Understanding the opponent's strategic competence in this way will likely highlight areas where risk of action may be greater or lesser for the state. Together, these features of risk assessment can inform the range of viable alternative courses of actions made available to top policy makers.[61]

Upon what basis do leaders come to understand the potential perils and opportunities in the strategic environment? How do governments come to understand the range of viable strategic course of action? These two issues have significant effects on the quality of strategic risk assessment, and both relate to how information flows among top policy makers and national security organizations. As James March and Johan Olsen note,

> Alternatives are not automatically provided to a decision maker; they have to be found. Search for alternatives occurs in a context in which problems are not only looking for solutions, but solutions are looking for problems. *Information about the consequences of alternatives is generated and communicated through institutional networks, so expectations depend on the structure or linkages within the system, as well as the ways in which biases and counterbiases cumulate.*[62]

When top policy makers obtain information from a single source, and when national security organizations withhold information from one another, the quality of risk assessments declines precipitously. Each of the four dimensions of risk assessment requires that analytical tasks be broken down, farmed out to different organizations, and then compiled to form a composite analytical product. Moreover, because top policy makers are ultimately responsible for the overall strategic performance of the state in limited war, risk assessments must be cast at the highest level. As such, strategic risk assessments are affected by the state's information collection and analysis capabilities and by the degree of military and diplomatic coordination. Thus robust information institutions provide the optimal structure for sound strategic risk analysis. This is so even when uncertainty about the strategic environment is pervasive. In short, robust information institutions better enable leaders to understand the limits of their knowledge, thereby affording them the ability to better evaluate the risks associated with a range of potential strategic options. "Empowered stovepipes," on the other hand, can never be omnicompetent. Any single organization that may be directly connected to top policy makers will inevitably conduct biased and limited information searches and provide skewed risk assessments in the direction of that organization's functional orientation. The ability to accurately evaluate strategic risk is at a premium in matters of national security. The information institution approach offers a way of understanding when and how decisions are made based on systematic calculations of strategic risk, and when they are likely to be shots in the dark.

PROPOSITIONS ON STRATEGIC OUTCOMES IN LIMITED WARFARE

When functioning, a robust information institution will more likely provide decision makers with accurate and timely information about the strategic environment and the behavior of the national security organizations within the state. Essential information will neither be hoarded at lower levels in the hierarchy, nor will leaders be provided with information in such a quantity that precludes high quality analysis.[63] Robust information institutions, in short, ameliorate the twin problems of information overload and of information scarcity. Truncated information institutions, on the other hand, are susceptible to these two information processing pathologies.

The information institution approach expects a state to experience double success from its limited war strategy when its information institution is robust. The prospects for military and diplomatic success in limited war are substantially increased when decision makers have as complete an understanding of the strategic environment as possible. Under these conditions, leaders are most likely to have an accurate understanding of the opponent's

strengths and weaknesses, the intentions of potential interveners and allies, and the challenges that will confront the state in the aftermath of the
war. Moreover, leaders can best ensure that the different components of
the broader strategy work in concert to achieve the political objectives of
the war. They are able to monitor the performance of their organizations
as they perform their respective missions and can guard against those organizations working at cross-purposes. In sum, robust information institutions (those where leaders have access to multiple sources of information
and where subordinate organs are laterally connected) produce comprehensive information collection and optimal analytic capabilities as well as
tight coordination of the military and diplomatic components of limited war
strategy.

Conversely, this approach expects double failure when a state's information institution is truncated. In these circumstances, state leaders have
access to very few sources of information pertaining to the military and
diplomatic elements of the limited war. Going to war without comprehensive information about the opponent and broader strategic environment
entails substantial risk. Not only is the state likely to adopt inappropriate,
ambiguous, and/or reckless military objectives, the chances are good that
the state will be unable to wage war in a benign strategic environment.
Militarily, the state runs the risk of defeat on the battlefield. Diplomatically,
the state courts third party intervention, the loss of support from key allies,
and ultimately, the inability to achieve its political objectives in the war.
Truncated information institutions (those where leaders receive information from a single organizational source and where subordinate organs are
disconnected from each other) produce limited information collection and
dysfunctional analytic capabilities, as well as a lack of coordination of the
military and diplomatic components of the limited war strategy.

Robust and truncated information institutions are extreme possibilities.
Between those extremes are "moderately truncated" information institutions. I use this term to capture instances were either the organizations
responsible for military strategy or those charged with diplomatic policies
function in relative isolation.[64] In cases where political leaders are closely
involved in the military aspects of the limited war, but where the diplomatic
aspects occur in relative isolation, this approach expects military success
and diplomatic failure (win the battle, lose the war). This outcome results,
first, from the state having only moderate information collection and fair
analytic capabilities, and second, from the poor coordination of the diplomatic component of limited war strategy. In cases where leaders are closely

TABLE 2.2. Information institutions—Propositions on strategic performance in limited war

| Independent Variable | Information Management Causal Mechanisms | Military and Diplomatic | Dependent Variable |
Information Institution	Information Collection and Analysis	Coordination	Strategic Performance
Robust—Multisourced and lateral connections	*Comprehensive collection* on opponent, potential interveners, allies, postwar challenges *Optimal analysis:* limited hoarding, vetting mechanisms, military and diplomatic tradeoffs confronted	*Tight:* military and diplomatic strategies work in concert with political objectives as focal point	Double Success
Moderately Truncated— Diplomatic isolated	*Moderate collection:* good on opponent, poor on potential interveners and allies; questionable on postwar *Fair analysis:* strong on opponent, weak on strategic environment. Military and diplomatic tradeoffs not confronted	*Poor:* diplomatic unresponsive, but military responsive to political objectives	Mixed: Win the Battle, Lose the War
Moderately Truncated— Military isolated	*Moderate collection:* good on potential interveners and allies, poor on opponent; questionable on postwar *Fair analysis:* strong on strategic environment; weak on opponent. Military and diplomatic tradeoffs not confronted	*Poor:* military unresponsive, but diplomatic responsive to political objectives	Mixed: Little Consolation
Truncated— Single sourced and stovepiping	*Limited collection* on opponent, potential interveners, allies, postwar challenges *Dysfunctional analysis:* widespread hoarding, no vetting mechanisms, military and diplomatic tradeoffs not confronted	*Uncoordinated:* military and diplomatic strategies work in isolation according to internally determined objectives	Double Failure

involved in diplomatic policies, but where the military as an organization operates in relative isolation, this approach expects military failure and diplomatic success (little consolation). Again, this outcome results from, first, the state possessing only moderate information collection and fair analytic capabilities, and second, the poor coordination of the military component of limited war strategy (see table 2.2 for a summary).

DIRECT AND INDIRECT COMPETITORS TO THE INFORMATION INSTITUTION APPROACH

Proper social scientific evaluations of an argument require, as Imre Lakatos argues, more than merely testing causal propositions against the empirical evidence. In addition, it is necessary to demonstrate that a preferred argument offers a more compelling explanation of a phenomenon than its competitors.[65] As such, two questions remain. First, what are the most compelling alternative explanations available of strategic success and failure in limited warfare? And second, what is the most effective means of structuring competitive tests of the information institution approach and its competitors against the empirical record? In this section, I address the first question; in the final section of this chapter, I answer the second pertaining to research design and methodology.

To make the case that the information institution approach offers a superior explanation of strategic success and failure in limited war, it is necessary to find alternative explanations that offer *direct* challenges to the causal processes involved in generating those outcomes. For my purposes, direct competitors speak not only to the outcomes I seek to explain (strategic performance), but also to the mechanisms that cause those outcomes (information management). Two direct competitors, both drawn from the literature on wartime civil-military relations, fit the bill: organizational culture theory and democratic civil-military relations theory. In addition to providing explanations of strategic performance in war, both theories feature information prominently in their explanations. Below, I derive specific propositions from these theories that can be tested against those of the information institution approach.

No matter how compelling arguments residing at the domestic or state level of analysis may be, there remains a prominent information-based explanation at the level of strategic interaction.[66] While not a direct competitor to my argument, rationalist bargaining theory nevertheless suggests that strategic outcomes in war are affected by information, albeit not through the information management capacities of states. Rationalist bargaining theory assumes that all states possess the ability to learn and update their strategies in light of new information. Rationalist bargaining theory is thus an *indirect* competitor to the information institution approach. Indirect tests are valuable because they establish when a preferred explanation is more or less relevant to a particular case.[67] In each of the empirical chapters that follow, I carefully examine the amount and content of the information available to the initiating state. If sufficient information existed for the creation of sound limited war strategies, but the state failed to respond to that information appropriately, then it can be concluded that the information institution approach is more relevant than rationalist bargaining theory in that particular case. Alternatively, if insufficient information existed to design a high quality limited war strategy at the start of the war, then the relevance of the information institution approach declines vis-à-vis rationalist bargaining theory. All else being equal, deference should be paid to extant approaches. The onus is on the new approach to demonstrate when and how its propositions should be taken over those already available.

Organizational Cultures

Organizational culture theory stands at the crossroads of two important literatures: traditional organizational theory and civil-military relations. On the one hand, traditional organizational theory argues that all organizational units, regardless of the state in which they are embedded, exhibit broadly similar behaviors.[68] Moreover, because of their bureaucratic nature, states conduct foreign policy as their organizations enact routines. Yet these arguments cannot explain substantial variation in military preferences and behaviors across time and space. Nor does traditional organizational theory offer a convincing explanation for why certain organizational routines, and not others, play a prominent role in determining the content of a given state's national security policies.[69] On the other hand, influential arguments in the civil-military relations literature posit that the nature of political leadership strongly affects how militaries behave, especially in times of war.[70] These arguments, however, have difficulty explaining how professional militaries often resist intentional direction even by the most the most gifted of civilian masters.[71]

As a variant of traditional organization theory, the organizational culture approach focuses on "the pattern of assumptions, ideas, and beliefs that proscribe how a group should adapt to its external environment and manage its internal affairs."[72] In so doing, this approach retains a strong organizational foundation, but one that is not tied to the assumption that all organizations (in this case professional militaries) see the world in the same way and have the same preferences. As a variant of the civil-military relations literature, this approach challenges the argument that the quality of leadership alone determines how and how well militaries will serve their civilian masters.

In order to derive specific propositions about the outcomes of limited war strategies from the organizational culture approach, two questions need to be answered. First, to what extent do a state's military organizations (as opposed to other state-level organizations) affect the content of limited war strategies? Second, how does military organizational culture influence the two information management mechanisms that affect strategic performance in limited war? With respect to the first question, organizational culture theorists argue that under certain conditions, state-level organizations can determine national preferences and choices. According to Jeffrey Legro, strategic decision making will be strongly conditioned by the culture of a military establishment when its "organizational salience" is high. Four factors bolster the relative salience of military organizations during times of war. First, the hierarchical nature of military organizations ensures that a dominant philosophy will serve as the guide to how they will act when called upon. Second, the monopoly of expertise militaries claim in their particular domain shields these organizations from outside pressures. Third, the complexity of warfare is especially high, and as a result civilians grant senior military officers substantial influence in strategic decision making when war is in the offing. Finally, due to the time constraints imposed on top policy makers both before and during war, leaders tend to accept military advice less critically than they would in times of peace.[73] In sum, organizational culture theory expects that professional militaries will play a decisive role in the design and execution of limited war strategies.

With respect to the relationship between organizational culture and information management, it is important to recognize that organizational cultures generate norms that pertain to specific preferences and behaviors. For example, Colin Kahl describes how the US military complied with a discrete norm of "noncombatant immunity" in the Iraq War.[74] Thus in order to derive propositions regarding the sources of success and failure in limited war strategies, it is necessary to isolate the relevant norms pertaining to, first, the military's conception of the nature of warfare, and second, the proper relationship between militaries and civilians.

Cultural understandings of the nature of warfare will have an effect on the type of information that militaries prefer to collect and analyze. Further, these views affect military behavior to the extent that militaries are sensitized to the problem of escalation. In general, militaries can have a culturally determined view of warfare based on whether military or political logics are understood to affect the nature of warfare. In a "military dominant" conception, warfare is understood to be an isolated human activity. This understanding holds that warfare is a starkly zero-sum, intensely competitive, and normal element of international political life. As such, the only information deemed relevant is that which pertains to the opponent on the battlefield.[75] Militaries captured by this culture, further, are desensitized to the problem of escalation largely because escalation and warfare are seen as being synonymous. The military dominant conception of war is thus akin to Carl von Clausewitz's ideal-typical war, where escalation in war is both inherent and natural.[76] At the other end of the spectrum lies a "balanced" conception of war. This cultural view understands war as an open and complex system where political and military logics interact extensively. Militaries holding this view will appreciate the value of information of all types, though they will tend to prioritize that which has direct military relevance. Moreover, they will be sensitized to the possibility of escalation and will not view it as inevitable. The balanced conception of war comes close to Clausewitz's understanding of war in reality, where elements apart from combat limit the behaviors of those engaged in direct fighting.[77]

Norms regarding the relationship between militaries and civilians will affect the degree of coordination between the military and diplomatic elements of limited war strategies. Modern professional militaries tend to be captured by one of two relational norms. The first, labeled "Jominian," holds that in times of war militaries should be afforded the maximum degree of autonomy possible. Because warfare is understood to be a wholly separate and isolated form of human interaction, politicians and other civilians are seen as having little to no legitimate role in the conduct of war fighting.[78] Militaries holding this relational norm will thus go to great lengths to shield themselves from civilian direction in wartime. The second, labeled "Clausewitzian," views warfare as an inherently political event, and as such militaries are instruments of politics, albeit unique ones. Because of the political nature of war, civilian oversight is deemed normal. To the extent that political leadership must be concerned with peace that follows a military contest, diplomatic concerns are apropos to the formation and execution of strategy.[79]

By combining these norms, it is possible to generate specific propositions about the likelihood of strategic success in limited war (see table 2.3
for a summary). The best chance for strategic success in limited wars occurs
when organizational cultures contain a balanced conception of warfare and
a Clausewitzian norm of civil-military relations. In this case, comprehensive collection and optimal analysis of information will result, and military-
diplomatic coordination will be tight. The worst chance for strategic success
occurs when organizational cultures contain a military dominant conception of warfare and a Jominian relational norm. In this case, limited collection and dysfunctional analysis of information will result, while the military
and diplomatic aspects of the war will be uncoordinated. The organizational
culture approach is capable of generating clear propositions for double success and double failure, yet it is capable of offering specific propositions
for only one of the two possible mixed outcomes. When military organizational culture entails a view of war that is balanced and a Jominian relational norm, the theory anticipates military success, but diplomatic failure
(win the battle, lose the war). In this case, the military will prefer to collect
and analyze information of multiple types but will be unwilling to tightly
coordinate its activities with those of civilian organizations. Although the
military will possess a comprehensive understanding of the strategic environment, it will nevertheless behave in ways detrimental to overall strategic
success. When military organizational culture entails a military dominant
conception of war and a Clausewitzian relational norm, the theory anticipates either mixed strategic outcome. Under these conditions, the impact of
military myopia will be lessened to some degree by its willingness to coordinate, but not completely. As a result, information collection and analysis
will be moderate and fair, while military and diplomatic coordination will
be tight. The less than ideal collection and analytical capabilities of the state
will likely generate either military or diplomatic failure; which outcome
results is logically indeterminate, however. What is clear is that the chances
of double failure are dramatically reduced.

Democratic Civil-Military Relations

The second variant of the civil-military relations literature that underscores
the importance of information management in crafting security policies
focuses on the power and preference relationships between civilians and
militaries in democratic states. With respect to the first information management mechanism, scholars of civil-military relations have attempted

T A B L E 2.3. Organizational cultures—Propositions on strategic performance in limited war

Independent Variable	Information Management Causal Mechanisms		Dependent Variable
View of War and Relational Norm → →	*Information Collection and Analysis*	*Military and Diplomatic Coordination* → →	*Strategic Performance*
Balanced and Clausewitzian	*Comprehensive collection* on opponent, potential interveners, allies, postwar challenges *Optimal analysis*: limited hoarding, vetting mechanisms, military and diplomatic trade-offs confronted	*Tight*: military and diplomatic strategies work in concert with political objectives as focal point	Double Success
Balanced and Jominian	*Comprehensive collection* on opponent, potential interveners, allies, postwar challenges *Optimal analysis*: limited hoarding, vetting mechanisms, military and diplomatic trade-offs confronted	*Uncoordinated*: military and diplomatic strategies work in isolation according to internally determined objectives	Mixed: Win the Battle, Lose the War
Military Dominant and Clausewitzian	*Moderate collection*: good on opponent, poor on potential interveners and allies; questionable on postwar *Fair analysis*: strong on opponent, weak on strategic environment. Military and diplomatic tradeoffs not optimally confronted	*Tight*: military and diplomatic strategies work in concert with political objectives as focal point	Either Mixed Outcome
Military Dominant and Jominian	*Limited collection* on opponent, potential interveners, allies, postwar challenges *Dysfunctional analysis*: widespread hoarding, no vetting mechanisms, military and diplomatic tradeoffs not confronted	*Uncoordinated*: military and diplomatic strategies work in isolation according to internally determined objectives	Double Failure

to clearly specify the conditions under which information collection and analysis are more or less likely to reflect organizational biases.[80] For example, Risa Brooks argues that the quality of "information sharing" among political elites and military officers is a function of the balance of political-military power in the states and the degree to which political-military preferences diverge. Information sharing among political and military leaders, those who occupy the "political-military apex," will be significantly hampered when domestic power is shared between politicians and military officers.[81] In other words, in democratic states (where the balance of power favors politicians), information sharing among leaders and top military officers tends to be fluid, regardless of the distance between political and military preferences. As Dan Reiter and Allan Stam argue, the political consequences of defeat on the battlefield motivate democratic leaders to promote officers in the military based on merit, thereby preventing the "commissarism" prevalent in authoritarian regimes. Commissarism has the effect of producing highly biased intelligence collection, "as military officers are more interested in maintaining the approval of the civilian leadership than in presenting sound military or strategic analysis"[82] In the best case, when preferences converge, neither side has any incentive to hoard information. When preferences do diverge, politicians can employ oversight mechanisms that allow them access to strategic information.[83] In short, while democracies may succumb to some problems in strategic assessment, the problem of blocked information exchange at the decision-making apex is not one of them.

With respect to the second information management mechanism, numerous studies have argued that the degree of integration between military policy and political objectives has a profound impact on the effectiveness of security policies. As Barry Posen argues, "Disintegrated grand strategies, in which political objectives and military doctrine are poorly reconciled, can lead to both war and defeat—jeopardizing the state's survival."[84] Again, Brooks posits that under the best conditions (when political dominance is high and when political-military preferences converge), strategic coordination is "relatively routinized, representative, and rigorous." Conversely, strategic coordination in democratic states breaks down when political and military preferences diverge. In the former case, strategic assessment is optimal because "advisory bodies include representatives from both the political and military apparatus of the state." In the latter case, strategic assessment suffers because of the oversight mechanisms political leaders employ to ensure access to information. These oversight mechanisms

TABLE 2.4. Democratic civil-military relations—Propositions on strategic performance in limited war

Independent Variable	Information Management Causal Mechanisms		Dependent Variable
	→ → Information Collection and Analysis	→ → Military and Diplomatic Coordination	Strategic Performance
Balance of Power and Preference Convergence			
Civilians Favored and Preference Convergence	*Comprehensive collection* on opponent, potential interveners, allies, postwar challenges *Optimal analysis*: limited hoarding, vetting mechanisms, military and diplomatic trade-offs confronted	*Tight*: military and diplomatic strategies work in concert with political objectives as focal point	Double Success
Civilians Favored and Preference Divergence	*Comprehensive collection* on opponent, potential interveners, allies, postwar challenges *Optimal analysis*: limited hoarding, vetting mechanisms, military and diplomatic trade-offs confronted	*Uncoordinated*: military and diplomatic strategies work in isolation according to internally determined objectives	Win the Battle, Lose the War
Shared Power and Preference Convergence	Not anticipated in democratic states	Not anticipated in democratic states	Not Anticipated
Shared Power and Preference Divergence	Not anticipated in democratic states	Not anticipated in democratic states	Not Anticipated

effectively marginalize senior military officials, which, in turn, "undermines the debate and rigor of analysis."[85]

Democratic civil-military relations theory expects double success in limited war strategies when political-military preferences converge, for two reasons. The first is that such democracies possess comprehensive collection and optimal analytic capabilities as a result of the fluidity of information sharing among military and political leaders. The second is that these democracies will experience tight military-diplomatic coordination stemming from the absence of factors that would otherwise generate friction between civilian and military leaders at the apex of the state. Further, democratic civil-military relations theory expects a mixed outcome when political and military preferences diverge: diplomatic failure, military success (win the battle, lose the war).[86] Because coordination is argued to suffer under these conditions, diplomatic activities are likely to be undermined by military behavior. But because of the fluidity of information exchange between political leaders and the military, it remains likely that military missions will be heavily influenced by political objectives, and further, those political objectives will be appropriate to the strategic environment.

The open exchange of information between civilian leaders and their militaries suggests that democratic civil-military relations theory is incapable of generating expectations for either the mixed strategic outcome of military failure, diplomatic success (little consolation), or the outcome of double failure (see table 2.4 for a summary of propositions). In light of recent scholarship on fortunes of democracies in war, this is not all surprising. To a considerable extent, it is the nature of democratic civil-military relations that has led to the conclusion that democracies possess information advantages over nondemocracies. These information advantages enable democracies to better estimate their probability of winning wars *ex ante*, and to thus outperform nondemocracies on the battlefield.[87]

THE NATURE OF THE COMPETING CAUSAL CLAIMS

None of the competing theoretical approaches addressed above offer deterministic causal explanations for the strategic outcomes of limited war. Rather, to varying degrees, all of the propositions specify a probabilistic relationship between independent and dependent variables. It is nevertheless important to recognize that for the information institution approach, the degree of indeterminism in the causal relationship between information institutional design and the outcomes of limited war strategies is far narrower than it is for either of the alternatives. This is so for two related reasons. The first pertains to the theoretical relationship between the possible ranges of limited war outcomes and the different forms that information institutions can assume. As discussed above, limited war outcomes are disaggregated into their military and diplomatic components. Similarly, the information institution approach recognizes that multiple state-level organizations make contributions to the overall limited war effort. In contrast, the two alternative approaches drawn from the literature on civil-military relations focus almost exclusively on the military aspects of limited war strategies. The result is a substantial difference in the size of the "causal gap" between strategy and wartime outcomes for the information institution approach and the two alternatives.[88] In cases where a third party intervenes in a war initially between two states, or where an insurgency erupts in the midst of a war, the causes of escalation are only partially attributable to the military component of limited war strategy. Political and diplomatic factors are likely to have been at work as well. By recognizing that both military and nonmilitary organizations contribute to the overall limited war effort, the information institution approach is able to offer a more comprehensive set of propositions pertaining to the varied causes of escalation in limited war.

Second, information institutions are conceived in such a manner as to account for the most important factors that induce escalation in limited wars. Again, information institutions affect the quality of strategic design and implementation through two mechanisms: the collection and analysis of information, and military-diplomatic coordination before and during war. Information collection and analysis affects whether or not the adopted limited war strategy incorporates information related to the likely sources of escalation in a given war. Military-diplomatic coordination affects whether or not the state will be able to ensure that all aspects of its strategy work in concert toward common wartime objectives. This approach posits that if information pertaining to the sources of escalation is available, then a state with a robust information institution will be optimally positioned to devise a strategy that avoids escalation. Conversely, states with truncated or moderately truncated information institutions will likely devise strategies that induce escalation. Critically, because the prewar availability of such information is a key parameter for the information institution approach, I am able to derive propositions pertaining to the causes of limited war escalation with a *relatively* high degree of certainty.[89] In sum, the information institution approach offers propositions with greater certainty in the causal relationship between strategic design and execution and the outcomes of limited war than either of the alternative theories drawn from the civil-military relations literature.

MEASURES, METHODS, AND CASE SELECTION

Having described the causal logics of the information institution approach and its competitors, we can now turn to the critical issue of how I plan to structure the empirical tests that constitute the remainder of the book. In this section, I provide detailed operational measures of each theory's variables and mechanisms as well as the indicators I will be using in the chapters that follow. I then describe my adopted research design and provide a justification of my selection of cases of American limited wars.

Measuring the Variables and Causal Mechanisms

This book seeks to explain the sources of strategic performance in limited warfare. The ability of a state to secure its military and diplomatic objectives in a limited war is important because it ultimately affects the likelihood of undesired escalation. Undesired escalation produces costs and risks that states want to avoid, and as such, I bound my explanatory focus by examining the outcomes of a state's *initial* strategic approach. To measure strategic outcomes, I ask three related questions. First, what are the specific political objectives sought in the war? Second, how are these political objectives reflected in the state's military objectives and missions? Third, how do these political objectives affect its diplomatic policies? In sum, we need to know why a state is fighting and how it prosecutes the war militarily and diplomatically.

I adopt the "score-keeping" procedure of evaluating strategic success and failure in limited wars. Score keeping offers the most objective measure of war outcomes available by examining whether or not the state secured the material *gains* and *aims* sought at the beginning of the war. Score-keeping evaluation commences with the first precipitating act of the crisis that led to the initial planning (and then execution) of the limited war strategy. Score keeping terminates either when the gains and aims sought have been achieved or when it becomes apparent to top policy makers that the desired aims and gains cannot be obtained, or cannot be obtained in the time or at the cost initially preferred. Finally, to be counted on the scorecard, "a gain or an aim achieved must be a direct product of the war. Including later gains [or losses] in the scorecard is often ill-advised because, as time goes on, confidence that these gains [or losses] were really caused by the war rapidly declines."[90] As such, in cases where a war escalated horizontally, I cut off my investigation at that point when the state finds itself combating additional belligerents, either other states or newly mobilized internal enemies. In cases where the war escalated durationally, I terminate the investigation at the point where it became clear to policy makers that they could either escalate the war vertically in the hope of achieving their political objectives sooner or continue the war at its present level of intensity in order to secure their political objectives much later than was initially anticipated. In cases where the state achieved both its initial military and diplomatic objectives, I examine the war in its entirety.

Turning to the operational measures of the causal variables, for the information institution approach, the pattern of information flow among top policy makers and national security organizations constitutes the primary causal variable. I measure the degree of multisourcing by examining the types of information that leaders considered. By examining this "paper trail," it is possible to determine which organization provided information to state leaders and at what point in the decision-making process. A second measure focuses on how state leaders responded to information made available to them. If state leaders actively considered information from a number of organizations in a comparative fashion, then the information institution is deemed to be multisourced.[91]

Lateral connections can take a number of forms, including: interdepartmental memoranda, the use of task forces, working groups, and interagency war games that comprise representatives from all affected agencies. For dense lateral connections to have the posited effects, the relations must be viewed by the individuals involved as being mutually beneficial and must include members who are charged with sufficient authority in the organization represented.[92] To have authority, these key individuals do not necessarily have to be the principals within an agency. Those individuals who receive and transmit the bulk of critical information are frequently those who are not at the pinnacle of the organization. When those information managers are included in interagency communications, then the density of lateral connections increases.[93]

It is important to note that my analytical focus is on the formal aspects of information institutions rather than on the informal social networks that form throughout governments. By formal information institutions, I refer to meetings, working groups, and such comprising principals and/or deputies who are formally sanctioned and charged with accomplishing specific interdepartmental objectives. Informal social networks are communication channels and relationships that exist to varying degrees in any large enterprise (either a state or a firm) that tend escape identification on an "organizational chart," but which nevertheless exert significant influence on the performance of the organization. Although recent scholarship has attempted to uncover these "hidden" informational relationships,[94] I consider them only to the extent that they emerge from the historical record. There are two reasons for my focus on formal information institutions. The first is pragmatic in nature: informal informational relationships are extremely difficult to uncover in any government and are even more so when that government ceased to exist over a half a century ago. Even when memoirs, oral histories, and diaries do reference informal communications among individuals, these sources are at best suggestive, and by no means definitive, as to the content of the information shared among individuals. Second, because my focus is on interdepartmental information sharing in the context of national security policy, there is strong reason to expect that individuals will refrain from revealing whom they shared information outside of the "chain of command." Ultimately, it is the formal arrangements, I argue, that affect the quality of strategy design and integration, and about which historical evidence exists in sufficient quantity and quality.

Organizational culture theory proposes that particular norms held by professional militaries strongly influences strategic performance in limited war. The two relevant norms embedded in military organizational cultures—the organization's concept of war and the norm of civil-military relations—can be ascertained by "reviewing available internal correspondence, planning documents, regulations, exercises and the memoirs of individual members. These multiple sources provide a composite picture of the hierarchy of legitimate beliefs within an organization."[95] Because of their importance to military organizations, the two culturally determined norms will likely emerge at the top of this hierarchy of beliefs.

Democratic civil-military relations theory highlights the importance of two primary causal variables. The first, the domestic balance of power between civilian leaders and the military, is held constant because in each case the United States was the state that initiated the limited war. As a democracy, the balance of political power favored civilian leaders. With respect to the preference convergence/divergence variable, I examine the historical record for "evidence of recurring, systematic cleavages over security goals, military strategy/policy, or corporate issues."[96]

All of the approaches under consideration hold that strategic outcomes are affected by a state's information management capacities. I argue that two information management mechanisms directly affect strategic performance in limited war: information collection and analysis and military-diplomatic coordination. For any explanation to be considered complete, the mechanisms generating outcomes must be clearly defined, accurately measured, and empirically verified.

The collection and analysis mechanism can take four forms.[97] At the extremes, a state can have comprehensive collection and optimal analysis, or limited collection and dysfunctional analysis. Information collection deals with intelligence pertaining to opponents, potential interveners, allies, and occupational challenges. The quality of analysis is affected by the degree of information hoarding, the presence of information vetting mechanisms, and the extent to which military and diplomatic trade-offs are explicitly considered in the design of strategy. Between these extremes lie two types of moderate collection and fair analysis. The first occurs when the military operates in isolation. In this case, leaders have access to information about potential interveners and allies but lack information on the opponent and possibly occupational challenges. Further, analysis is strong pertaining to the challenges and opportunities in the strategic environment, but is weak with respect to the opponent. The second occurs when diplomatic and intelligence agencies operate in isolation. Here, leaders have access to information about the opponent but lack information on potential interveners and allies and possibly occupational challenges. Further, analysis is strong pertaining to the opponent, but is weak with respect to the strategic environment. In both of these intermediate cases, military and diplomatic trade-offs are not explicitly considered in the design and execution of strategy.

The military-diplomatic coordination mechanism also comes in four types. At the extremes, coordination can be tightly coordinated or uncoordinated. When tightly coordinated, military and diplomatic organizations work in concert, with the political objectives of the war serving as the focal point of their activity. When uncoordinated, military and diplomatic organizations work at cross-purposes, motivated by internally derived objectives. Between these extremes are two types of poor coordination. The first occurs when the military is unresponsive to political objectives; the second occurs when diplomatic organizations are unresponsive to political objectives.

The Method

Having developed the competing theoretical positions, operationalized the independent and dependent variables, and described the causal mechanisms, I can now turn to how this study hangs together—the method by which I test the information institution approach against the evidence and its competitors. The approach I adopt is a combination of typological theory and process-tracing. According to Alexander George and Andrew Bennett, typological theory "specifies independent variables, delineates them into the categories for which the researcher will measure the cases and their outcomes, and provides not only hypotheses on how these variables operate individually, but also contingent generalizations on how and under what conditions they behave in specified conjunctions or configurations to produce effects on specified dependent variables."[98] By specifying the independent variables of each of the three competing approaches, the dependent variable (strategic performance in limited war), and the two causal mechanisms (information collection and analysis and military-diplomatic coordination) each in four ways, I am able to derive a "property space" of thirty-six cells (see table 7.1 in chapter 7). Each of the four rows constitutes a pathway through which the conjunction of the independent variable and causal mechanisms relates to specific outcomes. The four cases of limited war that I will be examining correspond to each of the four causal pathways.

By adopting a typological approach, I am able not only to clearly differentiate distinct causal pathways that link to specific cases, but I am also able to demonstrate the range of expectations for all of the competing explanations of success and failure in limited war strategies. Moreover, this research design facilitates fine-grained tests among theories by identifying the individual cells where propositions drawn from other approaches compete with those drawn from the information institution approach.[99] To adjudicate among competing propositions, in each case I will process-trace the causal pathways connecting the independent variable, causal mechanisms, and dependent variable.[100] Process-tracing is a valuable tool for uncovering causality because it enables investigators to view the microconnections between larger-scale causes and effects—in this case, by examining how individuals acquired and responded to information. Additionally, process-tracing enables the investigator to uncover additional theoretically relevant observations. As Gary King, Robert Keohane, and Sidney Verba note, "Such strategies link theory and empirical work by using the observable implications of a theory to suggest new observations that should be made to evaluate the theory," observations that reside at a lower level of aggregation but which bear directly on the implicated causal processes.[101] The implication here is that through process-tracing, additional theoretically relevant observations may emerge, and in the process, increase the size of the property space.

The combination of typological theory and process-tracing provides an optimal means of testing competing complex causal claims with a relatively small number of cases. On the one hand, by recognizing that outcomes result from causal conjunctions, typological theory provides clear and consistent procedures for competitive hypothesis testing. On the other hand, process-tracing enables the analyst to ascertain whether or not postulated causal conjunctions occurred in the cases under investigation. Because I argue that the causal association between information institutional design and the outcomes of limited wars is very close, we should insist on a very high bar for confirmation for the information institution approach in particular. Not only should information institutional design and the outcomes of limited war co-vary, but evidence of the two information management mechanisms should also receive empirical support.[102] Absent that strong support, the information institution approach should be jettisoned in favor of the alternatives.

Case Selection

The information institution approach is a general framework that should be applicable to all states. On what grounds do I select only post–World War II cases of American limited warfare? Six factors influenced my choice. First, as I will demonstrate in the empirical chapters, these cases provide complete variation on the dependent variable: double failure (Korea), "little consolation" (Vietnam), double success (Persian Gulf), and "win the battle, lose the war" (Iraq). Second, for each case a wealth of declassified evidence exists pertaining to the information management capabilities of the initiating state. Third, the historical span of these cases covers different structures of the international system (bipolar for Korea and Vietnam wars; unipolar for the Persian Gulf and Iraq wars), thus allowing me to control for the possible confounding effects of the polarity of the system in which these wars unfolded. Fourth, in each case, the United States was substantially more powerful than its primary opponent. Any observed variation in strategic performance can thus not be attributable to power imbalances. Fifth, as the United States is a democracy and possessed in each case a modern professional military, these wars provide a fair proving ground for the competing arguments. Sixth, and finally, the domain of limited warfare is one wherein American presidents possess a monopoly of policy authority. Not only do presidents possess the authority to direct all of the relevant national security organizations of the state, but also limited wars constitute an immediate and threatening challenge for all states involved. As such, information institutions are more likely than other domestic institutions to have a decisive influence on strategic performance in America's limited wars.

CHAPTER THREE

Military and Diplomatic Defeat
in the Korean War

The initial phase of the Korean War, the first American limited war in the post–World War II era, resulted in both military and diplomatic defeats for the United States. In response to North Korea's invasion, top policy makers quickly agreed to an American commitment to restore the status quo that prevailed on the Korean Peninsula prior to the attack. This war aim came under almost immediate fire from a select number of officials in Washington, and more importantly, from General Douglas MacArthur in Tokyo. In the ensuing weeks, top administration officials made the decision to dramatically scale-up American objectives in the war. Well before the expulsion of North Korean forces from South Korea, a consensus emerged around the goal of overthrowing the communist regime. The restoration of the status quo ante was hastily rendered a necessary, but by no means a sufficient, strategic outcome of the war. Yet this expanded war aim was predicated on fundamentally contradictory military and diplomatic objectives; preventing either Soviet or Chinese intervention in the war was deemed vital by officials in Washington. Despite the mounting and widely available information indicating that China would indeed intervene if the United States crossed the 38th parallel, MacArthur was given the green light to invade North Korea in early October 1950. America's limited war strategy in Korea was premised on a skewed and incomplete understanding of strategic environment, uncoordinated military and diplomatic objectives, and a flawed assessment of the risks entailed in its approach to the war. All of these problems stemmed from a single source within the truncated information institution that governed US strategic decision making. In the end,

American officials were incapable of designing a strategy that leveraged information different national security organizations possessed that clearly pointed to the looming disaster of undesired escalation in the Korean War.

This chapter proceeds in four parts. First, I provide a brief narrative of the war from June 25 to November 25, 1950, and show how the United States failed to achieve its military and diplomatic objectives. Second, I describe how the American information institution prior to the outbreak of the war was truncated. I make this case by illustrating how top policy makers were beholden to a single and highly biased source of information, and how the elements within the national security apparatus shared little critical information pertaining to the strategic situation in East Asia. Third, in order to test the causal logic of the information institution approach, I process-trace American strategic decision making at three critical points in the war: the decision to interpose the Seventh Fleet in the Taiwan Strait, the decision to cross into North Korea, and the decision not to halt the offensive at the "narrow neck" of the Korean Peninsula. I conclude by comparing this approach's explanatory logic of strategic performance in limited war to that of its competitors, democratic civil-military relations theory and organizational culture theory.

AMERICA'S STRATEGIC BLUNDERING: FAILING MILITARILY AND DIPLOMATICALLY IN KOREA

Although intelligence assessments convinced the Truman administration that a war on the Korean Peninsula was not likely in 1950, when the well-coordinated and tactically successful North Korean invasion did come it was quickly interpreted by leaders in Washington as being directed and controlled by the Soviet Union.[1] Confirming the expectations embodied in NSC 68,[2] officials in Washington thought the Soviets were testing the firmness of the United States' willingness to resist communist expansion.[3] Moreover, administration officials considered the Northern attack to be a ploy by the Soviets to wear down American capabilities in a nonvital area. Additional attempts could immediately follow on the heels of the North's attack, such as an invasion of Taiwan or the introduction of forces into North Korea by the Soviet's "proxy," the People's Republic of China (PRC).[4] Because the attack represented a challenge to the commitment made by the United States to an ally, President Harry Truman and Secretary of State Dean Acheson were convinced from the start that an American response was crucial.[5] For the president in particular, the Soviet-inspired North Korean attack smacked of

Hitler's piecemeal aggression in the late 1930s. To refrain from responding would be to invite a global war.[6]

Based on its estimates of the intentions of the two states that had the potential of intervening in the conflict, the Soviet Union and China, the Truman administration at first adopted a strategy designed to return the peninsula to the status quo ante. The actions the United States took early on were believed to be circumscribed and cautious. Because officials in Washington were uncertain of Soviet intentions,[7] and because it was hoped that the Republic of Korea Army (ROKA, South Korean Army) would be able to thwart the Northern attack (albeit, with limited American support), the United States undertook modest steps in committing to the conflict. Two factors prompted the administration to increase its efforts in the war, however. The first was the painfully obvious fact that the ROKA stood little chance in stopping the Northern advance. The second was mounting evidence that the Soviets were not inclined to overtly support the North Koreans, at least initially.[8] As the situation became clearer, Acheson recommended to the president that US air and naval forces provide extensive support to the ROKA below the 38th parallel and that the Seventh Fleet be used to prevent a Chinese communist attack on Taiwan, and vice versa.[9]

On June 29, Acheson clearly defined the limited nature of the US/UN response in Korea. The secretary of state labeled the attack "a cynical act of aggression" that posed "a direct challenge to the United Nations." Yet the United Nations' support of South Korea was "solely for the purpose of restoring the Republic of Korea to its status prior to the invasion from the north and of reestablishing the peace broken by that aggression."[10] Although the president soon approved the bombing of military targets north of the 38th parallel and the introduction of ground troops to South Korea, he was determined to keep the war limited and to prevent a direct US-Soviet confrontation.[11] Moreover, Truman and Acheson were intent on refraining from actions that would provoke hostilities from the PRC. Although the administration was concerned that the Soviets would have the PRC do the fighting for them, officials wanted to minimize the risk as much as possible (that is, to limit the PRC's involvement to indirect support).[12] This concern led Acheson to counsel against accepting Chiang Kai-shek's offer of 33,000 Chinese Nationalist troops for the defense of South Korea. Not only were these forces needed for the defense of the island, but also the introduction of Nationalist forces would surely have provoked the direct intervention by the Chinese communists.[13]

Throughout July and August, the military situation in South Korea steadily worsened for ROKA and US forces deployed against the advancing North Korean army. By the end of July, the North Korean army was bearing down on ROKA and American positions south of the Naktong River, an area commonly known as the Pusan Perimeter. For six weeks, the North Koreans launched multiple attacks against these defensive positions. At the end of August, the most violent attacks occurred all along the perimeter. Through the skillful manipulation of interior lines, however, General Walton Walker's Twenty-Fourth Division was able to withstand the North Korean offensive. By September 10, US forces in the Pusan Perimeter had grown substantially due to the continued buildup of troops and materiel. The North Korean forces, on the other hand, were badly diminished and significantly out-gunned. Moreover, the Far East Air Forces (FEAF) and the Seventh Fleet had total command of the air, meaning that no close air support was available to Kim Il Sung's forces.[14]

The fortunes of the North Korean army ultimately changed when the X Corps successfully landed on the beach at Inchon on September 15. For more than two months, MacArthur and his staff had been planning an amphibious attack in the enemy's rear, the intent of which was to envelop the North Korean army (which was vulnerable due to its badly stretched logistical supply route) and destroy it from multiple sides.[15] Although MacArthur was highly optimistic that the plan would succeed, the joint chiefs were wary. It was only on September 8, after MacArthur had repeatedly argued that Operation CHROMITE was viable and presented the best means of defeating the North Korean army in South Korea, that the chiefs relented, granting Douglas MacArthur, as commander in chief, United Nations Command (CINCUNC) the authority to commence the operation.[16] Although it took some time before North Korean forces along the Pusan Perimeter realized that they were vulnerable in the north, by September 22 resistance in the south crumbled and General Walker ordered the breakout with the intent of linking up with the X Corps.[17] By the end of September, the objective of restoring the status quo ante had been obtained. As it appeared to both MacArthur and officials in Washington, the North Korean army had been destroyed and Seoul had been returned to South Korean control.[18]

By this time, however, the restoration of the prewar status quo was not the American war aim. As will be discussed below, the United States was poised to initiate the war for rolling back communism on the Korean Peninsula. The United States would attempt to eradicate the Democratic People's Republic of Korea (DPRK) by occupying the peninsula in its entirety. To achieve this objective, the United States had to defeat the North

Korean army and establish a strong defensive position that would mitigate the impact of any foreign military assistance the North Koreans might receive. Additionally, the United States had to prevent both the Soviet Union and China from intervening in force. If the United States could defeat the North Korean regime militarily, and prevent third party intervention diplomatically, then the United States stood to capture substantial political gains. Not only would Soviet advances be checked, they would also be reversed. American credibility in the eyes of allies and adversaries alike would be substantially bolstered. Combined, these gains would have a salutary effect on the defense of Western Europe by strengthening the perception of American resolve while deterring any encroachment by the Soviets.

On October 8, seven days after ROKA forces, the United States undertook an invasion of North Korea. On October 17 the CINCUNC moved the line beyond which non-ROKA forces were prohibited from crossing thirty miles to the north. That line was roughly forty miles south of the Manchurian border and one hundred miles south of the Soviet border. Two days later he ordered a "maximum effort" by "all concerned" to seize positions along that front and to be "prepared for continued rapid advance to the border of North Korea." Unaware of the Chinese forces coming across the Yalu River, MacArthur ordered the lifting of all of the restrictions imposed on US forces in Korea on October 24. His commanders were "authorized to use any and all ground forces . . . as necessary to secure all of North Korea."[19]

Unknown to MacArthur, the Chinese were able to cross the Yalu with 260,000 troops in mid-October. From October 25 to November 8, the PRC waged what is known as the First Phase Offensive, the objectives of which were to test the strengths and weaknesses of its American and Korean opponents and to lure them in deeper into the northern reaches of the peninsula.[20] In the west, elements of two divisions from two Chinese armies nearly destroyed two South Korean divisions and badly mauled a third. Additionally, elements from one of the Chinese armies essentially destroyed the American Eighth Cavalry Regiment. In the east, Chinese troops moved into the area near the Chosin Reservoir to conduct defensive holding operations against the advancing X Corps.[21] On November 8, however, Chinese military resistance evaporated completely. The First Phase Offensive ended as suddenly as it had begun, leaving the Far East Command (FEC) no more certain of Chinese intentions and capabilities, and officials in Washington deeply concerned.

Significantly, while Korean and American military forces came in contact with Chinese forces from a number of different armies, US military commanders nevertheless believed that these troops were isolated volunteer units supporting the remnants of the North Korean army. By November 25, seventeen days after making their last contact with the Chinese, the United States faced roughly 380,000 Chinese forces in close proximity. But no one, especially those most in need of this information in Washington, had any idea.[22]

The immediate strategic effect of this dramatic underestimation of Chinese troop strength in North Korea was that limited consideration was given to the proposal of halting MacArthur's drive northward and establishing a strong defensive line at the "narrow neck" of the peninsula—an idea MacArthur detested.[23] Little weight was given to the proposal in Washington because MacArthur was certain the Chinese military action was insignificant. MacArthur explained the presence of the Chinese in North Korea in the most benign terms possible: China was attempting to provide covert assistance to the North in order to "salvage something from the wreckage."[24] The next day, MacArthur ordered an air assault intended to "isolate the battlefield" by bombing out the Korean ends of the bridges spanning the Yalu.[25] Although he warned the commander of the Far East Air Force "there must be no violation of the border," this directive violated previous instructions from the Joint Chiefs of Staff (JCS) to stay far away from Manchuria. Upon hearing word of the impending operation, Truman canceled the operation because, first, it violated a standing order from the JCS, and second, because Washington previously promised London that it would not act in ways that would threaten British interests in Manchuria. In the end, the decision was reached, pending further evidence of the PRC's intentions, to permit MacArthur to "continue the action" so long as there remained "a reasonable chance of success."[26]

The plan for MacArthur's "final" offensive consisted of two distinct operations. The first was the air campaign, which began on November 8, and was intended to knock out the bridges spanning the Yalu and to destroy the North Korean and Chinese forces between the United Nation's position and the Manchurian border. Despite the fact that the campaign was largely a failure, MacArthur believed the operation was succeeding. On November 17, the ambassador to South Korea, John Muccio, reported that "the General [MacArthur] . . . was sure the Chinese Communists had sent 25,000, and certainly no more than 30,000, soldiers across the border. They could not possibly have got more over with the surreptitiously covert means used. If they had moved in the open, they would have been detected by our Air Forces and our Intelligence." MacArthur assured Muccio that the air offensive was "destroying all resources in the narrow stretch between our present positions and the border. Unfortunately, this area will be left a desert."[27] The second operation of MacArthur's final offensive was a ground campaign with the objective of pressing on to the border. On November 15 MacArthur ordered General Edward Almond to begin planning for a westward movement toward the Chosin Reservoir to support the Eighth Army's advance in the east. Almond, however, temporized. Not only did he prefer to beat the Eighth Army to the border, but he also was fully convinced that Chinese forces in the Chosin area were meager, estimating that at most 20,000 poorly equipped and trained soldiers stood between his forces and X Corps (their actual strength was nearly 150,000).[28] The Eighth Army's offensive was scheduled to begin on November 15 and end at the Yalu on the twenty-fifth. Owing to significant logistical bottlenecks, however, the Eighth Army's offensive had to be delayed until November 24.[29]

In the meantime, Washington remained intent on finding a political solution to ending the crisis. Two factors affected how that "political solution" would be sought. The first was the expectation that the Chinese had no intention of launching a major attack in the short run.[30] Second, believing that the only way to successfully negotiate with the Chinese was from a position of strength, neither Secretary of Defense George C. Marshall (who had become defense secretary on September 21) nor Acheson was willing to urge a postponement or cancellation of the UN offensive. At a National Security Council (NSC) meeting on November 21, Marshall argued that MacArthur's "end the war" offensive should commence, and only when it was proven successful should negotiations with the Chinese begin. Acheson concurred with this assessment. No one, it appears, was willing to give any further consideration to abandoning territory already controlled by the United Nations in order to establish a defensive position at the narrow neck.[31] On November 25, a day after MacArthur's offensive began, the Chinese attacked in force and threw American and UN forces back across the 38th parallel.

Although Washington was well aware of the massive number of Chinese troops in Manchuria, it lacked an accurate accounting of the number of the Chinese Communist Forces (CCF) in North Korea itself. Strongly influenced by the inaccurate estimates of China's troop strength in the North, Washington held on to the belief that MacArthur's "end the war offensive" could handle the small number of troops in North Korea effectively. While administration officials recognized at this time that a political solution to the war was necessary, such negotiations could only be successful if the

United States bargained from a position of strength. Unfortunately, the United States had not been in a position of strength since October 19. By the time the PRC's Second Phase Offensive began, the Chinese had thirty infantry and three artillery divisions in Korea, with a total troop strength of 380,000.[32]

The result of the war for rollback was a double failure for the United States. Militarily, the United States adopted objectives and prosecuted a strategy that induced Chinese intervention. American and UN forces failed to defeat the North Korean People's Army (NKPA) and secure a strong defensive position to guard against Chinese interference. Diplomatically, Washington failed to convince the PRC that the United States had limited objectives (that is, that the United States had no intention of continuing the war into China), and to issue credible deterrence threats against intervention. In short, the United States adopted irreconcilable military and diplomatic objectives, and as a result the Korean War escalated horizontally and durationally. American military power quickly bogged down in a region that was deemed far from vital by virtually all American officials (save MacArthur).

A TRUNCATED INFORMATION INSTITUTION

I argue that the origins of the double failure of American limited war strategy lie in the truncated American information institution. In terms of leaders' access to information, top policy makers received intelligence pertaining to the strategic environment almost exclusively from a single source, General Douglas MacArthur's Far East Command. Moreover, the weakness of both the Central Intelligence Agency (CIA) and the National Security Council system ensured that little critical information was shared throughout the US government.

A Dearth of Lateral Connections and Information Mismanagement

Prior to the outbreak of the Korean War, American information management capabilities were severely limited, first, by the absence of communication channels connecting the various national security departments and agencies to each other. Two institutions existed at the time, which in theory, could have served as the conduits linking the national security bureaucracy together: the CIA and the NSC system. Yet, the CIA and NSC system were recent additions to the national security apparatus and as such lacked the power and authority to perform this function effectively. Because each con-stituted a threat to existing departments' autonomy and prerogatives, they stood little chance of overcoming bureaucratic resistance in the short run.

There were two ways in which the CIA was supposed to serve as the crit-ical information clearinghouse for top foreign policy officials. The first was to coordinate the intelligence collection activities of the various bureaus in the intelligence community (IC). The first Director of Central Intelligence (DCI), Roscoe Hillenkoetter, attempted to establish a forum wherein the intelligence chiefs from across the IC could coordinate collection activities and intelligence sharing. The mechanism through which coordination was to be achieved was the Interdepartmental Coordinating and Planning Staff (ICAPS), a body that reported to the DCI. From the perspective of the other intelligence chiefs, however, Hillenkoetter represented a threat to their au-tonomy. Representatives from the military and State Department refused to concede any coordinating authority to ICAPS largely because they viewed the DCI only as an equal player in the intelligence community.[33] From the start, intelligence collection was fragmented across the IC. No mechanism existed to establish government-wide intelligence priorities, to determine how scarce resources should best be used, or to respond to the most press-ing interests of top policy makers.[34]

If the direction of the intelligence activities of the IC was one side of the problem, the other was the coordination of the products of those depart-ments in reports and estimates of value to top policy makers in the ad-ministration. Among the CIA's primary objectives was the streamlining of intelligence production with the goal of correcting what had become clearly biased analyses by individual departments.[35] Toward this end, the Office of Reports and Estimates (ORE) was established to review raw intelligence and to transform it into objective estimates as an aid to determining future foreign-military policy.[36] This directive suited President Truman's desire to ensure that all of the intelligence pertaining to American national security policy would be centrally coordinated in an effort to prevent an attack as that suffered at Pearl Harbor.[37] At the same time, Truman wanted to reduce the burden of assessing the massive volume of cables, memos, and reports generated by the individual departments that came into him on a daily ba-sis. Truman requested that an intelligence digest be delivered to him daily that would reduce his workload while keeping him on top of developments around the world. Although these two demands had merit, they resulted in a conflict in mission of the ORE—a conflict between current and national intelligence.

In neither of these tasks did the ORE perform well. It quickly became apparent that the production of reports and estimates based on effective coordination would be an unattainable goal. In line with the American military's Jominian norm of civil-military relations, providing a civilian agency with critical information pertaining to the strengths and weaknesses of foreign forces was considered a breach of professionalism that was potentially dangerous, as civilians were understood to lack the training and expertise to understand such data. Compounding the problem was the fact that the military refused to provide information related to the capabilities and objectives of *American* armed forces.[38] As one ORE official lamented,

> The service agencies have always made a rigid distinction between *operational* and *intelligence* materials and have freely given CIA what they regard as intelligence materials but have refused to give CIA operational materials. Under this guise, they have withheld from CIA such sensitive materials as General MacArthur's reports from Tokyo, General Clay's reports from Berlin, Admiral Struble's reports from the Seventh Fleet, Admiral Badger's reports from Tsingtao, General Van Fleet's reports from Athens, etc. CIA does not receive reports made to the Joint Chiefs of Staff, many of which must, because of their origin and their subject, be worthy of the President's attention.[39]

The military services were not the only organs to block information to the ORE. Information management within the CIA itself was dysfunctional as well. The information collected by the CIA's own clandestine branch, the Office of Special Operations (OSO), was highly compartmentalized, and the ORE never gained access to the raw data elements within the CIA collected. The only information available to the ORE from within the CIA was overt in nature.[40] Confronted by both inter- and intradepartmental resistance, the ORE was unable to function as an information clearinghouse and began relying almost exclusively on its own resources to produce intelligence estimates.[41]

The final impediment to the ORE's performance was that it was charged with fulfilling the dual mission of producing both national and current intelligence. Because President Truman placed great stock in the daily and weekly intelligence digests prepared for him, the vast majority of ORE's efforts went to producing these reports. As a result, the estimating effort suffered greatly; national estimative analysis took on an "also-ran" status. This is not to imply that the *Daily* and *Weekly* digests were of the highest quality. In fact, because the editors of these reports lacked direct access to the policy makers who were purportedly reading them, the selection of topics for inclusion in each "was a shot in the dark." As R. Jack Smith notes, "The comic backdrop to this daily turmoil [the production of the *Daily*] was that in actuality *nobody* knew what President Truman wanted to see or not see. . . . How were we to judge, sitting in a rundown temporary building on the edge of the Potomac, what was fit for the President's eyes?"[42] Ray Cline aptly described the ORE's record during this period:

> It cannot honestly be said that it [the ORE] coordinated either intelligence ac-
> tivities or intelligence judgments; these were guarded closely by Army, Navy,
> Air Force, State, and the FBI. When attempts were made to prepare agreed
> national estimates on the basis of intelligence available to all, the coordination
> process was interminable, dissents were the rule rather than the exception, and
> every policymaking official took his own agency's intelligence appreciations
> along to the White House to argue his case. The prewar chaos was largely rec-
> reated with only a little more lip service to central coordination.[43]

The problems with intelligence direction and coordination did not go unnoticed by the administration. In January 1949, the Intelligence Survey Group (ISG), under the chairmanship of Allen Dulles, submitted a report that was highly critical of both ICAPS and the ORE.[44] Most importantly, this study contained a criticism of the CIA that would have a significant impact on the ability of the agency to perform its functions between 1949 and the outbreak of the Korean War. The report baldly stated, "Since it is the task of the Director to see that the Agency carries out its assigned functions, the failure to do so is necessarily a reflection of inadequacies of direction." In other words, Hillenkoetter was personally to blame for the dysfunctional nature of interdepartmental relations within the intelligence community.[45] If at this point DCI Hillenkoetter had resigned and was replaced by some-one with greater bureaucratic acumen, then this admonition would have been effective. However, Hillenkoetter would remain in his post for another year and a half. His competence had been called into question publicly, and as such, there was an even smaller chance that the bureaucratic obstacles to effective information transmission would be removed.

By the spring of 1950, the situation had deteriorated so completely that little in the way of actual national intelligence was being done. By this time, Hillenkoetter's stock had fallen to a depth so low the DCI was not invited to attend either of the Blair House meetings wherein the American response to the North Korean invasion was planned.[46] After Hillenkoetter requested that he be returned to active duty with the navy, General Walter Bedell Smith took over as DCI on October 7, 1950. Smith soon discovered that even after months of fighting, no current coordinated estimate of the situation in the Far East had been produced.[47]

The second institutional mechanism that could have served to connect the disparate elements of the national security apparatus together was the NSC system. Similar to the CIA, however, the NSC system failed in this task. There were two primary obstacles confronting the NSC system. The first was the formalistic manner of Truman's advisory system. By requiring individual department heads to report directly to him, Truman placed himself in a precarious information processing position as the sole arbiter of contending and conflicting intelligence (hence his desire for a daily intelligence digest that would assist him in making decisions).[48]

At its inception, the National Security Council was intended to be the primary advisory body to the president. Critical to the effectiveness of this body was the recognition by the president and council members alike that disagreements over policy should not be suppressed, but rather that they be clearly articulated at every stage in the policy-making process. Not only was this principle deemed crucial to providing Truman with multiple options, but just as importantly it was also seen as a means of preventing the council from foreclosing alternative policy avenues prematurely. In order for this advisory system to function effectively, it was incumbent upon the president to actively manage the council and its proceedings. Because he occupied a critical node in the information institution, Truman had to avail himself to as wide a range of information as possible.

Nevertheless, the National Security Council failed to operate effectively. Over time, attendance at council meetings grew to a substantial size. In addition to the heads of the representative departments, a number of NSC consultants and lower-level departmental advisers frequently attended the meetings. As a result of the sheer size of council meetings, open and focused discussion was easily inhibited. Council members quickly realized that their own departmental advisers were of greater value in providing them information than was to be gained at council meetings. Furthermore, in an effort to keep discussions at the meetings from being closed off, Truman eventually quit attending NSC meetings on a regular basis. The results, however, were less focused discussions and the frequent deferment of actions that required presidential approval. Finally, Truman's absence from council meetings prevented him from hearing council members' own direct expression of their views. Without the ability to query and prod his advisers, Truman cut himself off from a great deal of information and advice.[49]

This formalistic method of information delivery was only a general tendency, however, as Truman did convene a special working group to develop the most important strategic document of the early Cold War era, NSC 68.[50] The second, and more significant, obstacle to interdepartmental information sharing was the relative infancy and weakness of the NSC system. The impotence of the NSC system became clear when a personal feud erupted between Secretary of State Acheson and Secretary of Defense Louis Johnson, a long dispute that redounded negatively at the working levels of the government.[51]

One mechanism that could have bridged the Department of State (DOS) and Department of Defense (DOD) at the working level was the NSC Staff. Originally designed to serve as an executive liaison among departments, the NSC Staff—in theory—had the ability to maintain State-Defense coordination regardless of relations among departmental principals. Poorly funded and staffed, however, the NSC Staff soon proved itself to be a hindrance to achieving departmental objectives. Shortly after its inception, the Staff became irrelevant to the policy-making process as departments submitted policy papers directly to the NSC, bypassing the Staff entirely.[52] In sum, because the CIA and NSC Staff were incapable of fulfilling their crucial function, the Truman administration's information management system fell victim to personal disputes among departmental principals.

Single-Sourced Information Flows and Flying Blind

Leaders' access to information from multiple sources is critical to mitigating uncertainty in a complex strategic environment. With respect to the Asia-Pacific Theater, top policy makers received the vast majority of strategic information from MacArthur's Far East Command. To understand how the FEC assumed the dominant position in the American information institution, its relationship with three other national security organs needs to be evaluated: the CIA, State Department, and the Joint Chiefs of Staff. Ultimately, none of these organizations could serve top policy makers as an alternative source of information to that of the FEC.

The CIA, in particular its covert operations activities, was a potential alternative source of information that top policy makers could have tapped as the limited war strategy was designed and implemented. Yet consistent with the prevailing Jominian relational norm the American military held, MacArthur and his intelligence chief, Major General Charles Willoughby, had a long history of excluding other intelligence agencies from their domain. During the Second World War, MacArthur effectively barred the CIA's wartime predecessor, the Office of Strategic Services (OSS), from carrying out intelligence and propaganda operations. This pattern continued after the war ended. It was only after the outbreak of the Korean War that MacArthur reluctantly (and in a limited capacity) granted the CIA permission to operate on the Korean Peninsula.[53] In short, the dominant source of information pertaining to Chinese intentions and military capabilities before the outbreak of the Korean War was the intelligence organs within the Far East Command. According to Army Chief of Staff General J. Lawton Collins, an estimated 90 percent of the intelligence received before and during the Korean War came from the FEC.[54]

MacArthur's responsibility over intelligence matters grew dramatically after the North Korean attack. Following the UN Security Council vote to grant the United States authority over the multinational forces committed to combat, Truman selected MacArthur to command the coalition. The choice of General MacArthur would frustrate the president's ability to manage the limited war on organizational grounds. When MacArthur was selected to be CINCUNC, he was already saddled with the heavy burden of serving as the supreme commander, Allied Powers (SCAP) in occupied Japan, as the commander in chief, Far East Command of US ground, air, and sea forces (CINCFE), and as the commanding general, US Army Forces, Far East (USAFFE). MacArthur's United Nations Command (UNC) headquarters, located in downtown Tokyo, was staffed by officials who, like their superior, were already tasked with numerous responsibilities, only one of which was waging war. As the official army history notes, "with few exceptions, staff members of the Far East Command were assigned comparable duties on the UNC staff. In effect, the GHQ United Nations Command, was the GHQ, Far East Command, with an expanded mission."[55] These command decisions bolstered MacArthur's authority dramatically, and as such, no other military or civilian entity could effectively compete with MacArthur's estimates of the strategic situation in the Far East.

Yet information management within the FEC was dysfunctional. Surrounding MacArthur was a small group of intensely loyal advisers who served as the general's informational Praetorian Guard. In the words of MacArthur's biographer, D. Clayton James, "MacArthur was shielded by his GHQ senior staff officers in unfortunate ways; this was part of the legacy of their adulation of him from World War II." MacArthur possessed limited knowledge of the status of the Eighth Army under his command. "MacArthur's staff shielded the Far East commander from evidence suggesting the Eighth Army's progress toward combat readiness was not impressive, and he was quite shocked by the troops' poor performances early in the Korean War." Moreover,

MacArthur lived strangely isolated, apart from the activities of his Far East Command. Sadly, his trust in Willoughby was so deep by then that MacArthur's intelligence data came almost solely from his G-2, and Willoughby could be quite selective and sometimes erroneous in what he provided his commander. . . . It was as if MacArthur existed in Tokyo in a cocoon, perhaps of his own choosing but possibly created by his sycophantic staff chiefs. The price he would pay for such insularity would be tragically high.[56]

Willoughby's inability to accurately determine Chinese intentions was a contributing factor in the disaster that befell the United States in November 1950. While Willoughby's failure to correctly read the strategic situation from the evidence that was in his possession was certainly his fault, he was also hamstrung by deficiencies in intelligence collection—namely, a lack of signals intelligence (SIGINT) and communications intelligence (COMINT) resources in possession by the FEC G-2. In particular, the intelligence chief lacked trained Chinese linguists to translate Chinese radio traffic.[57] The paucity of such intelligence assets, it may be recalled, can be explained by the inability for ICAPS at the CIA to effectively coordinate the intelligence activities and assets of the broader intelligence community. Regardless, the primary point to be made is that the information that was made available to MacArthur by his intelligence chief was frequently erroneous (at times intentionally so), and often incomplete.

With respect to information from diplomatic sources, to some extent the State Department was hampered by the absence of direct state-to-state contacts between the United States and the PRC.[58] Nevertheless, DOS possessed a wealth of information pertaining to the broader strategic environment—much of which had direct military relevance. Ultimately, two factors inhibited the State Department from serving as a powerful alternative source of information to top policy makers. First, by virtue of the preeminence of the FEC in the Asia-Pacific region since World War II, the sheer volume of information provided by the DOS paled in comparison to that of MacArthur's command. To a considerable extent, State was beholden to information originating from the FEC, as was every other national security organization in the US government. Second, as will be discussed extensively below, the DOS was an organization divided along ideological lines: the Office of Northeast Asian Affairs was led by the hawkish anticommunist John Allison, while the Policy Planning Staff (PPS) was filled with officials who were more pragmatic (though still anticommunist). This ideological divide prevented the DOS from providing a clearly alternative interpretation of the situation in the Far East to that offered by MacArthur's command.

While those in the Policy Planning Staff made an attempt to undercut the prevailing wisdom originating from Tokyo, they lacked the broader institutional support to counter the tacit alliance between the FEC and the Office of Northeast Asian Affairs.

Finally, MacArthur's relationship with the Joint Chiefs of Staff and with other officials in Washington was itself problematic. On the one hand, MacArthur was senior to all of his supposed superiors in the JCS, and because of the tremendous authority he was granted at the time of the outbreak of the war, his ability to skew information sent to Washington to serve his own strategic objectives went unchecked. "MacArthur interpreted directives and guidance from all levels in Washington—Army, JCS, the secretary of defense, and the president—in ways that afforded him wider latitude of action and expression than intended." While his orders were frequently vague and contradictory, MacArthur's position as the primary source of information pertaining to the situation in the Far East afforded him the ability to conduct operations with only the most limited oversight.[59] Not only did MacArthur have meager awareness of Chinese intentions (as he received inaccurate information from Willoughby), but so too was Washington in the dark about the intentions and capabilities of the PRC. MacArthur's command was the dominant source of strategic information about China upon which administration officials relied. Without information derived from alternative sources pertaining to the Chinese military capabilities, top policy makers did not have the ability to question the veracity of MacArthur's reporting, nor were they able to exert moderating influence on military operations.

In sum, the American information institution prior to the outbreak of the Korean War was truncated. In terms of the two primary measures offered in chapter 2, the agencies and departments within the US government functioned largely in isolation from one another, and information pertaining to the strategic environment originated predominantly from a single source. Despite the best intentions of its creators, the CIA was unable to assume a position of power within the American intelligence community largely because of entrenched bureaucratic obstacles to effective information sharing. The result was that high quality national intelligence products were never produced before the outbreak of war on the Korean Peninsula. Without a solid informational foundation, there was a high probability that decision makers would be unable to craft a limited war strategy that was well suited to the strategic environment. Because of the weakness of the NSC system, dense lateral connections among the DOS and DOD were never created or maintained. The chances were slim that these two departments could have produced an effective limited war strategy in the summer of 1950. Finally, the ability of top policy makers to receive accurate political and military intelligence about the PRC was hampered by a near exclusive dependence on the FEC for strategic information. Even if the FEC's intelligence was of the highest quality, the inability to obtain information and estimates from alternative sources prevented officials in Washington from coming to terms with the PRC's intentions. As it was, the FEC's intelligence products were frequently biased, inaccurate, and incomplete. Thus the information institution approach expects the United States to enter the Korean War with limited information collection and dysfunctional analytic capabilities, and with uncoordinated military and diplomatic components of its limited war strategy.

WAGING WAR BY INEFFECTIVE INFORMATION MANAGEMENT

During times of crisis, information is typically incomplete, knowledge of the strategic environment tends toward uncertainty, and time is frequently of the essence. Under such situations, it is critical that effective information management procedures be in place so that policy makers can make decisions that are less error prone and stand less of a chance of redounding negatively in the future. This conclusion did not escape the Intelligence Survey Group's final report on the problems of the American intelligence community. In the section of the ISG's report pertaining to the functioning of the CIA's Office of Reports and Estimates, the following recommendation was posited:

> There should . . . be [a] provision for the prompt handling of major emergency situations so that, as a matter of course, when quick estimates are required, there is immediate consultation and collective appraisal by the Intelligence Advisory Committee on the basis of all available information.[60]

Such collaborative procedures did not emerge in the year and a half following the report's submission.

Compounding this problem, shortly after the North Korean attack President Truman instructed his advisers "that all proposals for presidential action in the current Korean crisis were to be forwarded to him through the NSC machinery; no unilateral proposals for his action were to be sent directly to him."[61] One effect of this directive was that the CIA's marginalization would be continued throughout the war. As noted, DCI Hillenkoetter was not included among the participants at the two critical Blair House meetings in late June, and there was no chance that his influence with the president could be bolstered as the war progressed. At working levels in the intelligence community, moreover, the CIA's advice and estimates would continue to be given short shrift as vital information would remain withheld from the agency's analysts.

In terms of the NSC machinery itself, Truman's order served to reify existing and dysfunctional information management processes. The lack of consultation and information sharing that characterized interagency relations prior to the war continued throughout. For example, in response to an August request from Dean Acheson for information related to aerial attacks in areas proximate to China's borders, Louis Johnson replied:

> I firmly believe in the importance of political considerations in politico-military decisions. However, I also believe that the conduct of military operations, once we are committed to such operations, are not subject to question in detail as long as they are conducted within the terms of the over-all decision and as long as our military commanders are held responsible for their successful conclusion. In short, once war operations are undertaken, it seems to me that they must be conducted to win. To any extent that external appearances are permitted to conflict with or hamper military judgment in actual combat decisions, the effectiveness of our forces will be jeopardized and the question of responsibility may well be raised.[62]

As a result, the strategy adopted was not based on a foundation of coordinated diplomatic and military intelligence—a foundation critical for effective limited war strategies.

From the Status Quo Ante to "Rollback"

Between June 25 and October 8, 1950, the Truman administration made two crucial decisions pertaining to how it would wage the American limited war in Korea. First, on June 27 the United States interposed the Seventh Fleet in the Taiwan Strait in an effort to prevent expansion of the war in that area. Second, on September 11 the administration gave its approval for waging war across the 38th parallel into North Korea with the president's signing of NSC 81/1. On October 8, American forces crossed the parallel seven days after the South Korean army's initial breach of the border. Together, these actions induced the PRC's intervention in the war,[63] an outcome the United

States wanted to avoid. While the initial decision was made in haste two days after the North Korean attack, the second decision was subject to intense discussion and debate in Washington and Tokyo. Significantly, these decisions were predicated on faulty estimates of how the PRC would likely behave throughout the course of the war. A more accurate understanding was available to American officials, one that would have prevented the United States from provoking Chinese intervention. This alternative perspective of Chinese intentions was never given a proper hearing, and the US military found itself fighting an entirely different war than was expected.

The initial American response to the outbreak of war on the peninsula was designed during two critical meetings in Washington at Blair House, the president's temporary residence. At these meetings, information on the current status of the PRC was scantily presented, and the possible future intentions of the PRC were barely discussed. To the extent that China was considered at all, it was viewed strictly as a pawn of the Kremlin. At the first Blair House meeting on June 25, a memorandum drafted by General MacArthur on June 14 (before the outbreak of the war) was the primary focus of attention, the effect of which was to narrow the participants' attention to the necessity of preventing Taiwan's fall and of "drawing a line" beyond which Soviet encroachments could not be allowed to cross. MacArthur posited that if the Soviets were allowed access to the island, American freedom of action in the Pacific and the security of the US defense perimeter would be placed in serious jeopardy.

> Formosa in the hands of the Communists can be compared to an unsinkable aircraft carrier and submarine tender ideally located to accomplish Soviet offensive strategy and at the same time checkmate counteroffensive operations by the United States Forces based on Okinawa and the Philippines.

Due to the island's strategic importance, MacArthur continued, "Unless the United States' political-military strategic position in the Far East is to be abandoned, it is obvious that the time must come in the foreseeable future when a line must be drawn beyond which Communist expansion will be stopped."[64] Moreover, while preemptive action in the strait could have provoked war with the Soviets (and by proxy, with the Chinese), the risk was deemed minimal because the Soviets were not seen as desiring war with the United States at the present time. Based on the analysis of this report, the Blair House attendees reasoned that while the Kremlin was certainly the force behind the North Korean attack, the Soviets would in all likelihood refrain from escalating if American action was swift and resolute.[65]

To the extent that American actions would prevent the PRC from taking Taiwan by force, it is surprising the minimal extent to which China was considered an independent actor in the unfolding crisis.[66] Moreover, when Chinese strategic calculations were explicitly considered, they were cast in the most favorable of terms for the United States. On the day that President Truman announced the Seventh Fleet decision, the State Department's Office of Intelligence Research (OIR) disseminated a wide-ranging assessment of the developing crisis. This document is of significance because it is among the few to refer to the PRC as having some degree of decision-making autonomy. According to the report, should the United States respond in a forceful manner (such as effective measures to forestall the PRC from capturing Taiwan) then the leaders in Beijing might come to see the Soviet's Korean adventure as a move that adversely affected Chinese interests. China might realize that the Soviets were incapable of outlasting the United States in the Cold War, and as a result, the newly formed Sino-Soviet alliance might weaken with a demonstration of American resolve and strength.[67]

The combined effect of these memos fundamentally altered Chinese-American relations, although administration officials did not recognize this. MacArthur's memo was more than a routine estimate of an existing strategic environment; it was a call for a revamped and expansive national security strategy. The problems were that its consideration came at a time when pressure for military action was extreme, and that it entered a decision-making framework incapable of conducting long-term forecasting. Specifically, no interdepartmental study had been conducted on the implications of such a strategic reorientation (that is, how securing Taiwan would complicate existing major war plans), no consideration was given to the likely effects it would have on the intentions of the PRC in light of the January 1950 declarations that Taiwan lay outside of the US defense perimeter, and no estimate was considered as to how the PRC would likely behave militarily given that the United States would soon be waging war on the Korean Peninsula. Rather, those present at the Blair House meetings simply grabbed onto MacArthur's recommendations because they *seemed* appropriate. Moreover, neither the MacArthur nor the OIR memo explicitly considered the possible downsides of the proposed course of action. It was entirely likely that the Chinese would interpret the interposition of the Seventh Fleet in the most hostile terms possible: as intervention in the yet unfinished Chinese civil war. While it was possible that a forceful US response would weaken the bonds between the two communist countries, it was just as possible that the opposite reaction could be induced—that American actions might force the Chinese to rely more heavily on the Soviets for support. As a result of the truncated information institution, American decision makers were not exposed to alternative recommendations and estimates as the United States began to chart its course in the Korean War. The president and his top advisers labored under a massive information burden, and without the benefit of effective information vetting mechanisms, decisions would be made only after cursory analysis.

Ultimately, China's intervention was motivated by what it saw as an increasing threat the United States posed.[68] As the United States undertook actions that were viewed as threatening to the Chinese, the belligerence of the PRC's policies increased accordingly. Unfortunately, American officials never came to terms with this logic. Rather, the Truman administration believed that Chinese intervention in the Korean War would be determined by a Soviet-centric, global logic wherein Chinese decision making was determined by Moscow and was conditioned by the Kremlin's desire to avoid sparking a global war with the United States. Although this perspective was off the mark, it did not necessarily rule out the possibility that the PRC would intervene in the war. Specifically, there were two strands of this Soviet-centric logic. The first, proffered by the CIA (and held by the State Department's Policy Planning Staff), saw the use of Chinese forces in Korea as a means by which the Kremlin could prolong the war, draining American political, economic, and military resources in the process, and at minimal risk of sparking World War III. The second strand, explicated by the Office of Northeast Asian Affairs in the DOS, held that the Soviets would not undertake *any* action that increased the possibility of global war with the United States. As such, the path was clear for the United States to impose unification of the two Koreas at low cost. Whereas the CIA's preferred logic was more accurate, it stood little chance of guiding US decision making because the agency was marginalized in the US information institution.

The CIA's version emerged relatively soon after the start of the Korean War, and remained throughout the period under consideration. Its clearest articulation is found in the agency's Intelligence Memorandum 302, "Consequences of the Korean Incident" of July 8. According to the CIA, the Soviet Union was seen as being an expansionist power, but one not prone to excessively risky behavior. Because Moscow was not materially prepared for a global war with the United States, it would take steps to avoid provoking direct conflict. As such, the Soviets were expected to employ strategies designed to wear down American military, economic, and political resources in ways that were considered to be of low to moderate risk. Further, the Soviets were considered to have nearly complete control over the foreign policy of the PRC, which was seen as being capable of deploying forces in multiple arenas even before the outbreak of the war.

The CIA expected that the Soviets would attempt to localize the fighting in Korea and refrain from initiating conflict elsewhere. Yet in order to prolong the American involvement in the war, Moscow would increase its military assistance to North Korea, "perhaps employing Chinese Communist troops, either covertly or overtly." In pursuing this course of action, the Soviet Union would be able to remain uncommitted to the war while enabling it to wage a propaganda campaign against the United States. This course of action was considered to entail only a moderate risk of global war with the United States.[69]

Significantly, the CIA's estimates and reports from the period July 8 to October 8 were guided by the logic detailed in Intelligence Memorandum 302.[70] For example, in response to the pressure being exerted by many in the government for an expansion of American war aims, on August 18 the CIA posited,

> Although an invasion of North Korea by UN forces could, if successful, bring several important advantages to the US, it appears at present that grave risks would be involved in such a course of action. The military success of the operation is by no means assured because the US cannot count on the cooperation of the non-Communist UN members and might also become involved in hostilities with Chinese Communist and Soviet troops. Under such circumstances there would, moreover, be a grave risk of general war.[71]

This cautionary warning became far more specific one month later—five days *after* NSC 81/1 (the enabling document permitting an invasion of North Korea) was signed by the president, but *before* American forces crossed the parallel.

> While it is doubtful that either Soviet or Chinese Communist forces will be committed south of the 38th parallel, both Moscow and Peiping [*sic*] have the capability of sending organized military units to reinforce the North Koreans at any critical juncture. They are much more likely, however, to aid the Communist cause in Korea by releasing large numbers of trained Chinese Communist . . . units, perhaps including small air units, for incorporation in the North Korean forces.[72]

In sum, while the CIA missed the regional, threat-based logic that would eventually drive Chinese intervention, from late June to late September the agency consistently advocated a cautious approach to American policy in the Korean War as a result of a logic that saw the introduction of Chinese troops as having only a minimal impact on the likelihood of global war.[73]

The CIA's consistent warnings had no appreciable affect on the US government's decision making with respect to crossing the 38th parallel. The primary obstacle to the CIA exerting influence on the course of strategic design was that it was largely isolated in the American information institution. Because the CIA was excluded from key strategic debates, those in the government who remained skeptical about an advance north of the 38th parallel could not use its assessments. Because many of the CIA's intelligence products were forced into the "NSC machinery," adjudication of contending estimates of likely Chinese behavior was left up to the NSC principals themselves, rather than at lower levels where the broader strategic questions were being debated. As such, top decision makers were saddled with the responsibilities of squaring dynamic intelligence with finished policy proposals (proposals that had by that time acquired significant bureaucratic support). In short, the isolation of the CIA prematurely closed off debate on the merits of expanding US war aims and dramatically increased the information burden of top policy makers as they made decisions on the course of the Korean War.

The official primarily responsible for forging a "consensus" on the viability of taking the war into North Korea was John Allison, the director of the Office of Northeast Asian Affairs in the State Department. In two critical memos, Allison argued that crossing the parallel, while potentially risky, was absolutely necessary to achieving peace and security in the region, and to punishing local acts of aggression.[74] On July 17, Allison was charged with the responsibility for guiding the effort that would eventually produce NSC 81/1.[75]

Allison's position was most clearly articulated in response to a paper drafted by the State Department's Policy Planning Staff on July 22. The stance that the PPS adopted in this first paper was strikingly similar to that which the CIA adopted in its critical Intelligence Memorandum 302 of July 8. According to the PPS, it was extremely unlikely that the Soviet Union would permit the existence of a noncommunist regime in North Korea that it could not dominate. As such, "When it becomes apparent that the North Korean aggression will be defeated, there might be some agreement between the U.S.S.R. and the North Korean regime which would mean in substance the U.N. military action north of the 38th parallel would result in conflict with the U.S.S.R. or Communist China." Given the inherent risks associated with crossing the 38th parallel, and because of the nature of existing American security commitments and military strength, the PPS concluded, "If U.N. forces were to continue military ground action north of the 38th parallel . . . the danger of conflict with Chinese Communist or Soviet forces would be greatly increased." In the final analysis, "The risks of bringing on a major conflict with the U.S.S.R. or Communist China, if U.N. military action north of the 38th parallel is employed in an effort to reach a 'final' settlement in Korea, appear to outweigh the political advantages that might be gained from such further military action."[76]

On July 24, Allison rejected the idea that any resolution to the Korean problem could be resolved through a political process based on the restoration of the status quo ante. "The aggressor would apparently be consulted on equal or nearly equal terms and the real aggressor, the Soviet Union, would presumably go unpunished in any way whatsoever. The aggressor would be informed that all he had to fear from aggression was being compelled to start over again." Among the failures of the PPS position, Allison noted, was its unwillingness to consider the fact that the North Korean regime was illegitimate in terms of international law and morality as it was a creature of the Soviet Union. Additionally, the PPS draft ignored the fact that the Soviet Union was currently in violation of the UN charter because it was providing aid to a regime against which the United Nations was acting. Finally, by failing to consider the "attitude of the 20 million people of South Korea who have been wantonly attacked, and the more than 2 million Koreans who fled from Soviet oppression in the North and sought refuge in the South," the PPS draft was barren of ethical content. Allison concluded,

> The paper assumes we can buy more time by a policy of appeasement—for that is what this paper recommends—a timid, half-heated policy designed not to provoke the Soviets to war. We should recognize that there is grave danger of conflict with the USSR and the Chinese Communists whatever we do from now on—but I fail to see what advantage we gain by a compromise with clear moral principles and a shirking of our duty to make clear once and for all that aggression does not pay—that he who violates the decent opinions of mankind must take the consequences and that he who takes the sword will perish by the sword.
>
> That this may mean war on a global scale is true—the American people should be told and told why and what it will mean to them. When all legal and moral right is on our side why should we hesitate?[77]

Despite the fact that Allison's willingness to run significant risks with the Soviet Union and China over Korea was completely out of step with objectives of Truman, Acheson, and the Joint Chiefs of Staff, this paper had the effect of killing any hope that the United States would refrain from crossing the 38th parallel. At no point after July 24 did State Department officials ever forward such cautious positions as those found in the PPS's initial draft memorandum.

The primary reason for this timidity was the fact that no support could be marshaled by the PPS that pointed to an increasing likelihood that crossing the 38th parallel would result in war with China or the Soviet Union. As Allison stated, the chances of global war were high no matter what course of action the United States adopted. This was, to repeat, not the position the CIA adopted. Yet because the PPS and the CIA were isolated from each other in the American information institution there was little chance of countering Allison's influence. On July 25, the PPS issued a second draft of its position that neither refuted Allison's claims—a task that could have easily been accomplished with estimates readily available from the CIA—nor retained the strong admonition against crossing the border.[78] Without the ability to counter Allison's charges, the PPS in effect retired from the bureaucratic battle, advocating that now was not the proper time to make such momentous strategic decisions.

Neither did the JCS share Allison's willingness to risk sparking global war. As the United States was currently deployed heavily in a region of marginal strategic importance, the JCS stressed that if the Kremlin were to enter the war or to indicate its intentions of doing so, "the U.S. should prepare to minimize its commitment in Korea and prepare to execute war [global] plans."[79] This sentiment was widely shared in the State Department. On August 25, a DOS meeting was held during which possible restrictions to US actions in North Korea were discussed. It was agreed that UN forces should remain well clear of the Soviet frontier. Specifically, State officials recommended that the narrow neck be the agreed northern stopping point, a point that would permit the most effective defensive consolidation and would provide the Soviets a sizeable and geographically suitable buffer zone.[80]

Allison submitted his final position paper to the NSC on August 30. Adhering to the warnings voiced by DOS officials on the twenty-fifth, Allison noted that the "risk of provoking a clash of Soviet forces with the UN forces will be inversely proportional to the distance between the front line UN forces and the Siberian-Manchurian borders." As such, General MacArthur should "refrain from any ground activity, either combat or occupational, in areas close to the international borders of Korea, or in any more distant areas the occupation of which might reasonably be construed as greatly increasing the military vulnerability of Vladivostok or any other strategic center in Siberia or Manchuria." The paper went on to specifically note that operations in the area behind the narrow neck (39th parallel) were considered to be those that would likely threaten those strategic centers. Despite these warnings, Allison's paper did provide a critical escape clause: "The UN Commander should not be denied the authority to carry out such operations in his discretion without conclusive reasons for such denial." With respect to the possibility of outside intervention in Korea, Allison argued that "if the intelligence available to the UN Commander should indicate that there will be important organized USSR or Chinese Communist resistance, he should not advance farther without specific authorization and should immediately refer the matter to the United Nations." In other words, critical strategic decisions were to be left to MacArthur's judgment based on intelligence estimates conducted by the Far East Command.[81]

On September 11, 1950, President Truman signed NSC 81/1, the enabling strategic document permitting US forces to cross the 38th parallel in an effort to destroy the North Korean regime and unify the peninsula. The objective of the next phase of the Korean War was to accomplish the "complete independence and unity of Korea . . . without substantially increasing the risk of general war with the Soviet Union or Communist China." With respect to possible intentions of the Soviet Union and China, NSC 81/1 stated that it was "unlikely that the Soviet Union will passively accept the emergence of a situation in which all or most of Korea would pass from its control, unless it believes that it can take action which would prevent this *and* which would not involve a substantial risk of general war or unless it is now prepared to accept such risk." Further,

> it is possible, but politically improbable, that no action will be taken by the Soviet Union or by the Chinese Communists to reoccupy Northern Korea or to indicate in any other way an intention to prevent the occupation of Northern Korea by United Nations forces before the latter have reached the 38th parallel. In this unlikely contingency there would be some reason to believe that the Soviet Union had decided to follow a hands-off policy, even at the expense of the loss of control of Northern Korea. Only in this contingency could the U.N. ground forces undertake to operate in or to occupy northern Korea without greatly increasing the risk of general war.

Despite the narrowness of the conditions under which the United States could advance across the border, NSC 81/1 went on to state that military action by the Soviet Union and the PRC was unlikely after the United States crossed into North Korea. "The Soviet Union may decide that it can risk reoccupying Northern Korea *before* United Nations forces have reached the 38th parallel, or the conclusion of an arrangement with the North Korean regime under which Soviet forces would be pledged to the defense of the territory of the 'People's Republic of Northern Korea.'" Significantly, no mention was given to the chances of Soviet action, *after* UN forces crossed the parallel. Moreover, the document noted that while the Soviets might use Chinese forces to occupy North Korea, such a course of action was deemed "politically unlikely" as the DPRK was considered to be in the Soviet sphere of influence, and was reasoned to increase the possibility of global war (the latter conclusion being the opposite of that reached by the CIA). NSC 81/1 authorized war in North Korea, "provided that at the time of such operations there has been no entry into North Korea by major Soviet or Chinese Communist forces, no announcement of intended entry, nor a threat to counter our operations militarily in North Korea."[82] In short, NSC 81/1 provided strategic guidance predicated on the Soviet-centric, global logic Allison offered, and was in consonance with the popular notion that the gains to be had in rolling back communism on the peninsula were worth the effort given the estimated risk of Soviet and Chinese intervention.[83]

It is striking that the estimates on likely Soviet and Chinese behavior the CIA produced were barely considered by those directly responsible for designing the next phase of the limited war strategy in Korea. Based on the evidence examined, the CIA's pessimism was referenced *only once* by American strategists. In a meeting of the NSC senior staff on August 25, Rear Admiral E. T. Wooldridge noted "that there was a very pessimistic CIA estimate dated August 18, regarding the dangerous consequences of any UN attempt at the military conquest of all of Korea." Wooldridge went on to state that the JCS would want to know the probable consequences of operations north of the 38th parallel.[84] This request is significant because it illustrates that the vast majority of the CIA's estimates had not been considered by the JCS up to that point. Furthermore, it is not surprising that the JCS representative on the NSC staff was the individual who made reference to the CIA's August 18 memo. Following the strictures of the "NSC machinery," this critical estimate was provided only to NSC staff for its consideration. The exclusion of the CIA from the bureaucratic process of strategic design was debilitating in two primary regards. First, the isolation in which the various agencies and departments operated precluded consideration of all of the evidence and estimates of the intentions of the PRC.

Without alternative estimates, the State Department's PPS was without the bureaucratic support required to counter Allison's proposals for extending the war into North Korea. Moreover, the JCS who continually expressed concern over the possibility that the United States would become engaged in a major war in Korea were never presented with sufficient evidence that the proposed course of action could indeed bog down the American military on the peninsula.

The second effect of the CIA's marginalization, and the general pattern organizational isolation, was that top policy makers were saddled with a tremendous information burden at a critical period before American troops crossed the parallel. As stated in NSC 81/1, the expansion of the war into North Korea was conditioned on the absence of Soviet and Chinese intervention, or the threat of intervention. Thus from September 11 to October 8, American officials were charged with the responsibility of carefully considering evidence that either communist power would enter the war. During this period, the administration did receive evidence from a number of sources indicating that the Chinese would enter the war if the United States crossed the 38th parallel. Yet not all of the evidence was clear cut; it was at times contradictory. Without a properly functioning information management system, top policy makers were forced to make sense of this information on their own. As a result, each piece of information was weighed on its own merits. At no time during this period was new information placed in a broader pattern of US-Chinese relations since the start of the war. In the end, American officials held on to their preexisting beliefs that the Chinese would refrain from entering the war, no matter what course of action the United States took.

In light of this perception, the available information was interpreted in generally optimistic terms or was dismissed outright if any doubt to its accuracy was evinced. Although the State Department received indications from sources in Hong Kong and Taipei that the PRC would intervene if US forces crossed the 38th parallel, officials were skeptical. On September 21, the DOS received word from New Delhi that the Indian ambassador to Beijing, K. M. Panikkar, who had just recently had a series of conversations with Zhou Enlai and other high officials, did not believe that Chinese intervention was likely. Shortly thereafter, the US consul general at Hong Kong argued that because representation at the United Nations was the PRC's highest political objective, and because of the government was busy with massive internal reconstruction efforts, the Chinese communists would only provide limited and indirect support to the DPRK.[85]

That pattern of reporting changed, however, on September 27. According to telegrams State Department officials received, Panikkar reversed his assessment of the PRC's intentions. Of significance was Panikkar's interpretation of the UN representation issue. In light of Zhou's comment on September 21 that "since the United Nations had no obligations to China, China had no obligations to the United Nations," Panikkar believed the probability of Chinese intervention had increased. Moreover, Indian Prime Minister Nehru pleaded for a halt at the 38th parallel by UN forces fearing the consequences of a clash between American and Chinese forces.[86] And, from the Dutch Charge in Beijing, US officials learned that the chief of staff of the Chinese army stated that China "had no choice but to fight if [the] 38th parallel [was] crossed; although [it was] realized war with USA would set back China's development 50 years or more, [in the] Chief of staff opinion if no resistance [was] offered at this time, China would forever be under American control."[87]

These messages matched public statements from the PRC concerning its interest in the outcome of the war in Korea. On August 26, in an article in *World Culture* (an official journal of the PRC), Zhou stated clearly that China was directly affected by the situation on the peninsula.[88] On September 22, the Chinese Foreign Ministry declared, "We clearly reaffirm that we will always stand on the side of the Korean people—just as the Korean people have stood on our side during the past decades—and resolutely oppose the criminal acts of American imperialist aggression against Korea and their intrigues for expanding the war."[89] In a public address celebrating the founding of the PRC, Zhou "branded the United States as China's worst enemy and stated that China will not allow a neighbor to be invaded."[90] On September 30, Zhou declared that "the Chinese people absolutely will not tolerate foreign aggression nor will they supinely tolerate seeing their neighbors being savagely invaded by imperialists."[91]

Finally, on October 3, Zhou held a midnight meeting with Indian Ambassador Panikkar in which he bluntly stated that if the Americans crossed the 38th parallel, the People's Liberation Army (PLA) would enter the war. "The American forces are trying to cross the 38th parallel and to expand the war. If they really want to do this, we will not sit still without doing anything. We will be forced to intervene."[92] Critically, based on available COMINT sources, the United States was able to know exactly the content of Panikkar's reporting and was thus not forced to rely on third parties for the details of his communications with New Delhi.[93] Despite the clarity of the warning Zhou provided, officials in Washington were skeptical that the Chinese had signaled their intention to intervene. Many distrusted Panikkar as he was considered to be a "fellow traveler" with the communists in Beijing. Regardless, this warning did prompt the DOS to request from a number of its consular offices "any info you have which [would] throw light on any intentions [Chinese] Communists or [Soviet] Union to intervene militarily [in] Korea or embark on other hostile course."[94]

In terms of its military capabilities, the PRC had been steadily augmenting its armed forces in Manchuria, and both the FEC and CIA were keeping close watch on these developments.[95] From July to September, the FEC continually reported on the steady buildup of PLA forces in Manchuria: July, 116,000 troops; August, 217,000 troops; late September, 246,000 troops with the possible overall strength as high as 450,000 (more than the entire UN command strength in Korea).[96] On September 8, the CIA reported that "certain of the Chinese Communist Military District forces in Manchuria may now be organized as field units."[97] Put simply, the Chinese had more than enough military power to effectively intervene in Korea.

Based on the evidence available, at no time during this critical period was there an effort to explicitly compare the steady increase in Chinese forces in Manchuria, the political intelligence available from Panikkar and other sources, and the increasing stridency of the PRC's public rhetoric. Rather, as time progressed, top decision makers considered each new development on its own terms. At the same time, State Department officials who were attempting to build a consensus in the United Nations for a move across the 38th parallel were under pressure from Republican officials in Congress to attack North Korea, and were attempting in vain to persuade the Indian government to use its leadership position among Asian nations to back the American effort (the Indians, in turn, were attempting in vain to dissuade the United States from attacking the North).[98] In short, this was a time when administration officials could have benefited most from a robust information institution. As things stood, there was little chance that China's intentions could have been discerned correctly; the information burden was simply too great for harried individuals to manage.

The War for Rollback and Chinese Intervention

On September 27, MacArthur received authorization from the Joint Chiefs of Staff to advance into North Korea. That directive, which had the backing of Truman, Acheson, and Marshall, stated that the UN forces were to destroy the North Korean army above the 38th parallel, "provided that at the time of such operations there has been no entry into North Korea by major Soviet or Chinese Communist forces, no announcement of intended entry, nor a threat to counter our operations militarily in North Korea." Significantly, the CINCUNC was given the responsibility for determining whether such intervention was likely or ongoing. "You [MacArthur] will continue to make special efforts to determine whether there is a Chinese Communist or Soviet threat to the attainment of your objective, which will be reported to the Joint Chiefs of Staff as a matter of urgency." Moreover, the final directive stated that "it should be the policy not to employ non-ROK forces in the North Korean provinces bordering on Manchuria and the Soviet Union." After the CINCUNC submitted his plan for military operations in North Korea and received the joint chiefs' approval, Marshall told MacArthur on September 29, "We want you to feel unhampered strategically and tactically to proceed north of the 38th Parallel. . . . I regard all of Korea open for our military operations unless and until the enemy capitulates."[99] While not intended by Marshall to supersede the specific directives sent on the twenty-seventh, MacArthur interpreted this seemingly open-ended endorsement of operations in North Korea as granting him extensive freedom as he prosecuted the war in the North. And, as the order stipulated, responsibility for determining whether or not the Chinese or Soviets would intervene in the war was placed squarely on MacArthur's shoulders.

The latitude granted MacArthur had the immediate effect of undermining military and diplomatic coordination by cutting the State Department out of the war. As American forces began closing on China's borders, two critical signals needed to be issued to the PRC. The first was that despite the decision to invade its neighbor, the United States had no intention of attacking China. This was already going to be a tough sell as the decision to cross the 38th parallel contradicted previous statements indicating that the United States sought only the restoration of the pre–June 25 border, and the interposition of the Seventh Fleet in the Taiwan Straight contradicted statements on America's refusal to interfere in China's civil war.[100] The second signal that needed to be sent was one of deterrence: that the United States had the power and resolve to thwart any intervention on the part of China. Because of MacArthur's autonomy, however, there was little chance that these signals would be sent. No matter how strenuously American officials might have tried to convince Beijing not to intervene, such precise signaling would have lacked credibility because they would not have reflected US military behavior. Only by retaining tight control over both the military and diplomatic aspects of the war could China's intervention be avoided.

The central position of the FEC in the American information institution prevented civilian policy makers from having any such influence on the conduct of military missions as evidence of the presence of Chinese forces in Korea mounted. An accurate depiction of Chinese force deployments was important because it could have prompted Washington to look favorably on a plan of establishing a strong defensive position at the "narrow neck" of the peninsula.[101] As it was, top policy makers in Washington were forced to depend on MacArthur's reporting and assessments for evidence that the strategy was succeeding or failing. MacArthur's reporting, however, was frequently contradictory and misleading. On October 15, Truman flew to Wake Island to briefly confer with MacArthur on the status of the war effort. When Truman queried MacArthur on the chances for Soviet or Chinese intervention, the general replied:

> Very little. Had they interfered in the first or second months it would have been decisive. We are no longer fearful of their intervention. . . . The Chinese have 300,000 men in Manchuria. Of these probably not more than 100/125,000 are distributed along the Yalu River. Only 50/60,000 could be gotten across the Yalu River. They have no Air Force. Now that we have bases for our Air Force in Korea, if the Chinese tried to get down to Pyongyang there would be the greatest slaughter.[102]

This assessment was familiar to officials in Washington who had been receiving intelligence from the FEC that corroborated MacArthur's numbers and judgment of possible Chinese reactions. In the midst of the First Phase Offensive roughly two weeks later, MacArthur explained the presence of the Chinese in North Korea in the most benign terms possible: China was attempting to provide covert assistance to the North in order to "salvage something from the wreckage." Only days later, in response to Truman's cancellation of MacArthur's order to bomb the Yalu bridges, however, the general's reporting changed dramatically,

> Men and materiel in large force are pouring across all bridges over Yalu from Manchuria. This movement not only jeopardizes but threatens the ultimate destruction of the forces under my command. . . . The only way to stop this reinforcement . . . is the destruction of these bridges. . . . Every hour that this is postponed will be paid for dearly in American and other United Nations blood.[103]

The striking difference between MacArthur's reports caught the JCS by surprise. The chief's response illustrates their concern that the CINCUNC had not been as forthcoming as their instructions demanded: "It is essential that we be kept informed of important changes in the situation as they occur."

Yet MacArthur had no further evidence that the Chinese had intervened in force. At no time before China's major offensive on November 24 did MacArthur have a clear idea of the number of Chinese forces in North Korea. Willoughby's theater intelligence estimates are largely to blame for this. During the October-November period, Willoughby continually received reports from both the Eighth Army and X Corps that indicated the Chinese were crossing the Yalu with full divisions. Because the FEC intelligence chief failed to accurately compare the evidence from the two sources, however, he retained a belief that American forces faced only individual "units." Although his reports to MacArthur did show an increase in the number of Chinese troops in the North over time, Willoughby's estimates were completely off the mark.[104]

Without an alternative source of information pertaining to the activity of Chinese forces in Korea, it was impossible for officials and intelligence organs in Washington to obtain a more accurate understanding of the strategic situation into which American and UN forces had stumbled. Put simply, had Washington been privy to the information provided by Chinese POWs and by frontline units, a more accurate understanding of Chinese intentions would likely have developed.

Under what conditions would an alternative understanding of Chinese intentions have been possible? Two conditions were necessary, both of which concern the manner in which information was shared among departments and agencies within the US government. First, a more complete picture of Chinese forces in Korea after the First Phase Offensive could have developed had information from the Eighth Army and X Corps been made available to intelligence organs in addition to Willoughby's FEC G-2. There are two reasons for optimism on this point. Initially, as a postmortem report conducted by the US Navy after the war concluded, a complete utilization of the resources and information, both of a military and political nature, "should have permitted of more accurate and timely information of the movements of enemy [i.e., Chinese] forces to the south." Given that this report does indicate that some strategic information was simply unknowable given the information at hand, its conclusions pertaining to Chinese intervention should not be dismissed lightly.[105]

Second, had information about the PLA's previous tactical, operational, and strategic methods been considered, it would have been possible to predict how the Chinese would likely behave when confronting a conventional force like the UN forces under MacArthur's command.[106] Astonishingly, as a DOD report of July 25, 1950, shows, the United States was not without valuable information pertaining to the PLA's approach to war fighting.

> In mounting and invasion of Taiwan the Chinese Communists would necessarily improvise and exploit their particular capabilities in order to overcome obvious amphibious shortcomings. The operation would not be an amphibious assault in the Western concept, mounted in highly specialized craft with extensive and well-coordinated air and naval support. Rather, with large resources of manpower and improvised small craft, including rafts for landing, at their disposal, the Chinese Communists would be expected to devise an operation designed to saturate the offshore defenses and to evade those defenses under cover of darkness and weather and through utilization of numerous embarkation and landing points. The operation will be planned to take advantage of key defections among the defenders and sabotage of key defense installations and communications at a critical time. Heavy troop losses would be an acceptable cost.[107]

In executing its intervention in the Korean War, the PLA employed many of these operational and tactical schemes to great effect. Specifically, their use of cover of darkness, exploitation of enemy weaknesses (that is, the division of UN forces as they proceeded toward the Yalu), capitalization of information asymmetries, and willingness to take heavy casualties, were all evident during and after the First Phase Offensive.

In the aftermath of the First Phase Offensive, officials in Washington were concerned that the objective of unifying the peninsula would induce Chinese intervention. On November 8 the JCS cabled MacArthur requesting his most recent assessment of the situation on the battlefield and indicating that his mission "may have to be re-examined." MacArthur's no-holds-barred response came on November 9. The CINCUNC stated, "In my opinion it would be fatal to weaken the fundamental and basic policy of the United Nations to destroy all resisting armed forces in Korea and bring that country into a unified and free nation. I believe that with my air power . . . I can deny reinforcements coming across the Yalu in sufficient strength to prevent the destruction of those forces now arrayed against me in North Korea." In response to the idea of halting operations at the narrow neck, MacArthur decried that such a move would in effect "appease the Chinese Communists" in the same manner as occurred at Munich. At the NSC meeting on that day, MacArthur's demand to seek total victory was at odds with the JCS's desire to seek a resolution to the war by "political means." In the end, the decision was reached, pending further evidence of the PRC's intentions, to permit MacArthur to "continue the action" so long as there remained "a reasonable chance of success."[108] As General Omar Bradley would later recount in his memoirs, "we reached drastically wrong conclusions and decisions. . . . The JCS should have taken firmest control of the Korean War and dealt with MacArthur bluntly. . . . At the very least the chiefs should have canceled MacArthur's planned offensive. Instead we let ourselves be misled by MacArthur's wildly erroneous estimates of the situation."[109]

As a result of the information monopoly held by the FEC pertaining to the military capabilities and behavior of the Chinese communist forces in Korea, officials in Washington labored under a pronounced scarcity of information. As William Stueck argues,

> In the end, it was President Truman and his top advisers, especially Acheson and Marshall, who most needed to know of the massive Chinese presence in Korea. Unlike MacArthur, they were Europe-firsters, and they genuinely wanted to avoid a confrontation with China. Had they known the magnitude of the Chinese presence in Korea, they might well have stopped UN ground forces during the second week of November.[110]

Without an accurate understanding of the extent of China's intervention in mid-November, top policy makers were forced to concede to MacArthur their acceptance of his "end the war" offensive. As a result of their concerns, however, the National Security Council submitted NSC 81/2 to President Truman on November 14. In that document, the NSC concluded, "It is of the utmost importance that the *real* intentions of the Chinese Communists be ascertained as soon as possible." Among the courses of action the NSC recommended were: continued military operations, intensified "covert actions to determine Chinese Communist intentions," and the use of "other available political channels" to "ascertain Chinese Communist intentions and, in particular, to determine whether there is any basis for arrangements which might stabilize Sino-Korean frontier problems on a satisfactory basis."[111] Unfortunately, by this late date, there was no room to bargain with the Chinese, given existing American objectives. That Washington did not know this was a direct result of the truncated information institution that prevented administration officials from understanding the strategic situation into which the United States had blundered in the autumn of 1950. On November 25 the Chinese communists launched their major offensive. Not only had the Chinese intervened in the Korean War, but as a result of

American strategic miscalculations, they had also done so with devastating effect.

INFORMATION INSTITUTIONS VERSUS CIVIL-MILITARY RELATIONS

The information institution approach finds substantial support in this case of limited warfare. The United States entered the Korean War with a truncated information institution. In terms of information sources, the top policy makers were forced to rely on a single and highly biased source, the Far East Command led by General Douglas MacArthur. With respect to lateral communication channels among the national security organizations, little information was shared as strategy was debated and executed. Under these circumstances, the information institution approach expects limited war strategies to fail both militarily and diplomatically. The evidence presented in this chapter confirms this expectation.

By process-tracing strategic decision making, this chapter also confirmed this approach's causal logic. As the war unfolded, the United States possessed limited collection and dysfunctional analytic capabilities. Prior to the crossing of the 38th parallel by the United States, the process of strategic design suffered from the incomplete utilization of the available information regarding Chinese intentions. Most importantly, the ability of MacArthur to provide the vast majority of strategic information pertaining to the situation in Korea enabled his command to assume a position of prominence in the design and execution of America's limited war strategy. As the information institution approach expects, when a single organization dominates the flow of information, top policy makers lose the substantial influence over the content and implementation of policy.[112] As a result, MacArthur's determination to expand the war met with surprisingly little resistance.

This is not to say, of course, that MacArthur's approach was without backers in Washington. Directly supporting the expansion of war aims was the director of the Office of Northeast Asian Affairs, John Allison. On the other hand, the CIA, JCS, and PPS in the State Department harbored reservations about any strategy that ran significant risks of inducing Chinese or Soviet intervention. The CIA and the PPS in particular were gravely concerned that the proposals for crossing the parallel would elicit such a response by Beijing. For their part, the Joint Chiefs of Staff feared that a major war on the peninsula (an area deemed to be of marginal strategic importance) would hamper the operation of global war plans should hostilities between the United States and Soviet Union erupt in open warfare.

While the CIA and PPS viewed the situation unfolding in Korea in similar terms, their ability to combine their bureaucratic influence was precluded by the absence of lateral connections between them and with the JCS. Because the CIA's reports and estimates were forced into the "NSC machinery," these strategic evaluations were largely unavailable to PPS officials when they needed them most—at the early phase of the "rollback debate." Moreover, while the JCS representative to the NSC did eventually receive some indication that the CIA considered expanding the war to North Korea was fraught with danger, it was simply too little, too late. By preventing these organizations from exerting any appreciable influence on the rollback debate, the absence of lateral connections increased the chances that strategic decision making would be guided by faulty risk assessments. In the end, the decision to expand American war aims was not based on a record of success on the battlefield, as a prominent realist analysis of the case concedes.[113] Rather, the decision resulted from an information institution that facilitated a skewed assemblage of evidence that highlighted the opportunities, but obscured the risks, of seeking to unify the peninsula under South Korea's control.

While the absence of lateral connections had a strong influence on the initial round of strategy design, the exclusive reliance on a single source of information prevented a reassessment and refinement to the strategy after American forces crossed into North Korea. Washington's inability to receive information pertaining to Chinese military behavior from sources other than the FEC had profound effects. Because of mistakes made in the FEC's intelligence branch, the US government was unable to determine the extent of Chinese intervention during and immediately after the First Phase Offensive. Had Washington been afforded a more accurate understanding of China's intervention, then the option of falling back to the narrow neck of the peninsula would likely have been pressed upon MacArthur. Ultimately, MacArthur's centrality in the American information institution prevented top policy makers from ensuring tight military and diplomatic coordination. Without the ability to send credible signals of assurance and deterrence, there was little chance that Beijing would perceive the United States as anything but a substantial threat to its physical security.

On its own terms, the information institution approach offers a compelling explanation of the sources of military and diplomatic failure in the Korean War. But how well does this approach fare against its competitors? Recall from chapter 2 that two primary variables constitute the heart of democratic civil-military relations theory: the balance of domestic power between civilians and the military, and the degree of preference divergence between political leaders and military officers. In the Korean War, as in all of the cases of limited war considered in this book, the balance of power clearly favored civilian leaders. Under these conditions, information sharing is anticipated to be open and fluid. Furthermore, this case demonstrates profound preference divergence between political leaders and the most relevant military officer, General Douglas MacArthur. While President Truman, Secretary of State Acheson, and Secretary of Defense Marshall all desired the unification of the peninsula under South Korean authority, none were willing to do so if the price of unification was direct Chinese intervention. MacArthur, on the other hand, was far more risk tolerant; his ultimate objective was the complete eradication of enemy forces before him no matter what their country of origin happened to be. Under these conditions, democratic civil-military relations theory anticipates substantial coordination problems between the military, diplomatic, and political elements of the limited war strategy. Finally, despite the lack of solid coordination, this approach does not expect double failure in limited war strategies primarily because of the information advantages that democratic states have over nondemocracies.

Only one of these expectations is borne out in the Korean War. The expectation of poor coordination is clearly confirmed by the available evidence. Yet the evidence also demonstrates that on numerous occasions, MacArthur's command failed to provide accurate, complete, and timely information pertaining to American fortunes on the battlefield. In response, top policy makers frequently suffered from an absence of knowledge from which sound strategic decisions could be made. Furthermore, the evidence demonstrates how ineffective American policy makers were in their ability to conduct any meaningful oversight of the war effort, particularly as it pertained to the sending of precise signals to Beijing. Finally, this case shows just how profoundly dysfunctional strategy can be, even when designed and executed by a democracy. The Korean War stands as an example of how a democratic state can completely misunderstand the strategic environment in which a war unfolds.

Organizational culture theory, on the other hand, finds strong support in this case. This approach anticipates military and diplomatic failure in limited wars when three conditions hold: when military organizations are deemed to the be the most salient of all national security organizations, when the cultural view of that organization conforms to a "military dominant" logic, and when the military follows a Jominian norm of civil-military relations. Organizational culture theory holds that during times of war militaries are likely to be considered the most salient of national security organizations, and as such are likely to have the most influence in matters of strategic design and execution. When the organization's concept of war is "military dominant," the most relevant information will be understood to be that which pertains strictly to the opponent on the battlefield. Moreover, the military dominant conception of war desensitizes military organizations to the problem of escalation, thus making escalation all the more likely. Finally, the Jominian relational norm views the wartime intrusion by civilians into military affairs as inappropriate. When combined, the military dominant concept of war and the Jominian relational norm increase the likelihood of double failure in limited war. Under these conditions, the two information management mechanisms are expected to operate poorly: information collection and analysis will be limited and dysfunctional, while the military and diplomatic elements of the war will be uncoordinated.

As numerous studies have demonstrated, among the most important aspects of organizational culture of the post–World War II American military was the military dominant conception of warfare.[114] Almost exclusively, the American military was focused on a future war with the Soviet Union; a war that would be all encompassing and fought for existential objectives. As Christopher Twomey notes, the emphasis by the American military on general war with the Soviets "led American strategists to avoid worrying about how to win a local, limited war of containment (which would very likely have involved a heavy focus on enhancing conventional capabilities) and rather to focus on ensuring that apocalyptic general war would be devastating to the Soviets."[115] Indeed, in the years immediately following World War II, few in the American military gave any thought to the likelihood of war with anyone other than the Soviets.[116] Given that any future war was likely to be fought at the highest level of intensity for nothing short of national survival, battlefield outcomes assumed far more importance than any restraint-inducing political logic. As such, the only type of information relevant to the military in its conduct of war pertained to those forces arrayed in front of it.

With respect to its relations with political authorities, the post–World War II American military adhered to a Jominian norm of civil-military relations. As Robert Cassidy argues, World War II had the effect of reifying the traditional notion within the American military of a "separation of political and military policy." Continuing, Cassidy remarks that

> the U.S. military culture that emerged [from World War II] is one that ostensibly embraced the Clausewitzian axiom of subordinating military modalities to the political but, in all actuality, was truly Jominian. Instead, the U.S. military,

once war breaks out, preferred to fight big conventional wars without limitations and without constraints imposed by its political masters.[117]

With such an understanding of the proper relationship between the military and its civilian "masters," it is unlikely that the military as an organization would be amenable to the careful tailoring of military missions with diplomatic policy in limited warfare.

The evidence presented in this chapter provides ample support for organizational culture theory. It is clearly the case that in the immediate aftermath of North Korea's attack, the American military—specifically, MacArthur's Far East Command—was viewed by top policy makers as the most salient of all national security organs. The latitude granted MacArthur as commander satisfies the first condition of the organizational culture approach. Moreover, the common desire by Truman, Acheson, and Marshall to avoid Chinese intervention had barely any effect on the strategic approach MacArthur adopted. For the latter, the appropriate strategy was to destroy any enemy forces south of the Yalu River, regardless of their origin. Battlefield information was given exclusive priority in this endeavor. Finally, the prevailing Jominian relational norm offers an alternative explanation for the absence of coordination between the military and diplomatic elements of the war. Because civilian intrusion into matters of war was deemed inappropriate, MacArthur was more than willing to ignore the pleas of many to either provide information or tailor his activities to avoid inducing Chinese intervention. In sum, both organizational culture theory and the information institution approach explain why the United States found itself fighting the PRC in this first limited war of the long Cold War era.

CHAPTER FOUR

The Vietnam War, Little Consolation

From 1964 to 1968, the United States waged war in Vietnam to contain the spread of communism, particularly China's direct and indirect expansion into Southeast Asia.[1] Believing that South Vietnam stood as the first of several dominoes poised to fall in the region, the United States committed itself to the protection of a noncommunist government in South Vietnam, the American army and marines' destruction of a communist insurgency in the South, and the application of coercive air power against the Democratic Republic of Vietnam (DRV, or North Vietnam). At the same time, and reflecting its ultimate diplomatic goal, the United States pursued these objectives in a manner intended to avoid Chinese intervention in the war. Overall, America's pre-1968 limited war strategy sought the political objective of establishing an independent noncommunist South Vietnam. In terms of military objectives, the United States sought to defeat the communist insurgency in the South and to coerce Hanoi into quitting its support for that insurgency. American diplomatic objectives were to ensure the political stability of the government of South Vietnam (GVN) and to avoid all-out Chinese intervention in the war.[2]

After 1968, however, these war aims were radically downgraded to the achievement of a "decent interval" whereby American forces could be withdrawn from the conflict.[3] The cause of this reduction in war aims was twofold. The first was the realization that the military objectives of defeating the southern insurgency and coercing Hanoi to cease its support for that cause had failed, as had its goal of achieving political stability of the GVN. The second was that despite these failures, the United States had successfully avoided Chinese intervention in the war. By preventing horizontal escalation, the United States was in a position to begin looking for a way out. The relationship between America's strategic failures and successes is a complex one; an adequate explanation for the outcome of the Vietnam War must be able to capture this complexity.

The air war against North Vietnam failed to achieve its military objective, first, because the amount of coercive pressure applied against the DRV was never sufficient to change Hanoi's behavior, and second, because the strategic concept Washington applied (gradualism accompanied by frequent bombing pauses) convinced Hanoi that it could outlast the United States in the war. Despite its inherent limitations, this approach was adopted because it was the only one available given the overriding diplomatic objective of avoiding Chinese intervention. Officials in Washington believed that too strong an application of air power would bring the People's Republic of China (PRC) into the war, and the adopted air strategy was a direct result of this concern. Significantly, the United States was *correct* in this belief: China was willing to intervene in the war under certain conditions. Leaders in Washington were well aware of Beijing's intentions on this score, and they worked to ensure that the American air campaign refrained from provoking China. The outcome of the American air campaign against the DRV was the result of a trade-off that privileged the avoidance of China's direct intervention over the objective of coercing Hanoi. I argue below that this outcome resulted from the tight integration of American national security agencies prosecuting the air war, and the multiple sources of information available to top policy makers pertaining to the intentions of the PRC as the air campaign was designed and waged.

Whereas the outcome of the air campaign resulted from a rational trade-off among competing objectives, the ground campaign failed because of the adoption of an inappropriate strategy by an insulated military organization immune to pressures by those outside. The US Army uncritically applied its "concept" of waging war in a manner that all but guaranteed defeat. The insulation and autonomy of the army meant that American political objectives could not be efficiently translated into military missions. Moreover, the absence of alternative sources of information (and the manner in which information was transmitted to Washington) meant that policy makers were unable to obtain an accurate understanding of the situation on the battlefield. Nor could they exert any meaningful pressure on the army to change its strategic approach in a more productive way. Moreover, the war-fighting concept of the US Army undercut the objective of providing the GVN with a measure of political stability. In the end, having failed in securing three of its four objectives, the United States could only take little consolation in the fact that its goal of avoiding Chinese intervention was achieved.

In broad strokes, the information institution approach finds strong support for its main propositions: moderately truncated information institutions, where military organizations are isolated from top policy makers and the rest of the national security bureaucracy, are likely to generate limited war strategies that result in diplomatic success and military failure—little consolation. More specifically, the information institution approach offers fresh insight into the nature and quality of American strategic decision making in the Vietnam War. This chapter demonstrates that top American officials were presented with multiple military and diplomatic trade-offs as they waged war on the ground and in the air. Some of these trade-offs were understood by top policy makers and were confronted head on; others went completely unnoticed and undermined American strategy in Vietnam. Finally, while the evidence presented in this chapter provides strong support for the causal logic of the information institution approach, it challenges the core claims of the organizational culture and democratic civil-military relations theories. In fact, this case illustrates precisely how information institutions determine the strategic influence of organizational cultures in wartime.

THE AIR WAR: DIPLOMATIC SUCCESS AND MILITARY FAILURE

The eleven-month period between August 1964 and July 1965 was critical in the American air campaign against the DRV. In this phase, officials in Washington formulated the air strategy, began implementing it in earnest, and made the most consequential decisions regarding how the campaign would be waged for the next three years.[4] Specifically, the American air campaign unfolded in three phases. First, in the aftermath of the August 1964 Gulf of Tonkin incident, Lyndon Johnson ordered retaliatory strikes against targets in the North and shortly thereafter bolstered American air power in South Vietnam.[5] Second, in response to the massive mortar attack on the US airfield and advisory compound at Pleiku, Washington responded again with sharp retaliatory strikes against the DRV, followed soon after by the prolonged bombing campaign known as Rolling Thunder.[6] Third, in early April 1965, the United States modified its strategy by leveling off the intensity of Rolling Thunder operations, opting instead to focus on waging the ground war in the South.[7]

Throughout, American objectives in the air campaign were twofold: to coerce Hanoi to cease supporting the southern insurgency, but to do so in a manner that avoided Chinese intervention. To square these objectives, Washington adopted the strategic approach known as "graduated pressure."[8] By applying steadily increasing doses of air power against the DRV, administration officials hoped to force Hanoi to the bargaining table, a move the DRV would take in order to avoid the future destruction of its industrial and military base. A critical assumption of the American strategy was that the defeat or destruction of the DRV was *not* a necessary condition to achieve victory, as negotiations would enable the United States to achieve the same political goals with the credible threat of more severe military action in the future.[9] Punctuating Rolling Thunder were bombing pauses designed to signal to Hanoi Washington's willingness to negotiate an end to the war. Washington's determination to send these signals, and its refusal to bomb the North to such an extent that the viability of the communist regime was threatened, enabled it to influence the level of threat posed to China. Top policy makers believed that Chinese intervention would result if the United States bombed China directly, invaded the DRV, or if the Hanoi government appeared to be at the point of collapse.[10] The graduated pressure strategy allowed the United States to refrain from engaging China's military assets in North Vietnam (a likely first step in a conflict spiral that could lead to an American attack on China) and to control the pressure exerted against the DRV itself. Soon after its inception, however, officials in Washington were forced to make a choice between the two objectives that Rolling Thunder was designed to realize. By April 1965 it became clear that the United States was likely to reach China's threshold of intervention well before it would reach Hanoi's threshold of coercion.

Although the PRC was growing concerned about the American course of action in Vietnam in first half of 1964[11] (leading to a spate of verbal threats in July[12]), Washington's post-Tonkin reprisals shook Mao and his comrades in Beijing profoundly. Mao could no longer believe with absolute certainty that his southern border was secure: the United States now had the power projection capability to strike from the air into the heart of China.[13] In response, Beijing ordered the Kunming and Guangzhou Military Regions, as well as the air force and naval units in south and southwest China, to begin mobilizing for potential combat.[14] Four air divisions and one antiaircraft division were dispatched to areas contiguous to Vietnam and were placed on high alert. Mao also agreed to the deployment of one naval fighter division to Hainan Island, and to the construction of three new airfields in Guangxi.

New long-range, early warning and ground-control-intercept radar systems were installed, one of which was positioned twelve miles from the Sino-Vietnamese border. Most importantly, the PRC sent a fighter regiment with 36 MIGs to North Vietnam; a significant development given that the DRV had no combat air force prior to this.[15] Finally, on August 13, Mao reiterated his pledge that if the United States did indeed attack the DRV, the PRC would commit troops to the war.[16]

The Chinese public reaction to the Gulf of Tonkin reprisal strikes was strident. For example, on August 6, an official statement was issued declaring

> U.S. imperialism went over the "brink of war" and made the first step in extending the war. . . . Aggression by the United States against the Democratic Republic of Viet Nam means aggression against China. . . . Whenever the U.S. imperialists invade the territory, territorial waters or airspace of the Democratic Republic of Viet Nam, the Chinese people, without hesitation, will resolutely support the Vietnamese people's just war against the U.S. aggressors. The Chinese Government has served serious warnings on the U.S. Government on many occasions that should it dare to launch an attack on the Democratic Republic of Viet Nam, the Chinese people will absolutely not stand by with folded arms or sit idly by without lending a helping hand.[17]

Two additional post-Tonkin developments are important to understanding the seriousness with which the PRC viewed developments in Vietnam. First, the PRC initiated its "Resist America and Assist Vietnam" movement with mass demonstrations from August 7 to 11. Second, Mao called for the creation of the Third Front, the major relocation of industrial bases from the periphery of China to its interior. The scale of this undertaking was tremendous, entailing major economic dislocations, with the goal of providing for greater security of the PRC's industrial capacity.[18] The relationship between the creation of the Third Front and the situation in Vietnam was underscored with the order given by Mao for the rapid completion of three new rail lines designed to provide more robust transportation links between China's interior and the Chinese-Vietnamese border regions.[19]

The period immediately following the Gulf of Tonkin incident was to date the most dangerous and held the highest probability of spilling over into armed conflict between the United States and the PRC. Conflict was avoided largely by the fact that after the American reprisals and force redeployment, the administration deliberately ratcheted down the level of international tension. There were three interlocking factors that determined the nature of US policy during this period, all of which were significantly conditioned by the accuracy of American perceptions of Chinese capabilities and intentions. The first was the recognition of the MIG deployment to North Vietnam and the major redeployment of air and ground forces from eastern to southern China. The second was that the weakness of the government of South Vietnam counterbalanced the desire of many in the American military to begin an offensive against North Vietnam. The third was the recognition that despite the scope of its military moves, the PRC was not going on the offensive in Vietnam and was willing to let tensions dissipate in the immediate future. This led Washington to conclude that it had time to spare in the hopes that the Nguyen Khanh government would right itself.[20]

On February 7, 1965, the National Liberation Front (NLF, Viet Cong) launched a massive mortar attack on the US airfield and advisory compound at Pleiku. In response, national security adviser McGeorge Bundy urged that a single retaliatory attack be initiated followed by "reprisal actions [which] would become less and less related to specific VC [Viet Cong] spectaculars and more and more related to a catalogue of VC outrages in SVN."[21] The first Rolling Thunder mission began on March 2. Six days later two marine battalions were deployed to South Vietnam to serve in the capacity of airfield protection.

The PRC's deterrent warnings became far more specific in response to Rolling Thunder. On March 25, *People's Daily* announced that the PRC would offer "the heroic Vietnamese people any necessary material support, including the supply of weapons and all kinds of military materials" and that, if necessary, China was prepared "to send its personnel to fight together with the Vietnamese people to annihilate the American aggressors." On April 2, the PRC issued its most serious warning to the United States. On a visit to Pakistan, Zhou Enlai requested that Ayub Khan convey several points to Washington during his upcoming visit:

> (1) China would not take the initiative to provoke a war against the United States; (2) China means what it says, and China will honor whatever international obligations it had undertaken; and (3) China is prepared.

Khan's trip to Washington was canceled, however, due to the Johnson administration's displeasure with Pakistan's increasing closeness to the PRC.[22] On May 28, the PRC made a second effort to convey to Washington the severity of its interests in preserving a viable North Vietnam. Meeting with Indonesian first deputy prime minister Subandrio, Zhou issued a statement reiterating the three points made above, but which also included a fourth point,

If the United States bombs China, that means bringing the war to China. The war has no boundary. This means two things: First, you cannot say that only an air war on your part is allowed and the land war on my part is not allowed. Second, not only may you invade our territory, we may also fight a war abroad.

To further clarify Beijing's position, foreign minister Chen Yi drew a clear line for the United States: if American military operations included only air attacks over the DRV, and did not come near the Chinese border, China would refrain from intervening in the war against the United States. By making sure that Washington would under no circumstances misunderstand the meaning of these messages, the PRC hoped to prevent the war's expansion into North Vietnam and, most importantly, into China itself.[23]

In early June, discussions were held in Beijing among leaders of the PRC and DRV to plan how, and under what conditions, the Chinese would assist the North Vietnamese in their war effort. According to their agreement: if the status quo remained in place, the DRV would fight the war on its own, while the PRC would provide material support as needed by the North; if the United States employed its air and naval forces to support a South Vietnamese attack on the DRV, China would reciprocate to support the DRV; and if US ground forces directly attacked the North, the PRC would use its land forces as strategic reserves for the North Vietnamese forces and conduct military operations as the need arose. The terms of the PRC-DRV air force cooperation took the following form: China would either, first, send volunteer pilots to Vietnam to operate Vietnamese aircraft; second, China would station pilots and aircraft at North Vietnamese airfields; or third, the PRC would fly aircraft from bases in China to join combat in Vietnam and land on North Vietnamese bases temporarily for refueling. Chinese ground troops would be employed to either bolster the defenses of the Northern forces in order to prepare for a counteroffensive, or would launch an offensive themselves to disrupt the American deployment and to win the initiative.[24]

Beginning on June 7, 1965, the PRC began sending antiaircraft artillery, railroad, engineering, minesweeping, and logistical units across the border into North Vietnam. These actions initiated a three-year period of extensive military support for the DRV, which included over 320,000 troops for the whole period (1967 was the year that witnessed the greatest number of PLA forces in the DRV at 170,000).[25] The presence of these troops, in addition to the large airbase at Yen Bai that China built in northwest Vietnam, added additional credibility to the Chinese deterrent.[26]

The period of spring to early summer 1965 was significant in the American war in Vietnam because at this time the decision to move to an offensively oriented ground strategy in the South was made. Although few in the administration expected that Rolling Thunder would produce the desired outcomes in the short run, the limited effects the bombing campaign appeared to have on the Hanoi leadership, along with new information concerning the strength of the NLF in the South, combined to create a sense of deep frustration among Johnson's top advisers. Disturbed by the lack of progress in the air campaign, the decision was made on April 6 to change the marines' mission from statically defensive base security to offensive "counterinsurgency," to increase the size and capabilities of US ground forces in the South, and to "plateau" the tempo of Rolling Thunder, at least temporarily.[27]

Based on their understanding of Chinese intentions, it was clear that the only aspect of the American strategy in Vietnam that was open to alteration was the intensity of the US ground effort. As such, the administration's primary focus between June 7 and July 28 was on the deployment of more troops to South Vietnam, specifically the extent of the total commitment and the timing of deployment. On only two occasions did proposals to significantly increase Rolling Thunder arise, and on both occasions the option was rejected. In the end, it was decided that LBJ would announce a commitment of an additional 55,000 troops, but would forego a call-up of reserves. The reason, McNamara stated, was to minimize "the actions which might induce Communist China or the Soviet Union to take initiatives they might not otherwise undertake," an attempt to reduce the probability of provoking extreme reactions by both of the communist powers. On July 28, LBJ announced at a press conference that he had decided to increase the American strength in South Vietnam to 125,000 men. Additional forces would be needed later, and the president stated they would be sent as requested. No mention was made of the air campaign because no fundamental change in strategy had occurred.[28]

Initially, the air campaign in the Vietnam War sought two objectives: the cessation of Hanoi's support for the southern insurgency and the avoidance intervention by China. As soon as it became clear that American air power was inducing hostility by China, Washington's attention turned to managing the Chinese threat. In so doing, the United States undermined its ultimate military objective, as Hanoi interpreted American restraint as irresolution. The DRV was neither prevented from assisting the southern insurgency materially, nor was its will to do so ever broken. Ultimately, the United States failed militarily, but succeeded diplomatically, in the air campaign, an outcome that resulted from a rational trade-off between competing objectives.

THE GROUND WAR:
MILITARY AND DIPLOMATIC FAILURE

The ultimate political objective of the United States in Vietnam was the creation and maintenance of an independent noncommunist South Vietnam. From a rational strategic perspective, American military and diplomatic resources should have been dedicated toward that end and tailored specifically to deal with the evolving threats and challenges confronting the southern regime. Whereas the prosecution of the air war against the DRV was heavily influenced by changes in the strategic environment, from 1965 to 1968 the United States waged the ground war in South Vietnam in a matter that was impervious to them.

The main threat to the GVN was a communist insurgency waged by the National Liberal Front and the People's Army of Vietnam (PAVN, North Vietnamese Army). By July 1965, it was becoming increasingly evident that the insurgency was moving away from small-scale, hit-and-run guerrilla operations (phase 2) and toward larger-scale conventional operations (phase 3).[29] With the introduction of US combat forces in mid-1965, the balance of forces quickly turned against the communists. Moreover, the primary manner in which the United States waged war in the South (larger-scale formations employing heavy doses of firepower, exploiting technologically advanced weapons systems) stood a good chance of defeating the GVN's opponents. Had the insurgents remained wedded to phase 3–style operations, then the United States would likely have been able to secure its political objectives in the war. Yet in relatively short order, the insurgents reverted to phase 2–style combat after it became clear they could not compete with American firepower and technology.[30] This strategic adaptation was not matched by the US Army. Rather, Military Assistance Command, Vietnam (MACV) continued to prosecute the ground war along the lines of the army's conventional doctrine.[31] The effect of this strategic rigidity would have profoundly negative effects on the ability of the United States to achieve its military and nonmilitary objectives in the ground campaign.

The insurgency's objective in reverting to guerrilla warfare was to expand its base of support among the population by attacking local government leadership and by gaining control over the population. The cultivation of links between the insurgency and the population was seen as critical given the introduction of American troops. Through coercion and persuasion of the population, the guerrilla forces attempted to protect and supply themselves effectively as well as demonstrate the GVN's inability to stem the tide of the revolution.

To effectively combat the insurgency at phase 2, the GVN and United States had to have population security as its primary objective. Only by severing the links between guerrillas and the population could the GVN/US deny the insurgency its primary source of strength. Larger-scale search-and-destroy operations, the kind the United States employed, were not simply unproductive in combating the NLF/PAVN, they were *counter* productive. The heavy reliance on firepower provided advance warning to the guerrillas that an attack was coming and ran substantial risks of alienating the population. Moreover, these types of operations could not achieve population security. Villages remained open for insurgents to exploit, and villagers were susceptible to coercion and indoctrination by the guerrilla forces.[32]

The US Army employed an attrition strategy against the NLF/PAVN with the intention of reaching a "crossover point" where the enemy's losses would exceed its ability to replace them with new forces. As MACV commander General William Westmoreland explained in 1965, "I see no practical alternative, short of nuclear war, to continue as we are, preparing for the long haul by building up our forces and facilities with [the] objective of gaining a qualitative and quantitative margin over [the] enemy which will wear him down."[33] Westmoreland's plan for achieving victory was to unfold in three phases. In Phase I, the United States would seek the stabilization of the war by the end of 1965 using the forty-four-battalion commitment that LBJ agreed to in July of that year. An additional twenty-four battalions would be employed in 1966 in order to resume the offensive against enemy forces. Finally, in Phase III mop-up operations would be conducted with the objective of destroying the remaining insurgent forces in the South.[34]

Critical to the success of this plan was the ability of the United States to force the NLF/PAVN to fight pitched battles. In so doing, American firepower could attrit the enemy's forces at a faster rate than they could be replaced. The primary metric by which this approach would be judged was the infamous "body count." By focusing on the numbers of enemy soldiers killed in action, MACV placed far more importance on the body count than it did on population security. Unfortunately, the attrition strategy neither succeeded in achieving the requisite "crossover point" nor did it provide army commanders with the incentive to report progress accurately. On the one hand, the use of heavy firepower gave advance warning to guerrilla forces of the army's intentions. As such, the insurgents retained the ability to dictate the timing and intensity of battles. And while the army did kill many NLF insurgents, the dominant American strategy was unable to delink the populace from the NLF/PAVN. As a result, political stability of the GVN continued to erode as insurgent forces were able to continually augment their numbers.[35] On the other hand, by relying on the body count as the key measure of success, commanders were given an incentive to inflate the number of enemy soldiers killed. Such inflated statistics were easily accomplished because of the inherent difficulty of differentiating between an insurgent and villager. Moreover, "upping the count often provided a graceful explanation for why a particular U.S. unit suffered heavy casualties in an engagement; it also provided MACV with welcome data in its struggle to reach the crossover point."[36]

As time progressed, American officials grew increasingly concerned over the viability of MACV's approach to the war. Despite the fact that many in the Office of the Secretary of Defense were convinced that the attrition strategy would not lead to military victory,[37] and regardless of the success that the Marines Corps was having in its limited pacification missions,[38] MACV's primary attrition strategy remained in place. Strategic continuity resulted largely because the army had not suffered a substantial battlefield defeat. For the Johnson administration that "defeat" came with the Tet Offensive in early 1968. Although American forces were able to withstand the offensive and deliver a substantial blow to the insurgency, the Tet Offensive demonstrated clearly the limits of the American strategy. In response to the attack, Westmoreland requested 10,500 additional troops be sent to South Vietnam. At the same time, the Joint Chiefs of Staff urged LBJ to take a step the president had heretofore rejected: the calling up of reserves. In the joint chiefs' view, the ability of the United States to meet the challenges posed by the Tet Offensive, and to ensure that the United States possessed a minimum level of readiness to meet additional contingencies, was in doubt if the president refused to mobilize the reserves.[39] Stunned by the NLF's ability to launch the offensive, and faced with the prospect shaking one of the critical limitations of the war, the president ultimately realized that success in Vietnam was not a possibility.[40] The army's approach had lost all credibility with the president and his top advisers. A plan for withdrawal was thus necessary.[41]

To achieve success in the ground campaign, American military operations had to be linked to its political objectives. Only by waging effective counterinsurgency warfare could the United States have had any chance of creating and maintaining a base of support for the GVN among the population. Yet from 1965 to 1968, American military operations were divorced from this strategic reality. The end result was that by 1968 the United States was no closer to achieving its objective of an independent South Vietnam. To the contrary, the government of South Vietnam was heavily dependent on the United States for its continued survival.

A MODERATELY TRUNCATED INFORMATION INSTITUTION

The Vietnam War was a mixed success for the United States. In the air campaign, although the United States succeeded in preventing Chinese intervention, it failed to coerce Hanoi to stop supporting the southern insurgency. In the ground campaign, the United States was neither able to defeat its primary opponent nor was it able to establish political stability of the GVN. I argue that this mixed case was produced by the moderately truncated nature of the American information institution. By the mid-1960s, the ability of the president to influence national security policy had grown substantially as a result of a series of institutional changes that brought more information to the highest reaches of the government and that bound many national security organizations together. These institutional changes enabled the White House to monitor the effects of the air war along multiple objectives, and to select among them when they became mutually exclusive. The United States was unable to effectively coerce Hanoi into ceasing its support for the southern insurgency because top policy makers realized that the air war was running an unacceptable risk of inducing Chinese intervention. The air strategy was designed and modified by Washington according to timely and accurate information pertaining to the PRC's intentions and capabilities.

Yet the substantial increase in the White House's ability to manage national security policy did not extend to the organization that was responsible for waging ground war in South Vietnam: MACV. To a considerable extent, the US Army (which commanded MACV) remained on the periphery of what was otherwise a robust information institution. MACV was largely insulated from pressures from above, and as a result, the adopted military strategy was ill suited to American political objectives. Because of MACV's role as the critical source of information pertaining to the progress of the war, Washington could intervene only when outright failure was evident.

Prior to that point, however, military operations in the South remained in the hands of MACV. Both Washington and the American embassy in Saigon were on the outside looking in.

Bolstering American Information Management Capacities

In response to what was considered a dismal performance in the Korean War, the Eisenhower administration enacted a series of reforms to the NSC system. To a significant extent, these reforms rationalized the foreign policy process and enhanced the information management capabilities of the United States.[42] Believing that much yet needed to be done, the Kennedy administration undertook a major overhaul of the NSC system. These reforms were crucial because they constituted the system that Lyndon Johnson inherited, through which America's Vietnam policy emerged. The Kennedy-era reforms focused on three primary aspects of the NSC machinery: the position of the national security adviser; the power and role of the NSC Staff; and the relative importance of the National Security Council vis-à-vis other ad hoc mechanisms for foreign policy development and implementation.

The first set of reforms substantially increased the responsibility of the national security adviser. Under Kennedy, McGeorge Bundy's duties expanded to include those assigned to six individuals in the Eisenhower administration.[43] In effect, the role that Bundy served in the Kennedy and Johnson administrations was that of a combined policy advisor and staff secretary, placing him in charge of both long-range planning and of managing the interagency decision-making process of American foreign policy. Such consolidation of roles resulted in a dramatic increase in the power of the national security adviser, and of the president to whom he was accountable. That power accrued from two primary sources. First, Bundy served as the information conduit running from the bureaucracy to the president, a relationship that provided Bundy with significant clout in the day-to-day management of the policy process. As Andrew Preston describes, not only was approval for high-level meetings between the president and departmental officials often granted by Bundy in advance, but also the national security adviser soon began clearing sensitive cables from the DOS to diplomatic posts abroad.[44]

The second source of Bundy's power stemmed from the reorganization of the NSC Staff, a series of overhauls that dramatically increased the scope and influence of the Staff's purview. Bundy created a powerful Staff that served as the president's eyes and ears, "no longer disinterested mediators working to push papers up to the NSC level."[45] According to Robert Komer, the Staff served a president who desired access to "a complete flow of raw information." Moreover,

> [the Staff served as a] shadow network which clued the President on what bidding was before a formal inter-departmentally cleared recommendation that got to him . . . the President had sources of independent judgment and recommendation on what each issue was all about, what ought to be done about it, from a little group of people in whom he had confidence—in other words, sort of a double check. [Finally, the Staff provided] follow through [working] to keep tabs on things and [seeing] that the cables went out and the responses were satisfactory, and that when the policy wasn't being executed, the President knew about it and he could give it another prod.[46]

The NSC Staff's ability to effectively assume this role was achieved via two institutional mechanisms. The first was the creation within the Staff of geographic and thematic sections that allowed members the ability to concentrate on specific areas of the globe or on discrete aspects of US foreign policy. This structure mirrored that of the State Department, leading Kennedy's press secretary, Pierre Salinger, to label the NSC Staff a "mini State Department."[47] With the addition of portfolio assignments, NSC Staff members became powerful figures in the foreign policy process. The second institutional mechanism, the famous Situation Room, gave the Staff the ability to obtain and control the information traffic in and out of Washington. The purpose of the Situation Room was to coordinate "the many information channels to the White House which sprang up in the early days of the Kennedy Administration, including those of the Central Intelligence Agency, the State and Defense Departments and the Chiefs of Staff through their aides in the White House."[48] In sum, the creation of geographic and thematic organs within the Staff and the establishment of the Situation Room enabled Kennedy and Bundy to know in much greater detail global events and trends that could impact the national security of the United States, as well as to keep tabs on the performance of the foreign policy bureaucracy in an unprecedented manner.[49]

The third aspect of the Kennedy-era reforms focused on the National Security Council itself—namely, its downgrading in importance as a body where the content of decisions were deliberated and decided upon.[50] In place of council meetings, the Kennedy team opted for ad hoc task forces to solve particular foreign policy problems. The value of the task force system as a means of decision making came from the "highly personalized and centralized basis of its assignment." As Dean Rusk explained, "since the authority for the task force stems directly from the President or other high officials, there usually results added urgency and a more thorough consideration of the problems than would other wise have been possible." Furthermore, task forces permitted more efficient interdepartmental coordination through the assignment of relevant personnel from different areas of the bureaucracy. Finally, because the management of the task force system fell to McGeorge Bundy, presidential oversight was ensured.[51]

With only a few notable exceptions, Lyndon Johnson did not fundamentally alter the manner in which the NSC system operated.[52] Where LBJ did institute change, it was in the relationship of the president to the NSC principals. LBJ's use of the (in)famous Tuesday lunches were, "indisputably an important institution in the foreign policy advisory process during the Johnson presidency."[53] Critically, the Tuesday lunches (whose primary attendees were the president, Bundy, Dean Rusk, and Robert McNamara) operated with the National Security Council, but not instead of it. Often, LBJ would hold these lunches immediately following full NSC meetings in order to provide a more open and frank discussion among the individuals whose departments were directly affected by the topics considered. Because the size of the lunches was limited, and because the war in Vietnam tended to be the primary matter under consideration, many in the government at the time, as well as subsequent scholarly treatments, disparaged the institution.[54] However, those arguing that the Tuesday lunches amounted to a dysfunctional advisory system fail to account for a number of critical facts. First, as indicated, the Tuesday lunches were not the sole organ for decision making; the NSC continued to meet throughout the Johnson presidency and, more importantly, frequently during the period under consideration. Second, as recent scholarship demonstrates, LBJ was not a captive of truncated discussions. His ability to acquire a wide range of information from his advisers pertaining to Vietnam was not diminished by the lunches.[55] Finally, the attendees of the lunches were in fact NSC principals, leaders of the departments involved in waging the war and managers of the interagency foreign policy process. What the lunches provided was an alternative, streamlined, and effective forum for decision making.[56]

Of course, to fully counter the claim that LBJ's informal advisory system was dysfunctional, it is necessary to demonstrate that the principals involved had access to information from a number of sources as decisions were being made. Three points stand out as being most important. First, one of the most important effects of Secretary of Defense McNamara's reforms in the Pentagon (that is, the establishment of a new system of budgeting based on long-range planning known as the Planning Programming Budgeting System—PPBS), was the dramatic increase of information from lower levels in the military to the Office of the Secretary of Defense (OSD). As one scholar notes, "PPBS gave the secretary of defense greatly increased power to make decisions on lower-order questions; the upward flow of information it generated gave him the ability to make such decisions, and McNamara's philosophy of management shows that he had the inclination to make use of his increased powers."[57] In other words, McNamara brought to the table a wealth of strategic, operational, and tactical information from the Pentagon, a point missed by those charging that the Tuesday lunches suffered from a lack of quality staff work.

Second, the Situation Room, the critical information hub connecting the military, diplomatic, and intelligence agencies of the government, was retained and its use increased in the period under consideration. As Michael Bohn, a former director of the Situation Room, notes, the Situation Room provided LBJ and his advisers timely information related to critical operations during the air war. "He [LBJ] met with military planners there to select targets. The duty officers became his personal bomb damage assessment team, gathering information from afar each night in order to answer the inevitable questions from the President, usually just before he went to sleep and again as he arose."[58] The ability for the president and his top advisers to obtain such information allowed for the unprecedented management of wartime operations from Washington. As the notes of the Tuesday lunches make clear, the charge that Johnson "micro-managed" the bombing of North Vietnam is definitely substantiated. "Johnson clearly feared that if the U.S. bombed near its border, China would enter the war, as it had in Korea a decade and a half earlier."[59] Access to such tactical and operational information from the Situation Room was a prerequisite for the president and his military and civilian advisers to play an active role in managing US operations in the skies above the DRV.

The final point pertains to the functioning of the intelligence community, in particular the role of the CIA in providing information to top government officials. In the early 1960s the intelligence community dramatically increased its technical capabilities in producing imagery and signals intelligence (IMINT and SIGINT, respectively).[60] Bureaucratic control over IMINT resources in particular was the subject of a great deal of debate and conflict during 1961–65. As a result of its mission, the US Air Force was intent on securing access to high-resolution photographic intelligence that would allow for greater accuracy and effectiveness of aerial bombing. Yet the CIA and OSD preferred IMINT resources that provided broader intelligence and information. For the agency, this meant area search capabilities—broad-spectrum coverage at lower resolution—in the service of analysts who produced longer-ranged intelligence products. For the OSD, such capabilities would be useful in Robert McNamara's efforts to acquire independent assessments of weapons systems procurement and strategic planning. As such, the CIA and OSD allied to press their case against the air force. By August 1965, an agreement was reached that provided the CIA and OSD joint decision-making authority over IMINT resources. The result of this conflict and eventual agreement substantially bolstered the position of the DCI in determining not only the utilization of IMINT resources, but just as importantly, drew the CIA and OSD into closer cooperation in other areas as well.[61]

The primary area of cooperation between the CIA and OSD was that of strategic research and analysis of a distinctly military nature. During the 1950s, the CIA at times produced military intelligence analysis, but the agency never challenged the Pentagon in this sphere. In the early 1960s, this situation changed, and with McNamara's approval. As Anne Karalekas argues, "the combination of Secretary of Defense Robert McNamara's reliance on the Agency for analysis and John McCone's insistence on the DCI's necessity to have independent judgments on military matters resulted in the expansion of the CIA's strategic intelligence effort and the acceptance of the Agency's role as a producer of military analysis." With McNamara's introduction of new management and strategic planning procedures, the CIA (and the Defense Intelligence Agency, DIA), provided the secretary of defense with intelligence assessments that were used in the service of "long-range program decisions by projecting foreign policy needs, military strategy, and budgetary requirements against force structures."[62] By August 1964, the CIA's Office of Research and Reports (ORR) was providing top policy makers with regular bomb damage assessments, and was taking an active part in the critical interdepartmental war games and task forces that produced the air war's graduate pressure strategy.

The Army Stands Apart

It is clear that by August 1964, the White House was in a strong position institutionally to exert substantial influence on the air campaign. The same cannot be said of the ground campaign. Whereas the design of the air campaign fell under the purview of the president and his top advisers (aided by the multiple sources of information available to top policy makers and the density of lateral connections among the agencies involved), the responsibility for designing the strategy of the ground war was MACV's alone. The autonomy of MACV was guaranteed from its inception. As the 1962 "terms of reference" for the commander, MACV stated, "the operational command of U.S. military personnel will be the direct responsibility of the senior U.S. military commander."[63] In short, Washington's ability to ensure that the air campaign accurately reflected a dynamic strategic environment was not replicated in the ground war in the South.[64]

The origins of this disjuncture lay again in the Kennedy administration's reform efforts, in this case a reform that failed. JFK entered office convinced that communist-inspired guerrilla warfare stood as a unique and significant threat to American national security. In May 1961, the president addressed Congress about his concerns this type of war embodied. Communist revolutionaries "have fired no missiles; and their troops are seldom seen. They send arms, agitators, aid, technicians and propaganda to every troubled area. But where fighting is required, it is usually done by others—by guerrillas striking at night, by assassins striking alone . . . by subversives and saboteurs and insurrectionists, who in some cases control whole areas inside of independent nations." To meet this new threat, JFK told the West Point graduating class of 1962, the United States needed "a whole new kind of strategy, a wholly different kind of force, and therefore a new and wholly different kind of military training."[65]

Toward that end, the administration endeavored to establish a government-wide counterinsurgency doctrine, one that necessitated combined military and political efforts, and the institutional apparatus for ensuring the coordination and unification of counterinsurgency policies.[66] A Special Group, Counterinsurgency (SGCI) was established in January 1962 to develop, monitor, and coordinate American counterinsurgency efforts.[67] The members of this group were high-level officials and were selected in part to reflect the president's determination to the effort.[68] In August, a widely distributed interagency policy paper titled "Overseas Internal Defense Policy" specified the roles and mission of American national security agencies in the field of counterinsurgency.[69] As Douglas Blaufarb notes,

> By August 1962, the administration thus had in place the main outlines of an organized national approach to the insurgency threat. Detailed and urgent instructions had gone out—and there had been persistent follow-up to insure

compliance—to revise the foreign affairs and military educational system, to develop a doctrine, and to establish responsive programs. High-level supervisory machinery had been put in place, and the agencies had been reorganized to assure a satisfactory response.[70]

While appearing to have all of the hallmarks of an effective interagency reform, the SGCI nevertheless failed along two crucial and interrelated dimensions: the army's cultural preference for waging midintensity conventional warfare was never shaken, and the political and military elements of counterinsurgency operations remained disconnected. The first problem manifested itself quickly, though surreptitiously. From the start, the army undertook a number of shallow reforms intended to demonstrate compliance with the administration's requirements, but never attempted to fundamentally alter its preferred doctrine. To a significant extent, the army was able to accomplish this because the members of the SGCI were either wedded to the traditional army culture, inexperienced in the nuances of counterinsurgency warfare, or both.[71] Kennedy's decision to name General Maxwell Taylor—the president's highly valued military advisor—as the chairman of the SGCI was perhaps the most problematic appointment. Thoroughly convinced that the solution to the insurgency in South Vietnam was to bomb the DRV, Taylor remained skeptical of the president's proposed doctrinal reorientation. Indeed, as Andrew Krepinevich points out, "Ironically, the effect of placing Taylor at so many of the junction points between the political leadership and the Army was not so much the application of pressure from above on the military as it was the insulation of the service from the very pressure that the president was trying to generate."[72]

The second problem with the SGCI—the inability to ensure political-military coordination—owed much to the meager size of its staff. Put simply, the absence of a permanent staff meant that little oversight capabilities existed in times when the high-level principals' attention turned to other matters. Without strong monitoring capabilities, little focus was given to the coordination of the military and nonmilitary components of counterinsurgency warfare. In the early 1960s, the absence of a coordinated political-military strategy resulted in the creation of two parallel approaches to the American advisory efforts in South Vietnam, one dedicated to the Strategic Hamlet program and the other focused on rooting out and destroying NLF forces.[73] Unfettered by the population security requirements of the hamlet approach, the army was free to employ its preferred firepower-intensive approach. Among the disastrous consequences of the absence of military-diplomatic coordination was the inability to receive accurate information pertaining to the Army of the Republic of Vietnam's (ARVN, South Vietnamese Army) performance. Trained and organized by American military advisers to fight conventionally, ARVN routinely supplied inflated statistics on enemy forces killed.[74] Unfortunately, these quantitative measures never captured the operational schemes that enabled vast numbers of NLF to escape detection, continue their recruitment efforts in the South, and systematically undermine the political stability of the GVN.[75]

The structural problems of the SGCI notwithstanding, the importance of this group in the American policy-making process declined when Taylor assumed the position of chairman of the JCS in October 1962. Unlike many of the Kennedy-era reforms, the SGCI stands out as a dramatic and important failure. Kennedy understood the importance of harnessing America's military and diplomatic resources to combat insurgencies around the world. In failing to accomplish this objective, the US Army—the organization that designed and executed the dominant strategy in South Vietnam—escaped incorporation into what had become an increasingly robust information institution. Indeed, it was only in October 1967 that General Earl Wheeler, chairman of the JCS, became a regular member of Johnson's Tuesday lunch group.[76] The army would continue to operate according to its internally derived strategic view, and would measure its success according to its criteria alone. In these ways, the US Army was an organization that responded only to "local knowledge," one characterized by closed circles of communications.[77] By failing to break through the army's insulated culture early on, American political objectives in the war stood little chance of being translated into military strategy after July 1965. As General Westmoreland noted, "the President [LBJ] never tried to tell me how to run the war. The tactics and battlefield strategy of running the war were mine."[78] As will be discussed below, the results of this organizational insulation were a military and a diplomatic failure in the South.

THE AIR WAR:
COMPETING OBJECTIVES AND RATIONAL CHOICE

Immediately following the Tonkin Gulf incident, the United States struck a number of targets in the DRV and bolstered American air power in South Vietnam. The Chinese, in turn, dramatically increased their material commitment to the DRV and began mobilizing for a potential war with the United States. The CIA carefully monitored the PRC's activity, making clear the dangers inherent to continuing the present course of action against

North Vietnam.[79] Additionally, Maxwell Taylor (now the US ambassador to South Vietnam) sent a series of memos to Washington from August 9 to 18 that urged the administration to continue pressuring the North Vietnamese, but not in the form of a dramatic military escalation. Noting that "the best thing that can be said about the present Khanh government is that it has lasted six months and has about a 50-50 chance of lasting out the year," Taylor argued that the most important objective for the United States was to do "everything possible to bolster the Khanh government." Taylor recommended that in the present, the United States should seek to strengthen the GVN politically and militarily, while being prepared "to implement contingency plans against North Vietnam with optimum readiness by January 1, 1965."[80]

In response to Taylor's memoranda, the State Department's William Bundy circulated the most important memo during this period, titled "Next Courses of Action in Southeast Asia." Bundy urged that for the next ten days to two weeks, the United States initiate a holding phase intended to prevent any further escalation by the communists. The solution to the problem in South Vietnam, Bundy wrote, "will require a combination of military pressure and some form of communication under which Hanoi (and Peiping [sic]) eventually accept the idea of getting out." Only after "a clear pattern of pressure hurting the DRV and leaving no doubts in South Vietnam of our resolve" should the United States consider negotiations aimed at resolving the Vietnam conflict.

As to the nature and timing of future actions, Bundy specified two categories of military operations: "limited pressures" and "more serious pressures." Limited pressures included the overt recognition and justification by the Saigon government of previously covert operations against the DRV, the reintroduction of American DeSoto patrols, and the initiation of cross-border operations into the Laotian panhandle on a limited scale and of "specific tit-for-tat actions of opportunity" in response to "any special VC or DRV activity." Accepting Taylor's proposed time frame of January 1 before moving beyond this scale of activity, Bundy noted that none of these actions would entail pressure strong enough to "change Hanoi's basic actions." In terms of more serious pressures, Bundy argued that barring a serious deterioration of the situation in the South, "systematic military actions against the DRV might start by progressive attacks keyed to the rationale of infiltration routes and facilities, followed by other selected military related targets."[81]

By mid-September, the administration had reached a consensus on three key issues:[82] first, the United States would eventually have to initiate overt military action against the DRV in order to convince the leaders in Hanoi to quit supporting the insurgency in the South; second, that at the present time, the GVN was too weak for such operations to begin in the near future; and third, that any escalation of the conflict ran the risk of provoking the Chinese into intervening in the war.[83] On September 10, LBJ endorsed the recommendations of the "Courses of Action" memo and the holding pattern recommended first by Taylor, and seconded by William Bundy and John McNaughton.[84]

The "consensus" reported to LBJ by McGeorge Bundy in a memo on September 8 notwithstanding, the Joint Chiefs of Staff retained serious reservations about the American strategy in Vietnam. From mid-August to mid-September, the chiefs expressed two primary objections. Initially, the chiefs (primarily Chief of Staff of the Air Force General Curtis LeMay and Commandant of the Marine Corps General Wallace Greene) rejected the idea that the United States should delay attacking North Vietnam. As the chairman of the JCS General Wheeler noted, "these two officers now felt that the situation would continue to deteriorate unless such drastic action [i.e., sustained bombing of targets in the DRV] was taken now."[85] Second, all of the chiefs objected to the notion offered by Walt W. Rostow (and adopted by William Bundy) that the key to victory was to be found in altering Hanoi's interest to continue supporting the NLF in the South by a controlled bombing program of the North. As General Wheeler reported on August 14,

> the Joint Chiefs of Staff are in general accord with the policy and courses of action contained in the paper [Bundy's "Next Courses of Action"] provided that more serious pressures . . . be implemented as necessary along with the limited pressures. . . . This will provide for military courses of action, to include attack of targets in the Democratic Republic of Vietnam (DRV), as necessary, *with the objective of destroying the DRV will and capabilities* to continue support of insurgent forces in Laos and the Republic of Vietnam.[86]

In line with the "military dominant" concept of warfare held by the air force, the chiefs' preference was to deny the enemy the ability to continue its support through strategic bombing, rather than punishment with the intention of altering its cost/benefit calculation.[87]

In an effort to reconcile the emerging strategy with the chiefs' objections, a political-military war game was conducted from September 7 to 18, called SIGMA II-64.[88] The objectives of SIGMA II were to, first, test the notion that graduated military pressures would induce the DRV to cease supporting the insurgency in the South, and second, to predict the likely changes of the PRC's strategy in the Vietnam conflict. SIGMA II took place over the nine-day period, with players meeting frequently from four to five hours per day. This time commitment alone is an indication of the seriousness with which the players approached the exercise. Following the game, the players met to critique each other's performance during play, and to draw broader lessons that could be learned and applied to the actual crisis unfolding. Because the participants in the game came from the military and civilian offices in the Pentagon (OSD), the State Department, and the intelligence community, the views and experiences of the players represented the range of organizations that had a role in determining and implementing policy in Vietnam.[89]

One of the most important findings of SIGMA II concerned the signaling process the blue and red teams employed as the war progressed.[90] Both sides attempted to communicate to the other that further moves were futile, given what each thought was a clear demonstration of its total commitment to achieving their respective objectives. The result, however, was a continued spiral of hostility, leading to a level of war fighting that neither side sought. According to one participant's commentary explaining this process, "You're there, you're committed. Your honor is at stake, now you've got to do something." In the game, that "something" turned out to be an American deployment of ten-plus divisions of ground forces in Southeast Asia, and the active consideration of an amphibious invasion of North Vietnam.[91] The implication of this dual failure at signaling was that to avoid a spiral of hostilities, it would be necessary to reach an understanding with the PRC that neither the destruction of the DRV nor an attack on the PRC was in the interest of the United States—an undertaking made more difficult by the concurrent necessity of signaling resolve.

Based on the game's outcome, the players concluded that when faced with the bombing of North Vietnam, aerial mining of DRV ports, and the introduction of a relatively modest strength of US forces in South Vietnam (six-plus divisions), the PRC would have no *need* for direct confrontation with the United States. The lack of a need to intervene directly in the war and confront US forces was predicated on the lack of political stability of the GVN and the general strategy of having South Vietnam cave in under the feet of the Americans. Not only was this the lowest-cost strategy, but it also enabled the red team to achieve its objective of ensuring that mainland China was not directly attacked by the United States.[92] However, a massive deployment of the PLA against US forces *was* considered to be likely if the

United States bombed China, if the United States invaded the North, or if the government of the DRV appeared to be at the point of collapse.[93]

The impact that SIGMA II had on the evolution of the US commitment to Vietnam was significant in two respects. First, the game enabled war planners to understand the *process* by which a direct confrontation with the PRC would come about—even when both sides wished to avoid that confrontation. Given that the perceived stakes of "losing South Vietnam" were seen to be significant, cutting a running at this stage was not desirable for the administration. Yet neither was a war with the PRC. Thus by playing this game, participants and planners were able to get a much better sense of how the PRC would likely respond to future American escalation and allowed the administration to better refine its strategy of graduated pressure in ways that avoided a conflict spiral with the Chinese. This conclusion, it should be noted, was reached seven months prior to the issuance by the PRC of its four-point deterrence warnings against substantial escalation in the air war over North Vietnam.

Second, the interagency nature of the game allowed the military and civilians from different agencies the opportunity to discuss future war plans and assess their likely implications *prior* to their actual implementation. The working group that was formed in November included many of the same participants of the SIGMA II exercise. Such intense familiarity with the way individuals from other agencies conceived of the problems attendant to the Vietnam conflict enabled a more thorough planning process to result; one that integrated all aspects of limited war fighting, and one that was dedicated to preventing Chinese intervention in the war.[94]

On October 31, the National Liberation Front launched a massive attack on the Bien Hoa airfield in South Vietnam. This event convinced the administration that planning for the war's escalation had to begin in earnest. LBJ ordered the creation of the working group headed by William Bundy that would systematically review the administration's Vietnam policy and draft a complete strategy for taking the war to the North. The importance of the working group's deliberations and policy recommendations are significant for three primary reasons. First, the working group was structured so that all of the relevant agencies and top policy makers had influence on the strategy that was ultimately put forward. Second, throughout November, close attention was paid to the most up-to-date intelligence available concerning the probability of Chinese intervention at different levels of American actions against the DRV. Finally, the strategy that the working group produced in early December was in fact the strategy that was applied beginning in February 1965.

The November working group was structured in a manner that enabled all of the agencies involved in the war to have influence in the process of strategic development. The outline William Bundy produced that directed the group's focus contained nine topics, the first three of which are the most important. Section I, the intelligence section, was prepared by the joint CIA/DIA/INR (Bureau of Intelligence and Research) intelligence committee. Section II, "U.S. Objectives and Stakes in South Vietnam," and Section III, "Southeast Asia and the Broad Options," were prepared by William Bundy, who worked closely with John McNaughton and who was assisted by the CIA and JCS.[95] In total, position papers were received from the OSD/ISA (International Security Affairs), JSC, Joint Staff, the combined intelligence committee, the ambassador in South Vietnam, the Policy Planning Staff, in addition to those papers written by Bundy himself.

As the November working group began its deliberations, it became apparent that the administration was divided as to how to proceed in Vietnam given that the PRC was now conventionally mobilized and had recently tested a nuclear device. The military clearly favored maintaining the option of employing nuclear weapons against the enemy should the situation require it.[96] On the other hand, a powerful argument had been circulated by Under Secretary of State George Ball that favored substantially decreasing American objectives in Vietnam in order to avoid that very contingency. At the outset, it was Ball's position that had the greater effect on the unfolding strategy. Ball's analysis on the stakes for the United States in Vietnam, coupled with the bleak picture in South Vietnam painted by the intelligence committee, led William Bundy to argue in his initial draft of Section II that the only way that the United States could achieve its objectives in Vietnam was by "committing ourselves to whatever degree of military action would be required to defeat North Vietnam and probably Communist China militarily." Such a commitment, however, would result in a ground war and would possibly require the use of nuclear weapons. With these consequences in mind, Bundy went on to question the whole notion upon which the US commitment to Vietnam was based: he substantially discounted the international political fallout that would result from the loss of South Vietnam.[97]

The initial drafts of Section III detailed three general options that the United States could adopt at this point. Option A, written by Michael Forrestal,[98] argued for maintaining the status quo. Option B, written by McNaughton and Bundy (but with the JCS reserving the right to make suggestions), called for "Present policies plus a systematic program of military pressures against the north, meshing at some point with negotiation, but with pressure actions to be continued until we achieve our central present objectives." Finally, option C, drafted by Bundy, argued for "present policies plus additional forceful measures and military moves, followed by negotiations in which we would seek to maintain a believable threat of still further military pressures but would not actually carry out such pressures to any marked degree during the negotiations."[99]

Because option A held very little chance for securing American objectives, it received scant attention after it was submitted. The initial draft of option B called for an immediate and hard military response against the North, and included the deployment of marines to Da Nang to protect the US base against a counteroffensive. Given that the potential for Chinese intervention was deemed to be the highest under option B, Bundy and McNaughton recommended that the United States be prepared to attack the PRC's air bases, nuclear production facilities, and other military targets. Recognizing that the chances for a substantial DRV move southward would likely result with such a strong American response, option B called for both air and naval strikes against the North, a naval blockade, and "an early ground attack northward to seize, liberate and occupy North Vietnam." Should the Chinese counterattack, the United States would immediately go to a full-scale war footing. According to Bundy, option B held the highest probability of achieving US objectives and of dramatically escalating the war.[100]

Option C sought a gradual and limited application of force against the North in the hopes of securing peace through negotiation. Initially, the United States would conduct limited air attacks against infiltration routes in Laos and North Vietnam and would deploy ground forces to the northern portion of South Vietnam with the intent of deterring a DRV invasion. Should these actions fail to produce DRV capitulation, Bundy recommended bombing additional targets from a list of ninety-four, mining northern ports, and establishing a naval quarantine. Ultimately, option C "seemed to aim at saving American face by making a show of force but avoiding a long-term commitment even if Washington had to abandon its main objectives."[101]

On November 10 and 14, the military offered its responses to these proposals. Initially, the Joint Staff offered a biting critique of Bundy's draft of Section II, arguing that the United States was permanently committed to the defense of South Vietnam, and that South Vietnam was just as important a symbol as Berlin was (and that militarily, it was more important).[102] The chiefs urged a major deployment of troops to South Vietnam, attacks on Phuc Yen and petroleum, oil, and lubricants (POL) storage facilities near Hanoi, and then a prompt follow through with attacks on all ninety-four targets as well as infiltration targets. Believing that US nuclear power would deter intervention, the chiefs argued that "DRV and CHICOMs [Chinese Communists] would be unlikely to expand the conflict," although they did note that existing military plans would permit the United States to meet any move made by the opposing side.[103]

The joint intelligence committee submitted a final preliminary paper on November 16 that attempted to clearly specify the conditions under which the DRV and PRC were likely to intervene in the war. With respect to option C, the intelligence memo noted that the probability of communist intervention would substantially increase as the tempo and severity of American military actions increased. At the upper reaches of option C, which included "attacks on some or all of the 94-List targets, and amphibious or airborne operations to seize coastal lodgments in the DRV," the possibility of Chinese involvement in the war was considered to be unlikely, "unless they felt it was necessary in order to prevent destruction of the Communist regime in North Vietnam" or if air bases in China were attacked. Sounding a note of caution, the committee stated that "there is always a chance that Peiping [sic] might so intervene either for reasons that seem irrational to us or because it miscalculated the objectives of U.S. moves in the area. Communist China's capability for conducting a ground war in adjacent areas of southeast Asia is formidable."[104] In considering the likely reaction by the DRV and PRC to option B, the committee noted that "the risks of a U.S.-DRV war and of U.S.-Chinese Communist hostilities would be considerable, perhaps greater than in the case of the highest-level option C measures above."[105]

By November 18, the initial round of intelligence analysis and policy proposals had been drafted and debated at the subcabinet level. Over the next two days, the president and his senior advisors considered the various positions. After William Bundy's briefing to the president on the nineteenth concerning the progress that had been made on scenarios A, B, and C, the principals showed a clear preference for a continued focus on B and C.[106] In light of the preferences of top policy makers, and based on the comments received from the JCS and Joint Staff, McNaughton and William Bundy took to reformulating options B and C.

On November 21, Bundy issued a redraft of his proposals concerning the options available to the United States, suggesting a preference for option C. Key in this document was a section concerning the possibility of an American invasion of the DRV. Bundy suggested that prior to such a decision, the United States should consider lessening its objectives, based on "the volume of international noise and desire for a peaceful settlement."

Should the DRV demonstrate no willingness to modify its position after attacks against targets from the list of ninety-four, aerial mining, and a naval quarantine, the United States ought to be willing to settle for less than what had long been America's stated objectives.

On November 23, the JCS issued a full-scale critique of Bundy's proposals, which began with a rejection of the idea that the United States settle for anything less than what was entailed in National Security Action Memorandum (NSAM) 288. According to the chiefs, Bundy's reworked option C did not indicate the extent to which the United States would go if the DRV failed to respond to American pressures at higher levels, nor did it clearly specify the terms that the United States would seek in negotiations with Hanoi. In a response that reflected the Jominian norm of civil-military relations, the chiefs proposed option C':graduated military pressures that would include "an advance decision to continue military pressure, if necessary, to the full limits of what military actions can contribute toward US national objectives." Although C and C' entailed similar military actions, two significant differences emerged in the chiefs' memo. First, under C', the pace of the pressure applied on the DRV would be much faster than under C. Second, and far more importantly, the chiefs were demanding that a decision be made a priori for the use of nuclear weapons should Hanoi refuse to capitulate.[107] Additionally, the chiefs rejected Bundy's option B and proposed "a controlled program of intense military pressures against the DRV, swiftly, yet deliberately applied, designed to have a major military and psychological impact from the outset . . . [and] carried through, if necessary, to the full limits of what military actions can contribute toward US national objectives." Because option C' failed to "eliminate DRV air and DRV facilities available to CHICOM air at the outset," the chiefs reasoned that their option B stood the best chance of achieving US objectives while diminishing the likelihood of Chinese intervention.[108] Thus while they were willing to go with option C', their option B was the preferred choice.

On November 24, the intelligence committee issued a paper examining the political factors that would likely lead to Chinese intervention in the war. In their judgment, as the United States imposed increasingly severe pressure against the DRV,[109] Hanoi would be faced with a number of crucial questions pertaining to the interests of the United States. At issue was whether or not Hanoi believed the United States was intent on securing its objectives regardless of the possibility of war with the Chinese, or whether the American escalation was designed to secure a favorable bargaining position. More fundamental to this, Hanoi would likely wonder whether

American war aims were in fact limited. Based on the scenarios presented, the committee noted that "comprehension of the other's intentions would almost certainly be difficult on both sides, and especially so as the scale of hostilities mounted." In addition to Hanoi's perceptions of US intent, the committee struck a pessimistic cord in its assessment of the DRV's capacity to sustain punishment over time. Noting that the interdiction of the North's imports, transportation facilities, and industrial plants would in fact cripple its industry, the committee stated, "We do not believe that such actions would have a crucial effect on the daily lives of the overwhelming majority of the North Vietnamese population . . . [nor would] attacks on industrial targets . . . greatly exacerbate current economic difficulties as to create unmanageable control problems." In short, the panel considered the DRV "willing to suffer some damage to the country in the course of a test of wills with the U.S."[110]

The implications of Hanoi's willingness to suffer were significant. If Hanoi was unlikely to alter its behavior due to its capacity to sustain major damage, and the United States was forced to go to extreme measures in its attempt to force the DRV over the cost/benefit divide, the viability of the northern regime would be called into question. Under these conditions, any hesitancy that Hanoi might have in requesting assistance from the PRC would be overcome. In addition to the DRV's willingness to have the PRC intervene on its behalf at this point, the PRC as well would likely find it in its interest to do so. Should the Hanoi government be threatened with collapse, the Chinese would likely intervene for two reasons: out of fear for the security of their southern frontiers, and because of their need to strongly support "wars of national liberation" in the continuing Sino-Soviet split. Finally, the committee noted that in the present, the Chinese did not have the capacity to bolster the DRV's offensive or defensive capabilities, "short of [a] large-scale introduction of ground forces." Thus if faced with the possibility of Hanoi's collapse, the Chinese would likely intervene in force. Over time, however, China's ability to augment the DRV's fighting capabilities would grow. As China's internal force redeployment continued, more military hardware and troops could be made available to the DRV without significantly degrading China's own combat effectiveness.[111]

Two principal-level meetings were held on November 24 and 26, which together winnowed the strategic options down to one. Two primary issues were settled on the twenty-fourth. First, a "consensus" was reached concerning the objectives and stakes for the United States in Vietnam. The participants rejected William Bundy's (and George Ball's) sanguine assessments of the "loss" of South Vietnam, noting that because the United States had a long-standing commitment to Saigon, its fall to communism would be dire to American prestige. Second, despite having scored a bureaucratic victory over American objectives, the military's preferred course B lost out to option C/C'. A number of reasons stood behind the rejection of option B, most important was the consensus view that "in the light of all factors," B did not stand the best chance of achieving "our full objectives."[112] As the intelligence committee argued, the Chinese were more likely to intervene in response to an American escalation that threatened the viability of the DRV. Should that occur, then the long sought after objective of a stable and independent South Vietnam would be placed in jeopardy. On the twenty-sixth, Ambassador Taylor joined the principals and "urged that over the next two months we adopt a program of Option A plus the first stages of Option C."[113]

On November 29, William Bundy circulated a proposal for action in Vietnam that condensed the various options into one, reflecting the consensus of the two NSC meetings. Bundy's redraft contained plans that were very close to option C. In phase I (thirty days long), the United States would intensify existing military actions, including armed reconnaissance in Laos and reprisal strikes against the DRV for any major NLF attacks in the South. In phase II, the United States would conduct anti-infiltration strikes into the DRV. If Hanoi showed no signs of moderation, and if the stability of the Saigon government improved, then the United States would implement a series of air strikes of progressive intensity (two to six months long). Concurrently, the United States would watch for any indication that Hanoi was yielding and would be prepared to cease its attacks if the DRV was willing to capitulate on American terms. Bundy's proposal reflected the bureaucratic compromise reached in the NSC meetings: although it was stated at the outset that the United States was committed to whatever level of violence was necessary to secure its maximum objectives, there was no specific indication that the United States would go to the "full limits" of its power. As such, a substantial amount of strategic flexibility was retained.[114] On December 7, LBJ approved the strategy.[115] On February 26, the decision to initiate Rolling Thunder was made.[116]

Strategy Modified

On March 13, DCI McCone submitted a memo to the president covering the nature of communist reactions to attacks against the DRV. While noting that to date such reactions had been as predicted, McCone informed LBJ that the probability of the DRV capitulating to American coercion was spiraling downward. McCone reminded the president that the general view of the intelligence community was that the DRV would likely succumb to US airpower if they lacked the ability to undermine the GVN. However, "If Viet Cong military strength and capabilities are greater than we have supposed, as a review of the data now in process suggests, this factor might alter the general situation."[117] That review, a joint CIA/DIA/INR assessment of NLF strength, had a profound effect on top policy makers in Washington. The report stated that there was a strong possibility that the total NLF strength in South Vietnam was 150,000 (50,000 regulars and 100,000 irregulars), a full 50 percent greater than had been estimated for at least eighteen months.[118] On the eighteenth, McCone met with Rusk and McNamara individually to brief the two secretaries on the new estimate. Both were shaken, with McNamara realizing that the US and South Vietnamese forces were "simply outmanned."[119]

The new estimate of NLF strength had a direct effect on the US strategy against North Vietnam. McCone got to the heart of the problem in his memo to LBJ: based on *previous* estimates, the DRV was expected to look for a way to avoid the fate of suffering significant punishment through some form of political negotiations, rather than intensify the struggle while "accepting the destructive consequences in North Vietnam in the expectation of early victory in the South."[120] American perceptions of the DRV's calculations changed with the new assessment of NLF strength. If the DRV believed that an early victory could be gained, or if the struggle in the South could at least be intensified over the long run, the willingness of Hanoi's leaders to withstand American punishment might be similarly bolstered. The question confronting Washington now was how to respond to the new assessment of NLF strength.

The administration had three options available: it could drastically step up its air attacks on the DRV (an option that included hitting the major military and economic targets) in an effort to get Hanoi to call off the NLF in the South; it could initiate a significant ground offensive in the South with the objective of defeating the military threat to South Vietnam; or, the United States could do both. The two options of increasing Rolling Thunder and initiating a ground offensive were forwarded by John McNaughton to McGeorge Bundy, McNamara, and others on March 10. Not only did this memo present the strategic options available to the United States, but also just as importantly McNaughton attached detailed risk assessments attending to each option. If the United States chose to "progressively squeeze North Vietnam" by striking north of the 20th parallel, then the likelihood that the MIGs at Phuc Yen would be drawn out rose dramatically as did the chances that China would introduce fighters from Hainan. This latter possibility made salient the question of "hot pursuit" into China and striking airfields in the PRC itself. Finally, such a strategy also entailed a risk of DRV and Chinese air and ground intervention in the South (although the probability that the PRC would take such a course was lower than that of North Vietnam). On the other hand, if the United States went with a massive ground effort, then McNaughton forecasted only a Chinese deployment of troops into the DRV. Although the ground strategy was deemed to be less provocative, McNaughton suggested that this approach was less controllable: "Once US troops are in, it will be impossible to withdraw them or to move them . . . without admitting defeat." McNaughton's suggestion was to combine the two approaches by beginning an initial progressive squeeze on the DRV, all the while being prepared to "shunt to 'circuit-breakers' . . . either to deploy large numbers of US forces in South Vietnam or to Thailand and Laos."[121]

McNaughton offered a strategy composed of *consecutive* operations: first in the air, and then on the ground (holding the air operation constant). In response to the new estimate of NLF strength however, the JCS urged that the United States move to a *concurrent* ground offensive in the South and a massive air attack in the North. On March 15, in a memo to McNamara discussing the conditions under which the United States should seek negotiations with DRV, Wheeler stated that the chiefs were of the belief that "there should be no attempt to negotiate a settlement until US/Government of Vietnam forces have achieved a strong position of military advantage." Such an advantage could only come from the full implementation of the "program designed to destroy the will and capabilities of the DRV to support the insurgencies in the RVN [Republic of Vietnam, South Vietnam] and Laos,"[122] a manifest example of the military dominant concept of warfare the US armed forces held. Five days later, Wheeler sent McNamara a second memo calling for the introduction of US combat forces "in such strengths as to achieve an effective margin of combat power, and provide a clear indication that United States intends to support South Vietnam and intends to achieve its objectives." In addition to increasing the pressure on the North from the air, the chiefs urged a ground offensive in the South designed to deter Chinese intervention and to "gain effective operational superiority and assume the offensive" against the NLF.[123]

Thus by March 20, the administration had before it two strategic options. The essential difference between the two programs turned on the assessment of the risks entailed in dramatically stepping up attacks on the DRV. In the end, the president agreed to a variant of McNaughton's plan. This decision was heavily influenced by information that strongly pointed to growing Chinese material assistance to the southern insurgency,[124] indications that the PRC was beginning to equate NLF success to its own national security,[125] continuing augmentation of China's air and ground force projection capabilities,[126] and the increasingly hard line that Beijing was taking toward the Vietnam conflict as it attempted to outcompete Moscow in the widening Sino-Soviet split.[127]

In a memo to the president, McGeorge Bundy argued that as a result of the revised estimates of NLF strength and the prediction of an impending major spring offensive,[128] it was critical that "we put every possibly useful resource into the effort in the South," including: (1) an 18,000 to 20,000 man increase in US military forces to fill out existing units and provide for increased logistics capabilities, and (2) the deployment of two or three divisions "to take on limited missions, to release government forces for wider use, and to deter large-scale DRV attacks on South Vietnam." At the same time, Bundy recommended that the United States should plateau the intensity of Rolling Thunder operations. Air missions should remain out of the operational range of the MIGs in the North, while limiting attacks to lines of communication (LOCs) and perhaps to rail lines north and northeast of Hanoi.[129] These recommendations were formally adopted in NSAM 328 on April 6.[130] At this point the United States assumed direct responsibility of the offensive ground war against the NLF in South Vietnam.

At a high-level meeting with the president on April 21, McNamara presented a plan for the implementation of NSAM 328. Noting that the number of US forces currently deployed in the South was inadequate to the task of meeting the NLF threat, the secretary of defense pressed for the deployment of additional ground forces and urged that Rolling Thunder *not* be extended to include "industrial targets, POL centers, or anything in the Hanoi-Haiphong area" for the next six months to a year. In effect, McNamara proposed maintaining the interdiction focus of the air campaign, and Rusk concurred that this was the proper course to follow. Although he did not indicate that he was opposed to the recommendations, McGeorge Bundy suggested that an estimate be conducted that would gauge the reactions of Hanoi, Beijing, and Moscow to the deployment of a significant number of US combat forces.[131]

The Board of National Estimates submitted its report the next day. This memorandum presented a stark but accurate depiction of how the Vietnam War would unfold. Should the United States refrain from increasing the scale and tempo of Rolling Thunder while at the same time begin committing more and more ground forces to South Vietnam, Washington could expect the communists to attempt to bog down American forces in the jungles of Southeast Asia. At the same time, however, this course of action did not pose a direct threat of a substantially wider war with the Chinese.[132] In a second high-level meeting held on the twenty-second, McNamara indicated that he agreed with the assessment, and by implication, noted that he preferred the course of action that provided room for maneuver well short of Chinese intervention.[133]

Thus by the end of April 1965, the United States made a critical alteration to the limited war strategy in Vietnam. Rather than placing the bulk of war effort on the bombing campaign against the DRV, the United States opted to plateau Rolling Thunder operations and to focus instead on waging the ground war in South Vietnam. This decision was based on the acquisition of new information pertaining to the strength of NLF in the South, specifically on how the revised estimate of NLF combat power affected the likelihood that Rolling Thunder would achieve its objectives. Significantly, the evidence demonstrates that the change in strategy occurred *before* Washington officials received the Chinese four-point message.[134] By piecing together intelligence from a number of different sources, the United States was able to make a critical change to its strategy in a timely and effective manner. This is not to say that China's direct warning was of limited value to American policy makers. China's message was important because it *reinforced* conclusions that had been made prior.

In response to the initiation by the NLF of a major offensive and the astonishingly poor performance of the ARVN to counter the advance, General Westmoreland sent a cable to Washington on June 7 requesting a buildup to forty-four battalions of US and third country troops. Given the urgency of the memo, and the clear indications that the NLF offensive threatened to render the ARVN combat ineffective, there was little doubt at the highest levels that Westmoreland's request had to be granted. On June 12, the JCS approved the request and asked McNamara that he endorse the plan to send 117,000 American soldiers to South Vietnam by the fall of 1965. Five days later, McNamara agreed and in a meeting on the eighteenth with LBJ, McGeorge Bundy, and Rusk, the secretary of defense secured the president's approval for the full complement suggested by the chiefs and for 20,000 additional non-American forces by November 1.[135] It is important to recognize that this decision did not represent a change in strategy by the United States: the plan sought to exert military pressure on NLF forces solely in the South but did not entail a change in the air campaign. Although the specifics of the plan were not made public until late July, the United States was now committed to seeking its political objectives in the ground war in South Vietnam.[136]

"COUNTERINSURGENCY" IN SOUTH VIETNAM

The flexibility exhibited in the air war was in no way matched in the ground war. Throughout the period under consideration, the US Army and MACV ensured that the preferred strategic approach, large-scale conventional search-and-destroy missions, would take center stage. True to the military dominant concept of warfare, this approach was inappropriate to the strategic context of Vietnam, and as a result, the United States was unable to secure its political objectives. Significantly, alternative approaches were known to MACV. Yet because of the autonomy and isolation that characterized MACV's position in the information institution, top commanders in the field successfully resisted pressures from outside, inside, and above the army.

One example of the weakness of external pressures on MACV was the appointment of Edward Lansdale to the American embassy in Saigon in 1965. Lansdale was tapped to oversee pacification efforts, advise various American agencies, and to assist the South Vietnamese government in winning over the allegiance of the populace. A prominent figure with direct experience in waging counterinsurgency warfare in Asia, Lansdale's appointment to Saigon held the potential of influencing US military and diplomatic strategies in a more effective manner. Prior to his appointment to the American embassy, Lansdale authored a critique of the American approach in the war. While not criticizing the objectives of the war, Lansdale attacked the attrition strategy the American army had adopted. Noting that the conventional attrition strategy turned more peasants toward the insurgency, Lansdale argued that the United States should focus on winning the hearts and minds of the population.[137] His preference for pacification over body counts met stiff resistance from the army—an organization that held strongly to the Jominian norm of civil-military relations. Lansdale's attempt to reorient the American approach was hampered by a number of factors, including the lack of a clear mission, the absence of both autonomy and a direct channel back to Washington (he reported to Ambassador Lodge and not the president), and no independent control of the funds necessary to influence either his American or Vietnamese counterparts.[138] As a result of MACV's near monopoly over the course of American military operations and strategy, Lansdale's efforts were bound to fail. As a result, there was little chance that American military and diplomatic objectives could be effectively coordinated in South Vietnam.

In March 1966, roughly one year after the American commitment of ground forces to the war, an army staff study titled "Program for the Pacification and Long-Term Development of South Vietnam" (PROVN) was completed. The PROVN study was highly critical of the attrition strategy and recommended that pacification and population control assume top priority of American efforts in South Vietnam. Noting that there was "no unified effective pattern" to the war effort, the report urged that unity of command over all aspects of counterinsurgency efforts be achieved quickly. Because the PROVN study was conducted under army auspices, it stood the best chance of inducing changes in strategy and doctrine.[139] Yet this was not to be the case. As the Pentagon Papers note,

> The study was intended for internal Army use, and was for a while after its completion treated with such delicacy that Army officers were forbidden even to discuss its existence outside DOD. This was unfortunate, because in content it was far-ranging and thoughtful, and set a precedent for responsible forward planning and analysis which should be duplicated in other fields.[140]

The impact of the PROVN study was thus negligible.[141] The document was downgraded from a study to a "conceptual document" and was submitted to the NSC for its "consideration."[142] Westmoreland had little to fear that such a move would hamper MACV's preferred course of action. Indeed, "the second half of 1966 saw MACV utilize its maneuver battalions almost exclusively in search-and-destroy operations."[143]

The army's approach remained that of attrition for three primary reasons. The first was that MACV was disinclined to adopt an approach that ran counter to its organizational cultural concept of war and its preference for conventional search-and-destroy missions.[144] According to its own, internally derived, evaluative metrics, search-and-destroy operations were succeeding in capturing and killing increasing numbers of enemy combatants at rates that outstripped the enemy's ability to recruit new members. Yet as former Defense Intelligence Agency official Patrick McGarvey noted, these analyses were far from objective.

> The military in Saigon sent all the facts back to Washington eventually. During the buildup period, infiltration data and recruitment data came in via General

Westmoreland's daily cablegram. Data from field contact with enemy units came amid the more mundane cables or by courier up to five weeks later. Cables from Westmoreland, of course, were given higher priority in Washington. When we started "winning," detailed reports highlighting "body counts" and statistics on how many villages were pacified were cabled with Westmoreland's signature; recruitment studies were pouched or cabled with the reports on the fluctuating price of rice. It was all a matter of emphasis.[145]

Second, because of the prevailing Jominian relational norm, MACV rejected any notion of "unity of command" that entailed the American ambassador having the ability to determine army priorities and missions. As Robert Komer, the special assistant to the president for pacification, lamented to McNamara in September 1966,

> While I'm proud of at least getting the civil side moving in the last 5 months [on implementing the recommendations of the PROVN study], one man in Washington—with a fuzzy grant of authority—can only do so much. The real bottleneck is not back here (where I have the President behind me and your support) but in Saigon, where there are real and legitimate questions as to how much I can get our theater commanders to swallow.[146]

Third, because MACV—the organization that bore direct responsibility for designing and implementing ground operations in South Vietnam—operated nearly autonomously in the American information institution, it was largely immune from pressures (from either the top or from competing organizations) to deviate from its preferred strategic approach.[147]

At most, MACV was willing to adopt the rhetoric of pacification and population security, all the while maintaining the conventional approach. In late August 1966, Westmoreland cabled Washington with a proposal for modifying the strategy in South Vietnam. After noting that "the enemy has launched a determined campaign to gain control of South Vietnam—its land, its people, and its government," and that there was no indication that its resolve or capabilities had been seriously degraded, Westmoreland offered a proposal that in effect would provide a "shield" under which Vietnamese forces could more effectively protect pacification activities. The manner in which Westmoreland envisioned this strategic "revision" taking place, however, was fully consistent with the extant strategic course. The nature of American operations contemplated fell along traditional lines,

> The essential tasks of revolutionary development and nation building cannot be accomplished if enemy main forces can gain access to the population centers and destroy our efforts. US/Free World forces, with their mobility and in

coordination with Vietnamese Armed Forces, must take the fight to the enemy by attacking his main forces and invading his base areas. Our ability to do this is improving steadily. Maximum emphasis will be given to the use of long range patrols and other means to find the enemy and locate his bases. Forces and bases thus discovered will be subjected to either ground attack or quick reaction B-52 and tactical air strikes. When feasible, B-52 strikes will be followed by ground forces to search the area. Sustained ground combat operations will maintain pressure on the enemy.

Westmoreland concludes the memo as follows:

In summation, the MACV mission, which is to assist the Government of Vietnam to defeat the Viet Cong/North Vietnamese Army forces and extend Government control throughout South Vietnam, prescribes our two principal tasks.

• We must defeat the enemy through offensive operations against his main forces and bases.
• We must assist the Government to gain control of the people by providing direct military support of revolutionary development in coordination with the other agencies of the U.S. Mission.

The simultaneous accomplishment of these tasks is required to allow the people of South Vietnam to get on with the job of nation building.[148]

Possibly sensing that a pacification-based approach was gaining support in Washington,[149] Westmoreland attempted to square the strategic circle. Nevertheless, the twin components of his proposal were clearly at odds with each other. With US forces engaging the enemy conventionally, there remained little chance that population security would be dramatically enhanced. What was required was a full-scale restructuring of the American command structure in theater (along the lines detailed in the PROVN study), and a dedication to the objective of rural development as a means of decoupling the insurgents from the population. Given that the army was disinclined to engage in such far-reaching organizational and strategic reforms,[150] OSD's efforts (along with others inside and outside the Pentagon[151]) had little impact on the main course of the ground war.

Although PROVN had no significant impact on MACV's behavior, the study did have an influence on many in Washington. After Westmoreland submitted his force requests for the next calendar year in June 1966, McNamara demurred and requested in return a "detailed line by line analysis for these requirements to determine that each is truly essential to the carrying out of our war plan." Attached to McNamara's request was a study conducted by the Office of Systems Analysis (OSA) that called into question Westmoreland's proposed troop requirements. On August 10, Westmoreland replied that he could not justify the reduction in forces the OSA suggested.[152]

In the ensuing months, the OSD waged a battle of numbers with MACV and the JCS in an attempt to demonstrate that the attrition approach was not fulfilling American objectives and to force the army to adopt a pacification-based approach. In March 1967, Westmoreland requested an increase in American forces of at least 2 2/3 divisions in order to combat an enemy whose ranks had been steadily growing. On April 27, Westmoreland briefed his proposal to the president, complaining that with the force restriction facing MACV, the adopted "meat-grinder" approach, would yield no further positive developments. The editor of the Pentagon Papers sums up Westmoreland's presentation in the following terms.

> He [Westmoreland] then predicted that "unless the will of the enemy is broken or unless there was an unraveling of the VC infrastructure the war could go on for 5 years. If our forces were increased that period could be reduced although not necessarily in proportion to increases in strength, since factors other than increase in strength had to be considered. For instance, a non-professional force, such as that which would result from fulfilling the requirement for 100,000 additional men by calling reserves, would cause some degradation of normal leadership and effectiveness." Westmoreland concluded by estimating that with a force level of *565,000 men, the war could well go on for three years. With a second increment of 2 1/3 divisions leading to a total of 665,000 men, it could go on for two years.*[153]

LBJ then inquired of Westmoreland the likely result of not providing the general's requested 2 2/3 division force. Westmoreland responded that American momentum would die, the enemy would recapture the initiative in certain areas, and that while the United States would not necessarily lose the war, it would certainly drag on for a longer period of time.[154]

The civilians in the OSD remained unconvinced, however, that MACV's forces should be augmented. OSA studies conducted between January and May 1967 demonstrated that the enemy had initiated a whopping 88 percent of combat actions (a clear indication that the initiative was not with the United States).[155] Furthermore, OSA studies made the case that a pacification-based strategy was the less costly approach in terms of casualties, and that search-and-destroy operations were not enabling the government of South Vietnam to provide population security from the insurgents.[156] Critically, the OSA derived these conclusions based on information provided by MACV itself, as the latter was the dominant source of information pertaining to the situation in the theater.

The army's response to OSA analysis was sharp and defensive. As Krepinevich explains,

> The Army rejected the OSA evaluation out of hand. Furthermore, it sought to exclude other individuals and organizations from having access to the SEA [Southeast Asia] Reports. On at least two occasions General Wheeler strongly recommended to McNamara that the reports "be limited to internal OSD use only" in order to "reduce the dissemination of incorrect and/or misleading information to senior officials of other government agencies, as well as commanders in the field."

Despite the alternative analysis OSA provided, neither the army nor MACV systematically evaluated it.[157] Doing so would have required a full-scale reconsideration of the conventional strategy.

Perhaps the best indicator of MACV's insularity in the American information institution is the performance of the Defense Intelligence Agency. As an agency, DIA was created to provide critical intelligence assessments to both the JCS and to the secretary of defense. Throughout the war, however, DIA was subject to extensive pressures to conform to the army's view on matters of intelligence, and DIA complied. According to McGarvey,

> It [DIA] paid little or no attention to what Hanoi was saying on the radio, discounting it as propaganda. It made little effort to perceive the enemy's view of the war. It made little effort to reason out what the enemy's strategy was, why he believed he was winning, what he was saying publicly about how he was going to fight the war, or how the bombing was affecting his morale. It was too busy keeping up with the flow of numbers from Saigon.[158]

As the agency placed between the competing camps within the Pentagon, DIA could have served as an objective arbiter of the contending strategic approaches. Yet because of the extensive pressures exerted on DIA to conform to the strategic view of MACV, there was little chance that thorough and objective analyses of the efficacy of the conventional approach to waging the ground war would be conducted. The predictable result was American strategic rigidity in the face of a highly adaptable and competent opponent.

Ultimately, it took the Tet Offensive to convince President Johnson that American military objectives in Vietnam could not be achieved. In response to the offensive, Westmoreland pressed LBJ to have American reserves put into active duty. For Westmoreland, additional deployments were necessary to exploit opportunities presented by the offensive, which could "materially shorten the war." Disinclined to take such a drastic step, the president committed only to sending an additional 10,000 troops. It then fell to General Wheeler to make the case to LBJ. Upon his return from Saigon, Wheeler informed the president that Westmoreland needed a commitment of an additional 190,000 forces. Again, civilians in the OSD were dead set against approving MACV's request. According to their analysis, no American force level could produce victory unless the conventional strategy was abandoned in favor of one that focused on population control and pacification. With his military and civilian advisers clearly split, and with domestic support for the war eroding, LBJ recalled Westmoreland to Washington, placed stringent limits on the air war and future troop deployments, and declared that this would be his final term in office.[159] In the aftermath of Tet, American objectives were scaled back dramatically and the United States began to search for a way out of the war. That process would be slow, painful, and costly. America's inability to secure its military and nonmilitary objectives induced a dramatic durational escalation of the Vietnam War.

INFORMATION INSTITUTIONS VERSUS CIVIL-MILITARY RELATIONS

The outcome of America's limited war in Vietnam, a military defeat and diplomatic success—little consolation, resulted from the moderately truncated nature of the American information institution under LBJ. The components of the information institution that produced the strategy for the air campaign afforded top policy makers with information from multiple organizational sources, and those organizations widely shared information with each other. By contrast, the components of the information institution that produced the strategy for the ground campaign provided top policy makers with information from a single organizational source that operated autonomously from the rest of the national security bureaucracy.

The evidence presented strongly confirms the causal logic of the information institution approach. The United States went to war with a moderately truncated information institution, wherein the military (the army in particular) was isolated from top policy makers and from what was otherwise a tightly knit national security bureaucracy. Under these conditions, this approach expects American information collection and analysis to be moderate and fair. Specifically, information pertaining to the state that stood the highest chance of intervening against the United States, China, was plentiful and was subject to rigorous evaluation. Information regarding the principal military opponent, the NLF/PAVN, was never afforded the same treatment. Moreover, the information institution approach expects military and diplomatic coordination to be poor, particularly in the ground war. American efforts to avoid horizontal escalation were far more successful than those directed to defeating the southern insurgency and to the bolstering of political stability of the GVN.

The Vietnam War is a particularly useful test case for the information institution approach. Put simply, the strategic outcomes of the air and ground campaigns diverged dramatically, and the information institution approach should be able to explain this variation. First, the design of the strategy of the air campaign benefited from access to multiple sources of information pertaining to the DRV and to the PRC. Both the SIGMA II war game and the November working group incorporated military and civilian agencies of the US government. This broad range of information meant that top policy makers were not beholden solely to the military for analysis and options. Furthermore, the density of communication channels among these agencies proved invaluable because the massive amount of information flowing into Washington could be evaluated and vetted with greater precision. Together, the multiple sources of information and the density of lateral connections provided, first, comprehensive information collection of the strategic environment and optimal analysis. As the air strategy was being designed, leaders were provided with information regarding the PRC in addition to that of the primary opponent, the DRV. Further, because all of the relevant agencies were included in the strategic design process, top policy makers were able to assess the likely benefits and risks of a wide range of alternative approaches, not simply those the military preferred. As it turned out, this wide range of perspective proved beneficial because the US Air Force's cultural preference for strategic bombing would in all likelihood have threatened the viability of the regime of North Vietnam and would have induced Chinese intervention. Additionally, the prosecution of the air campaign exhibited tight coordination between military and diplomatic objectives. Given the strategic situation in Southeast Asia, the graduated pressure strategy was the only option available that could balance the perceived need to coerce the DRV into ceasing its support for the southern insurgency and to prevent Chinese intervention.

Optimal or not, Rolling Thunder was incapable of delivering both of these strategic objectives. As new evidence of the NLF's strength made its way to Washington, combined with that of the PRC's ongoing preparations to intervene in the war, Washington had to make a choice between coercing Hanoi and managing the Chinese threat. Consistent with the logic of the information institution approach, the decision in April 1965 to plateau Rolling Thunder and to concentrate on the ground war in South Vietnam was rational, a decision based on the comprehensive collection and optimal analysis of information. Moreover, the alteration in strategy reflected the tight coordination between diplomatic and military objectives. The administration made a clear choice: managing the Chinese threat and avoiding a major war against the PRC was more important to American interests than was the attempt to coerce the DRV. As such, the air war was scaled back in a manner that reflected that political objective.

By way of comparison, the ground war was managed in an exactly opposite fashion. Because of MACV's autonomy in the information institution, top policy makers received information pertaining to the fortunes of American combat forces from only one source. For its part, MACV received and shared little information with other departments and agencies in the national security bureaucracy. The result was a military strategy based exclusively on biased and incomplete information, a strategy that undermined American political objectives in the ground campaign.

Turning to the competing explanations, democratic civil-military relations theory performs poorly in this case. When political and military preferences diverge (as was clearly evident in the Vietnam War), the theory expects political-military coordination to suffer. At the same time, information sharing will remain fluid due to the oversight mechanisms political leaders employ to monitor the behavior of their military organizations. In the case of the air campaign, the evidence presented supports the expectation of fluid information sharing. However, the expectation of a lack of political-military coordination receives little support. Despite the complete lack of faith in the graduated pressure strategy by top military officials, Rolling Thunder thoroughly embodied American military and diplomatic objectives. In the case of the ground war, the opposite pattern holds. While the theory correctly identifies a profound lack of coordination between civilians and the military, the expectation of fluid information sharing found little support. Indeed, civilians in Washington were largely ignorant about the ineffectiveness of American combat forces over a period of years. To a significant extent, the reason for this case of information asymmetry was the inability of top policy makers to exercise meaningful oversight over a military organization that was isolated and autonomous. In sum, democratic civil-military relations theory runs into three major problems in the case of Vietnam: it does not anticipate the outcome of military failure and diplomatic success, it cannot explain tight military-diplomatic coordination when military and political preferences diverge, and it cannot account for persistently blocked information channels between the military and political leaders when the domestic balance of power favors civilians.

Organizational culture theory anticipates mixed strategic success in limited war under two possible conditions: when a "balanced" conception of war interacts with a Jominian norm of civil-military relations, or when a "military dominant" concept of war interacts with a Clausewitzian relational norm. Yet evidence presented above demonstrates, as do multiple independent studies, that the US Army and Air Force both held a cultural concept of war that was "military dominant" and both adhered to a Jominian relational norm. Under these conditions, the organizational culture approach anticipates not a mixed outcome, but rather double failure in limited wars

The American army's approach to warfare in the Vietnam era can be boiled down to a focus on midintensity conflict with a strong preference for the massive use of firepower to destroy the enemy and to mitigate American casualties. For the army, the wars of the recent past confirmed the efficacy of the "Army Concept." In both World War II and Korea, the army employed massive firepower in an attempt to substitute materiel for combat forces. In terms of the opponent in a future war, the US Army focused nearly exclusively on the Soviet Union and planned extensively for general war in Europe. The predominance of the Soviet threat meant that the army constantly based its peacetime planning on worst-case scenarios. Over time, this focus was translated into a threat preference: army officers considered planning for war with the Soviet Union to be *the* objective of their careers. Attention to other potential opponents, and consideration of other modes of warfare, was given short shrift.[160] Although the Korean War vindicated the army's preferred approach to waging war, the scale and scope of military operations imposed by civilian leadership were deemed unacceptable. Following the Chinese intervention in that war, civilian leaders placed limitations on the military's conduct. The prolonged stalemate and eventual terms of the armistice contributed to a pronounced "never again" attitude within the army.[161] This attitude meant that in the future, army officers would go to great lengths to avoid being placed in a position of waging wars without a significant degree of autonomy.

Similar to the army, air strategists approached the entire notion of limited war with distain. In particular, American air chiefs believed that their preferred approach to war, strategic bombing, was vindicated in the Second World War. American air chiefs believed that large doses of air power, focused against an opponent's nation rather than its armed forces per se, constituted the best means of prevailing in any conflict.[162] These perceptions became institutionalized with the rise of the US Strategic Air Command (SAC) and with the publication of Manual 1–8 "Strategic Air Operations," the guiding doctrine of the air force that remained fundamentally unchanged until December 1965.

Under the leadership of General Curtis LeMay, SAC planning focused strictly on the worst-case scenario of a general, nuclear war with the Soviet Union. By 1955, LeMay had acquired virtual autonomy in target selection in a future war, and in the autumn of 1960, SAC's influence rose dramatically with the development of the Single Integrated Operational Plan (SIOP) for nuclear war. With the Pentagon focused on waging nuclear war with the USSR, air planners devoted little attention to other, more limited contingencies. In 1961, LeMay assumed the position of US Air Force chief of staff. As this service's top officer, the air force raised the profile of strategic bombing to a new level. Indeed, in the air force's manuals pertaining to limited warfare, the use of nuclear weapons to achieve strategic effects was emphasized.[163] More broadly, the air force's "Basic Doctrine" at the time clearly articulated the preference for general war planning. According to that document, "The best preparation for limited war is proper preparation for general war. . . . The latter is the more important since there can be no guarantee that a limited war would not spread into general conflict."[164]

To the extent that both the army and air force held a concept of warfare that was "military dominant" and adhered to a Jominian relational norm, organizational culture theory cannot explain the strategic outcome of the Vietnam War—military failure and diplomatic success. When we turn attention to how the air force and the army influenced the air and ground strategies respectively, however, an interesting pattern emerges. While the army was afforded near-total influence over the ground campaign, the same cannot be said of the air force. The information institution approach offers an explanation for this pattern. I argued in chapter 2 that among the benefits of robust information institutions is the ability to break through cultures that separate organizations that respond to "local knowledge," such as professional militaries. Specifically, when leaders receive information from multiple sources, organizations that are characterized by closed circles of communication are prevented from dominating policy formulation and execution. In the absence of multiple sources of information, those types of organizations will have the ability to isolate themselves from policy makers and other organs within the information institution. In this case, the American army exercised substantial influence over the strategy in the ground war because top policy makers did not have the institutional capacity to counter the cultural elements that induced MACV's separation from the rest of the national security bureaucracy. While a nearly identical cultural predisposition to isolation existed in the air force, top policy makers had the ability to override those cultural preferences effectively. In neither the ground nor air campaign did top policy makers see the military as the only "salient organization," because both campaigns had to be limited and controlled in significant ways. Only in the air campaign were policy makers able to exert their preference, however. In short, the evidence presented in this chapter demonstrates precisely how information institutions determine the strategic influence of organizational cultures in wartime.

Of the four limited wars examined in this book, Vietnam stands out in terms of the scale of its impact on American domestic and international politics. It is for good reason that this war has been described as an "American tragedy." As such, it is worth considering whether the Vietnam War could have turned out differently for the United States. Specifically, given my conclusion that the ground campaign's failures are attributable to the weakness of the information institution that guided American strategic decision making, could a robust information institution have delivered an across-the-board strategic victory for the United States? Cast at such a high level of abstraction, this counterfactual question cannot be answered with any degree of precision. The reason is that it violates the rule of "historical consistency," or the "minimal-rewrite rule," that must be followed when conducting counterfactual thought experiments. There are simply too many historical facts, over too many years, that would have to be altered for this question to be answered either way with any degree of confidence.[165]

At the same time, two conclusions from the preceding analysis can be reached. The first, of course, is that the *particular* information flow patterns that governed American strategic decision making in the ground campaign directly contributed to the *particular* military failure in the war. The evidence provided in this chapter demonstrates that MACV's autonomy in the information institution prevented President Johnson and his top advisers from understanding how counterproductive American strategy in South Vietnam actually was. Their inability to come to terms with the US Army's dysfunctional approach caused the durational escalation of the war. The second is that had the information flow pattern that governed the conduct of the ground campaign resembled the pattern that governed the air campaign, top policy makers would likely have made substantial—and potentially productive—strategic adjustments early on. Given the receptiveness and flexibility to new information top American officials exhibited in the air campaign, it is reasonable to conclude that alternative strategic approaches to the ground campaign would have been entertained by top policy makers if they had been rigorously evaluated. For example, had the recommendations contained in the PROVN study been subjected to the same type of risk assessments that informed the air strategy, it is likely that top policy makers would not have accepted Westmoreland's recommendations as favorably as they did. Had the American army adopted a full-fledged counterinsurgency strategy in the ground campaign, the outcome may have indeed been more favorable for the United States. Yet given the length of time that successful counterinsurgencies typically take,[166] there is no guarantee that the United States would have had the domestic political will for an extended conflict in Southeast Asia.

CHAPTER FIVE

Military and Diplomatic Success in the Persian Gulf War

The Persian Gulf War was a double strategic success for the United States. In terms of its military objectives, the United States sought to evict Iraq from Kuwait, severely degrade Iraqi combat power, and pave the way for the restoration of the legitimate Kuwaiti government. In terms of its diplomatic objectives, the United States attempted to construct and maintain a massive international coalition to isolate and pressure Iraq and to achieve the explicit approval of the United Nations in the process. In all of these objectives, the United States was successful; the war ended with the satisfaction of all American war aims and without experiencing undesired escalation. I argue that these strategic successes resulted from the robust nature of the American information institution that was firmly in place when the crisis erupted in early August 1990. Information flowed remarkably freely among top policy makers and national security organizations. The strategy that resulted was based on comprehensive collection and optimal analysis of information, and resulted in tight coordination between the military and diplomatic aspects of the war.

Neither of the competing theories is able to explain American strategic performance in the Persian Gulf War as well as the information institution approach. While democratic civil-military relations theory's expectation of fluid information sharing between the military and top policy makers is confirmed, the theory is at pains to explain the tight coordination between the military and diplomatic aspects of the broader war effort. Organizational culture theory fares particularly poorly in this case. In the wake of Vietnam, the American military's adherence to a "military dominant" concept of warfare and to the Jominian norm of civil-military relations was reinforced. Under these conditions, organizational culture theory anticipates double failure in the Persian Gulf War—an outcome clearly at odds with the empirical record. Indeed, it was because of the robust American information institution that the organizational culture of the military had little direct influence on the content and execution of US strategy in the Persian Gulf.

A CASE OF DOUBLE SUCCESS

On August 1, 1990, Iraq quickly invaded and occupied Kuwait. Despite the extensive record of belligerent rhetoric by Saddam Hussein and the overt nature of his military mobilization and deployments, the United States was taken off guard by the attack. Almost immediately, President George Bush and his top civilian advisers came to the conclusion that under no circumstances could Saddam's action go unanswered. Over the next few days and weeks, the president would lay out a bold set of political objectives to deal with the crisis and eventual war in the Persian Gulf. In a nationally televised address on August 8, and then again to a crowd of military and civilian employees at the Pentagon, Bush laid out four principles that would guide American policy:

1 The immediate, complete, and unconditional withdrawal of all Iraqi forces from Kuwait
2 The restoration of Kuwait's legitimate government
3 A commitment to the security and stability of the Persian Gulf, and
4 The protection of the lives of American citizens abroad.

Those principles were codified in National Security Directive (NSD) 45 on August 20.[1]

Yet for Bush and his national security adviser, Brent Scowcroft, these four principles were ultimately means to a much larger end. At a meeting of the National Security Council on August 3, the second of the crisis, Under Secretary of State Lawrence Eagleburger argued that Iraq's invasion of Kuwait constituted the "first test of the post–Cold War system" and that direct American involvement in the crisis was necessary so that future attempts at aggression (by Iraq or other states) would be deterred.[2] The president, Scowcroft, and Secretary of Defense Dick Cheney each concurred that the stakes for the United States in the crisis extended far beyond the region, as important as those were. Indeed, many in the administration believed that the evolving post–Cold War era presented numerous opportunities for the United States to extend its influence around the globe in order to better secure American national interests.[3] While this fifth principle of attempting to facilitate the emergence of a "new world order" was clear from the very beginning of the crisis, its articulation came in the president's address to a joint session of Congress on September 11:

> We stand today at a unique and extraordinary moment. The crisis in the Persian Gulf, as grave as it is, also offers a rare opportunity to move toward an historic period of cooperation. Out of these troubled times, our fifth objective—a new world order—can emerge: a new era—freer from the threat of terror, stronger in the pursuit of justice, and more secure in the quest for peace.[4]

Understanding the motivations that underlay these five objectives is essential to piecing together the strategic approach the United States adopted in the Persian Gulf War. First, if Iraq were to swallow Kuwait completely, it would eventually come to exert substantial power over international oil markets. Richard Haass, former special assistant to the president for Near East and South Asian affairs and member of the Deputies Committee, argues that the administration sought to avoid this outcome not because the United States had direct financial interests at stake. Rather, administration officials viewed American access to Persian Gulf oil in strategic terms.[5] Washington feared that a disruption in the flow of oil could lead to turmoil in the international political economy, as was the case in 1973 and 1979. A spike in oil prices threatened a downturn and possible recession in the American economy, something the administration worried would preclude American activism in foreign policy as it sought to manage the end of the Cold War.[6]

In terms of regional security, top policy makers believed that acquiescing to Saddam would set a dangerous precedent. As the Soviet Union's power waned, the restraint on regional actors enforced by the bipolar distribution of power was evaporating. The United States thus needed, first, to clearly demonstrate its commitment to its allies who might be the target of future aggression. It was clear to administration officials that regional security could only be maintained by the recalibration of the balance of power in the Persian Gulf. Among the consequences of the Iran-Iraq war was the rise of Iraqi power and the sharp reduction of Iranian power. To many in the administration, this imbalance of power led to Saddam's aggression against Kuwait; rectifying the balance of power between Iraq and Iran was key to longer-term regional stability. The outcome of the current crisis could not result in Saddam's retaining substantial military power. Eventually, the destruction of Iraq's Republican Guard and weapons of mass destruction (WMD) were adopted as key American war aims.[7]

For Bush, Scowcroft, and Secretary of State James Baker, the opportunity to don the mantle of leadership in the post–Cold War era was one that could not be missed. For Scowcroft, Saddam's invasion stood as a direct challenge to the credibility of American commitments to its allies. A failure to act would undercut a central tenet of US leadership in the world.[8] Yet the administration's understanding of American leadership was also cast strongly in terms of exploiting new diplomatic opportunities and preserving and enhancing existing international institutions.[9] The United States would seek to construct a broad coalition, and to confront Iraq through bilateral diplomacy and through the UN Security Council. For Baker, the prime opportunity for cooperating with the Soviet Union came early on in the crisis when he and Soviet foreign minister Eduard Shevardnadze issued a joint statement condemning Iraq's aggression.[10] While Bush, Baker, and other officials would be constantly engaged in bilateral diplomacy with potential partners, the United Nations was a key element in constructing the coalition. As Haass notes, the administration understood that

> for most people around the world and their governments the U.N. is an important and at times essential source of authority and legitimacy. Its endorsement can constitute a prerequisite for the participation of others, be it to make sanctions effective or to lend support to U.S. military efforts or to introduce forces of their own.[11]

From the very beginning, top policy makers saw the Persian Gulf crisis as presenting a means of enhancing American leadership in the new era. To achieve that objective, the cultivation of allies and institutions was seen as a critical ingredient.[12]

A final motivation for confronting Saddam was held primarily by Bush, and it was personal. The president believed he had a strong moral obligation to punish a bad actor in the international system, one who violated all standards of decency by "annexing" smaller neighbors and who took civilian hostages. In attacking Kuwait, Saddam appeared to Bush as a latter-day Hitler. Much of the president's public rhetoric reflected this analogy.[13] Moreover, as president, Bush believed it was ultimately his responsibility to protect the well-being of American citizens abroad. By taking American and other Western hostages, Saddam played to one of Bush's worst fears, and as a result, had to be punished.[14] As will be discussed below, this last motive threatened to transform the war into one for regime change rather than one for the restoration of the status quo ante.

In his memoirs, Baker offers a succinct description of America's strategy in the Persian Gulf crisis. The first order of business was to deter an Iraqi attack on Saudi Arabia.

> In combination with that mission, however, was the undoing of Iraq's invasion of Kuwait by the pursuit of a policy of coercive diplomacy against Saddam Hussein. We would begin with diplomatic pressure, then add economic pressure, to a great degree organized through the United Nations, and finally move toward military pressure by gradually increasing American troop strength in the Gulf. The strategy was to lead a global political alliance aimed at isolating Iraq. Through the use of economic sanctions, we hoped to make Saddam pay such a high price for his aggression that in time he would be forced to release his Western hostages and withdraw from Kuwait. If he didn't, we would expel him by military force.[15]

In terms of its diplomacy, the United States endeavored to create a global coalition to isolate and pressure Iraq. The desired composition of the coalition was comprehensive. The United States sought and received support from all of the great powers and, with the exception of Jordan, all of the states in the Persian Gulf region. When Desert Shield became Desert Storm, the maintenance of the international coalition was seen as critical, and American officials were able to hold the alliance together despite strong counterpressures from Iraq.[16]

Three states in particular were seen as key to maintaining the coalition. First, to prevent Saddam from trying to play the superpowers off one another, the support of the Soviet Union (Iraq's Cold War patron) was deemed essential. Second, Saudi Arabia, which would eventually host hundreds of thousands of American servicemen and women on its soil, had to be firmly on board. Finally, Israeli intervention in the war had to be avoided at all costs because participation by the Jewish state would in all likelihood undermine the support of the other countries in the Middle East.

To assemble and cement a coalition of this magnitude and complexity, the administration engaged in extensive bilateral and multilateral diplomacy. Top administration officials (including the president) worked individual leaders tirelessly. Much of the diplomacy toward the Soviet Union was handled by Baker, who at every stage attempted to accommodate Soviet sensitivities with respect to the wording, timing, and nature of UN resolutions toward Iraq.[17] While Soviet cooperation was sought, many in the administration (namely Scowcroft) wanted to ensure that the Soviets cooperated by lending support to the United States but did not become actively engaged in the crisis. Threading that needle proved difficult at times, but ultimately the Soviets played the role that Washington desired.

Active Saudi participation was in no way guaranteed at the start of the crisis. The first order of business for the United States was to convince Riyadh that Saddam posed a direct threat to the kingdom and that appeasement would be disastrous. Second, the United States needed to secure Saudi permission to host a massive military force on its territory from which the eventual war would be launched. The United States shared top-secret intelligence with the Saudis and sent a high-level delegation to meet with King Fahd to cement the relationship early on.[18] Given the special role that Saudi Arabia had in the Muslim world, American officials understood that military operations against a Muslim state during Ramadan and the Hajj would pose a substantial challenge to the cohesion of the alliance. Throughout the crisis, the American ambassador to the kingdom, Charles Freeman, pressured his superiors not to offend their hosts by stationing American forces too close to Mecca and insisted that military actions be taken sooner rather than later in order to maintain Saudi support.[19]

American efforts to restrain Israel from entering the war were extensive, and were made all the more difficult by the fact that relations between the two states had cooled substantially by fall 1990. Moreover, in response to Israeli security forces killing twenty-two Palestinians on Temple Mount in early October, the United States cosigned a UN Security Council resolution calling for an investigation of the incident.[20] Despite this, the United States was able to restrain Israel from entering the crisis and war by employing both positive and negative inducements. On the positive side, Bush promised Israeli prime minister Yitzhak Shamir in December that the United States would make sure that in the event of war, Iraq's military power would be substantially degraded and that its WMD program would be destroyed. And in an effort to ensure the Israelis that the United States would keep them fully informed of Saddam's likely attack on them, a secure phone line was established between the American and Israeli defense chiefs. Finally, during the war the United States would devote forces away from the main battle area to search for mobile Iraqi Scud launchers in an effort to assuage the quite understandable Israeli desires to end Saddam's aerial attacks.[21] On the negative side, the United States refused to provide Israel the codes that would enable it to identify American aircraft and limited Israel's access to intelligence pertaining to ongoing operations.[22] This balance ultimately succeeded in preventing Israel's entry in the war, thereby further stabilizing the coalition.

The American decision to use the United Nations as the forum to build the coalition paid substantial dividends internationally. In all, the United Nations passed twelve individual resolutions pertaining to the crisis, including the initial condemnation of the invasion, the placement of economic sanctions on Iraq, and the authorization of states to "use all necessary means" to force Iraq's withdrawal from Kuwait. Critically, the UN resolution permitted states only to force Iraq from Kuwait, but did not sanction the overthrow of the regime. The benefits of working through the United Nations occurred largely because of the constraints that were placed on American objectives. American policy makers realized that in order to obtain consensus in the Security Council, more ambitious war aims could not be sought. Additional constraints included policy changes and delays, numerous economic side payments and political concessions to member states, and the ability of "Saddam to prepare for hostilities and consolidate his defenses, requiring the size of the allied force to be revised upward." At the same time, however, the United States was able to deftly navigate UN politics in such a way that resistance to American objectives was dealt with easily.[23] Finally, as Alexander Thompson shows, UN approval of intervention against Iraq *preceded* the international support that the United States achieved. By using the United Nations as the primary forum for confronting Iraq, the United States was able to construct and maintain a sizable and complex international wartime coalition. In the end, forty nations contributed some combination of military and/or medical personnel, military equipment, and financial support for the war.[24]

On January 15, 1991, the day of the UN Security Council's imposed deadline, Bush signed NSD 54, which authorized "military actions designed to bring about Iraq's withdrawal from Kuwait." In terms of its military objectives, the United States and coalition partners sought to:

1 Defend Saudi Arabia and the other GCC [Gulf Cooperation Council] states against attack
2 Preclude Iraqi launch of ballistic missiles against neighboring states and friendly forces
3 Destroy Iraq's chemical, biological, and nuclear capabilities
4 Destroy Iraq's command, control, and communications capabilities
5 Eliminate the Republican Guard as an effective fighting force; and
6 Conduct operations designed to drive Iraq's forces from Kuwait, break

the will of Iraqi forces, discourage Iraqi use of chemical, biological or nuclear weapons, encourage defection of Iraqi forces, and weaken Iraqi popular support for the current government.

NSD 54 did state that if Iraq employed WMD, supported terrorist acts against the United States or coalition partners, or destroyed Kuwaiti oil fields, "it shall become an explicit objective of the United States to replace the current leadership of Iraq."[25]

The military strategy adopted to deliver these objectives combined an initial air campaign followed by a ground assault. The first phase of the bombing campaign would initially be aimed at Saddam's regime and would be intended to undermine confidence in the government, disrupt Iraqi command and control, and significantly degrade Iraqi military capabilities. The second phase of the air war would aim to create an opening for the ground offensive by confusing Iraqi forces in the theater and tilt the balance of forces in favor of the coalition. The ensuing ground offensive would entail, first, a deceptive attack by US Marines and the armies of Arab states into Kuwait from Saudi Arabia. Second, the main army attack would come in the west, its aim being the destruction of the Republican Guard.[26]

Operation Desert Storm, launched on January 17, 1991, began with a thirty-eight-day bombing campaign that destroyed military command and other infrastructure targets in Iraq, and which pounded Iraqi military forces and supply lines in Kuwait. The next day, the first Iraqi Scud missiles were fired at Israel. This prompted Cheney to order the deployment of air, ground, and Patriot missile assets in an effort to prevent Iraqi Scuds from raining down on Israel (and thus keep them out of the war).[27] The ground phase began on February 24 and lasted four days. By end of the fourth day, the Republican Guard had ceased to be an effective military force and, on February 28, a cease-fire was ordered. Despite the fact that Saddam did order the burning of Kuwaiti oil wells—an act that clearly crossed a war aims threshold in NSD 54—the United States refrained from taking direct military actions designed to topple the regime. As Haass recalls, there was no dissent among the top policy makers in Washington on this point. The United States had succeeded militarily in the war, and any attempt to remove Saddam promised to shatter the coalition. Moreover, there was the prevailing belief that what had been accomplished was likely to lead to Saddam's ouster by the Iraqis themselves.[28] In the end, Operation Desert Storm was a historically lopsided military victory: Iraqi forces had been decimated and were forced to leave Kuwait at the price of sixty-three American lives.[29]

The Persian Gulf War was a military and diplomatic success for the United States. In terms of diplomacy, the United States assembled a massive and complex international coalition to confront Iraq and expel its forces from Kuwait. Through extensive bilateral and multilateral diplomatic efforts, the United States achieved the support of all of the great powers and the vast majority of the regional states in the war effort. Moreover, the United States actively sought to keep Israel from entering the war, and this too was achieved. In terms of military objectives, the United States sought to physically expel Iraqi forces from Kuwait, eliminate the Republican Guard as an effective fighting force, and degrade Iraq's WMD programs. All of this was achieved with an astonishingly low level of coalition casualties. Despite the pressures and opportunities to expand American war aims, the United States remained wedded to those endorsed by the United Nations.

A ROBUST INFORMATION INSTITUTION

The origins of the double success in the Persian Gulf War lie in the robust nature of the American information institution. In terms of leaders' access to information, top policy makers received information pertaining to all aspects of the war from multiple organizational sources from the beginning of the crisis to the termination of the war. Moreover, the organizations responsible for waging the military and diplomatic aspects of the war widely and routinely shared information with one another. Critically, the structure of the National Security Council system was such that leaders' access to information and interagency information sharing functioned in tandem, placing top policy makers in an optimal position to design and implement sound national security policy. Of the four cases of limited war considered in this book, the information institution of the first Bush administration functioned the most effectively.

Organization of the National Security Council System

On January 30, 1989, the president issued NSD 1, which formally established the elements of his interagency policy process. Four bodies constituted the core of this system: the National Security Council (NSC), the Principals Committee (PC), the Deputies Committee (DC), and the Policy Coordinating Committees (PCCs). Central to this system were the PC and DC. The PC was the senior interagency forum for national security policy and was tasked to "review, coordinate, and monitor the development and implementation of national security policy." Its membership included the secretaries of state and defense, the national security adviser, the Director of Central Intelligence (DCI), the chairman of the Joint Chiefs of Staff, and the president's chief of staff. The DC was the "senior sub-Cabinet interagency forum," whose members included the deputy national security adviser, under secretary of defense for policy, under secretary of state for political affairs, deputy Director of Central Intelligence, and vice chairman of the Joint Chiefs of Staff. The responsibility of the DC was to ensure "that all papers to be discussed by the NSC or the [PC] fully analyze the issues, fairly and adequately set out the facts, consider a full range of views and options, and satisfactorily assess the prospects, risks, and implications of each." Toward that end, NSD 1 noted that additional departmental representatives could attend DC meetings where appropriate. Finally, a number of functional and regional PCCs were established at the assistant secretary level and were tasked with identifying and developing policy issues for the NSC.[30]

By virtue of the stipulation contained in NSD 1 to expand participation in DC meetings to include relevant personnel from across the government, and with the assignment of crisis management responsibility to this body,[31] the Deputies Committee quickly emerged as the most important policy-making body in the government. Significantly, the actual policy-making process that characterized the Bush administration functioned in ways not envisioned by NSD 1.[32] To understand how this structure evolved and functioned, attention must be given to the relationship between the principals and deputies along three dimensions: the collegiality and trust among the president's top advisers, the role and power of Bush's national security adviser Brent Scowcroft, and the dedication to due process and quality control at all levels in the development and implementation of national security policy.

Among the most widely noted characteristics of Bush's foreign policy team is the high degrees of collegiality, cooperation, and trust among those at the top. As in all administrations, the president set the tone for working relationships among his advisers. Bush expected "collegiality and openness from his team and would tolerate nothing less."[33] The president demanded loyalty and insisted that his foreign policy team functioned as a *team*. The paralysis induced by the ideological battles waged by Caspar Weinberger and George Shultz in the Reagan administration were not to be replicated in the Bush administration. Trust and cooperation were facilitated, to a considerable extent, by the genuine friendships built over the years among this group of individuals. Throughout their respective careers, Bush and

Baker had forged deep professional and personal bonds, so much so that "these two men were outwardly so close in personality and interests that they themselves viewed each other more like brothers than mere friends."[34] Bush and Scowcroft, too, had developed a close personal friendship to the extent that one NSC staffer subsequently commented that the national security adviser was closer to Bush than Baker was, "to the point that there were times at which I thought Bush and Scowcroft were almost like two dimensions of one person. He was almost like a kind of doppelganger for Bush."[35] Reflecting on the dynamics of the entire team, deputy national security adviser Robert Gates noted, "The unique distinction was that the whole inner circle was composed of old friends who went fishing and golfing together."[36]

Of course, the pressures of governmental service can easily shatter old friendships. The benefits that personal bonds can offer will only be had, and the pitfalls they can entail will only be avoided, if the foreign policy process is effectively managed. It thus fell to Scowcroft to put these pieces together. To effectively serve as the president's chief adviser on national security and to oversee the day-to-day functioning of the foreign policy process, Scowcroft had to overcome three main obstacles. First, he had to deal with a hands-on president—one who saw himself as a player-manager of the foreign policy team. Second, he had to navigate the tricky relationship between the president and his secretary of state. Finally, Scowcroft had to overcome the potential dysfunctions of a closed, informal decision-making process at the top. According to Ivo Daalder and I. M. Destler, Scowcroft's formula entailed three elements: maintaining the trust of the key players, cultivating a strong professional relationship with the president, and establishing a cooperative policy process at all levels.[37]

Scowcroft was able to secure the confidence and trust of his colleagues by maintaining a transparent policy-making process.[38] Scowcroft went to great lengths to represent the views of others fairly, to allow open access to the president, and to set clear limits on his own role. Scowcroft met weekly with Baker and Cheney over breakfast to resolve any outstanding differences that had not been resolved in other forums. As the chair of the PC, Scowcroft was able to ascertain where key players stood on the issues at hand so that he could fairly represent those views to Bush. Whenever one of the principals desired to make his case to the president directly, Scowcroft ensured that a direct meeting would be granted. Finally, Scowcroft recognized that the public face of the administration's foreign policy had to be that of James Baker. By playing a behind-the-scenes role, Scowcroft made sure that the prerogatives of the secretary of state were not infringed upon.[39]

At the same time, the national security adviser never let his influence with the president diminish. Scowcroft made sure that in times of crisis, power and influence flowed through him and the NSC staff. In so doing, Scowcroft attempted to prevent any specific aspect of foreign policy from driving policy generally. Crises, such as that in the Persian Gulf, involve military and diplomatic roles, but it is only the president who can balance the competing demands that inevitably emerge.[40] Scowcroft understood this and worked to keep the president at the center of national security strategy.[41] Toward this end, Scowcroft benefited from the president's activism in matters of foreign policy. For example, access to real-time information via the Situation Room, and the ability to have that information analyzed and evaluated by a highly competent NSC staff, enabled Bush to conduct constant telephone diplomacy during the Persian Gulf crisis.[42] By placing the president at the center, and Scowcroft and Gates as the chairmen of the two most important foreign policy committees, Bush and Scowcroft guaranteed that all critical business would be managed through the White House.[43]

National security advisers wear two hats: one of foreign policy adviser to the president and one of manager of the foreign policy process. Among all of America's national security advisers, Scowcroft is widely seen as the one who most effectively balanced these two responsibilities. Scowcroft's insistence on transparency enabled him to offer his own policy preferences to Bush without engendering distrust among the other key players on the president's foreign policy team. Ironically, it was just this role that Scowcroft himself criticized in the recommendations section of the final report of the Tower Board. Convened in the wake of the Iran-Contra scandal, the Tower Board argued that the primary responsibility of the national security adviser was that of policy coordination, not policy design.[44] Yet by the time of Iraq's invasion of Kuwait, Scowcroft had become Bush's closest policy adviser. Far from instilling discord and dysfunction in the policy-making process, however, Scowcroft managed a well-designed and effective system. In short, going into the Persian Gulf War, Bush's NSC system had all of the hallmarks of a robust information institution discussed in chapter 2.

Dense Lateral Connections: Up and Down Bush's Policy Ladder

The information institution that emerged was characterized, first, by the widespread sharing of information among the relevant departments and agencies responsible for national security policy. According to one member of the NSC staff, Scowcroft's success as national security adviser can be attributed to his "dispensing due process and exercising quality control."[45]

In terms of due process, NSD 1 envisioned a hierarchical National Security Council system centered in the White House. Initial policy issues and proposals would be identified by the various PCCs and then sent up to the DC. The DC, comprised of representatives from all of the key departments and agencies involved in national security affairs, would then conduct a full assessment of these policy proposals and ensure that all options (and their associated costs and benefits) had been fully considered. The PC would review the options and forward recommendations to the NSC. Additionally, the PC was tasked with monitoring the implementation of the policy adopted at the NSC level. On its face, this system had much to commend, most importantly the inclusion of all of the relevant agencies involved in foreign policy design and implementation.

This system was substantially, though informally, upended not long into Bush's term. The two top bodies, the NSC and PC, saw their roles substantially diminished. Formal NSC meetings were infrequent during the first two years of the Bush administration. The reason for this was largely due to the fact that formal NSC meetings tend not to be conducive to open and frank discussions, a recurrent complaint among presidents and their national security advisers. Additionally, while the PC remained an important institution, the frequency of its meetings declined as well. Two factors explain the diminished role of the PC. First, its structure contained a glaring flaw—the absence of the president. Scowcroft's intention in forming the PC was to have a body that "could help clarify issues and positions among the principals before the issues were taken to the President. It could save him considerable time, and time, I [Scowcroft] believed, was his most valuable commodity."[46] Yet by excluding the president, his interests were not explicitly incorporated into the structure of the PC. Not being one to stand aside in matters of national security, Bush preferred to be involved at this level of the policy process. Presidential involvement thus obviated the need for the PC. In its place, an informal grouping known as the Big 8 took the place of the PC. The Big 8 included Bush, Scowcroft, Baker, Cheney, chief of staff John Sununu, chairman of the Joint Chiefs of Staff Colin Powell, Gates, and vice president Dan Quayle.[47]

The second reason for the decline in the PC's role was that the DC quickly emerged as the engine of the foreign policy process. Five permanent members represented the core of the DC: Gates (who chaired the committee), Paul Wolfowitz from DOD, Robert Kimmitt from DOS, Admiral David Jeremiah from the JCS, and Richard Kerr from the CIA. During the Persian Gulf War, Haass joined the DC due to the fact that the Persian Gulf region fell within his purview.[48] The responsibilities of the DC were extensive in the policy process. According to Philip Zelikow, the DC served as the key mechanism for vetting information.

> One of the reasons the system ran so well was the system actually didn't do policy analysis at the table, at the level of the principals. People actually wrote down analysis, and analysis got vetted up. The key place it got commissioned and vetted was this deputies committee.[49]

Further, with the downgrading of the PC, the DC assumed the responsibility for monitoring policy implementation. As DC member Kimmitt remarked,

> During the Gulf crisis, there would be a PCC meeting at 9 a.m. Then at 11 a.m., the deputies committee would get on the video conference and talk. That would go until about 12:00 p.m. You can get about seventy-five percent of your work done there. And then we'd get together in a small group, in the situation room, just seven or eight of us. Gates would then attend the meeting of the Big Eight. Importantly, very importantly, we would also meet on the way back down, and have another small group meeting, back to a video conference with deputies, and then we would meet inside the department, because, frankly, policy implementation is much tougher than policy formulation. Making sure what people say should be done gets done is crucial to the policy process.[50]

Finally, because the DC included representatives from all of the relevant agencies, it was able to evaluate all aspects of the policy issues at hand, conduct thorough analysis with the benefit of multiple sources of information, and was able to monitor the compliance with policy directives issued from the top. According to Gates,

> If there were a problem between CIA and the military, Dick Kerr and Dave Jeremiah could deal with it directly. And their subordinates knew that their bosses were trying to solve a problem. You had a dialogue among the members of the Deputies Committee that extended to bilateral issues between agencies that really changed the culture or atmosphere of the way the government was run.[51]

To a significant extent, the "dialogue" among the members of this committee explains the absence of bureaucratic infighting and hold-up problems that characterized the Bush administration's foreign policy process.[52]

That the DC was able to perform these functions well is attributable to three primary factors. The first is the access that the deputies had to their principals. The chair of the committee, Robert Gates, was the first deputy national security adviser to be given the title "assistant to the president," which gave him ready access to Bush, the first deputy to be included in the president's morning intelligence briefing, and the only nonprincipal to sit in on meetings of the Big 8. Others were similarly empowered by their principals to speak on their behalf in DC meetings. According to Daalder and Destler, the reason why the PC met so infrequently was that the DC was able to resolve most issues at its meetings. Any unresolved issues necessitated presidential decision.[53]

The second source of the DC's effectiveness centered on the procedural norms—due process—established by Bush, Scowcroft, and Gates. The determination to conduct thorough intelligence and policy assessments was established at the top by Bush. The president made it a point to read the president's daily brief (PDB) in the presence of a CIA briefer and either Scowcroft or his deputy, most often Gates. As Bush remarked, "That way I could task the briefers to bring in more information on a certain matter or, when the reading would bring to mind policy matters, ask Brent to follow up on an item of interest."[54] Scowcroft too exhibited a dedication to thorough analysis. According to Haass,

> During the Gulf crisis of 1990-91, every Saturday morning, Brent and I, or Brent, Bob Gates, and I, used to gather in Brent's office. And Brent would be lying down on his couch, and he'd basically say, Okay, what do we do now? What do we do next? What aren't we thinking about? And we just institutionalized it. Every Saturday morning, the two or three of us would spend time taking a step back, saying okay, here's my list. Here's everything we're working on. What are we comfortable with? What could happen that we're not thinking of? And we just tried to do that, to stay one step ahead of events.[55]

The high value placed on rigorous analysis extended down from the national security adviser to the DC through its chairman. Gates never let the DC stray into policy matters that had not been thoroughly analyzed. The reason for this was to ensure that the principals' desire for high-quality analysis was met. As Zelikow notes,

> That they [the principals] were receptive to input from below doesn't even capture it. They demanded input from below. One of the most singular characteristics of this group was that they were committed to analysis and they were disciplined about getting it. And that has all kinds of implications all the way down. If you have a deputies committee that says we're not going to discuss this issue until somebody's written a decent quality paper on this that's more than just a few bullet points, then that means the paper has to be tasked and drafted . . . when you're not making it up and when you insist on have that kind of analysis going in you get better policy.[56]

The final source of the DC's effectiveness was the high degree of quality control enforced by Gates and Scowcroft. Gates's capacity to ascertain the critical from the merely important was well known and respected. More than this, however, was the deputy national security adviser's insistence that his boss be fully prepared for all aspects of his job. As Gates describes,

> Let's just say that managing the paper flow was not one of Brent's strengths. And so, it fell to me. The stuff would come through me. A lot of stuff I would sign off on myself. And then the policy-oriented papers, a lot of the more important decision papers, I would send on to Brent. Then, what I would usually do at the end of the day is go into his office, rifle his in box, pull out the stuff that had to be acted on, make him sit down and sign them, or read them. One deputy national security advisor that I worked for referred to this process as the Strasbourg Goose Process as I shoved this stuff down his throat.[57]

Armed with the information provided to him from the DC, Scowcroft was better able to identify and pressure the source of flawed policy ideas, even when the source of those ideas was the president himself. As will be discussed at length below, it was Scowcroft who intervened to convince Bush not to seek the overthrow of Saddam's regime when the opportunity presented itself.

In sum, by insisting on both rigorous and thorough analysis of policy options and comprehensive implementation oversight, Bush's national security policy process sought to capitalize on the core strengths of Eisenhower's "policy hill." By fusing together these responsibilities in a powerful committee that represented all of the relevant departments and agencies involved with national security policy, Bush's "policy ladder" was an even more effective model for designing and implementing policy. As will be discussed below, the DC played crucial roles in the building of the coalition, in determining American war aims, in assisting with the development of the military strategy, and in terminating the war. Moreover, all of the members of the Big 8 understood in intimate detail the various objectives the United States sought in the war.

Multiple Sources of Information

In terms of their access to information, top policy makers sought and received information pertaining to the military and diplomatic aspects of the war from multiple organizational sources. Three key relationships would be critical to the diplomacy in the Persian Gulf War: those with the Soviets, the United Nations, and the states in the Persian Gulf region. In all of these, top policy makers had in place a system of acquiring information in a timely fashion. It was Baker who would take a direct lead in managing US-Soviet relations. Baker had worked tirelessly in the months prior to the war to build a cooperative relationship with the Soviets.[58] This effort resulted in a substantial reservoir of goodwill between Baker and Gorbachev/Shevardnadze. Despite the fact that Thomas Pickering, the United States' permanent representative to the United Nations, did not have a seat on Bush's cabinet, his role in the administration's foreign policy was critical. As a former ambassador to the United Nations, Bush had a deep commitment to the institution, and the president sought a "real professional" for the post. The value Bush placed in US-UN relations ensured that Pickering would have direct access to the top players in the policy process.[59] Finally, the president himself assumed an active role in the diplomatic relations with many countries, especially those in the Persian Gulf region. This direct access to foreign leaders provided Bush with insight into and influence with leaders in the Middle East.[60] With the key state in the region, Saudi Arabia, Scowcroft made a point of providing Prince Bandar bin Sultan direct access to Bush because Bandar had direct access to King Fahd.[61]

Unlike presidents Truman and Johnson, George Bush made it clear that he was the ultimate decision maker when it came to matters of military policy. That included permitting civilians to question, probe, and criticize the military in matters of strategy. In fact, it was Bush and his top advisers who rejected General Norman Schwarzkopf's initial war plan. Bush's relationship with the military ensured that he and his top advisers had access to the information necessary for them to provide guidance on such matters. On the one hand, Bush believed strongly in the chain of command running through the secretary of defense, the chairman of the JCS, and the regional commanders. The president refrained from involving himself *directly* in operational and tactical matters. Nevertheless, civilian influence in the planning and conduct of the war was extensive.[62] On the other hand, Powell was a member of the Big 8, and was included in all of the major decisions during the Persian Gulf crisis and war. Powell's access to the president allowed him to impress upon Bush the importance of issuing crystal clear orders, thereby enabling the military to perform the exact missions their commander in chief desired.[63]

The at-times-uneasy relationship between Cheney and Powell was an important factor in structuring the flow of military information to top policy makers. Prior to the Gulf War, the two ironed out an understanding as to how information would flow. As Powell recounts in his memoirs,

Cheney had called me to his office alone. "You're off to a good start as chairman," he said, offering me a seat. "You're forceful and you're taking charge. But you tend to funnel all the information coming to me. That's not the way I want it." He went on to say that he expected information from numerous sources. He had me dead to rights. Information is power. He knew it as well as I did. And I tended to control it. I told him I understood, as long as we both recognized my obligation, as his senior military advisor, to give him my counsel. Matters could get choppy if he were to operate on military advice or information of which I was unaware. "Fine," he said, "as long as we understand each other . . . Colin." The slight hesitation let me know that the relationship was still familiar but that I was being shown my place in it.[64]

Ultimately, this professional tension would be highly productive. Cheney would make good on his promise to seek information from multiple sources. Indeed, it was Cheney who, after having consulted with Henry Rowen and Wolfowitz from the Office of the Secretary of Defense, made the strongest initial pitch for the inclusion in the war plan of a western attack into Iraq.[65] Powell would work to ensure that Schwarzkopf had the flexibility he needed from Washington.[66] Reflecting on this relationship, Scowcroft noted that Powell "managed brilliantly the sometimes awkward relationship between the secretary of defense and the chairman in NSC discussions with the president, serving as an NSC principal alongside his own immediate boss."[67] The same could be said of Powell's ability to manage the relationship between the chairman and the commander in chief (CINC). Although Powell stood outside the chain of command between the president, secretary of defense, and the CINC, the chairman played the crucial role of intermediary between the fiery-tempered Schwarzkopf and civilian leadership.[68]

Finally, top policy makers sought and received access to countless intelligence products pertaining to national security affairs. As noted above, Bush was the consummate consumer of the intelligence contained in his PDB. Much of this is explained by the fact that he was the only former DCI to become president. This experience gave him a clear understanding of what was reasonable to expect from intelligence products, which questions to ask, and how to go about getting answers to issues left open. CIA analysts quickly discovered that they had an unprecedented amount of contact with the president. It was the president's style to phone analysts directly with questions and comments on the reports submitted to him.[69]

The CIA was not the sole agency within the intelligence community providing information to the president and his chief aides. On numerous occasions, CIA analysis and estimates proved completely inaccurate.[70] At such times, the information provided by the Defense Intelligence Agency (DIA) and the State Department's Bureau of Intelligence and Research (INR) proved to be highly influential in guiding American policy.[71] Moreover, it appears that top policy makers benefited from the success that the National Security Agency had in decrypting the communications of Middle East leaders as the Persian Gulf crisis unfolded.[72] Finally, in an effort to guarantee that the White House had access to military and diplomatic information during the Persian Gulf crisis, Bush and Scowcroft "set up an NSC structure that encouraged the free flow of information, both up to the President and down to the Situation Room." In addition to the daily briefings that he would receive from Powell, Cheney, Scowcroft, and CIA director William Webster, "Bush still either called the duty officer [in the Situation Room] early every morning or went downstairs for a personal briefing." In effect, the Situation Room became Richard Haass's office and was also the location of DC meetings during the war.[73]

Taken together, the president and his top advisers went to war against Iraq with a robust information institution. Top policy makers received information pertaining to the military and diplomatic aspects of the crisis from multiple sources, and information was widely and routinely shared among all of the relevant national security organizations prior to and during the war. Thus the information institution approach outlined in chapter 2 expects the United States to enter the war with comprehensive collection and optimal analytic capabilities, and with tightly coordinated military and diplomatic components of its limited war strategy.

A MANAGED VICTORY

Although Iraq's invasion of Kuwait caught Washington by surprise, within a week the foundation for the American response to the crisis was set. By the end of August, America's strategic objectives were clearly articulated. Throughout the crisis, top policy makers were determined to prevent events from spiraling out of control, and to a significant extent, they succeeded.

Upon learning of Iraq's invasion on August 1, Brent Scowcroft chaired the first of at least fifty-five Deputies Committee meetings held from August 1990 to March 1991.[74] The DC quickly decided that the first order of business was to offer a squadron of twenty-four F-15s to Saudi Arabia as a means of demonstrating America's determination to defend the kingdom. Moreover, it was agreed that Iraqi and Kuwaiti financial assets in the United States should be immediately frozen.[75] Later that evening, after being prompted by Baker and Kimmitt, Bush decided that the first diplomatic step taken by the United States would be at the United Nations. In the early morning hours of August 2, the Security Council passed Resolution 660 condemning Iraq's invasion.[76]

The first formal NSC meeting pertaining to the situation in the Gulf, held on August 2, was a disappointment for Bush and Scowcroft. DCI Webster presented a dire assessment of Iraq's ability to swallow Kuwait whole and then punch through the meager Saudi defenses on the border. Following Webster's assessment were Kimmitt's and Pickering's briefs on the unfolding diplomatic efforts at the United Nations and elsewhere. Schwarzkopf then laid out in brief detail the off-the-shelf plans for the defense of Saudi Arabia. Much of the meeting, however, was devoted to the likely effects the invasion would have on the price of oil and the likelihood that neighboring states would seek a compromise solution with Iraq that left Kuwait in the lurch.[77] Reflecting on the meeting, Scowcroft noted,

> I was frankly appalled at the undertone of the discussion, which suggested resignation to the invasion and even adaptation to a *fait accompli*. . . . The remarks tended to skip over the enormous stake the United States had in the situation, or the ramifications of the aggression on the emerging post–Cold War world. . . . The tone implied that the crisis was halfway around the world and doing anything serious about it would just be too difficult.[78]

At that moment Scowcroft took command of the interagency process. While Bush, Baker, and Pickering would take the lead in assembling the international coalition, and while Cheney and Powell would manage the mobilization and deployment of troops to Saudi Arabia, it was Scowcroft who took the lead in designing and managing the comprehensive strategy.[79]

By the time of the second NSC meeting on August 3, the president's attitude toward the crisis had hardened, especially so in light of Baker's securing an American-Soviet joint statement condemning the invasion. Scowcroft, Cheney, Eagleburger, and Haass were determined to focus the administration's attention on the price the United States would have to pay if it refrained from acting forcefully. It was agreed that Scowcroft would deliver the "Churchill speech, that is, a rousing call for the imperative of resisting and, in the end, reversing Iraqi aggression."[80] Following Scowcroft's line were Eagleburger and Cheney who offered their rationales for taking a strong stand against Saddam. Powell presented Central Command's (CENTCOM) plan in more detail, but warned that if the United States were to indeed go to war, Iraqi forces would put up a stiff fight requiring the United States to substantially bolster its troop presence in the region. Powell then asked,

"One question is how individualized is this aggression? If he [Saddam] is gone, would he have a more reasonable replacement?" Scowcroft and Haass recoiled at the possibility of the crisis becoming one about the nature of the Iraqi regime. "Iraq could fall apart," Scowcroft noted. "It's unlikely anyone else would have the same cult of personality" needed to hold the country together, Haass added.[81] The second NSC meeting concluded without a formal decision being made, but with a clear path being established. Scowcroft and Haass had stated for the record that the United States should seek to expel Iraq from Kuwait, and not seek the overthrow of Saddam. Moreover, given that any military response required Saudi approval, the United States would employ economic sanctions as the primary coercive tool in the short run. Three days later, the UN Security Council passed Resolution 661, which put into effect a broad sanctions regime against Iraq.[82]

Camp David was the site for the third NSC meeting on August 4, which dealt primarily with American military options. Schwarzkopf presented, first, a detailed description of Iraqi military capabilities, noting that Iraq possessed an army "ranked in size behind only those of China, the Soviet Union, and Vietnam." Iraq's primary strengths were in its chemical weapons stockpile. Iraqi weaknesses included its "feeble logistics and a centralized system of command and control in which important decisions, even in the heat of battle, could be made only by Saddam personally." Schwarzkopf warned that it would take nearly three months to assemble a sizeable enough contingent in Saudi Arabia to fully ward off an Iraqi attack, a force size totaling some 200,000 to 250,000 troops from all branches. Turning Bush's attention to the option of forcibly removing Iraq from Kuwait, Schwarzkopf noted that the United States would have to more than "double the size of the projected force, pulling at least six additional divisions out of the United States and Europe." The earliest such an army would be ready to fight was estimated at eight to ten months.[83] Following the larger session, the Big 8 met to discuss new intelligence indicating that Saudi leaders were inclined to consider buying their way out the current situation. Following the meeting, Bush and Scowcroft remained at Camp David to phone King Fahd, telling him that Iraqi forces were amassing on the border and that the time had come for the Saudis to act.

As gaining Saudi support had to be secured sooner rather than later, it was decided that Cheney would lead a high-level delegation to meet with King Fahd in an attempt to get Riyadh's formal invitation to host American combat forces. Two days prior to Cheney's departure, Prince Bandar had been given a thorough briefing of the intelligence pertaining to Saddam's forces in Kuwait and Iraq as well as CENTCOM's OPLAN 90-1002. Meeting with Powell, Cheney, Wolfowitz, and Haass, Bandar was told just how seriously the United Stated viewed the situation in the Gulf, in particular the defense of Saudi Arabia.[84]

At the end of the August 4 NSC meeting, it was apparent that Bush had come to the conclusion that a hard line had to be taken against Iraq. The president made this clear to a group of reporters assembled outside the White House on August 5: "This will not stand, this aggression against Kuwait."[85] Later that day, the NSC met for a fourth time. Initially, the topic to be considered was covert operations that could be taken against Iraq. That issue was pushed aside when DCI Webster made it known that based on recently gathered CIA intelligence, Iraq was prepared to move immediately against Saudi Arabia. Both Powell and Baker rejected the CIA's analysis, however. Based on DIA analysis, Powell argued that the key elements that would enable such an attack were missing. "We would need to see more missiles, logistics, and tanks to conclude an invasion is imminent." Baker concurred, noting, "INR agrees with DIA about the key missing pieces of intelligence."[86]

The discussion then turned to the issue of Saddam's understanding of the situation facing him. Bush wondered if Saddam was riding a postinvasion emotional high and was not appreciating the fact that he was becoming increasingly isolated in the world community. Secretary of the Treasury Nicholas Brady suggested that someone, possibly French president François Mitterrand, be used as an envoy to the Iraqi leader. "We don't want to appear to be negotiating," warned Scowcroft. Baker concurred, "We could lose momentum with the Arabs." But, the secretary of state then added, "Should we ask the Soviets to weigh in?" In response, Scowcroft argued that bringing the Soviets directly into the crisis would "send a bad signal." For Scowcroft, the United States had to be seen as completely self-sufficient in protecting Gulf security—especially to the Soviets. Sununu then countered that by bringing the Soviets in, the pace of the crisis could be slowed down. Scowcroft responded to the president's chief of staff that, "I am not sure we want to slow things down." Recognizing the dilemma, Bush stated, "If he [Saddam] slows down, our side will slow down." Baker then withdrew his recommendation. "The only thing that will influence Saddam is our deterrent."[87]

On August 6, Cheney received the formal invitation from the Saudis to host American combat forces in the kingdom. Later that day, Bush formally ordered the implementation of OPLAN 90-1002, thereby commencing

Operation Desert Shield. Before returning to Washington, however, Cheney and Gates were redirected to Egypt and Morocco in order to further entrench those states in the growing coalition. It was Bush's personal telephone diplomacy that cleared the way for Cheney's visits. As Gates remarked later, "It showed how the president was really working it in real time."[88]

On August 14, Bush met with Powell at the Pentagon to discuss the progress of the military buildup. Powell noted that within a couple of weeks, sufficient forces would be in place to deter Saddam from attacking Saudi Arabia. By early December, the chairman stated, the United States would have roughly 184,000 troops in place, and there would be little doubt that Saudi territory could be defended. To reach that force level, however, the president would have to issue an order calling up the reserves, "a major political decision" that Bush had to consider soon. If his objective were simply to defend Saudi Arabia, then force levels needed to be capped in October. Powell then stated, "If we are going to eject Saddam, is the objective only to free Kuwait or, while we're at it, to destroy his war-making potential at some level?" Depending on the option selected, decisions about timing and force levels could not be delayed indefinitely. On August 22, the president ordered the call-up of reserves.[89]

Debating War Aims and Military Strategy

As early as mid-August, pressures began to mount on the administration to think beyond the objective of restoring the status quo ante. The Saudis insisted upon a direct meeting with the president, and on August 16 foreign minister Saud al-Faisal and Bandar met in Kennebunkport, Maine, with Bush, Sununu, Scowcroft, Gates, and Haass. At the start, the Saudi envoys made clear they were speaking not only for Riyadh but for Cairo and Damascus as well. As Haass recalls,

> Their message was blunt: "Our assessment is that it will take more than economic sanctions to liberate Kuwait." What they wanted was for us to do whatever was necessary to liberate Kuwait by force, preferably under U.N. auspices, in the process destroying enough of Saddam's war-making machine so that they wouldn't have to continue to live in fear and in Saddam's shadow.

A complete withdrawal from Kuwait was no longer sufficient for these coalition members. Additionally, the Saudis were growing impatient with the pace of events, partly out of concern that the "Arab street" would turn against them, and partly because of their lack of confidence in American staying power.[90]

Two days later, the administration was placed under further pressure to act militarily when five tankers with Iraqi oil refused to turn back to port when confronted by the US Navy. Cheney and the British prime minister, Margaret Thatcher, urged Bush to take military action against the tankers unilaterally. Baker, however, was adamantly opposed to this course of action. Baker argued that without additional UN authorization to enforce the embargo by force, the United States would threaten the stability of the coalition. In particular, Baker feared that the Soviets would likely pull out, and in the process, other states might follow suit. Bush acceded to Baker's plea for more time, and on August 25 UN Security Council Resolution 665 was passed, which allowed for the use of limited naval actions to be used to enforce the embargo.[91] By securing UN authorization for the embargo's enforcement, the United States dramatically winnowed Iraq's ability to split the coalition by increasing the pressure against Saddam at a critical point in time.[92]

As the individual responsible for managing the passage of Resolution 665 through the United Nations, Pickering grew increasingly concerned that the administration's diplomatic and military tracks were beginning to diverge. On August 30, he submitted a strategy memo to Bush and Baker that sketched out a political-military course that the United States and United Nations could follow in the aftermath of the Persian Gulf crisis. Pickering's main objective was to draw policy maker's attention to the longer-term issue of regional stability in the event that Saddam survived the war. In broad strokes, the strategy called for the creation of an exclusionary zone in southern Iraq, off limits to Iraqi forces and monitored by a UN peacekeeping force, and the reduction in size of Iraq's overall military capabilities—including Iraq's WMD programs. The latter pillar was essential, Pickering argued, to ensuring the stability of the Persian Gulf.[93]

Taken together, top policy makers were being pressured not only to act more forcefully against Iraq in the short run, but also to give serious thought to the substantial reduction of Iraqi military capabilities as a condition for the settlement of the crisis. President Bush had resisted pressures from members of his own cabinet and closest international ally to act unilaterally to enforce the embargo. Yet the issue of the final status of Saddam's military forces demanded attention. Few believed that a substantial reduction in Iraqi military power could be achieved via sanctions alone. Indeed, the president was skeptical that sanctions would have any positive effects in an acceptable amount of time.[94] Much had been achieved on the diplomatic front by the end of August. The time had come to give serious consideration to the content of American war aims should sanctions ultimately fail to remove Iraq from Kuwait on acceptable terms.

The DC was given the responsibility for drafting a formal list of war aims for a possible war against Iraq. Gates recalled that "the idea of a significant reduction of Iraqi military power, on a permanent basis, was a significant element of the whole discussion." After weeks of meetings, the DC recommended to Bush two of three agreed-upon war aims. First, and least contentious, was the forcible removal of Iraq from Kuwait. Second, the United States would seek to eliminate the Republican Guard as a military force. According to Haass, the DC endorsed this aim to ensure that Iraq "did not emerge as the principal power of the Gulf" in the war's aftermath. This objective strongly influenced the manner in which the war was to be waged.

> There was a rationale for not simply fighting the war narrowly in Kuwait, but for taking the war to Iraq and to Saddam, because you could argue it tactically: that it was necessary so he couldn't bring them to bear in Kuwait. So it was a totally legitimate tactical argument. But I'm not going to sit here and say it didn't occur to some of us that there was also a strategic rationale for it, because it was a way of to some extent cutting Saddam down to size, so he couldn't do it again quite so easily.

This logic extended to Iraq's WMD program. The DC argued that "a significant degrading" of these capabilities was a realistic goal and should be sought. The final war aim, not endorsed by the DC, was debated for weeks: replacing the Iraqi regime. Gates recalled that the members of the DC "unanimously recommended to the president and to our bosses that that not be a war aim . . . because we couldn't figure out how to guarantee that we could achieve it. That was for us the Vietnam scenario."[95] Recognizing these difficulties, Haass remarked that the overriding objective "was to fashion a set of aims that were militarily do-able and that were politically sustainable."[96]

Based on intelligence obtained by CENTCOM in mid-September, it was clear that Iraq had neither the intention of attacking Saudi Arabia nor of withdrawing from Kuwait. Iraqi Republican Guard and armored units had backed away from the border and were being replaced by tens of thousands of entrenched and barricaded infantry. Behind them, Iraqi armor was placed in reinforcing positions, while the Republican Guard was repositioned back in Iraq.[97] At the same time, Saddam was almost completely isolated diplomatically, and, based on the available intelligence, economic sanctions had cut off nearly 95 percent of Saddam's exports and imports. For Powell, this evidence suggested that a strategy of containing Iraq was appropriate. Powell believed that sanctions would likely provoke an Iraqi response within a month. When he suggested this time frame to Wolfowitz, the under secretary of defense countered that for sanctions to work, Saddam had to believe they would be in place indefinitely. Nevertheless, Powell believed this approach had to be considered at the highest levels. The chairman made the case for containment first to Cheney, then to Baker (who Powell knew was sympathetic to a diplomatic solution to the crisis), and then finally to Scowcroft. Powell told Scowcroft explicitly that if there was an alternative to war, the principals had to give it their full consideration.[98] Clearly, Powell was concerned that the president was not hearing all that he needed to make an informed decision. Finally, on September 24, Powell met with Bush, Scowcroft, Baker, and Cheney to make it clear to the president that he had more than one option available. The first was for an offensive option, the second was containment. Containing Iraq would take longer, Powell noted, but either policy would ultimately be successful. No one at the meeting embraced containment, and Bush appeared skeptical. "I don't think there's time politically for that strategy."[99]

At this point CENTCOM began its initial planning for an eventual offensive operation against Iraqi positions in Kuwait. While the White House was fully involved in designing the diplomatic approach and in drafting the list of war aims that would be sought in a possible war, the initial military planning efforts were conducted in isolation by a small staff within CENTCOM. This staff, which excluded the marines and which did not have direct contact with Powell's staff in Washington, was responsible for planning the ground offensive against Iraqi forces. Planning for the air campaign was the responsibility of the air force.[100] The initial ground planning effort was guided by a number of assumptions, the most important of which was the belief that the Republican Guard had been redeployed just inside Iraq in order to gain operational flexibility should the United States mount an attack from Saudi Arabia into Kuwait. Three proposals were drafted: the first and preferred plan called for a direct attack up the middle into Kuwait; the second and third for some variation of an attack west of the Wadi al-Batin on the Iraq-Kuwait border. The latter two options were rejected internally because they appeared to be too logistically demanding and because this approach would leave US supply lines badly stretched and vulnerable to an Iraqi counterattack. Schwarzkopf was briefed on these plans by Lieutenant

Colonel Joseph Purvis, who made it clear that he was not comfortable with any of the three options. To strike successfully, an additional army corps would be needed.[101]

Despite Schwarzkopf's objections that the plan was not ready, Powell instructed that he, Cheney, and Jeremiah be briefed on the draft. On October 10, Schwarzkopf's chief of staff, Major General Robert Johnston, led the briefing team on behalf of the CINC, who remained in Riyadh. At the Pentagon, the team was met with substantial skepticism over the land component.[102] While plans for the air campaign escaped substantial criticism overall, Powell and marine commandant Al Gray raised substantial concerns over the ability of air power to punch a hole in the Iraqi defenses and the absence of marine amphibious capabilities. At the end of the brief, Purvis presented Schwarzkopf's assessment: the CINC was happy with the air plan, but not with the ground-war plan. Ultimately, an additional corps was needed.[103]

The next day, the team met in the White House to brief the plan to the Big 8. Lieutenant General Buster Glosson presented the air-war plan, arguing that at the end of the campaign, Saddam would be incapable of communicating with his army and would be unable to send reinforcements to Kuwait. Bush indicated that he was comfortable with the approach but wanted to make sure that no targets of religious or historical import were included on the target list. During Glosson's briefing, Powell made sure to impress upon the president the limits of American air power. Glosson noted that there was a very good chance that Saddam would survive the bombing campaign, as the United States was not including him personally on the target list.

Purvis then presented CENTCOM's plan to attack Iraqi defense from the ground. Immediately, Scowcroft objected to the idea of American forces running headlong into the teeth of Iraqi prepared positions. Would not a western flanking maneuver be more effective? Powell interjected at this point, stating that an attack from the west was not logistically sustainable nor did the United States have an adequate force to pull the move off. Bush asked what it would take to make a western attack possible, and Powell responded that an additional corps would be needed, and that it could be in place by January 1. The meeting adjourned when Cheney recommended that further conversations take place in a smaller setting.[104]

The October 11 meeting at the White House was a critical event in the run-up to the Persian Gulf War. The single-corps plan was ruled unacceptable and a preference for a two-corps, western-flanking plan had been registered.[105] More significantly, however, was the effect the briefing had on the principals and their resulting determination to more rigorously monitor and influence CENTCOM's planning. As Scowcroft noted,

> I was not happy with the briefing. It sounded unenthusiastic, delivered by people who didn't want to do the job. The option they presented us, an attack straight up through the center of the Iraqi army, seemed to me to be so counterintuitive that I could not stay silent . . . I was appalled with the presentation and afterwards I called Cheney to say I thought we had to do better. Cheney shared my concern and sent the planners back to the drawing board.[106]

The next morning, Cheney informed Powell that Schwarzkopf's plan would not fly. Powell promised to stay on top of CENTCOM, and in an effort to push him to think harder about the land component planning, the chairman informed Schwarzkopf just how badly the briefing went.[107] For his part, Cheney would begin devising his own strategic alternative.[108]

In his meeting with Powell in late September, Bush stated that he did not believe there was sufficient time politically for a strategy of containment to work effectively. Intelligence sources made clear that Iraq was digging in and reinforcing its positions in Kuwait. On September 28, Bush met with the Kuwaiti emir, who gave a firsthand account of the atrocities Iraqi forces were committing. According to Bush, "It was during this period that I began to move from viewing Saddam's aggression exclusively as a dangerous strategic threat and an injustice to its reversal as a moral crusade."[109] In any event, the longer Iraq remained in Kuwait, the less of Kuwait there would be to save. Finally, in the latter half of October, the US ambassador to Saudi Arabia, Chas Freeman, sent a series of cables to Baker and Bush that made it clear that Riyadh was growing increasingly impatient to have the crisis resolved—by war if necessary—as quickly as possible. In a memo to Freeman on October 22, Baker made the case that sanctions were indeed working, and that although more time was needed for them to be completely effective, it was Saddam who stood most to lose as the crisis dragged on. On October 29, Freeman made it clear why he felt the secretary of state's preferred policy courted disaster. As time dragged on, Saddam would be able to more effectively split the coalition and turn the region against the United States. Further, Freeman noted that the longer offensive military operations were delayed, the less likely it was that they could be carried off at all. Two factors militated against delay: the weather and the upcoming religious season in Saudi Arabia. Any military operation against Iraq had to be *completed* by the first week of March, though sooner would be better. Ultimately, given the lead times involved in additional U.S. and Arab deployments, judgments must be made NOW on whether we need to have an offensive option in order to resolve this crisis, because the favorable window for utilizing such an option begins to close just three months from now, by end of January.[110]

Earlier in October, the DC was tasked with figuring out a way for moving from containing Iraq to liberating Kuwait. Three basic options were outlined:

1   Sticking with sanctions in the hope they would pressure Saddam to exit Kuwait
2   Giving an ultimatum to Iraq to leave Kuwait by a date certain or be forced out (ideally, one backed by the United Nations)
3   Waiting until Saddam did something new and then using that provocation to oust him from Kuwait.

The pros and cons of each of these actions were considered in the DC's memo. It was noted that DC members held little confidence in the ability of sanctions to force Iraq out, and even if they did work, there would be little left of Kuwait to salvage. Moreover, waiting for a new provocation would in effect give the initiative to Saddam and put the United States in an "odd position of responding militarily to what would seem to many to be a lesser offense than the taking over of Kuwait."[111]

With the Freeman and DC memos in hand, the Big 8 met in the Situation Room on October 30 to discuss the next move. In a memo submitted to Bush before the meeting, Scowcroft argued that

our basic objective at this point ought to be to regain momentum and take the initiative away from Saddam. This requires a two-track strategy: on the diplomatic side, a renewed push for full and unconditional Iraqi withdrawal as called for by Security Council resolution 660; on the military side, accelerated preparations that provide a real alternative should diplomacy fail. One way of implementing this strategy would be giving an ultimatum to Saddam demanding that he withdraw fully from Kuwait (and release all hostages while permitting the legitimate government to return) by a certain date. I would argue that the date certain should be around the end of the year, some five months since the attack and the imposition of sanctions.

Scowcroft went on to note that the end of November would be the optimal time to announce the ultimatum. That way, additional military preparations could be made and it would dispel the argument that the United States had not given diplomacy a chance. "It would also bring matters to a head before Iraq had much more time to work on its biological and nuclear weapons capability, dig in completely in Kuwait, or before we found ourselves heading into poor weather, Ramadan and the Hajj." Scowcroft concluded that the ultimatum approach was appropriate because the "coalition shows signs of fraying at the edges" for the reasons stipulated in Freeman's memo.[112]

At the opening of the meeting, Scowcroft presented the options the DC had laid out. In response to a question from Bush on the efficacy of continuing with sanctions, Baker responded, "I believe sanctions will not get him out in a time frame we can accept." Cheney then stated that to conduct "a real offensive, we will need significant additional forces—three more divisions." Powell added that military planning was well advanced for more forces.[113] "We could have an additional hundred and forty thousand people in place by 15 January. I also intend to send whatever else I can get in. We are talking about a major war against Iraq. I want to send in five or six carrier task forces." At that point, the discussion turned to the timing of the ultimatum. January 15 appeared the appropriate date, given Powell's time frame for assembling additional forces. The meeting concluded with Baker stating, "We will announce the troop build-up on Monday [November 5] if the Saudis say yes." In the mean time, the secretary of state would press coalition partners to support the ultimatum approach.[114] On November 8, after Baker's meeting with the Saudis, the president formally announced that American combat strength in the Gulf would be doubled. The results of Baker's diplomatic efforts more generally were, in Haass's words, "remarkably successful." On November 29, the UN Security Council passed Resolution 678, after the president made a trip to Paris to meet with Mikhail Gorbachev to secure the Soviets' support. The resolution authorized member states to use "all necessary means"[115] to oust Iraq from Kuwait if a withdrawal did not occur by January 15.[116]

As the administration was debating the efficacy of sanctions and designing its new diplomatic approach to the crisis, efforts were underway to overhaul the military's strategy. Three separate planning efforts were begun simultaneously: civilians in the OSD began working on a plan that was known colloquially as the "western excursion," Powell and the Joint Staff developed an option that would use overwhelming force and include a substantial western flanking component, and CENTCOM worked on both a one- and two-corps plan in case no additional forces would be committed to the region. That there were three independent planning efforts underway is a clear indication that CENTCOM had lost its monopoly over military planning.[117]

As discussed above, Cheney made it clear to Powell that he intended to seek military advice and information from multiple sources. Sticking to that promise, Cheney began searching for an alternative approach to that briefed by CENTCOM on October 11. In mid-October, Henry Rowen, assistant secretary of defense for international security affairs, approached Wolfowitz with an idea for a plan that would have CENTCOM send one or two divisions to the far western reaches of Iraq. This would have the benefit of drawing the Iraqi army's attention away from the main battle that would occur in Kuwait; a scheme Rowen likened to MacArthur's landing at Inchon in the Korean War.[118] Wolfowitz briefed Cheney on the plan, and Cheney ordered the creation of a small planning cell to develop the idea even further. The result of that planning was Operation Scorpion. By placing coalition forces deep into western Iraq, planners believed that Iraqi high command would perceive a direct threat to Baghdad. Even if Baghdad wasn't the target, the United States could ransom the city in exchange for a political settlement on favorable terms. Should Iraqi forces be turned to meet the threat, it was believe they would be easy targets for coalition air power. And with US forces so far to the west, the coalition would be able to meet any Scud threat Iraq posed to Israel.[119]

After being presented with the western excursion plan, Powell's planning efforts got underway in earnest. For Powell and his staff, the western excursion idea was fundamentally flawed to the extent that it did not entail a massive use of force to crush the opponent's armed forces. With that principle in mind, Powell's team devised a scenario entailing a massive sweep through the desert west of the Wadi al-Batin, which would then turn east to envelop the Republican Guard. To the east, the marines would hold Iraqi forces in place temporarily, thereby allowing the western envelopment to take place. Finally, Schwarzkopf's planners work on the two-corps plan that also included an attack to the west, but not as far as Powell had outlined. To the CENTCOM team, an attack as far west as Powell's plan envisioned had the short-term effect of diverting combat power from the main attack. From Powell's perspective, the CENTCOM plan was not the "roundhouse punch" the army should seek to deliver.[120]

Powell met with Schwarzkopf on October 22. Neither held Cheney's western excursion in high esteem.[121] For them, the notion of holding Iraqi territory as a bargaining chip was a nonstarter, largely because it did not focus on the key strategic issue: the destruction of the Republican Guard. After a few rounds of debate over how far the attack to the west should be pushed, Schwarzkopf informed his planning staff to plan the attack as far west as logistically possible. According to Michael Gordon and Bernard Trainor, "Even if the Western Excursion was not the perfect plan, it had already accomplished one of Cheney's goals: it had lit a fire under the military." They would not be coming back with a plan that called for a major attack up the middle.[122]

Another of Cheney's goals was to closely monitor the progress of the military's planning effort from this point forward. Cheney would seek to understand and question the evolving war plan in excruciating detail.[123] Explaining his approach to Wolfowitz, Cheney commented that he had no desire to micromanage the planners and did not want to redo the plan. "But I intend to own it when it's finished." In a period of less than a month, beginning on November 26, Cheney was given fifteen extensive briefings related to every aspect of the war plan. The result of this effort was that the president and his top civilian advisers were kept fully informed of the nature of military operations planned for the coming war in the Persian Gulf. Finally, on December 19, Cheney and Powell met with Schwarzkopf and his planning team for a final briefing on the war plan. It quickly became apparent to Schwarzkopf that despite Cheney's detailed understanding of the war plan's intricacies, and his willingness to ask many pointed questions about the plan, both he and Powell were fully on board.[124] Toward the end of the meeting, Cheney and Powell reassured Schwarzkopf that should war come, he would be given a free hand to execute the plan. "The President, Cheney and Powell had to sign off on the plan, but once it was approved, it would for the most part be in Schwarzkopf's hands."[125]

In mid-December, with the January 15 deadline looming, the United States turned its attention to Israel. Over the previous four months, the United States had exerted pressure on Israel to maintain a low profile. Relations between the United States and Israel were less then optimal at this point, especially given the consent the United States gave in the UN Security Council for an investigation of the Temple Mount incident in October. On December 11, Prime Minister Shamir visited the White House. The week prior, Shamir had made clear Israel's price for staying out of the conflict if Iraq were to attack: the elimination of Iraq's WMD program. In their meeting, Bush assured Shamir that under no conditions would Saddam be allowed to escape the crisis with his army intact. Shamir replied that Israel was not thinking of preemptive strike, but that the United States and Israel should share military intelligence in any event. Shamir added, "But if something should happen, we should try to consult beforehand, before something is launched."[126] This was as close as Bush would come to getting a pledge of restraint from Israel. Keeping Israel out of the war, and keeping the coalition together, would continue to influence American actions well into the war.

On January 9, 1991, in what was billed as an "extra mile for peace," Baker met with Tariq Aziz in Geneva. In terms of US-Iraqi relations, the meeting changed little. The event did have the effect of fraying nerves in Riyadh, however. Regardless, American diplomacy had run its course. On January 15, President Bush signed NSD 54, the document that laid out American aims in the war. On January 16, the Persian Gulf War commenced.[127]

Waging and Ending the War

As soon as the first coalition attacks began, intelligence reports of Iraqi Scud attacks on Israel made their way to Washington. The Israelis were incensed and appeared to be on the verge of responding militarily. Cheney was of the mind to allow them a free hand and recommended that the US military pass along the codes identifying friendly forces to the Israel Defense Forces (IDF). Haass countered that to permit the Israelis to respond would "raise a host of messy tactical issues (such as overflight of Arab countries) and would add a new dimension to the crisis and a new challenge to coalition management."[128] There was also the question as to what an Israeli attack could accomplish. The United States had already a substantial air presence in the theater and could retaliate just as effectively, if not more so, than the Israeli air force. Numerous calls were made to Israeli officials over the ensuing hours and days that expressed sympathy, concern, and the importance of restraint.[129] Eagleburger and Wolfowitz were dispatched to Israel in an effort to look for ways the United States and Israel could cooperate short of Israel's active intervention in the war.[130] Finally, the Israelis were promised that a significant number of military assets would be devoted to hunting down and destroying Scud launchers. As Haass remarked, "This scenario—Iraqi Scuds landing in Israel, Israeli desire to retaliate, U.S. urging restraint, and more U.S. military effort devoted to taking out the Scuds—would be repeated throughout the war."[131] Ultimately, Israel's restraint proved to be disastrous for Saddam. Not only had his ploy to draw Israel into the war failed, but it also led to the intensification of American-Israeli relations, with the tacit approval of the Arab states.[132]

The attacks on Israel coincided with commencement of the DC's effort in drafting a memo on the termination of the war. Magnifying the difficulty of this assignment was the apparent willingness on the part of the president to consider expanding American war aims. Prior to the onset of war, Bush's rhetoric had become increasingly harsh. On numerous occasions, the president had equated Saddam to Hitler, prompting Scowcroft and his advisers to caution Bush that such language would inevitably lead to raised expectations pertaining to what the United States should seek in a war.[133] For Bush, the conflict had become personal, Saddam was squarely to blame, and as such the United States was obliged to topple the Iraqi dictator.

The American intelligence community had been working to forecast the likely regional effects of such an outcome.[134] In an estimate released prior to the initiation of the air campaign, the DIA noted that even in the event of Saddam's ouster, the problem of Iraqi aggression would in all likelihood persist. According to the DIA's memo, "A successor government would display hostility toward the U.S., Israel, Egypt, and the Gulf Cooperation Council states, and also continue to promote Iraq's role in the Arab world." Toward that end, any successor regime "would resume pursuit of weapons of mass destruction to support its ambitions." Compounding the problem were the threats Iran and Turkey posed to a post-Saddam Iraq. "The most significant Iranian threat would be Tehran's potential support to Iraqi Shia and Kurdish separatists. Iran could be expected to support Kurdish separatists, who would likely resume an insurgency aimed at independence or autonomy from Baghdad." In order to preserve the territorial integrity of the country, a new regime would have to devote substantial military assets to put down an insurgency in the north, thereby opening the door to a possible Iranian attack in the south. A report filed by the Kuwaiti Task Force/US Army Civil Affairs Reconstruction Group seconded this conclusion, arguing that "political and military collapse could make Iraq vulnerable to the predatory ambitions of its immediate neighbors." In that event, the United States would lose any hope of managing postwar events and would be forced to watch as the region descended into turmoil. The danger to regional security and stability was highlighted by other assessments, one of which stated that "the whole fertile crescent—Iraq, Syria, Lebanon, Jordan—is in question."[135]

As the point person designated to draft the DC's war termination memo for the president, Richard Haass was fully cognizant of Bush's desires to punish Saddam as well as the assessments made by the intelligence community. Unfortunately for the president, the case could not be made that this option was cost free. In three separate memos (the first two of which the president rejected), Haass impressed upon Bush the danger associated with expanding American war aims. On the issue of taking Saddam out, Haass noted, "It goes beyond our domestic writ; it goes beyond our international writ; it goes beyond what the Coalition would sustain; and most important of all, it would require an indefinite occupation of Iraq by U.S. forces." On January 23, Scowcroft arranged for a meeting between Bush and Haass. Speaking to the president, Haass confessed, "Mr. President, I know what you want, I just don't see how it's going to happen. I don't think we're going to get our battleship *Missouri* here," a reference to the location of the surrender ceremony wherein General MacArthur dictated the terms to the Japanese at the end of the Second World War. Rather, Haass stated that the president would have to accept something far less conclusive: a de facto end of the war, when the United Nations endorsed conditions had been met. Critically, those conditions had nothing to do with the nature of the Iraqi regime. Haass concluded his case to the president by noting that the rest of the world would be satisfied with the liberation of Kuwait; to demand more "was beyond the do-able."[136] Significantly, at that point the conversation turned to the issue of the extent to which the American military should advance into Iraq. The possibility of limiting the scope of the ground advance was contemplated because extending too far into Iraq might unintentionally bring down the regime. That scenario was disastrous for Haass and Scowcroft: a situation in which US troops would be responsible for maintaining civil order in a country on the verge of a multisided civil war, one in which all sides would view the Americans as occupiers.[137]

On January 29, the stability of the coalition was challenged when Baker and Soviet foreign minister Alexander Bessmertnykh issued a joint statement that offered a cease-fire in exchange for Iraq's complete withdrawal from Kuwait and its compliance with all UN Security Council resolutions. This statement, which was not cleared by Bush or Scowcroft, threatened to dramatically alleviate the pressure on Saddam to the extent that the cease-fire would have gone into effect with the mere promise by Saddam to vacate Kuwait.[138] Shortly thereafter, the White House issued a "clarifying statement" that indicated that the United States' position had not changed. Still, there were numerous problems associated with the joint communiqué. One of which surfaced on February 15 when Saddam indicated that he was prepared "to deal with U.N. Security Council Resolution 660, with the aim of reaching an honorable and acceptable solution, including withdrawal from Kuwait." Saddam quickly added conditions to this, however, including Israel's withdrawal from the occupied territories and the demand to terminate all UN resolutions against Iraq. For their part, the Soviets were attempting to halt the eventual transition to the ground phase of the war by working to get Saddam to offer something the Americans would find at least moderately acceptable, and in the process, retain their ability to influence the politics in the region.[139] Although European governments evinced little support for these efforts, European public opinion did register some backing. The Arab states, on the other hand, were keen to continue pressuring Saddam. The response to these diplomatic complications was another ultimatum to Saddam: Iraq had twenty-four hours to begin its withdrawal of Kuwait. As the administration was debating the terms of the ultimatum, Saddam began torching Kuwaiti oil wells.[140]

The ground war against Iraq began on February 25. Soon thereafter, the Big 8 met to debate the war's duration and the terms that would be acceptable for surrender. It was decided that the United States would seek a public declaration that Saddam supported all UN resolutions and the agreement by the Iraqis to lay down their arms. Four days after the ground war began, horrific images of what came to be known as the "Highway of Death" were broadcast on CNN. Bush met with his top advisers, and all came to the conclusion that no further military action was necessary.[141] Bush then ordered that a cease-fire be arranged, despite Schwarzkopf's objection that doing so would prevent coalition forces from completely destroying the Iraqi army.[142]

Ending the war now presented numerous advantages. First, with the coalition still intact, the administration hoped that it would be able to capitalize on the goodwill banked with the Soviets and Arabs states. The administration planned to refocus on the peace process in the near future, and the support by the Soviets and key Arab countries would be much needed. Second, while beaten badly, Iraq was still powerful enough to balance Iran should the latter embark on a future bid for regional hegemony.[143] As Scowcroft later noted, "It wasn't a matter of destroying the whole army, they had over 20 divisions up north that weren't involved at all, so that wasn't the issue. But, we really did want to destroy their most capable units." Third, there was a prevailing view that Saddam's days were numbered in any event. With respect to its war aims, the United States had just liberated Kuwait, badly mauled the Republican Guard, substantially degraded Iraq's WMD program, and rallied the international community behind Washington's leadership. All of this was achieved with an astonishingly low level of coalition casualties. In short, the United States achieved both military and diplomatic successes in the Persian Gulf War.[144]

INFORMATION INSTITUTIONS VERSUS CIVIL-MILITARY RELATIONS

The information institution approach finds substantial support in this case of limited war. The United States entered the Persian Gulf War with a robust information institution. In terms of their access to information, top policy makers were presented with information pertaining to the primary opponent and to the wider strategic environment from multiple organizational sources. With respect to interorganizational information sharing, the Bush administration's National Security Council system ensured that all of the agencies responsible for designing and executing the limited war strategy in the war widely and routinely shared information. Under these circumstances, this approach expects double success (both military and diplomatic) in limited war. The evidence presented in this chapter confirms this expectation. The United States succeeded militarily and diplomatically in the war, and in the process, was able to prevent the war from escalating in any way.

The evidence presented also confirmed the causal logic of the information institution approach. During the crisis and throughout the war, the United States possessed comprehensive collection and optimal analytical capabilities. During the initial phase of the crisis, top policy makers received a wealth of information pertaining to America's diplomatic targets and primary opponent. To facilitate the construction of the coalition, the United States was able to secure Saudi Arabia's cooperation by sharing up-to-the-minute intelligence on Iraqi military activity. Moreover, the open lines of communication between Washington and Riyadh and other Middle Eastern capitals allowed the United States to understand the pressures and constraints under which those states labored. American diplomacy with the Soviet Union provided valuable information about the Kremlin, which was put to good use as the United States maneuvered its way through the UN Security Council and dealt with the numerous diplomatic challenges America's Cold War rival posed. Finally, although relations with Israel were not optimal, the United States was able to secure Israeli restraint through careful diplomacy and military-military contacts. The diplomatic relationships the United States cultivated prior to the crisis proved to be its most important source of information about the broader strategic environment. At the same time, the availability of signals and communications intelligence proved valuable as the United States sought to manage those relationships during the crisis.

As the United States began to develop its offensive military strategy, top policy makers were afforded with information from multiple sources pertaining to Iraq's capabilities and intentions. In addition to the CIA, the DIA, and INR routinely provided information pertaining to Iraq's military deployments, and at times that information proved immensely valuable.

CENTCOM's intelligence resources produced products that were widely respected within the intelligence community and were routinely digested by officials in Washington.[145] At critical points in the run-up to the war, information from diplomatic sources enabled American strategists to fully understand and incorporate the sensitivities of key regional states into their military planning. By employing the Situation Room's technical capabilities, and by acquiring information from sources at lower levels in the chain of command, the president and his top advisers were never in the dark about the status and content of the military's war-planning effort. Finally, information from multiple sources was employed as the DC debated the specific war aims the United States should seek and as it prepared the critical memorandum on the termination of the war. This information allowed top policy makers to understand the coalition's limitations, the difficulties that would be faced if the United States sought to oust Saddam from power, and the regional consequences that would result if Iraq were utterly destroyed by the war. In sum, information pertaining to nearly all aspects of the war—military and diplomatic—was available to top policy makers. And due to the structure of the administration's interagency process, information hoarding was rare, information vetting was efficient and effective, and military and diplomatic trade-offs were confronted squarely.

Throughout the crisis and war, top policy makers were able to maintain tight coordination among America's political objectives and its military and diplomatic policies. First, the objectives of forcing Iraq from Kuwait and of restoring Kuwait's legitimate government significantly affected the diplomatic and military strategies employed. American demands were clearly articulated to Iraq and were buttressed by numerous UN Security Council resolutions. The sheer size of the coalition supporting those demands provided a clear signal to Iraq that it was isolated and prevented Saddam from cutting side deals that would allow it to hold on to chunks of Kuwaiti territory. The objective of using the war as a means of ushering in a "new world order" influenced the administration's coalition building efforts. By working through the United Nations, the United States was able to secure worldwide support for its leadership in the crisis, and through deft diplomacy, was able to avoid substantial rifts from developing in its relationship with the Soviets over the war. Finally, its commitment to the security and stability of the Persian Gulf influenced the military objectives that were sought in the war. Despite the president's personal preference to punish Saddam for his transgressions, American policy remained focused on the objective of forcing Iraq from Kuwait. And in an effort to recalibrate the balance of regional power between Iraq and Iran, the United States endeavored to cut Iraqi power down, but not to the point of rendering Iraq incapable of defending itself. At times, maintaining the balance among these objectives required that diplomacy give way to the demands of military planning, and vice versa. For example, to accomplish its military objectives completely, American diplomats were tasked with the responsibility of wrangling more from Saudi Arabia than the kingdom would have desired. On the other hand, in an effort to prevent Israel from entering the war, the military was forced to devote assets to engage in a hunt for mobile Scud launchers, a job that Schwarzkopf believed to be of limited military value. Most importantly, it was the diplomatic imperative of keeping Saudi Arabia, Egypt, and Syria in the coalition that resulted in the inclusion of the destruction of the Republican Guard in America's war aims.

How well does the information institution approach perform when compared to the competing theories of strategic performance in limited warfare? Democratic civil-military relations theory expects double success when political and military preferences converge. When preferences converge, policy advisory bodies will be widely representative, resulting in "relatively routinized, representative, and rigorous" coordination. Conversely, when political and military preferences diverge, coordination will suffer because the oversight mechanisms civilians employ to ensure access to information have the pernicious effect of marginalizing senior military officials.[146] In either case, this approach expects information sharing to be fluid among civilian leaders and senior military officials.

The first mechanism, fluid information sharing among civilians and officers, is strongly confirmed by this case. From the beginning of the crisis to the end of the war, top policy makers received a wealth of information from the military that had a direct influence on the content of the broader limited war strategy. With respect to the second mechanism, military and diplomatic coordination, democratic civil-military relations theory encounters numerous problems. The first is that the Persian Gulf case is one where political and military preference diverged strongly. Based on the evidence presented above, both Powell and Schwarzkopf evinced preferences well short of the use of force against Iraq. Prior to the war, Powell and Schwarzkopf made it clear that they were not in favor of going to war. Moreover, it was Powell who repeatedly pressed the case to the president and his top advisers for containing Iraq—an approach that contradicted stated policy. This hesitancy did not escape Scowcroft's and Cheney's attention. As noted, the national security adviser saw American military planning as being "unenthusiastic, delivered by people who didn't want to do the job." For his part, the secretary of defense reminded Powell that his job as chairman of the Joint Chiefs of Staff was emphatically not to concern himself with political matters.[147] In response, civilian leaders implemented what could only be considered intrusive oversight mechanisms on the military to ensure access to information. For example, Dick Cheney insisted that he be constantly briefed on all aspects of the military strategy as it was being designed. And, it was the secretary of defense who pressed the military to consider a broad envelopment of Iraqi forces through Saudi Arabia—a move that senior military officers viewed with disdain. The intrusiveness of these oversight mechanisms notwithstanding, the extent of military-diplomatic coordination was exceptionally tight. Both before and during the war, American military and diplomatic policies went forward with remarkable harmony. In short, democratic civil-military relations theory is only partly confirmed in this case.

Of the three approaches, organizational culture theory performs the worst in the Persian Gulf case. This approach anticipates double success in limited war strategies when the military holds a "balanced" concept of warfare—where both military and political logics are seen as being central to nature of warfare—and when the organization follows a Clausewitzian norm of civil-military relations. Under these conditions, information collection and analysis is anticipated to be comprehensive and optimal, and military-diplomatic coordination is likely to be tight.

Neither of these cultural elements was present in the American military prior to the Persian Gulf War. As was the case in both Korea and Vietnam, the American military's concept of warfare was "military dominant," a view that held little room for political nuance.[148] The evidence presented above demonstrates the presence of this concept. Top policy makers repeatedly insisted that military missions be specifically tailored to satisfy diplomatic objectives, over the strong objections of Schwarzkopf. For example, civilians demanded the redeployment of American forces to areas near the Israeli border in order to assuage its security concerns. These diplomatic concerns were far from trivial—Israeli restraint was crucial to the maintenance of the international coalition—but they were substantially downplayed and resisted by military commanders on operational and strategic grounds.

Additionally, the initial military plan Schwarzkopf's team devised was predicated on an attrition-based operational logic. Militaries that adopt attrition strategies perform strategic calculations that consider only the balance of military forces: attrition is the preferred strategy of the strong and not the weak.[149] Attrition strategies deliver success through the sequential accumulation of tactical victories. Such an approach reflects an organizational culture that does not see escalation as a fundamental problem of war. Rather, escalation is the natural result of military contests. Attrition strategies are not politically nimble insofar as military missions are designed to serve only one purpose: the outright destruction of the enemy.[150] In sum, the "military dominant" concept of warfare generated military plans that were ill suited to American objectives in the Persian Gulf War. In response, civilians in the Office of the Secretary of Defense designed Operation Scorpion—the plan to insert coalition forces deep into western Iraq, which would constitute a threat to the capitol city. This plan ultimately threatened to sideline the military in the strategic planning process. To avoid this fate, the military immediately shifted away from its initial attrition-based frontal attack scheme toward one that incorporated substantial elements of strategic maneuver. Top policy makers required a military approach that was tailored to multiple political and diplomatic considerations. The American military on its own was incapable of delivering that strategy due to its prevailing concept of warfare.

With respect to the proper form of civil-military relations, many scholars have demonstrated how the post-Vietnam American military remained powerfully wedded to the Jominian relational norm. The primary lesson the military learned from that war was that it had fought "with a hand tied behind its back." Obtrusive and unwarranted civilian involvement in military matters caused the United States to lose that war. In response, the military went to great lengths to ensure that future civilian leaders would no longer be able to hamstring the military in the ways Johnson and Nixon (though, primarily the former) had done.[151] By far the clearest articulation of the Jominian norm was offered by secretary of defense Caspar Weinberger in 1984 (himself a veteran of the Second World War who served under General Douglas MacArthur). The "Weinberger Doctrine" became, in the words of Eliot Cohen, "canonical within the defense establishment; they embodied, for a generation of officers, the 'normal' theory of civil-military relations."[152] Boiled down to its essentials, the Weinberger Doctrine served as a military-derived template that civilian leaders were to follow when making decisions pertaining to the use of force. It embodied a preferred approach to warfare, one that viewed the stark separation between military and political affairs as appropriate. At the same time, the Weinberger Doctrine stacked the deck in favor of the military as an organization in the traditionally civilian realm of wartime decision making. By insisting that civilians make decisions on the use of force in a particular manner (regardless of whether some consider those criteria sound, or not[153]), the military's Jominian relational norm was exposed.

The organizational culture of the American military thus contained both a "military dominant" concept of warfare and a Jominian norm of civil-military relations. Under these conditions, this approach anticipates double failure in limited war—an outcome clearly at odds with the empirical record. Perhaps most striking is the degree to which organizational cultural factors mattered *so little* in the strategic outcome of the Persian Gulf War. The reason is that because of the robust nature of the American information institution, top policy makers were able to penetrate the military's culture in important ways. While the military was thoroughly Jominian in its understanding of the proper relationship between it and civilians, their masters were died-in-the-wool Clausewitzians. Top policy makers prevailed in this contest because of their institutional capacities to acquire and employ information from military and nonmilitary sources as strategy was designed and executed. Civilians were not forced to rely solely on the military for strategic information (as was Truman with respect to MacArthur). Moreover, because the limited war strategy was thoroughly owned by the White House, top policy makers could ensure tight military and diplomatic coordination from beginning to end. The robust information institution further enabled civilians to modify the military's war planning in ways that were beneficial to them—but in ways that ran against the military's concept of warfare. As was the case in the air campaign in the Vietnam War, the military was neither viewed by civilian leaders as the only salient national security organization, nor were civilians beholden to what the military preferred to give them. In the Persian Gulf War, the robust information institution exerted powerful countervailing pressures against the military's organizational culture, pressures that were not manifest in either the Korean War or the ground campaign in the Vietnam War. Ultimately, it is the salience of the organization that determines when militaries will have a predominant role in strategic decision making. The evidence presented in this chapter demonstrates how salience is a product of the information flow patterns within governments at limited war.

CHAPTER SIX

Iraq—Win the Battle, Lose the War

On May 1, 2003, from the flight deck of the USS *Abraham Lincoln* and under a banner declaring "Mission Accomplished," President George W. Bush declared an end to major combat operations in Iraq. In the narrowest of senses, Bush was correct. In a few short weeks, the United States and its coalition partners waged an intense and successful conventional battle, the objectives of which were to eradicate the Iraqi military as an effective combat force and to overthrow the regime of Saddam Hussein. Had the conventional military element been the only salient measure of US strategy in the Iraq War, then in all likelihood the anticipated early withdrawal of American combat forces would have begun on schedule. Yet in a larger sense (most likely the way that Bush had intended), that declaration proved to be premature at best. Not only did American combat operations continue, but they also intensified as a hydra-headed insurgency emerged in the wake of American military operations. The rise of the Sunni insurgency, the complete collapse of Iraqi civil society, and the eventual outbreak of communal civil war, was precisely the opposite political outcome the United States sought. Top administration officials desired the emergence of a stable and democratic Iraqi state—a democracy in the heart of a region dominated by authoritarian states, from which the majority of militant jihadists originate. By mid-2003, the battle against Saddam had been won. The war the administration desired and envisioned, however, was lost with the explosion of the insurgency, the continued infiltration of foreign terrorists, and the realization that American forces would have to be committed in Iraq for far longer than the president and his most influential advisers believed would be necessary. In short, the limited war in Iraq escalated, first, horizontally with the introduction of a host of new combatants, and then durationally as the United States began the slow process of waging counterinsurgency warfare.

The causes of the Sunni insurgency stemmed directly from the contradictory military and diplomatic objectives that were sought prior to and during the initial phases of one of America's longest wars. In turn, the causes of these faulty strategic choices originated from a dysfunctional decision-making process that was incapable of incorporating information within the US government that clearly showed how postconflict stabilization and reconstruction efforts would be stymied unless that United States committed a large number of troops to the war and was prepared to incorporate Iraqi administrative and security institutions into the occupation phase of the campaign. At the same time, however, that structure of strategic decision making generated a war plan that achieved the stated, if limited, military objectives. Understanding the relationship between America's military success and diplomatic failure is the objective of this chapter.

In the pages that follow, I first present an overview of America's conflict with Iraq to demonstrate how despite having achieved its military objectives, the United States failed to secure its diplomatic objectives. Second, I describe how the American information institution prior to and during the war was moderately truncated. Specifically, I show that while the military and top administration officials widely shared information with each other, the agencies and departments responsible for the diplomatic aspects of the war were systematically excluded from the process of strategic decision making. Third, in order to evaluate the logic of the information institution approach, I process-trace American decision making at three critical junctures: the development of a military strategy that was predicated on achieving speed and surprise in the march to Baghdad; the decision to delay concerted postwar planning until after the American diplomatic activity at the United Nations ended in December 2002–January 2003; and the "debate" over the issuance of the two critical orders by the Coalition Provisional Authority (CPA) in Iraq that disbanded the Iraqi military and that thoroughly scoured former Baath Party members from key Iraqi institutions. I argue that while individually these decisions created major hurdles for the United States, their combined effects rendered unattainable the ultimate strategic objectives the United States sought in its limited war against Iraq. I conclude by assessing the explanatory power of the information institution approach compared to that of democratic civil-military relations theory and organizational culture theory.

WIN THE BATTLE, LOSE THE WAR:
MILITARY SUCCESS, DIPLOMATIC FAILURE

Although regime change in Iraq had been desired by many in the administration for quite some time (and was a declared policy of the Clinton administration),[1] the origins of the Iraq War lay in the terrorist attacks on September 11, 2001.[2] The events of 9/11 had a profound influence on top American policy makers: the terrorist attack affected the goals the United States would seek in the war and the manner in which the United States would seek them. Written in the aftermath of 9/11, the National Security Strategy of the United States of America (NSS) is the best source for understanding the overriding strategic objectives that would guide American strategy in the Iraq War.[3]

According to the NSS,[4] the primary national security objective of the United States in the post-9/11 era was not simply the physical safety of the country, but rather "to help make the world not just safer but better. [America's] goals on the path to progress are clear: political and economic freedom, peaceful relations with other states, and respect for human dignity." This last goal, the explicit championing of human dignity, was critical. According to the document, human dignity was understood to be: the rule of law, limits on the absolute power of the state, freedom of speech, freedom of worship, equal justice, respect for women, religious and ethnic tolerance, and respect for private property. These sweeping objectives crystallized into the concept of a "balance of power that favors freedom." The primary obstacle to this grand objective came from rogue states, those that were determined to acquire weapons of mass destruction (WMD), sponsored terrorism around the globe, threatened their neighbors, and violated international treaties, inter alia. In the context of 9/11, the NSS argued that the threats such states posed were immense: not only could rogue states not be deterred or contained, but they also constituted an imminent threat to the physical security of the United States and its allies.[5] While the NSS contains a lengthy justification for the use of preemptive and preventive military force against rogue states,[6] there is no direct reference to changing the regimes of those states once attacked. Yet when considering the ultimate objective of the strategy—to promote a balance of power favoring freedom—and the explicit goal of championing the aspirations of human dignity, the implication was clear that once a rogue state was slated for attack, the objectives would be to overthrow the regime and to create the conditions for democracy to take root. Critically, and presciently, the NSS posited that rogue states were not the only threat to human dignity around the world. Regional instability could also lead to disastrous consequences for the United States' primary strategic objective:

> Concerned nations must remain actively engaged in critical regional disputes to *avoid explosive escalation and minimize human suffering.* In an increasingly inter-connected world, *regional crises can strain our alliances, rekindle rivalries among the major powers, and create horrifying affronts to human dignity.*[7]

As the guiding strategic document in the post-9/11 era, the 2002 NSS held that should a rogue state appear either ready to employ WMD, or even seek to acquire the precursors of a WMD program, the United States would have little option but to use military force to overthrow the regime and fa-cilitate the transition to democracy. At the same time, the strategy strongly advocated steps that mitigated the explosive violence and the associated af-fronts to human dignity that result from local and regional instability. By fundamentally altering the nature of rogue states, the United States would make great strides in creating a balance of power that favors freedom—the ultimate objective of American foreign policy. Although not explicitly stated in the NSS, the region that exhibited a manifest *im*balance of power favor-ing freedom was the Middle East. And the state that most closely matched the definition of "rogue" was Iraq.

Overthrowing Saddam became a top administration priority shortly after 9/11, and the reasons for war closely matched the criteria laid out in the NSS.[8] Many in the administration saw Saddam as posing both an immedi-ate and a long-term threat to the United States. While the underlying public rationale for war centered on Iraq's actual possession of WMD stockpiles, Saddam's past possession of such materials, use of them against his own population, past instances of aggression against his neighbors, repeated vio-lations of his treaty obligations, and known links to terrorists were sufficient to classify Iraq as a significant rogue threat. Still, it was widely believed among administration officials that Saddam did indeed possess chemical and biological weapons programs and, possibly, a nuclear infrastructure.[9] While this bill of particulars against Saddam had been issued before 9/11, American threat sensitivity became far more acute in the aftermath of the terrorist attack. As a result, the bar against an American military response was lowered substantially.[10]

For the president and his most influential advisers, the alternatives to war did not appear as effective means of dealing with the threat Saddam's Iraq posed. The status quo containment approach was quickly unraveling.

The international sanctions regime was weakly constructed and afforded Saddam the ability to exploit loopholes in his attempts to acquire prohibited items. United Nations–authorized weapons inspectors had been kicked out of the country, and as a result, accurate information pertaining to Saddam's WMD capabilities was difficult to acquire. Finally, the ongoing no-fly zone patrols exposed American and British pilots to hostile Iraqi fire on a daily basis. Measures beyond the status quo, but short of war, similarly appeared ineffective. Smart sanctions, an approach the State Department favored, were seen by most in the administration as a continuation of the failed containment policy. American sponsorship of a coup to oust Saddam had a number of drawbacks, most notably the absence of certainty that any post-Saddam leader would abandon the policies adopted by the Iraqi dictator.[11]

On the other hand, a successful war for regime change offered the administration two interrelated and substantial prizes. First, by attacking Iraq, the United States would be able to demonstrate clearly that its response to 9/11 was both offensive in nature and global in scale. Second, in line with the ultimate objective of American foreign policy established in the NSS, a democratic Iraq in the Middle East could serve as the precipitating event for democratic transformation throughout the region.[12] Ultimately, as John Owen argues in his study of the history of foreign imposed regime change, the administration believed itself to be enmeshed in a war with radical Islam. The only way the larger war could be won was by transforming the political history of the region.[13] President Bush and his most influential advisers were looking for a victory in the first battle in what was likely to be a two-generation war. Iraq appeared to be the most promising target.[14]

The United States went to war against Iraq with a set of military and diplomatic objectives that were heavily influenced by the NSS. With respect to military objectives, the United States sought the overthrow of the Iraqi regime, the eradication of Iraqi WMD stockpiles and infrastructure, and the capture and/or killing of any terrorists the regime was believed to be harboring. In terms of its diplomatic objectives, the United States would seek to provide humanitarian aid to Iraqi citizens and an end to the international sanctions regime, secure Iraq's oil fields for the purpose of using oil revenues to aid in the country's economic reconstruction, and "help the Iraqi people create the conditions for a rapid transition to a representative self-government that is not a threat to its neighbors and is committed to the territorial integrity of that country."[15]

From November 21, 2001 (the point at which the American military began planning for war[16]), to summer 2003 (the time frame during which the Sunni insurgency emerged[17]), the American confrontation with Iraq unfolded in four stages. In the first stage, from November 2001 to August 2002, the United States began to step up international political pressure against the regime by laying out the rationale for war, engaging in a process of iterated military planning, and conducting a slow and quiet campaign of military deployments to the region. On January 29, 2002, Bush delivered the annual State of the Union address wherein the president declared that Iraq, Iran, and North Korea constituted an "axis of evil" due to their steadfast determination to acquire WMD. Bush made clear his intention to eliminate the threats these states posed, noting that "America will always stand firm for the nonnegotiable demands of human dignity." On June 1, Bush delivered the commencement address to the graduating class at West Point. The president's purpose was to introduce the concepts contained in the NSS, and in so doing, Bush stressed the imperative of taking "preemptive" action against threats to American security, rather than attempting to contain and deter them.[18]

In terms of military preparations, Secretary of Defense Donald Rumsfeld and General Tommy Franks, commander of US Central Command (CENTCOM), began to thoroughly reformulate existing war plans against Iraq. Two overriding principles guided their efforts. First, in order to limit the chances that Saddam would act in a hostile manner and obstruct planned American military operations, Rumsfeld and Franks sought to compress the time between the president's decision to go to war and the commencement of hostilities. Second, in order to avoid a long war in the heart of the Middle East, military operations had to be conducted with as rapid an operational tempo as possible.[19] To achieve both of these objectives, Rumsfeld urged Franks to design a plan that required a minimal amount of force and to begin deploying military platforms and hardware in a manner that would avoid public scrutiny.[20] By December 2001, the military objectives of a war on Iraq had been communicated to CENTCOM: regime change and the eradication of the threats Saddam Hussein posed.[21] By August 2002, a consensus among Bush and his closest advisers had formed that war in Iraq was necessary and desirable.[22]

The second stage in the US confrontation with Iraq featured an extensive and prolonged American diplomatic engagement with the United Nations. Although Secretary of State Colin Powell hoped that coercive diplomacy conducted under UN auspices might result in a solution short of war, Bush and Vice President Richard Cheney saw UN diplomacy as a means of reducing the international political costs that would result in an attack on Iraq, generally, and of facilitating British participation in the war effort, specifically.[23] After seven weeks of diplomatic wrangling, the UN Security

Council passed Resolution 1441 on November 8, 2002, which found Iraq to be in violation of its disarmament obligations under Resolution 687 passed after the Persian Gulf War. Iraq was given an opportunity to comply with those obligations or face "serious consequences." In order to demonstrate its compliance, Iraq was to allow international weapons inspectors unfettered access to all suspected WMD cites and to provide the Security Council with a declaration as to the status of its weapons programs within thirty days. On December 7, Iraq submitted its declaration, a twelve-thousand-page document that the United States deemed wholly unsatisfactory. At that point, extensive internal and international negotiations began as to whether a second UN Security Council resolution would be necessary before the war could commence. On March 12, 2003, after it became evident that France would veto any additional resolution, Bush informed the British prime minister, Tony Blair, that American diplomacy at the United Nations was finished.[24]

American diplomacy at the United Nations had a direct, and pernicious, effect on the US planning effort for postwar Iraq. Throughout this period, planning for postwar stability and reconstruction efforts began to take place across the US government. Yet these planning efforts occurred in isolation and were not drawn together under centralized direction until very late. Although Rumsfeld originally ordered CENTCOM to begin postwar stability and reconstruction planning in September 2002, it did so only in earnest after the final war plan, Cobra II, was published in February 2003.[25] The State Department had been engaged in a wide-ranging program, known as the Future of Iraq (FOI) project. The objective of FOI was to draw together Iraqi exiles, academics, and other experts to discuss critical issues that would confront the United States after a war with Iraq.[26] During the summer and fall of 2002, the under secretary of defense for policy, Douglas Feith, urged Rumsfeld repeatedly to create an interagency planning office that would coordinate the work being done across the government and to assume responsibility for postwar Iraq. On October 18, Rumsfeld directed Feith to begin setting up that office, but soon thereafter, Rumsfeld reversed his order. The reason for Rumsfeld's reversal was that President Bush made the decision that the establishment of an interagency office dedicated to Iraqi reconstruction at such an early date would be counterproductive to the diplomatic efforts at the United Nations.[27] It wasn't until January 20, 2003, that the president signed National Security Directive No. 24, the document that ordered the Office of Reconstruction and Humanitarian Assistance (ORHA) into existence.[28] In sum, on the eve of the Iraq War, the United

States possessed a military strategy that had been extensively scrutinized and reworked for a little less than a year and a half, but with a postwar office that had been in existence for only a matter of weeks.

On March 17, 2003, President Bush delivered an ultimatum to Saddam Hussein to either abdicate power peacefully or face an American-led invasion bent on overthrowing the regime. On March 19, the Iraq War commenced with an attempted decapitation strike against Saddam.[29] Having failed to take Saddam out quickly, the US-led coalition began the joint air and ground invasion of Iraq with a force size of roughly 162,000 the next day.[30] The invasion took place on two main fronts.[31] Special Operations Forces (SOF) linked with allied Kurdish fighters to secure a northern position designed to prevent thirteen Iraqi divisions from effectively moving southward.[32] In the south, the primary avenue of advance, US and British forces invaded Iraq from Kuwait along three axes. These forces moved quickly through the country despite facing tough battles at key river crossings and in the southern cities of Nasiriyah, Najaf, and Samawah. As coalition forces advanced, they witnessed many of Iraq's army units "melt away" among the civilian population and were surprised to find themselves in close contact with an irregular force loyal to the Iraqi dictator known as the Saddam Fedayeen.[33] On April 3, American forces began the first of two probes (known as Thunder Runs) into Baghdad, the effect of which was the dismantling of the city's defenses.[34] By April 9, Saddam's rule had effectively ended.

Major combat operations in Iraq lasted a mere twenty-one days and resulted in a military victory for the United States and its coalition partners. Two factors are responsible for this outcome. The first is that the Iraqi Army possessed little capacity for sustained combat effectiveness. The Iraqi military suffered from pathological behavior by officers throughout the ranks, was subject to tyrannical harassment by Saddam, and was organized in a manner that prevented concerted and efficient strategic planning.[35] The second is that the American military was particularly well suited to capitalize on numerous Iraqi military mistakes. At the tactical level, the lopsided outcome in major combat operations (MCOs) resulted from the absence of combat skill on the part of the Iraqis and the ability of coalition skill and technology to subject Iraqi forces to withering firepower.[36] Operationally and strategically, the American war plan was built on a sufficient base of information pertaining to support structures of the Iraqi regime and the nature of the deployment of Iraq's army. CENTCOM possessed solid intelligence on the Iraqi military formations coming from signals, imagery, and human intelligence sources. The available intelligence showed clearly that Saddam had not deployed his forces to counter a ground assault, and coalition forces exploited Saddam's failures to the fullest.[37]

The salutary effects of the coalition's military success in Iraq were short-lived, however. Almost immediately after the displacement of the regime, sporadic violence and widespread looting took place in Baghdad and other major centers throughout the country. This pattern of lawlessness continued for three weeks, the cumulative effect of which was the essential destruction of the state's administrative capacities.[38] The rapid deterioration of the security situation in Iraq resulted from a number of factors, including the civilian population's desperation after years of brutal governance, the release by Saddam of tens of thousands of prisoners from Iraqi jails before the war began, and the widespread availability of unguarded arsenals that criminals, civilians, and former regime loyalists could readily access.[39] Most critically, however, was the inability of the US military to respond to the security vacuum due to the relatively small size of the occupation force and the absence of appropriate rules of engagement for that force in the new environment. As a result, many Iraqi Sunnis—who constituted the vast majority of the state's governing structure—saw the American-led invasion, and the chaos that ensued, as a direct challenge to their standing in the country. Not only were Sunnis now denied the material privileges afforded to them by the regime, but also the overthrow of the regime amounted to a direct challenge to their identity as the rightful leaders of Iraq.[40] In short order, Sunni imams began directing popular frustration toward the Americans who had failed to provide basic security in the aftermath of major combat operations, and in some instances, gave vocal support to anticoalition attacks.[41]

By mid-May, the situation in Iraq had become precarious for American objectives. Despite the collapse of the Iraqi state, the exacerbation of the deep rifts within Iraqi society, and the rapidly deteriorating security situation, the insurgency in Iraq had yet to materialize. On May 23, L. Paul Bremer, head of the Coalition Provisional Authority, issued two directives that would effectively "catalyze" the Sunni insurgency.[42] The first order initiated an extensive program of de-Baathification of what remained of Iraq's governing structures. The second order called for the immediate disbanding of the entire Iraqi army. With the first order, up to 100,000 individuals were relieved of their positions due in large part to the manner in which the de-Baathification order was implemented. With the second order, at least 400,000 soldiers (trained and armed) were dismissed from duty. The purpose of these two orders was, in short, to facilitate the transition from dictatorship to democracy, the United States' most important diplomatic objective of the Iraq War. According to Bremer, the de-Baathification order was intended to prevent former regime loyalists from corrupting the process of creating an interim government that would design a new Iraqi constitution and legal code, as well as oversee economic reforms. The disbanding of the Iraqi Army was intended to pave the way for a New Iraqi Army, an organization that represented all aspects of Iraqi society and that would convince the civilian population that the old instruments of Saddam's repressive apparatus were gone for good.[43]

The effect of these two orders, however, stood in stark contrast to the desires and expectations of American officials. The scale of the CPA's de-Baathification policy effectively ripped apart the vital "administrative glue" of the Iraqi state, belied the fact that many party members had joined simply for personal advancement or survival, and was widely interpreted as an act of anti-Sunni bias on the part of the United States. The disbanding of the armed forces had an even more detrimental effect. For many Iraqis, the armed forces had become an "integral part of the identity of the state of Iraq." For the Sunni officer corps in particular, this order was a personal affront and a threat to their material well-being.[44] As one American official noted, the CPA's disbanding of the army "made 450,000 enemies on the ground in Iraq."[45] Combined, the CPA's two orders served as the proximate cause for the rise of the Sunni insurgency.[46] With no way to arrest the escalating violence in the country—due to the limited number of coalition forces committed to the invasion and to the inability to create an army from scratch in the short run[47]—the United States played the role of witness as Iraq's Sunni and Shia communities turned on each other. Based on the expectations and assumptions of top American officials, the diplomatic objectives of the Iraq War were lost by August 2003. At that point, American civilian and military officials began the painfully slow process of attempting to identify and navigate the complex environments of insurgency and communal civil war.[48]

A MODERATELY TRUNCATED INFORMATION INSTITUTION

Of the four limited wars considered, Iraq was the most ambitious in terms of the political objectives sought. To achieve success, the United States had to have all of the components of its strategy—for the war and its aftermath—fully integrated in the planning process and synchronized in their execution.[49] I argue that the United States was incapable of achieving such broad-scale integration due to the moderately truncated information institution through which strategic decision making was made. In terms of leaders' access to information, the information made available to top policy makers originated primarily from a single channel, the Defense Department. Critically, that channel possessed and transmitted a wealth of information to top policy makers, especially information pertaining to the war planning process. At the same time, the departments and agencies responsible for waging the military and diplomatic aspects of the war shared very little information and operated in near isolation from each other.

The Empowered Stovepipe

The defining feature of information management in the George W. Bush administration was the hybrid decision-making proclivities of the president. In general, Bush valued order and hierarchy, and as a "CEO President" he was inclined to delegate authority to his subordinates rather than to micromanage from the Oval Office. On issues that Bush deemed of lesser importance, his attention to detail was slight, thereby placing the onus on governmental departments and agencies to provide him with information.[50] Yet Bush was more than willing to insert himself directly into the policy process and engage an issue in detail, especially on matters that were central to his agenda. This decision-making style generated an advisory system that was an admixture of the hierarchical forms Eisenhower and Nixon employed, and the collegial system the Kennedy administration adopted.[51] Given the importance of presidential influence in spurring the bureaucracy to purposive action, the decision by the president to engage or delegate had a substantial effect on the quality of policy enacted.

There is widespread agreement among scholars and former administration officials that the NSC system was fundamentally broken in the George W. Bush administration. There are two primary reasons for this. The first was that critical elements of past NSC systems were either downgraded or terminated outright soon after Bush took office. On February 13, 2001, Bush signed National Security Presidential Directive (NSPD) 1, the initial document that laid out the structure of the National Security Council system for the administration. In many respects, NSPD 1 replicated organizational features of the George H. W. Bush and Clinton administrations. Most notably, the Principals Committee (PC) and Deputies Committee (DC) structure was retained. Yet in at least one critical respect, NSPD 1 was a definite break from the past. The president ordered the termination of the Clinton-era interagency coordinating forum for smaller-scale contingency operations. The purpose of this working group, known as Presidential Decision

Directive (PDD) 56, was to ensure tight coordination between the military and political components in armed conflicts. In deciding not to retain this working group, which proved successful in Kosovo in 1998–99, the incoming administration put on hold the explicit consideration of military and diplomatic coordination in limited warfare.[52]

The second reason for the NSC system's dysfunction was that it lacked effective management at the top. The twin responsibilities of the national security adviser, to serve the president as an honest broker of information and to effectively manage the interagency policy process, were never performed well by Condoleezza Rice. Rice recognized early on that her primary source of power and influence in the administration was to "translate Bush's instincts and intuitions into policy, to make sure his wishes became the government's commands." For Rice, communicating the president's agenda was her primary purpose.[53] Moreover, the information that Rice presented to Bush pertaining to the positions of PC members frequently papered over the sharp points of disagreements. As Feith notes,

> Rather than pass along to the President a disagreement in all its naked disharmony, Rice often crafted what she called a "bridging proposal"—an option that borrowed both from Powell's position and from the differing views of Rumsfeld or Cheney. This was supposed to mollify all the principals and relieve Bush of having to choose one department's position over another.[54]

The effects of this type of information reporting were detrimental in two ways: first, it presented the president with a false sense of concurrence among his senior advisers, granting the illusion of consensus when none was there; second, it prematurely cut off debate at the highest levels and prevented the president the opportunity to more fully probe the contending positions his top advisers held.[55] In understanding her role in this manner, Rice was unable to provide sufficient, unbiased information to Bush so that his decisions were based on more than gut reactions and to ensure that the multiple organs that constituted the government worked harmoniously to fulfill the president's commands.

In the hybrid advisory system of the George W. Bush administration, the role of the national security adviser was especially crucial. As the adviser to the president on national security affairs, Rice was the individual best suited to direct Bush's attention to matters that demanded presidential attention. Further, as the manager of the foreign policy process, Rice was the only administration official who could have ensured that those issues Bush preferred to delegate to others were handled properly, and not left to languish. In neither respect did Rice, nor the NSC system for which she was responsible, function effectively. In terms of directing presidential attention, the more powerful actors in the administration—Cheney and Rumsfeld—had far greater influence with Bush than Rice. And in terms of managing the foreign policy process, those more powerful actors had the ability to systematically influence which aspects of national security policy were acted upon, and which were not. Finally, in those instances when others were able to obtain presidential attention against the preferences of Cheney and Rumsfeld, little coordination among the various aspects of national security policy resulted.

Taken together, information management in the George W. Bush administration functioned as an empowered stovepipe. On matters the president deemed critical, his attention was focused and his influence keenly felt. On matters Bush considered less important, the president freely delegated to his subordinates. In terms of understanding the nature of the information institution in the George W. Bush administration, two critical issues must be addressed. First, who had sufficient influence over Bush to make sure that his attention was focused, thereby facilitating presidential influence on an important policy matter. Second, if the president were to delegate on a particular policy matter, to what extent would interagency coordination result?

Privileged Sources of Information

The center of gravity in the information institution of the George W. Bush administration was the alliance between Vice President Cheney and Secretary of Defense Rumsfeld. Cheney was the most influential administration official in directing Bush's attention to particularly important foreign policy matters.[56] Cheney possessed three critical assets that afforded him substantial influence. The first was the explicit trust that Bush placed in him. The two shared a deep-seated conservative outlook, and Bush respected and relied on Cheney's wealth of expertise and keen intellect.[57] Second, Cheney went to considerable lengths to expand the size and power of the Office of the Vice President (OVP). At the center of this office was the vice president's national security staff, an organization that was far more ideologically cohesive than the NSC staff, and which was empowered with direct policy-making responsibilities. The individual responsible for coordinating the work of Cheney's national security staff was I. Lewis "Scooter" Libby. Libby's influence within the government was extensive. In addition to serving as Cheney's national security adviser and his chief of staff, Libby was also granted the title of "assistant to the president." This last role afforded Libby access to meetings of the formal NSC and PC; he was one of only two individuals below the principal level who had such access (deputy national security adviser Stephen Hadley was the other). Libby's position placed him at the apex of two parallel channels within the White House. Although he reported to Cheney, he outranked everyone who reported to the president, except Rice, Bush's chief of staff Andrew Card, and political adviser Karl Rove—who were his peers. As Barton Gellman explains, "Libby would see and have the right to challenge any speech, legislation, or executive order before it reached the Oval Office."[58] Libby was a "force multiplier" for Cheney, so much so that in the words of one former NSC staffer, "Libby is able to 'run circles around Condi.'"[59]

The third of Cheney's assets was his powerful information network that enabled him to know better than any other administration official what was going on across the government. This network included Rumsfeld, Paul Wolfowitz, Feith, and William Luti in the Defense Department; Hadley, Zalmay Khalilzad, and Elliott Abrams on the NSC staff; John Bolton at the State Department; and of course any member of the vice president's national security staff who attended interagency meetings. Together, these assets enabled Cheney to exert more influence over Bush and the foreign policy process than any other official. Either directly, through his staff, or through his allies, Cheney was afforded unparalleled access to, and direction of, the foreign policy process.[60]

If Cheney was the individual who focused Bush's national security agenda most effectively, Rumsfeld was the most influential official to translate that agenda into policy and strategy. Rumsfeld was determined that the Office of the Secretary of Defense (OSD) serve as the central information conduit linking the president to the military. Rumsfeld insisted that he act as the sole source of information pertaining to military affairs for the president and the NSC, and that through him, Bush's policy objectives be effectively translated into military missions of all sorts.

Rumsfeld was able to secure this position in the information institution in two ways. First, he was intent on preventing any potential information competitors throughout the government from influencing military affairs. Rumsfeld's initial efforts focused on reducing what he saw as undue influence afforded to the Joint Chiefs of Staff (JCS) during the Clinton administration. Rumsfeld's early relations with General Hugh Shelton, the chairman of the JCS selected during the previous administration, were exceptionally tense. On numerous occasions, Rumsfeld lambasted Shelton and his Joint

Staff for failing to make him aware of ongoing military operations, charging that the military was flouting the proper chain of command. On October 1, 2001, Bush replaced Shelton with General Richard Myers. The Myers appointment signaled that the JCS would no longer have an independent voice in military policy. Under Myers, the Joint Chiefs were extraordinarily deferential to Rumsfeld, so much so that the chairman of the JCS lost the ability to select officers on the Joint Staff.[61] The secretary of defense was now the sole source of advice to the president on military matters.[62]

Similarly, Rumsfeld succeeded in diminishing the authority and influence of the NSC staff shortly after 9/11. In a memo to Rice pertaining to the appointment of Wayne Downing to head the NSC's new counterterrorism position, Rumsfeld charged that it was "dangerous, exceedingly dangerous" for anyone outside the chain of command to influence mission planning and execution. As Daalder and Destler note, Rumsfeld pointedly made Rice aware that she was not in the chain of command.[63] As Rumsfeld's pique over Rice's handling of the interagency process grew, he began bypassing her altogether, preferring to obtain access to Bush through his chief of staff, Andrew Card. Finally, to prevent the NSC staff from providing the president with independent information, Rumsfeld granted little authority to his deputies, preventing the DC from serving as an independent source of information to the PC and the president.[64]

Rumsfeld was in constant contact with Franks as the Iraq war plan took shape, taking a hands-on approach by questioning the assumptions guiding the use of force and pushing Franks on highly detailed matters ranging from air targeting, troop deployments, operational concepts, and such. By February 7, 2002, the day on which Franks first briefed the president on the state of CENTCOM's war plan, the commander's concept had been through five iterations, each of which had been thoroughly evaluated by the secretary of defense. At the same time, Rumsfeld went to significant lengths to include Bush in the military strategic decision-making process. On multiple occasions, Franks briefed Bush on the status of the evolving war plan, and Bush provided Franks with feedback regarding his overall objectives and political concerns.[65]

Rumsfeld's intention was to serve as an effective bridge between the combatant commander and the president, to be a "true channel" of information so that Bush's policy objectives would be effectively translated into military strategy.[66] Yet information within that channel flowed primarily from Rumsfeld to Franks. In order to provide Bush with as much flexibility as possible in deciding when to initiate hostilities, Rumsfeld set highly restrictive conditions on how the military could conduct the war. The secretary set those conditions without seeking or receiving advice from the uniformed military apart from Franks and his team, even going so far as to forbid Franks from consulting with the former commander of CENTCOM, General Anthony Zinni, "the man who knew more about Middle Eastern history, culture, and leaders than any other senior officer in the U.S. military." Rumsfeld's determination to ensure that the president's preferences dominated the war planning process had the effect of isolating Franks from the rest of the US military. The result was a war plan for major combat operations only, not one capable of handling the full spectrum of military operations necessary to achieve the strategic objectives of the war.[67]

Additionally, the bulk of the government's postwar planning efforts, as well as the administration of Iraq in the aftermath of MCOs, fell under Rumsfeld's purview. In October 2002, Bush made the decision to tap the DOD to take the lead in postwar planning, but it was not until January 20, 2003, that this directive was made official in NSPD 24. In short, preparing for the two critical postwar challenges, providing security and political/economic reconstruction, were the primary responsibility of the DOD.

Two elements within the US military were tasked with planning postcombat stability operations. The Combined Forces Land Component Command (CFLCC) was given the lead in this mission in January 2002. After a CENTCOM-sponsored war game in December demonstrated that little attention had been paid to the relationship between combat and stability operations, Lieutenant General George Casey, J5 director on the Joint Staff, created a planning cell known as Task Force IV (TFIV). The relationship between CFLCC and TFIV was confused and dysfunctional, however.

> CFLCC's planning staff envisioned that TFIV would only assume responsibilities for Phase IV [stability] operations after the CFLCC redeployed to the United States. However, the commander of TFIV believed he was given full responsibility for Phase IV planning. As a result, the CFLCC C5 and the TFIV conducted parallel planning for the same mission. Little direct coordination occurred between the two planning staffs, though the TFIV commander met regularly with the C5 and the deputy commander of CFLCC to share information . . . instead of working closely with CFLCC. . . . Task Force IV never effectively coordinated its work on Phase IV with the CFLCC planners responsible for Phase I through III [MCOs].[68]

With respect to postwar reconstruction, the head of the Office of Reconstruction and Humanitarian Assistance, Jay Garner, was given only a few weeks to set up his office and establish ties with CENTCOM and the various entities across the government that had been conducting aspects of postwar planning. According to NSPD 24, Garner's mission was to help the United States meet the "humanitarian, reconstruction, and administration challenges facing the country [Iraq] in the immediate aftermath of the combat operations." ORHA would be responsible for "detailed planning across the spectrum of issues that the United States Government would face with respect to the postwar administration of Iraq," including all of the security, economic, and political matters. Although the directive stipulated that ten agencies immediately provide ORHA with experts, and that it would be the responsibility of the ORHA administrator to coordinate the interagency process pertaining to postwar Iraq, ORHA's location in the information institution fell squarely under Rumsfeld, coequal to CENTCOM.[69]

ORHA was disbanded only a few months after its inception, and the Coalition Provisional Authority was established in its place. CPA's mission was similarly wide ranging. CPA's two primary objectives were "to set Iraq on the path to a more open, humane and democratic society . . . [and] to reform Iraq's closed and moribund economy."[70] Bremer described his role: "As the senior American in Baghdad, I would be President George W. Bush's personal envoy. My chain of command ran through Secretary of Defense Donald Rumsfeld and straight to the president." Bremer discovered quickly that this reporting and command structure prevented him from communicating with other relevant US government agencies. Reports and memos sent to Rumsfeld were not shared with anyone outside the Pentagon. This situation began to improve only after the two crucial CPA directives had been issued. Even so, Rice found it necessary to instruct NSC staffers to bypass formal channels (that is, to circumvent the DOD) in order to receive any information from the CPA. Furthermore, although Bremer had no authority over the 170,000 troops in Iraq, whose mission it was to provide for the country's security, CENTCOM "had orders from the president and Rumsfeld to coordinate their operations with the CPA and me [Bremer]."[71] Nevertheless, relations between the staffs of the CPA and military were fraught with tension, a situation described by Ricardo Sanchez, commander of Combined Joint Task Force 7, as "devastating" to effective political-military operations in Iraq.[72]

As secretary of defense, Rumsfeld's most important objective was to enact the president's military transformation agenda, a complete overhaul of the military's principles and policies pertaining to procurement, budgeting, and the use of force. To Rumsfeld, the primary threat to the United States in an era of global military preponderance was not located abroad, but rather in the sprawling Pentagon bureaucracy. In this mission to transform the military, Rumsfeld's appetite for raw data and analysis was immense, and he was indefatigable in his search for information. Rumsfeld adopted what was known as the "snowflake" system. Short and terse, Rumsfeld's "memos served to give lower-ranking officials a more direct window into the secretary's thinking than they might otherwise have had," and allowed him to acquire a great deal of information quickly by cutting through multiple layers within the Pentagon's bureaucracy.[73]

Rumsfeld was intent on having his subordinates rethink long-standing assumptions, to transform the American military in ways that would enable it to act more effectively in the post–Cold War security environment, and to ensure that the he was squarely in the chain of command (at the expense of the uniformed military and other departments and agencies). Guiding all of this were Rumsfeld's own ideas pertaining to how the president should deal with the military and how the United States should use force. Despite his disdain for the Pentagon's bureaucracy, Rumsfeld was influenced by his own parochial preferences, which prevented him from subjecting his ideas to the rigorous tests he imposed on others. Rumsfeld was a decision maker empowered to the hilt by virtue of his access to both Bush and Cheney, and armed with a massive amount of information. But this was information with a particular purpose and was narrowly focused. Contradictory information and advice, especially if it originated from outside Rumsfeld's understanding of the "chain of command," was seen as irrelevant at best, threatening at worst.[74] In short, Rumsfeld was able to serve Bush as a powerful source of information. But the information he presented originated from a system that was prone to allowing rosy scenarios to dominate.[75]

The absence of a fully empowered and effectively managed NSC system enabled the alliance of Cheney and Rumsfeld to become the center of gravity in the information institution. The result was that the information these sources provided dominated the assessments of the key decision makers in the administration. Under these circumstances, information originating from the intelligence community (IC) and State Department had little influence in determining whether and how the United States would wage war against Iraq.[76]

Neither Cheney nor Rumsfeld wanted the CIA to play an influential role either in the decision to go to war or how that war would be prosecuted. Cheney in particular held the CIA in low regard. Not only was the former secretary of defense dismayed when it was revealed how precious little the agency knew about the state of Iraq's WMD program in the aftermath of the Persian Gulf War, but he also found the CIA's risk-averse culture to be dangerous in the post-9/11 world. For his part, Rumsfeld was intent on having the Defense Department take the lead in Iraq, as it was unable to do in Afghanistan.[77] Through their efforts, the CIA's participation in the decision-making process, both at the highest levels—over whether to go to war, and if so, what the likely challenges would be—and at the military-strategic level—over how to manage contingencies during and after major combat operations—was severely restricted.[78] To the extent that information from the intelligence community contradicted the policy preferences of Cheney and Rumsfeld, it was manipulated so as to lessen its impact.[79]

For the most part, the ability of the State Department to influence decision making through information was limited. The primary channel through which the DOS could exert influence was through the NSC system. Yet as will be discussed below the NSC system had very little impact on the design and implementation of Iraq policy. Powell never developed a close working relationship with Bush, and as a result, was unable to acquire as much access to the president as Cheney, Rumsfeld, and Rice had.[80] The clearest indication of this is when, in July 2002, Powell learned from his deputy Richard Haass that, according to Rice, Bush had concluded that a confrontation with Iraq was all but inevitable. The circuitous manner in which the secretary of state came about this information epitomizes the extent to which the DOS was without influence at the upper reaches of the administration.[81] Still, Powell was able to affect American policy toward Iraq in a profound manner. On August 5, 2002, Powell met with Bush and Rice alone to make the case that war with Iraq would have substantial implications for American foreign policy. Powell urged Bush to seek international and congressional backing before making the decision to go to war. Bush was determined to retain the main outlines of his policy. Nevertheless, the president agreed to follow the advice of his secretary of state, but only to the extent that it enabled key allies to participate in the war effort.[82]

Within the American information institution, the State Department and CIA had few points of access to the strategic decision-making process. The information that the president received came almost exclusively from the OVP and OSD. The dominance of the OVP/OSD information alliance—the empowered stovepipe—would prevent top policy makers from receiving an accurate understanding of the dynamic strategic environment in Iraq.

Severed Lines of Communication: An NSC System in Name Only

In addition to serving as the dominant source of information in national security affairs, it was the Cheney/Rumsfeld stovepipe wherein the vast majority of war and postwar planning efforts took place. Because these crucial elements of the Iraq War did not fall under the purview of the NSC system, the relationship between postwar planning and American diplomacy at the United Nations failed to attract much administrative attention. The departments and agencies responsible for planning and executing the various aspects of America's Iraq strategy were not connected by lateral channels of communication, as would have resulted if the political-military working group in PDD 56 had been retained. In the George W. Bush information institution, the NSC system existed in name only.

Nominally, Iraq policy fell under the purview of a number of hierarchically situated interagency groups. As stipulated in NSPD 1, the PC and DC remained intact and were represented by all of the relevant agencies. Under the DC, an Executive Steering Group (ESG) for Iraq policy was constituted that focused on strategic planning and policy recommendations for DC meetings. Under the ESG, the Iraq Political-Military Cell (IPMC) was charged with integrating planning efforts regarding postwar stabilization and the transition to Iraqi sovereignty. The Iraq Relief and Reconstruction (IR+R) task force was responsible for planning immediate humanitarian relief operations as well as reconstruction over the long term. Finally, the Coalition Working Group was tasked with coordinating the military and diplomatic elements necessary to build and maintain the international coalition. Each of these groups was represented by the responsible operational department, including the NSC staff, DOS, DOD, CIA, and OVP. This interagency structure took shape in July 2002.[83]

On paper, this was a system that had all of the hallmarks of a robust information institution. It was situated within the interagency NSC system, was widely represented, and was established well before the commencement of hostilities. However, this system was never empowered with actual policy-making responsibilities, suffered from a lack of competent management, and the actual quality of the products of each group was spotty at best. Ideally, the PC and DC existed to provide the president and NSC with options and advice at the highest level of decision making. These committees function best when all views are represented clearly and when the principals and deputies are able to establish the contours of coordination for their staffs at lower levels. These committees become dysfunctional when particular agencies are systematically marginalized in the decision-making process, or when the performances of agencies are not monitored effectively. Marginalization was the fate of the State Department on the PC.[84] For its part, the DC was the exemplar of dysfunction, a conclusion reached by those in the State and Defense Departments alike. Deputy secretary of state

Richard Armitage made Rice aware of this directly. As Daalder and Destler recount, Armitage told Rice she was running a "dysfunctional" process.

> "You don't resolve things," he told her. Defense was running roughshod over the interagency process. Rumsfeld and his aides were conducting their own foreign policy. Deputies and Principals Committee meetings were useless. "We'd get on the gerbil wheel every morning getting ready for these DCs and PCs," Armitage said later. "Then we'd get off the gerbil wheel and wait for an answer. No answer would ever come from the NSC, so we'd get back on the gerbil wheel the next morning." And when decisions were made, there was no follow-through by the agencies and no price to be paid for failing to do so. The problem, Armitage told Rice, was an absence of execution and a complete lack of accountability—especially on the trio of issues that mattered most: Iraq, Iran, and North Korea.[85]

Feith was also of the opinion that the performance of these committees was lacking, and he too points to the absence of quality leadership at the top as the reason.

> Regarding Iraq, the interagency process made it easier for Powell and Armitage to affect Administration policy through passivity and delaying tactics. When Cabinet consensus was required to bring forward a particular proposal to the President . . . it was easy for State officials to block the initiative for weeks or months—without having to explain themselves to the President.[86]

To be sure, the Defense Department exhibited similar behavior at DC meetings, especially on matters Rumsfeld was determined to control. As Rumsfeld's aide, Steve Herbits, described, "The fighting between State and Defense was so bad that interagency meetings were at times little more than shouting matches"[87]

In the summer of 2002, the Joint Staff conducted a series of war games to assess the status of the war and postwar planning efforts. Realizing that no interagency structure existed to support these exercises, Casey urged creation of the ESG and IPMC. In August, Frank Miller began leading the ESG, and until March 2003 the group met three times per week. ESG's responsibility covered a host of political and military planning issues, all of which required intensive interagency collaboration. If the members of the ESG could not reach consensus on particular matters, the issue was to be sent to the DC, and PC if necessary, for resolution. ESG meetings were not always attended by every agency, however, nor were there dedicated ESG representatives assigned by the participating departments. OSD, for example, had inconsistent representation, and many of the officials who did attend lacked the authority to actually make decisions. Interagency coordination suffered in the ESG because OSD was the only organization that could connect those planning the war (CENTCOM and CFLCC) to those responsible for issuing strategic guidance.[88] Miller soon discovered that much of his time would be dedicated to attempting to coordinate elements within the DOD. Feith's policy office in the OSD, the Joint Staff, and CENTCOM, for example, operated independently from each other. "Communications between the civilian and military sides of the Defense Department," Miller noted, "are catastrophically broken."[89] Finally, the IPMC, which had responsibility for postwar stability and reconstruction planning, was not well integrated into the structure as defined by Casey and empowered by the DC. The vast majority of its focus dealt with postwar humanitarian issues, and the work of the IR+R proved valuable in this endeavor. But because ESG was unable to offer much in the way of political-military guidance on postwar stability and reconstruction, this critical planning component languished.[90] Nor was the Future of Iraq project run by the State Department represented in the IPMC. In the end, the interagency structure within the NSC system proved ineffective in coordinating the planning efforts for the war and its aftermath.

The three crucial areas that together prefigured diplomatic failure in Iraq—troop size, UN diplomacy, and postwar planning and operations—were treated as isolated policy matters rather than as interrelated components of a broader strategic plan. Planning for war took place strictly within the Rumsfeld-Franks channel. At the initial phases, war planning was limited to a small number of senior officials at CENTCOM and CFLCC. During the 2002–early 2003 period, the number of planning staffs within CENTCOM and CFLCC grew in size, but it wasn't until October 2002 that the classification level of OPLAN 1003V was downgraded to "Secret," the level at which the most detailed planning could be conducted. The primary problem that would plague the military's planning efforts, especially for the postwar phase, was the lack of clear strategic guidance for integrating political, economic, and military efforts for stabilization and reconstruction.[91] There are three reasons for this. First, Rumsfeld was determined to prevent concerns over the postwar phase from influencing the war planning process, especially if those concerns affected the timing of the start of the war.[92] DOD officials were barred from participating in postwar war gaming exercises sponsored by other agencies (that is, the CIA), and elements within the DOD itself which voiced concerns pertaining to postwar planning were not incorporated into the planning process (that is, the Strategic Studies Institute at the Army War College). Second, within the Pentagon there was a persistent lack of coordination between civilian and military officials over the nature of postwar strategy.[93] Finally, there was confusion as to who was actually responsible for postwar stability and reconstruction.[94]

With respect to actual postwar planning, NSPD 24 was clear that an interagency staff would constitute ORHA and that the office would report to the secretary of defense. Nevertheless, Rumsfeld and Cheney went to great lengths to prevent ORHA from being a true interagency organization. For example, Rumsfeld sought to exclude numerous DOS officials who had been selected by Garner to critical posts in ORHA.[95] And the director of the Future of Iraq project, Tom Warrick, was barred from ORHA over Garner's strong objections.[96] Evidently, neither Bush nor Rice understood the implications of the postwar administration established under NSPD 24. As Powell explained to them in early March 2003, Rumsfeld sat at the apex of two chains of command, one military and one diplomatic.

> When you have two chains of command and you don't have a common superior in the theater, it means that every little half-assed fight they have out there, if they can't work it out, comes out to one place to be resolved. And that's in the Pentagon. Not in the NSC or State Department, but in the Pentagon.[97]

This situation placed Rumsfeld in the position of responsibility for all aspects of the combat and postwar phases of the war in Iraq.

The one issue that played a key role in delaying the creation of a truly empowered postwar planning office, American diplomacy at the United Nations, was the subject of intense interagency deliberation. Throughout the summer and fall of 2002, the DC and PC debated the merits and content of UN Security Council resolutions, and it was Rice's NSC staff that produced the "Ultimatum Strategy" that the United States would pursue through the United Nations.[98] Despite the intensity of interagency input, the connection between American diplomacy and postwar planning efforts was never addressed directly. There are two reasons for this lack of coordination. The first is that unlike UN diplomatic initiatives, postwar planning fell under the purview of Rumsfeld's OSD and were not the direct responsibility of any interagency forum. Second, extant interagency bodies were not sufficiently empowered to reconcile the various strands of the evolving Iraq War strategy. The logical place for coordination to have occurred was the DC, ESG, IPMC, and Coalition Working Group channel. Because Rumsfeld retained possession of war and postwar planning matters, explicit coordination of the diplomatic and postwar efforts never occurred. Perhaps unwittingly,

Powell abetted the critical lapse in oversight by agreeing to have DOD take the lead in postwar stability and reconstruction efforts.[99]

In sum, the United States entered the war with a moderately truncated information institution. Information pertaining to the multifaceted strategic environment originated primarily from the Cheney/Rumsfeld stovepipe. Because of the wealth of information the DOD possessed, however, the president and his top advisers were fully advised on the war planning process and had the capacity to ensure that military strategy accurately incorporated the military objectives determined by the president. On the other hand, information from the intelligence community and State Department was largely given short shrift due to the marginalization of these entities at the top. Moreover, few information channels connected agencies and departments together and, as a result, information sharing occurred only at the margins. Again, the notable exception to this pattern was the war planning process. Information from the intelligence community pertaining to the state of Iraq's military and regime support structures flowed directly to CENTCOM. Combined, America's information institution contained an empowered stovepipe, one that would guide strategic decision making by selecting and privileging information based on its source and preferred nature of its content. Thus the information institution approach expects the United States to possess moderate collection and fair analytic capabilities, and to experience poor coordination among the military and diplomatic aspects of the war.

DECISION MAKING IN THE EMPOWERED STOVEPIPE

American strategic performance in the critical early phase of the Iraq War was powerfully affected by decisions made on three key issues: (1) the nature of the American military's approach to waging the ground campaign, (2) when and how to plan for postwar reconstruction, and (3) the future status of Baath Party members in the government and the size and mission of the Iraqi Army after the war.

Planning for Combat and Postcombat Stabilization—Failure to Confront Trade-Offs

Between November 2001 and December 2002, Rumsfeld and Franks continuously developed the Iraq war plan. A number of objectives influenced the planning process, all of which derived from guidance Franks received from top policy makers through Rumsfeld. The ultimate military objective in the war was the overthrow of Saddam's regime. Toward that end, Rumsfeld pressed Franks to design a war plan that compressed the time from presidential decision to the commencement of hostilities. Moreover, in order to avoid undercutting American diplomatic efforts (either at the United Nations or elsewhere), the deployment of forces to the region had to be done in as quiet a fashion as possible, entailing the piecemeal positioning of forces over a period of many months. For Rumsfeld, these latter two objectives required the United States to go to war with the fewest number of troops as possible. Finally, in order to avoid a long and bloody war, Rumsfeld insisted that the operational tempo of the war be a rapid as possible. If the United States were able to launch the war (and achieve at least tactical, if not strategic surprise) and advance to Baghdad expeditiously, civilian officials at the Pentagon expected the war to be won in a very short period of time.[100] After a relatively brief period of postcombat occupation, American troops could begin withdrawing from the theater.

Early in the planning process, Rumsfeld made it clear that that United States was not going to be caught off guard should the president make a decision to go to war against Iraq. In the winter of 2001, Rumsfeld impressed upon Franks the necessity of compressing the decision-to-invasion time as much as possible. To some extent, Franks concurred, yet informed Rumsfeld that rapidly transforming OPLAN 1003 (the extant Iraq war plan) would be dangerous. Any changes to the war plan would have to be methodological, though not necessarily slow. Rumsfeld ordered Franks to begin that work, as well as to commence planning for the quiet prepositioning of military assets to the region.[101]

Franks briefed the first iteration of the war plan, Generated Start, to Bush's war cabinet on February 7, 2002. The concept entailed three phases: a ninety-day period to prepare and position forces in the region; a forty-five-day period of combined air and Special Forces attacks designed to prepare for the ground invasion; and a ninety-day ground assault phase with two (possibly three) corps.[102] The total invasion force envisioned started with 145,000 troops, but would grow overtime, possibly to as high as 275,000.[103] Neither Rumsfeld nor Franks were pleased with this initial concept. For Cheney, the proposed plan took far too long to unfold.

At the same time that CENTCOM was working on the Generated Start concept, Franks was already thinking of ways to reduce the number of troops necessary and to shorten the first two phases of the war to reduce the decision-to-invasion window. On April 20, Franks indicated to Bush that such revisions were possible. Bush was encouraged with the prospect but urged Franks to think about ways to wage war in the shortest amount of time possible. Top on the list of presidential concerns was the prospect of a long war and the myriad regional problems that would ensue. On May 11, Franks briefed Bush again on the latest iteration of the Generated Start plan. At that meeting, Bush, Card, and Rice expressed concerns that Saddam might respond to an American invasion by withdrawing his troops into the city of Baghdad, thus forcing the United States to engage in bloody and slow-going urban warfare. Dubbed the "Fortress of Baghdad" scenario, Franks was urged to consider ways of avoiding this outcome. Finally, on May 24, Franks briefed Rumsfeld, Bush, and his combatant commanders on the alternative to Generated Start. The alternative concept, Running Start, was appealing to the secretary of defense and president because it short-ened the decision-to-invasion window by trimming the number of forces committed to the early periods of the invasion and contained measures to counter the Fortress of Baghdad contingency.

Running Start was a plan that could be employed if a decision to go to war was made in the very short run. The problem was that it entailed a great deal of risk, especially for the lead elements of the invading force. Franks thus prodded his planners to consider ways of reducing the risk while simultaneously ensuring that the objectives and conditions Bush and Rumsfeld gave him were met. A third planning variant, the Hybrid plan, was the result, and on August 5 Franks briefed Bush and the NSC on its elements. Hybrid contained four phases. Phase I was made up of a five-day period to establish an air bridge into Iraq and an eleven-day period to transport the initial troops into the country. In Phase II, Special Forces and air operations would take place for sixteen days to prepare for the ground invasion and secure oil fields from sabotage. Phase III envisioned a 125-day-long ground assault period. During the first week, a division would bear the brunt of the operations, but would be augmented with additional forces thereafter. Phase IV, postcombat stability operations, would follow, but the specific mission and duration were unknown to Franks at the time.

After hearing the briefing, Bush declared that he "liked the concept." Franks went on to discuss matters that could significantly challenge the plan, as well as issues that CENTCOM still had to address. One of these was the number of troops required for Phase IV stability operations. Recognizing that events in Iraq would determine the timing of the withdrawal of forces, Franks believed that the invasion force of up to 265,000 would be drawn down to 50,000 over an eighteen-month period. On August 6, Franks made it clear that Hybrid would be the plan. Tellingly, Franks referred to this iteration as the "5-11-16-125" plan.[104] Those were the number of days that made up phases I–III. Phase IV was clearly an afterthought.

To CFLCC commander David McKiernan, Franks's Hybrid plan was essentially the same as the Running Start plan and did little to alleviate the substantial risks the latter entailed. Specifically, Running Start contained so little combat power at the opening of the invasion that lead elements would have to delay their advance shortly after it began and wait for reinforcements to flow in. Moreover, the overall plan called for far too few troops to deal with the possible postcombat instability should Saddam's regime collapse completely and quickly. Because the president had decided to take the Iraq issue to the United Nations, McKiernan recognized that a compressed decision-to-invasion window was unnecessary, given the risks entailed. There was time to build up more forces prior to the onset of war.[105]

CFLCC then began work on the fourth iteration of the war plan, Cobra II, which was closer in size to the original Generated Start concept. Reflecting the objectives of Bush, Rice, and Card, Fortress Baghdad countermeasures were built in, as were plans to bypass Iraq's southern cities so that the invading force could advance through the country as quickly as possible. Although he was convinced of the merits of this final variant, Franks recognized two issues straightaway. First, because of its relatively larger force requirement, Cobra II would necessitate a "chunky TPFDL," or the Time Phased Force Deployment List—the process by which the US military mobilizes and deploys for combat. Second, based on his frequent interactions with his civilian masters, there would be significant pressures to stem the flow of follow-on forces should the regime collapse quickly.

Rumsfeld approved Cobra II in December 2002. The secretary of defense insisted, however, that he control the number, composition, and timing of the forces deployed in the upcoming war. Rumsfeld insisted on keeping the TPFDL in his hands in part because he wanted to avoid undermining ongoing American diplomacy at the United Nations.[106] At the same time, Rumsfeld considered the TPFDL to be an anachronism of the Cold War that took decision making out of his hands. In assuming responsibility for the military's deployment scheme, Rumsfeld was able to winnow down the number of forces ultimately deployed to the battle. The United States invaded Iraq with a force size of 145,000 troops.[107]

CFLCC planning for postwar stability operations began in earnest in February 2003 after Cobra II was officially published. A number of assumptions informed this planning process, among them was that additional forces beyond those slated for the invasion would be necessary for Phase IV operations. Additionally, surrendered Iraqi army units would have to be remobilized and employed in security operations. The plan identified seven areas of concentration in the postwar period: ensuring the rule of law, providing security, supporting civil administration, providing assistance to civilian governance, maintaining and enlarging the coalition, providing emergency humanitarian assistance if necessary, and assisting in the restoration and repair of Iraqi infrastructure.

A number of problems plagued the postwar stability component of the plan. The first and most glaring problem was that the plan was completed at the end of April 2003, after the fall of the regime and the widespread looting that followed. Moreover, the required augmentation of American forces did not occur after the fall of the regime. Lastly, the plan assumed incorrectly that the US military would be in a supporting, rather than leading, position in the postwar period.[108] Nevertheless, at the end of major combat operations, Franks was of the opinion that US forces could be drawn down to 32,000 (the size of a single division) by September, assuming all went well.[109]

Iraq war planning was the product of the Rumsfeld-CENTCOM-CFLCC stovepipe. Through this channel the president and his top advisers received the vast majority of their information pertaining to the strategic environment, and as a result the assumptions held by those in that channel were imposed on those at the top.[110] Few other sources of information influenced the manner in which top policy makers viewed the upcoming war, and as a result, the president's attention was directed to the first three phases of the war, at the expense of the fourth. Rumsfeld was able to thwart other departments and agencies from influencing the war planning process in ways that cut against the secretary of defense's preferences. For example, Rumsfeld prevented other principals from having access to the war plans prior to their being briefed on it, and insisted that all copies of the briefing slides be returned to him after PC meetings.[111] Frank Miller at the ESG made repeated attempts to circumvent Rumsfeld's grip on the planning process. Using back channels through the Joint Staff, Miller quietly shared information regarding the war plan with Powell and Armitage in December 2002. As Bradley Graham notes, "such surreptitious tactics to ensure that senior officials remained up-to-date on important planning elements reflected the dysfunctional nature of the interagency process—both Rumsfeld's wariness of sharing and Rice's inability to enforce great cooperation and information flow."[112]

At most, information from other sources was allowed to factor in to the planning and execution of the offensive in a support capacity. To a considerable extent, this information proved valuable in the war. From satellite and other imagery intelligence, communications and signals intelligence, and human assets from the CIA, Franks had an accurate understanding of the tactical formations of the Iraq's military.[113] As the authors of the military's official history of Operation Iraqi Freedom conclude,

> On balance, military intelligence and national intelligence, surveillance, and reconnaissance means worked well. For the most part, CFLCC knew where the Iraq uniformed forces were, could target them, and could provide data on their whereabouts to tactical units.

The tracking of Iraq's paramilitary units (that is, the Saddam Fedayeen) proved more difficult, however.[114]

Ultimately, this empowered stovepipe generated a war plan that was capable of obtaining America's military objectives but was incapable of securing its diplomatic objectives. Due to Rumsfeld's near information monopoly in the war planning process, contrary information was prevented from influencing top policy makers' understanding of the strategic environment or from affecting the war plan in any meaningful sense. Information that challenged the assumptions of the war planners was available within the US government. Yet due to the isolated nature of the war planning process, that information did not receive a comprehensive hearing at the top, nor was it incorporated into the war planning process. Information from the State Department, intelligence community, and even from within the Defense Department was available that, if heeded, would have enabled the United States to be in a much better position to secure its nonmilitary objectives in the Iraq War.

Run by the DOS, the Future of Iraq project generated a massive amount of information pertaining to a host of issues that the United States would likely confront in the event of war. As many scholars and commentators have noted, the project's conclusions were not actual planning documents— but they were never intended to be such. Yet the project constituted the most comprehensive attempt by the US government to grapple with postwar issues, and a number of the conclusions and recommendations were solid and prescient. With respect to postwar stabilization, the project warned that "the removal of Saddam's regime will provide a power vacuum and create popular anxieties about the viability of all Iraqi institutions." FOI went on to note that "the period immediately after regime change might offer these criminals the opportunity to engage in acts of killing, plunder, and looting."[115] It was essential that the US military have the capability of dealing with this likely contingency. FOI also concluded that a great deal of care had to be taken when demobilizing Iraq's army. While many of Saddam's "henchmen" had to be removed, a functioning army would be necessary for public order.[116] Where CFLCC planners assumed that the defeated army would be available for such services, FOI offered a series of recommendations as to how best to plan for "disarmament, demobilization, and reintegration" of the army.[117] As it was, FOI had no impact on the war planning effort. As Rumsfeld explains,

> The Future of Iraq papers were likely circulated at lower levels within the government, as is often the case with concepts and proposals. But I was not aware of an effort by any senior official at State to present these papers for interagency review or evaluation, as would certainly have been needed had they been intended as a plan. The notion that a few in the State Department may have alerted people to potential problems in postwar Iraq—even if quite helpfully—was not on its face a seminal achievement.[118]

The director of policy planning at the State Department, Richard Haass, drafted memos that warned of similar outcomes in postwar Iraq. One in particular examined the history of nation building and the lessons that could readily be applied in the current context. Among its conclusions was the recognition that all successful national building efforts in the past were based on "a bedrock of basic security," and that everything possible had to be done to avoid the creation of a postwar power vacuum. Not only did this imply that the United States had to commit a substantial number of forces for the stabilization effort, but also that the "rebuilding of police and military forces making use of many of those who had been serving in existing forces" had to occur quickly. This memo was circulated in September of 2002, but its impact on the war and postwar planning process was negligible.[119]

Information from the CIA was similarly disconnected from the military planning efforts and did not make its way to the top policy makers. In May 2002, the CIA initiated a long series of war games, the intention of which was to assess the likely outcomes in the aftermath of a war for regime change. Among the recurring themes of the war games was the risk of chaos after major combat operations terminated. Representatives from the DOD participated very early on in these exercises, but when the OSD learned of their participation, they were barred from any further involvement in the project.[120]

Throughout 2002, the intelligence community issued a number of reports warning that the objectives the United States sought in the war would be undermined if the stabilization mission failed. In August, the CIA produced an assessment of the challenges that would likely face the United States in postwar Iraq drawing on the lessons learned from its experience in managing postwar Germany and Japan. The CIA assessed that the challenges in Iraq would likely be more difficult than those after World War II. Critical to success would be "the ability of the occupation forces to control the security situation." This task would be so difficult because "the religious and cultural gap between occupying Western forces and the Iraqi population" would be wider than what was the case in Germany or even Japan. The report stipulated that "the transformation of Iraq to a true democracy could require a US role lasting a generation."[121] In October the CIA produced a report of a simulation exercise on postwar challenges. The report noted that Iraq's Sunni population were the "most likely targets of score-settling" and are "likely to perceive the United States as the enemy."[122] Finally, in January 2003, the National Intelligence Council (NIC) issued a report titled "Principal Challenges in Post-Saddam Iraq." Among the NIC's key judgments was the finding that

> Iraq would be unlikely to split apart, but a post-Saddam authority would face a deeply divided society with a significant chance that domestic groups would engage in violent conflict with each other unless an occupying force prevented them from doing so.[123]

The last and most comprehensive of these reports made clear that the occupying force had to have postcombat stabilization as a key objective. These conclusions, however, never made their way into the war planning process. As the Scope Note states, the NIC produced this paper at the request of the director of policy planning at the Department of State. These forecasts were based on sound regional and country experience, proved to be accurate, but had no discernable impact on the decision-making process.[124]

Among the deleterious effects of Rumsfeld's control over the war planning process was the isolation of CENTCOM and CFLCC from the rest of the American military.[125] Many within the DOD harbored concerns that the United States would enter the war with insufficient forces and that Phase IV planning was incomplete. In February 2003, the Strategic Studies Institute at the Army War College published a lengthy paper on the likely challenges that would confront the United States in the aftermath of war. The conclusions, stated clearly on the first page of the document, note that "to be successful, an occupation such as that contemplated after any hostilities in Iraq requires much detailed interagency planning, many forces, multi-year military commitment, and a national commitment to nation building." The paper warned that although a honeymoon period would likely follow Saddam's ouster, it would be brief. "A force initially viewed as liberators can rapidly be relegated to the status of invaders should an unwelcome occupation continue for a long period of time." Occupation challenges would be particularly acute if a postwar international force did not implement the bulk of the occupational duties. With respect to America's objective of supporting the growth of democracy, the report noted that "the establishment of democracy or even some sort of rough pluralism in Iraq, where it has never really existed previously, will be a staggering challenge for any occupation force. . . . It is also reasonable to expect considerable resistance to efforts at even pluralism in Iraq" due to the fact that the Sunni population will assume that a democratic agenda would come at their expense. And the report warned against the wholesale elimination of Iraq's army. "To tear apart the Army in the war's aftermath could lead to the destruction of one of the only forces for unity within the society. Breaking up large elements of the army also raises the possibility that demobilized soldiers could affiliate with ethnic or tribal militias."[126]

OSD was intent on preventing information pertaining to postwar challenges from affecting either the content of the war plan or from having an impact on strategic decision making at the highest levels. On February 25, 2003, the army chief of staff, General Eric Shinseki, appeared before the Senate Armed Services Committee. When asked to give his estimate on the number of troops that would be required for postwar occupation, Shinseki said he thought it would be "something on the order of several hundred thousand soldiers." Shinseki's estimate was based on the fact that Iraq was a large state with the potential for violent communal conflict. Two days later, deputy secretary of defense Paul Wolfowitz testified before the same committee that Shinseki's estimate was "outlandish" and "wildly off the mark." Wolfowitz stated that "it is hard to conceive that it would take more forces to provide stability in post-Saddam Iraq than it would take to conduct the war itself and to secure the surrender of Saddam's security forces and his army—hard to imagine."[127] Wolfowitz's public admonition of Shinseki had a chilling effect on the uniformed military. The message was clear that further discussions about what might go wrong in the aftermath of the war were unwelcomed.

Ultimately, no alternative sources of information were presented to top policy makers that would focus the president's attention to postcombat matters with the intensity that he focused on plans for major combat operations. Rather, the information that Bush did receive indicated that postwar Iraq would be largely immune from the debilitating strife predicted by the DOS, intelligence community, and even from within the DOD.[128] For example, on January 10, 2003, Bush and Cheney met privately with three leading Iraqi dissidents. At that meeting, all of the Iraqis insisted that the United States would be greeted as liberators of their country. They stated that the divisions between Sunnis and Shiites were not as pronounced as many outside Iraq believed. Reflecting these sentiments, Cheney concluded that the United States had "to have a light hand in the postwar phase," and all agreed.[129]

Moreover, the absence of lateral connections across the government prevented the military war planners from considering how the stabilization mission could go awry if not dealt with thoroughly. As it was, the nature of the war planning process played to the worst tendencies of military planning. As the authors of the US Army's official history for the postwar phase concluded, there was an

> incorrect belief that stability and support operations meant the sequential use instead of the simultaneous use of offense, defense, and stability and support operations during a campaign. This misunderstanding has also led to the mistaken belief that stability and support operations were somehow less difficult and required less planning and preparations. These ambiguities and assumptions affected how military planners thought about the design and conduct of [Operation Iraqi Freedom].[130]

The report notes that in general, military war planners tend to concentrate on major combat operations at the expense of postwar stability operations. Ensuring that all aspects of war planning are given adequate intention is a matter that civilians had to attend to. Rice recognized this, yet was incapable of convincing either the military or the president that postwar stabilization had to be addressed early and extensively in the planning process.

> My several attempts to get the Pentagon to address the rear-area security issue seriously always led to uninformative slides and a rather dismissive handling of the question. When I finally arranged a briefing on the issue before the President in early February [2003], he started the meeting in a way that completely destroyed any chance of getting an answer. "This is something Condi has wanted to talk about," he said. I could immediately see that the generals no longer thought it to be a serious question.[131]

The empowered stovepipe guaranteed that postconflict stabilization would not be considered in sufficient detail.

American Diplomacy and Postwar Reconstruction—Coordination Failure

Postwar reconstruction and governance in the aftermath of war received a substantial amount of attention by various entities across the US government prior to the onset of war. As nearly all of the participants understood, the rapid stabilization and then reconstruction of the country after the war (and after decades of brutal dictatorship) would be essential to Iraq's democratic future. Critical to the success of this planning effort was the early centralization of the various planning efforts, which encompassed the breadth of American instruments of power and resources. Yet the centralization of planning occurred only weeks before the onset of hostilities. The result was the saddling of ORHA with a crushing load of responsibilities that stood little chance of being handled effectively.

Ostensibly, a centralized forum for postwar reconstruction planning was created in July–August 2002 with the constitution of the ESG and its subordinate working groups, the IPMC and IR+R. The IPMC was not intended to conduct independent postwar planning per se, but rather to provide guidance for the individual departments' planning efforts within a coherent strategic framework. To facilitate this mission, the IPMC had a dedicated staff, but members of this staff were drawn from the Joint Staff, not the NSC staff. The IPMC's primary focus was on humanitarian relief, though longer-term reconstruction efforts did fall within the cell's purview. Nevertheless, IPMC dedicated itself almost exclusively to the humanitarian relief mission, allowing the reconstruction planning effort to languish. The principal cause of this oversight was that the ESG—the organization to which the IPMC reported—had as its primary focus matters relating to war planning. Together, the ESG and IPMC received far less high-level guidance on reconstruction work than did the ESG on war planning, and the IR+R on humanitarian work.[132]

The major obstacle to effective and comprehensive planning was that the Deputies Committee—which was empowered to give strategic guidance to the IPMC through the ESG—was mired in an endless series of debates, the vast majority of which were never resolved. Throughout 2002, the DC's focus in matters relating to the postwar period pertained almost exclusively to the status and role of "Iraqi externals" in the new Iraq: whether to create among them a transition government that could be installed in the aftermath of war, to use them in carrying out intelligence and humanitarian relief projects, and to incorporate them into CENTCOM's war planning so that the invasion force would benefit from their language skills and country knowledge. The DC was incapable of resolving these debates, and as a result, guidance for lower-level organizations was never generated.[133] The primary advocate for the extensive use of Iraqi externals was the DOD's Office of Special Plans (OSP), headed by Feith. In addition, OSP was tasked with providing policy guidance on the status of Iraq's army and the nature of postwar de-Baathification policy. OSP, along with CENTCOM, assumed that the Iraqi military would continue to exist and be used for reconstruction projects as its units were reconstituted after the war.[134]

For its part, the DOS participated in the interagency process, but on most issues it (and the CIA) took diametrically opposed positions to the OSD, especially on matters related to the status of the Iraqi exiles. Moreover, the Future of Iraq project was never incorporated into extant interagency planning, remaining stovepiped in the DOS. In fact, the project was not allowed to receive an interagency briefing until October 2002.[135] With respect to postwar reconstruction, the members of the FOI urged a number of crucial policies at a very early date. For example, project members called for the rapid reform and training of Iraq's police forces, and for using Iraqi military personnel "not associated with torture and corruption in police activities" in this policing function.[136] On de-Baathification, FOI concluded that such a policy was essential, but warned that it should not be done as a wholesale abolition of the administration due to its role in creating a framework for social order.[137] Further, FOI urged the gradual halving of Iraq's army, and not its immediate and total abolition, and for its use in creating a democratic state.[138] Finally, the project warned against the dangerous consequences that would result from prolonged water and electrical shortages, as these conditions would degrade the population's willingness to support the United States and any new Iraqi government.[139] Many in the DOS hoped FOI would serve as the foundation for the postwar reconstruction planning process. This sentiment was echoed by Feith, who spoke favorably of FOI due largely to the fact that it was constituted by Iraqi externals.[140]

The United States Agency for International Development (USAID), the organization within the US government with extensive experience in reconstruction efforts, was not officially tasked with postwar planning until early 2003. Nevertheless, USAID began its work unofficially in the summer 2002. Its planning efforts focused primarily on the tasks of providing and rebuilding electrical, water, and sewage infrastructure, as well as on public health and local governance issues. In its frequent meetings with CENTCOM commanders, however, USAID was told that the US military would have no responsibility for public sector security and policy, humanitarian relief, or civilian government affairs. Responsibility for these matters was not formally assigned prior to the issuance of NSPD 24, though the military assumed that USAID would take on a prominent reconstruction role.[141]

In short, postwar reconstruction planning did occur at a relatively early date, though those efforts took place in isolated pockets across the US government. In the summer and fall of 2002, Feith peppered Rumsfeld with requests to establish a single office that would coordinate the government's efforts. Bush denied Rumsfeld's request to create such an entity on the grounds that the existence of a single office dedicated to postwar planning would undermine the administration's diplomacy at the United Nations.[142] This decision was momentous because it guaranteed that the United States would enter the Iraq War with few resources and disjointed plans for postwar reconstruction.

The decision to delay the creation of ORHA is puzzling for a number of reasons. First, a centralized interagency planning structure already existed within the US government. The ESG-IPMC-IR+R constellation of working groups was created in the summer of 2002 and could have easily assumed the coordinating role Feith envisioned. That it wasn't considered to serve in this capacity speaks to the influence the NSC system had in strategic decision making regarding Iraq policy. Second, FOI was also in existence well before US-UN diplomacy began, and, due to the composition of its membership, was conducting its work in the open. Third, at the same time that UN diplomacy began, Cheney gave a speech to the Veterans of Foreign Wars wherein the vice president declared that Iraq was in possession of WMD and then went on to lay out the case for war.[143] Cheney suffered no consequence for delivering this speech despite having clearly taken steps to undermine American diplomatic efforts at the United Nations. Fourth, it evidently occurred to no one in the administration that American coercive diplomacy at the United Nations could have been bolstered by an "open secret" of the existence of an office dedicated to postwar reconstruction planning. In sum, to effectively coordinate US war planning, diplomatic initiatives, and postwar reconstruction planning, high-level interagency attention and authority was essential. This type of effort could only have occurred through an empowered NSC system. Absent that, the creation of ORHA had to wait until January 2003.

The Empowered Stovepipe: De-Baathification and Disbanding the Iraqi Army

Upon being tapped to head ORHA, Garner was informed by Rumsfeld that one of his primary missions was the coordination of the interagency postwar planning process. That mission was delayed for weeks as ORHA staffers attempted to set up their own office and prepare for deployment on very short notice. At the end of February, ORHA conducted a "rock drill" at the National Defense University, which was attended by several hundred people from every agency that would have a role in the reconstruction effort. The purpose of the meeting was to discuss issues that had already received attention and attempt to discover those matters that had been missed in the various planning efforts. In Garner's words, the meeting uncovered "tons of problems." Among the most acute was ORHA's staff. Despite the official guidance in NSPD 24, ORHA lacked highly qualified staff members from a number of critical agencies. In fact, Garner was first introduced to the director of the FOI project, Tom Warrick, at that February meeting. Moreover, it was made clear at the meeting that the responsibility for providing post-conflict security was an issue that had yet to be resolved. When ORHA staff members deployed to Kuwait in mid-March, no one in the theater was expecting them. McKiernan refused to allow ORHA to locate its staff with CFLCC at Camp Doha, and the two staffs were never able to establish close working relations. The inability to coordinate with the military at an early date meant that ORHA was without clear guidance in the face of the massive looting and ongoing combat operations throughout April. Unknown to Garner, within days of his arrival in Baghdad on April 21, the decision had been made to disband ORHA and set up the Coalition Provisional Authority in its place.[144] Due to its inability to coordinate existing postwar planning efforts, and to ensure tight working relations with CENTCOM well before the start of the war, ORHA had little impact on the postwar administration of Iraq.[145]

On May 6, Bush announced Bremer's appointment to head the CPA. Initially, plans for ORHA's successor entailed collaboration between Zalmay Khalilzad, who had been attempting to lay the groundwork with Iraqi leaders for the creation of a new government, and Bremer, who would focus on postwar reconstruction issues. Bremer, however, convinced Bush that a collaborative effort would be detrimental to unity of command in Iraq. Bremer was tapped to be essentially an American viceroy to the country, a decision that was made without Powell or Rice even being notified in advance.[146] CPA would serve alongside CENTCOM in Iraq and would report to Rumsfeld in Washington.

Among the first official actions Bremer took was the issuance of the two crucial orders pertaining to de-Baathification and the dismantling of the Iraq's army. Preparations for these orders were months in the making. On March 10, Frank Miller, the chair of the ESG, briefed the NSC on plans for dealing with Baath Party members in the aftermath of war. Miller stressed that "those who ran Saddam's Iraq cannot work for us, and cannot run the future free Iraq, but we need to keep the state running." Miller noted that according to intelligence estimates, there were approximately 25,000 top-level Baathists in the country that should be removed once Saddam was overthrown. This amounted to just about 1 percent of the two million government employees in Iraq. Removing them, Miller argued, would not render critical public institutions leaderless. Bush concurred with Miller's plan and stated that it was critical for the United States to show Iraqis that Americans trusted them. Bush indicated his desire to have some government ministries under Iraqi leadership as quickly as possible. The next day, Rice issued to the NSC principals a "Summary of Conclusions" memo pertaining to what had been agreed at the meeting. Included in the memo was the consensus on the plans to reform Iraq's bureaucracy.[147]

On May 9, Feith presented Bremer with a draft plan for de-Baathification. The consensus at the March 10 NSC meeting notwithstanding, Feith's OSP drew up a plan, in cooperation with Ahmed Chalabi, that contained the seeds of a far wider-scale de-Baathification agenda. The next day, Rumsfeld issued Bremer an order to implement the draft plan. The order banned all senior party members from serving in government positions, along with the top three layers of officials of all ministries even if they were not members of the party. Bremer was of the belief that this amounted to around 20,000 individuals who were "true believers" in Saddam's regime. The US military in Iraq thought the order would affect merely 6,000 people. The actual number affected was 85,000–100,000, including some 40,000 schoolteachers who found joining the party to be the surest route to employment stability.[148] Many in the administration were unaware that the any policy change had occurred between March and May. Director of Central Intelligence George Tenet noted that the CIA was unaware of the order until after it was issued because no PC meeting was convened to discuss this critical topic.[149] Moreover, the order was made after the CIA station chief warned Bremer that his order would fire the technocrats responsible for running Iraq's vital infrastructure. "By nightfall," he told Bremer, "you'll have driven 30,000 to 50,000 Baathists underground. And in six months, you'll regret this."[150]

Initially, the vast majority of the Iraqi population was in favor of at least "some" Baathists being removed from office. Yet the manner in which de-Baathification was implemented generated a substantial amount of hostility toward the United States in the early summer. De-Baathification was not implemented consistently across the country and was being used to purge far more than the most hard-core supporters of the old regime. Making matters worse, the decision was made at the end of the summer to name Chalabi as the head of the High National De-Baathification Commission. Under Chalabi's leadership, the commission took an extremely hard line, eventually forcing the CPA to conclude that Chalabi was using the commission to further his own political ambitions by barring tens of thousands of Iraqis from serving in a myriad of capacities.[151]

On March 12, Feith briefed the NSC on the status of the planning effort for handling Iraq's foreign ministry, military, and intelligence services. The NSC agreed that the Special Republican Guard, Republican Guard, and Special Security Organization had to be completely and immediately disbanded. The regular army, however, would be subject to a slower demobilization and employed as a reconstruction force under American oversight.[152] As Feith's presentation warned, the United States could not "immediately demobilize 250k–300k personnel and put on street [*sic*]."[153]

The decision to retain the Iraqi regular army, or at least a sizable portion of it, reflected not just the judgment of Feith and Rumsfeld but also of CENTCOM, the intelligence community, and the DOS. The regular army could be used, as a practical matter, to assist the United States in reconstruction efforts. For CENTCOM, the use of the army in such a capacity was essential given the relatively few numbers of American troops in the theater. According to the intelligence community, the members of FOI, and the DOS, the Iraqi army—for all of its noted faults—was a national force, the sole institution in Iraq that stood the best chance of unifying the disparate elements of Iraqi society.

By mid-April, the situation in Iraq had deteriorated to such a point that, according the US military, the national army had ceased to exist as a functioning entity. Contrary to the expectations and desires of American war planners, the Iraqi army appeared to be unavailable to serve in any postwar reconstruction capacity. One of the causes of the army's disappearance was the highly effective US psychological operations program during the combat phase of the war, which urged Iraqi soldiers to return home or be treated as hostile. The US military adopted this policy because it lacked the requisite troop strength to capture and detain Iraqi soldiers in the midst of major combat operations. According to James Dobbins and colleagues, "this disjuncture between combat- and post-combat phase planning was symptomatic of the larger failure to align ends and means through the transition from conventional combat to postconflict reconstruction."[154]

In response to the deteriorating security situation, Bremer and his senior adviser, Walter Slocombe, began working on a new policy to deal with the

Iraqi army. Bremer and Slocombe, in conjunction with senior OSD officials, believed that it would be ill advised to recall the former army under
the existing conditions for three reasons. First, and to them the most obvious, was the fact that the Iraqi military had disbanded itself and ceased to
exist. Second, for CPA officials, disbanding the army had symbolic importance—namely, sending a clear signal to the Iraqi population that Saddam's
regime was gone for good. Third, CPA believed the infrastructure (bases,
barracks, and equipment) had disappeared along with the army. Thus a
new army would need to be created from scratch, a force that would be
drawn from all of Iraq's ethnic groups and that would effectively serve the
new democratic Iraqi regime.

On May 10, Slocombe circulated a draft order disbanding the entirety
of the Iraqi army among Rumsfeld, Wolfowitz, Feith, Franks, and Garner.
One day *prior* to that, however, Rumsfeld sent a memo to the PC titled
"Principles for Iraq-Policy Guidelines." That memo stated ambiguously
that the coalition "will actively oppose Saddam Hussein's old enforcers—the
Ba'ath Party, Fedayeen Saddam, etc." and that "we will make clear that the
coalition will eliminate the remnants of Saddam's regime." Garner received
the draft order on May 15, whereupon he raised a number of objections to
Bremer. Most notably, Garner indicated that ORHA was in the process of
recalling soldiers from the army. In fact, by mid-May, 137,000 Iraqis had
applied with the US military to return to their posts.[155] Regardless, Bremer
insisted that his policy go forward.[156]

On May 19, Rumsfeld received from Bremer the final version of the order
disbanding the army. On May 22, Bremer sent Bush a letter informing the
president of his intention to dissolve "Saddam's military and intelligence
structures." At an NSC meeting that same day, Bremer again informed Bush
of his plan. Receiving no verbal response from the president, Bremer assumed the path was clear for him to issue the directive. On May 23, Bush sent
Bremer a letter stating that he fully supported Bremer in his mission.[157]

Later that day, Bremer issued CPA Order 2, which disbanded all of Iraq's
security forces. This applied to Iraq's regular army, which as the president
believed, was to have been demobilized slowly. Evidently, Rice was unaware of the content of Bremer's order and Powell was out of town when it
was finally issued. In fact, the order had not been vetted by the interagency
process in any capacity. Myers, McKiernan, vice chairman of the JCS Peter
Pace, and national intelligence officer for the Near East and South Asia Paul
Pillar have all stated that they received no indication of the content of the
order, nor was their input solicited in advance.[158] The decision was made

against the long-standing advice of the DOS, CIA, and Army War College. As to the rationale for the decision, Powell later noted that the Iraqi soldiers' refusal to fight did not amount to the wholesale dissolution of the army as an institution. "The troops might have been gone, but the army was not going. There was a structure there. There were units. There was an infrastructure."[159] Garner knew this as well, though he was unsuccessful in convincing Bremer to abandon his policy. In describing the process by which CPA Order 2 was issued, Frank Miller stated, "most of us had no advanced warning that it was coming. No one from the Pentagon had brought this to our attention. It was blown through the system."[160] Additionally,

> Anyone who is experienced in the ways of Washington knows the difference between an open, transparent policy process and slamming something through the system. . . . The most pretentious decision of the occupation, disbanding the Iraqi army, was carried out stealthily and without giving the president's principal advisors an opportunity to consider it and give the president their views.[161]

Combined, the effects of CPA orders 1 and 2 were profound and debilitating in terms of America's diplomatic objectives in Iraq. The de-Baathification policy and the decision to outsource its implementation to Ahmed Chalabi fundamentally transformed the nature of political power in Iraq along religious lines. The new Shiite majority, with strong religious and political ties to Iran, stood the most to gain in the short run. In response, many in the Sunni minority followed the militant appeals of Sunni imams to resist the US occupation. More damaging was the dissolution of the Iraqi army. To many in the Sunni community, this act constituted a direct challenge to their identity as the rightful leaders of the Iraqi state. With too few troops to contain the growing unrest in the country, the United States was unable to respond to activities of the newly unemployed Sunni group. Under threat from a newly empowered Shiite majority, many Sunnis filled the ranks of the growing insurgency. By the time the United States began to take seriously the need to create a new national army in 2004, the insurgency had effectively destroyed the possibility for the emergence of a stable and democratic Iraq.[162]

INFORMATION INSTITUTIONS VERSUS CIVIL-MILITARY RELATIONS

The strategic outcome of the Iraq War was a military success but diplomatic failure for the United States. This outcome resulted from three interrelated decisions top American officials made. First, in terms of war planning, the United States designed a strategy that was intended to achieve the objective of regime overthrow as quickly as possible. Toward that end, the number of forces committed to war was kept to a bare minimum. While the United States was able to achieve its military objectives, the manner in which it accomplished them prevented the US from effectively stabilizing the country in the aftermath of major combat operations. Second, while elements of the American government did conduct postwar reconstruction planning prior to the onset of war, those efforts were incomplete and disjointed. The United States went to war with an interagency office, ORHA, that was merely weeks old, but which was tasked with a monumental set of objectives. Top administration officials intentionally delayed the formation of ORHA because they believed that an interagency office for postwar planning would undermine American diplomacy at the United Nations. Third, as a result of the inability to provide basic security for postwar Iraq, and without the benefit of a comprehensive and thoroughly vetted postwar reconstruction plan, the decisions to conduct extensive de-Baathification and to disband Iraq's armed forces were made with little understanding of the devastating consequences that would result.

The information institution approach finds substantial support in this case of limited warfare. The United States entered the Iraq War with a moderately truncated information institution. In terms of information sources, top policy makers were largely beholden to a single source of information, the Office of the Secretary of Defense and—through it—US Central Command. Unlike the Far East Command under MacArthur, however, top policy makers were directly connected to the war planning process and received a wealth of information pertaining to the plans and operations of the American military. And, through this channel, top policy makers were able to ensure that military operations squared with American political objectives. With respect to lateral channels of communication among key departments and agencies, little information was shared as the strategy was debated, refined, and executed. Under these conditions, this approach expects a mixed strategic outcome: military success and diplomatic failure in the war.

The evidence presented in this chapter further confirms the causal logic of the information institution approach. During the war planning process, the United States possessed moderate collection and fair analytical capabilities. As a result of a closed circle of communication among the president, vice president, the OSD, and CENTCOM, the United States was able to devise a war plan that was adequately designed and resourced to accomplish its military objectives—but only its military objectives. Drawing from a wealth of information pertaining to the capabilities and disposition of Iraq's army, the United States designed a plan that overthrew the Iraqi regime with as few American troops as possible. At the same time, information originating from the intelligence community, the DOS, and even from within the DOD that challenged the rosy expectations of the OSD and CENTCOM was never incorporated into the planning process. Ultimately, the war planning process was blind to the trade-offs that were unintentionally being made. In waging war, the United States purchased a light military footprint and rapid operational tempo at the expense of sufficient forces to provide security in the aftermath. While it is the case that top policy makers expressed concern that things might not go as planned, these concerns were afterthoughts and not incorporated into the planning process.[163]

The absence of lateral communication channels had a debilitating effect on military-diplomatic coordination, especially in terms of postwar reconstruction. Due in large part to the weakness of the NSC system, the decision was made to delay the creation of a centralized office responsible for postwar reconstruction until mere weeks before the onset of war. In the interim, postwar planning continued, but in isolation across the US government. By the time ORHA was created, little time, guidance, and resources were available to conduct postwar reconstruction planning effectively. In the wake of the regime's overthrow, ORHA was incapable of providing even the rudiments of what Garner had hoped to accomplish. Moreover, despite having subjected both of the plans for de-Baathification and the future status of the Iraqi Army to interagency scrutiny, the CPA enacted policies that catalyzed the Sunni insurgency. The failure to subject the newest variants of these policies to intense interagency vetting and oversight stemmed from the control the OSD exercised over postwar operations in Iraq.

Finally, the evidence presented above confirms the expectation that high-quality strategic risk assessments are unlikely when the information institution is characterized by an "empowered stovepipe." The case of the Iraq War differs from the three others considered in this book to the extent that this particular information flow pattern emerged in almost ideal-typical form. Cheney and Rumsfeld endeavored successfully to serve as the dominant providers of information to the president. While it is the case that some information from nonmilitary sources did make its way to the top, that information was not subjected to honest and comprehensive vetting procedures. Rather, it was groomed extensively, allowing information from privileged sources, and of preferred content, to affect strategic decision making. The results were decisions made without the benefit of thorough and accurate risk assessments of various courses of action. The presence of such an empowered stovepipe, and its deleterious effects, further supports the logic of the information institution approach.

On balance, the evidence presented in this chapter poses substantial challenges to both democratic civil-military relations theory and organizational culture theory. It is important to recognize that democratic civil-military relations theory anticipates the outcome that was observed in the Iraq War: military success, diplomatic failure. Moreover, this approach captures many important features in the relationship between the military and civilian leadership. When political and military preferences diverge greatly—as occurred in this case—military and diplomatic coordination is likely to suffer (though, because the domestic balance of power favors civilians, information flows will remain fluid). The ability for top policy makers to receive sufficient and timely information from the military increases the chances that the military objectives will be achieved in the war. But because military and diplomatic coordination is likely to suffer, diplomatic objectives are unlikely to be secured.

Specifically, Risa Brooks argues that democratic civil-military relations theory offers a powerful explanation for the failure of the United States to obtain its political objectives in the Iraq War. According to her account, the oversight mechanisms civilians employed to ensure access to military information hampered military-diplomatic coordination to such an extent that the military failed to prioritize planning for postwar Iraq. Brooks details three ways in which strategic coordination suffered due to the high degree of political-military preference divergence. First, civilians—and Rumsfeld in particular—were not privy to the full range of assessments pertaining to likely outcomes of the postwar environment. Due to the rather oppressive oversight mechanisms Rumsfeld employed, an "ethos of self-censorship" emerged among senior military officers. Second, because senior military officers who were concerned with the postwar environment were cut out of the strategy design process, Rumsfeld was incapable of influencing those officers who denigrated postwar stabilization planning. Third, the Iraq war plan was subsumed in the "underlying bureaucratic battle between the secretary and his generals."[164]

In the narrowest of senses, Brooks's analysis is correct. Relations between Rumsfeld and his generals all but guaranteed that critical information pertaining to the likely outcomes in a postwar Iraq would not be considered by the OSD, and that by excluding those who were concerned with postwar stabilization from participating in the planning process, little strategic attention would be devoted to Phase IV of the Iraq war plan. Yet this conclusion fails to address the critical structural problem of American war and postwar planning: the exclusion of virtually *all other agencies* in the national security bureaucracy that had information pertaining to, and operational responsibility for, postwar Iraq. Civil-military relations were only one part, albeit an important part, of a much larger institutional problem. As the evidence presented in this chapter shows clearly, nonmilitary organizations possessed a wealth of information strongly suggesting that postwar stabilization had to be a top priority for the US military. Democratic civil-military relations theory simply cannot explain why those nonmilitary bureaus were systematically excluded from influencing the Iraq war plan. It should be recalled that nonmilitary organs within the national security bureaucracy played an extensive role in designing and executing the limited war strategy in the Persian Gulf War. Moreover, the failure to achieve the key objective in Iraq, the emergence of a stable and democratic Iraqi state, cannot be explained by the failure to achieve immediate postcombat *stabilization* solely. Postwar *reconstruction* (a mission that primarily demanded the participation of diplomatic instruments) was destined to fail due to the exclusion of the nonmilitary agencies and departments in the overall planning effort. Ultimately, the strategic outcome of the Iraq War was the product of far more than dysfunctional civil-military relations. A complete explanation of the horizontal and durational escalation of the Iraq War must take into consideration the role of military and nonmilitary intelligence collection and analysis, and military and diplomatic coordination. Democratic civil-military relations theory is simply too narrowly cast to provide such an explanation.

If democratic civil-military relations theory encounters difficulty in explaining the lack of coordination between the military and diplomatic elements of America's Iraq War strategy, could it be that the specific individuals involved—and not civil-military relations, generally—caused the mixed outcomes of the war? After all, Cheney and Rumsfeld played integral roles in structuring the pattern of information flows to and from the president. And the secretary of defense erected many of the obstacles to information sharing. Again, however, such an approach can only take the analysis a short distance. Rumsfeld's "successes" in structuring information flow patterns interacted with the "failures" of Rice, Powell, and Tenet and were abetted by Bush's inability to fully appreciate the dysfunctional strategic decision-making procedures that characterized his administration's handling of the war. Moreover, the downstream implications of the choices particular individuals made can only be glimpsed at through the lens provided by theories that reside at the individual level of analysis. While it may be the case that institutionalized patterns of information flow resulted from individual choices in this case, the whole of the information institution exhibited properties and behaviors that are not reducible to those prior choices.[165] The information institution approach thus provides a more complete and compelling explanation for America's strategic performance in the Iraq War than is offered by individual level approaches.

As discussed in chapter 2, the organizational culture of professional militaries affects strategic performance in limited war through two critical mechanisms: first, the content of a military's culture as it pertains to the concept of war ("military dominant" or "balanced") and to the embedded norm of civil-military relations (Jominian or Clausewitzian); and second, whether top policy makers consider the military to be the most salient organization in the national security bureaucracy. In terms of its culture, studies of the American military in the post–Persian Gulf era have concluded that to a considerable extent, the reigning concept of war was "military dominant." In ways that are by now familiar, the American military had a pervasive tendency to "separate war and politics—to view military victory as an end in itself, ignoring war's function as an instrument of policy."[166] For the military, the "lessons" of Desert Storm reinforced this concept. As Steven Metz describes,

> Pointing to the Gulf War, the military argued that the United States needed a military organized, sized, equipped, and trained much like the one it had. Why tweak success? . . . It [the Persian Gulf War] showed that techniques developed for European battlefields worked in other environments (at least against proto-Soviet adversaries). It showed that the seminal shift in American military strategy begun in the 1970s was successful. The grinding approach of Grant and Eisenhower gave way to a mode of fighting where finesse, speed, and precision bewildered the enemy; avoided his strengths; capitalized on his weaknesses; and eventually, shattered his will. Ironically, though, precisely because of the military success of the Gulf War, this style of military operations became so deeply etched in the American mind that later change was difficult.[167]

This concept of war holds little to no space for the consideration of the untidy element of politics. Indeed, for the American military, those messy conflicts were not considered to be warfare, per se; rather, "military operations other than war."[168] No better reflection of the prevailing "military dominant" concept is Franks's admonition to Rumsfeld's civilian advisers, "You pay attention to the day after and I'll pay attention to the day of."[169] Concurring in this assessment, Rumsfeld notes that "Franks admittedly had little enthusiasm for setting up a postcombat government or dealing with the related tangle of bureaucratic and interagency issues."[170]

Despite the consistency of the cultural concept of war across the cases considered here, there is strong evidence to suggest that in the years prior to the Iraq War, the influence of the Jominian relational norm had given way to its Clausewitzian counterpart. While the military as an organization disparaged those "military operations other than war," it had grown quite accustomed to participating in them. To a considerable extent, America's position in the post–Cold War international system guaranteed that the American military would be heavily involved in a range of violent conflicts necessitating close military and diplomatic coordination. As such, American military commanders had become habituated to the diplomatic rigors of waging coalition warfare, participating in (coercive) diplomatic negotiations, and arranging terms of peace that were far from cut and dry, at least from the military's perspective.[171] And as the forward presence of American military forces was maintained in the years after the Persian Gulf War, senior military officers were routinely drawn into de facto peacetime diplomatic service, particularly in the Middle East.[172] Finally, the military-diplomatic intricacies of America's post–Cold War foreign-military policy prompted the Clinton administration to create an interagency coordinating forum for smaller-scale contingency operations.[173] Far from viewing civilian participation into its domain as abnormal, the post–Cold War American military was well on its way to firmly establishing a Clausewitzian norm of civil-military relations.

An organizational culture that contains a "military dominant" conception of warfare and a Clausewitzian norm of civil-military relations is, however, only one of two necessary conditions for the production of a mixed strategic outcome in limited wars. The second necessary condition is that top policy makers view the military as the most salient organization for waging limited wars. On this score, organizational culture theory encounters problems. The evidence presented in this chapter demonstrates that it was the American military that was beholden to the strategic direction of the OSD. Far from taking what the military gave him, Rumsfeld was determined to design and implement a war (and postwar) plan that served his objectives. Critically, while the military as an organization may have been far more receptive to diplomatic coordination than it had been in the limited wars of the past, the information institution in which it was embedded prevented thorough information sharing and tight coordination with American diplomats and intelligence agencies. In sum, the moderately truncated information institution, and not the military's organizational culture, caused the mixed strategic outcome of the Iraq War.

CHAPTER SEVEN

Information Institutions Matter!

The Nobel Prize–winning political economist Elinor Ostrom argued in 2005 that to satisfactorily explain the origins and outcomes of important social behavior, the context of the relationships among actors must be explicitly incorporated in our theoretical frameworks. Toward this end, Ostrom noted that several fundamental questions must be answered, among them are, "whether the situation is stable or changing, conveys substantial information about its structure and the behavior of participants, tends to invoke norms such as trust and reciprocity (or those of an eye for an eye), and allows participants to adapt more effective strategies over time?" Reflecting on the massive literature dedicated to answering these questions, Ostrom concludes with these thoughts:

> Two fundamental lessons from the vast empirical and theoretical research of the last several decades are: first, humans have complex motivations including narrow self-interest as well as norms of proper behavior and other-regarding preferences; and second, *institutions matter!*[1]

My intention in this book has been to show how a particular type of institution, one involving the pattern of information flow among hierarchically arranged actors in the context of the state, affects strategic performance in war. The empirical findings presented in the preceding chapters demonstrate clearly that information institutions do indeed matter.

The purpose of this final chapter is twofold. The first is to summarize the findings of the previous four empirical chapters pertaining to strategic performance in limited war. I will show how the information institution approach offers superior explanations of the sources of American strategic performance compared to those of its direct competitors drawn from the civil-military relations literature. Following that, I evaluate my argument against its indirect competitor, rationalist bargaining theory, to determine the relevance of exogenous information in explaining strategic performance in the cases under consideration. The second purpose of this chapter is to spell out the implications of the information institution approach for international relations (IR) theory and for foreign policy.

THE SOURCES OF STRATEGIC PERFORMANCE IN AMERICA'S LIMITED WARS: INFORMATION INSTITUTIONS VERSUS THE DIRECT COMPETITORS

Under what conditions are states able to design and execute limited war strategies that defeat the opponent and avoid escalation simultaneously? Securing these wartime objectives constitutes the central challenge of limited warfare. An evaluation of strategic performance in limited war requires an assessment of the extent to which *both* a state's military and diplomatic objectives were achieved. Restricting the focus to either the military or the diplomatic component alone can only result in incomplete analysis of a state's (mis)fortunes in these conflicts. Thus, as I discussed in chapter 2, it is the sinews of limited war strategy—the threads that tie the political, military, and diplomatic aspects of the limited war effort together—that must be examined in order to explain overall strategic performance. Specifically, I argued that two information management mechanisms have a direct effect on strategic performance in limited war: the extent to which states collect and analyze information pertaining to the strategic environment (outside information), and the ability of states to ensure that the military and diplomatic elements of the limited war strategy are coordinated (inside information).

In chapters 3–6, I examined four cases of American limited warfare, each of which corresponded to distinct strategic performance outcomes. By process-tracing how information was collected, analyzed, and shared among top policy makers and their national security organizations, I was able to uncover distinct causal pathways that generated these particular outcomes. In this section, I present those causal pathways and then ask three analytical questions. First, which of the three competing approaches offers a potential explanation for the causal pathway under consideration? Second, to what extent did the evidence validate these explanations? Third, for the approaches that were not validated by the evidence, where specifically did they fall short? Table 7.1 summarizes the causal logic of the information

TABLE 7.1. Competing expectations (outcomes) of strategic performance in limited war

Theory	Case	Independent Variable	Collection/Analysis	Coordination	Strategic Performance
		Information sources/ Lateral connections			
Information Institutions	(1) Persian Gulf: Double Success (‡)	Robust	Comprehensive and Optimal (+)	Tight (+)	Double success (+)
	(2) Iraq: Win battle, lose war (‡)	Moderately Truncated Diplomacy isolated	Moderate and Fair (+)	Poor (+)	Win battle, lose war (+)
	(3) Vietnam: Little consolation (‡)	Moderately Truncated Military isolated	Moderate and Fair overall (+) • Air (+) • Ground (+)	Poor overall (+) • Air (+) • Ground (+)	Little consolation (+)
	(4) Korea: Double Failure (‡)	Truncated	Limited and Dysfunctional (+)	Uncoordinated (+)	Double failure (+)
		View of war/ Relational norm			
Organizational Culture	Persian Gulf: Double Success (≠)	Military dominant/ Jominian	Limited and Dysfunctional (−)	Uncoordinated (−)	Double failure (−)
	Iraq: Win battle, lose war (†)	Military dominant/ Clausewitzian	Moderate and Fair (+)	Tight (−)	Either mixed case (+)

		Power distribution/ Preference convergence			
	Vietnam: Little consolation (†)	Military dominant/ Jominian	Limited and Dysfunctional (+/-) • Air (-) • Ground (+)	Uncoordinated (+/-) • Air (-) • Ground (+)	Double failure (-)
	(4) Korea: Double Failure (‡)	Military dominant/ Jominian	Limited and Dysfunctional (+)	Uncoordinated (+)	Double failure (+)
Democratic Civil-Military Relations	Persian Gulf: Double Success (†)	Civilian/diverge	Comprehensive and Optimal (+)	Uncoordinated (-)	Win battle, lose war (-)
	Iraq: Win battle, lose war (≠)	Civilian/diverge	Comprehensive and Optimal (-)	Uncoordinated (-)	Win battle, lose war (-)
	Vietnam: Little consolation (†)	Civilian/diverge	Comprehensive and Optimal (+/-) • Air (+) • Ground (-)	Uncoordinated (+/-) • Air (-) • Ground (+)	Win battle, lose war (-)
	Korea: Double Failure (†)	Civilian/diverge	Comprehensive and Optimal (-)	Uncoordinated (+)	Win battle, lose war (-)

(‡) Theory was able to offer a compelling explanation of the complete causal pathway leading to strategic performance.

(†) Theory was able to offer a compelling explanation of only a portion of the causal pathway leading to strategic performance.

(≠) Theory was unable to offer a compelling explanation of any portion of the causal pathway leading to strategic performance.

(+) Specific expected outcome met and explained.

(-) Specific expected outcome not met and/or not explained.

institution approach and its direct competitors in each case of limited war. The Independent Variable column contains the specific form that each causal variable assumed in the cases. The three columns to the left specify the expected outcome, followed by whether the approach offers a compelling explanation of that expected outcome in parentheses (+ for a compelling explanation of the expected outcome, - for an inaccurate explanation of the expected outcome). Rows identified by (‡) indicate where a theory was able to offer a compelling explanation of the complete causal pathway leading to strategic performance, while rows identified by (†) indicate where a theory offered a compelling explanation of only a relevant portion of a causal pathway. Rows identified by (≠) indicate where a theory was unable to offer a compelling explanation of any portion of the causal pathway leading to strategic performance.

Causal Pathway 1: Comprehensive Collection and Optimal Analysis of Information + Tight Military-Diplomatic Coordination → Double Success (the Persian Gulf War)

The Persian Gulf War was a double strategic success for the United States. Not only was its military objective secured (the defeat of the Iraqi Army) but so too was its diplomatic objective (the construction and maintenance of a massive and complex international coalition throughout the crisis and war). The evidence presented in chapter 5 showed that this level of strategic performance was generated by high quality information management: the United States was able to comprehensively collect and optimally analyze information about its primary opponent and the broader strategic environment, and was able to ensure tight coordination between its military and diplomatic approaches to the initial crisis and war. The effectiveness of these information-processing mechanisms generated sound strategic risk assessments both prior to and during the war. Top policy makers were able to thoroughly evaluate the strengths and weaknesses of alternative courses of action, and as a result, the quality of strategic decision making was particularly high.

Each of the three competing theoretical approaches anticipates this outcome, but under different conditions. The information institution approach expects this causal pathway when the information institutions are robust: when leaders have access to multiple organizational sources of information, and when national security organizations widely and routinely share information with each other. Organizational culture theory predicts this outcome when the military's organizational culture entails a balanced conception of war and when it abides by a Clausewitzian norm of civil-military relations. Finally, democratic civil-military relations theory anticipates this outcome when the balance of domestic power favors civilians (as is the case in all democracies) and when political-military preferences converge.

Only the information institution approach received strong confirmation in this case. Information flows among President George H. W. Bush, his top advisers, and all of the national security organizations were remarkably robust. Due to the power and competence of the National Security Council system, top policy makers were afforded a wealth of strategic information from multiple organizational sources, and that information was meticulously vetted through extensive information sharing throughout the foreign policy bureaucracy. Information collection and analysis was comprehensive and optimal, and it had to be given the strategic stakes involved. Moreover, this case exhibited a high degree of military and diplomatic coordination from the beginning of the crisis to the end of the war. On the other hand, the evidence presented offers little support for either organizational culture theory or democratic civil-military relations theory. Given the military dominant conception of war and the Jominian norm of civil-military relations (a cultural combination that spanned across the first three limited wars considered in this book), organizational culture theory expects strategic performance (and the associated two information management mechanisms) to be the exact opposite of that which occurred. While democratic civil-military relations theory is able to correctly anticipate fluid information sharing among policy makers and the military, it incorrectly expects an absence of military-diplomatic coordination. Thus its overall projection of military success and diplomatic failure (win the battle, lose the war) was not realized.

Causal Pathway 2: Diplomacy Isolated—Moderate Collection and Fair Analysis of Information + Poor Military-Diplomatic Coordination → Win the Battle, Lose the War (the Iraq War)

American strategic performance in the Iraq War was mixed. Although the United States was able to secure its initial military objectives of destroying the Iraqi Army and overthrowing the regime of Saddam Hussein, it was unable to achieve its diplomatic objectives pertaining to postwar reconstruction. The Iraq War expanded first horizontally with the emergence of the Sunni-based insurgency, and then durationally as the United States found itself in the midst of a brutal and costly sectarian civil war. The evidence presented in chapter 6 demonstrates that this outcome resulted from America's limited collection and fair analysis of strategic information. While the United States was able to achieve a remarkably clear understanding of the strengths and weaknesses of its military opponent, it had scant understanding of the motivations of potential spoilers to its efforts to create a viable and democratic Iraqi government. Additionally, the evidence shows that America's military and diplomatic efforts were only poorly reconciled, specifically in the areas of postwar security and reconstruction.

Each of the three competing explanations expects this outcome, though only two with specificity. The information institution approach expects this causal pathway when the information institution is moderately truncated, wherein diplomatic organizations are disconnected from the communication channels that constitute the domain of strategic decision making. Democratic civil-military relations theory anticipates this causal pathway when political and military preferences diverge. Although it is not capable of identifying this causal pathway precisely, organizational culture theory does anticipate a mixed strategic outcome when the military holds a military dominant conception of war and when it abides by a Clausewitzian relational norm.

The Iraq War provides strong confirmation for only the information institution approach. America entered the war with a moderately truncated information institution, where the organizations responsible for the diplomatic component of the broader strategy were systematically isolated from the locus of strategic decision making. Top policy makers received the vast majority of their information from the Department of Defense, which in turned received its information primarily from the US Central Command. Unlike the information institution in Korea, however, top policy makers monitored and managed the war planning process and were kept fully informed of the American military's intentions and actions. Yet this "empowered stovepipe" was incapable of providing senior governmental officials with a comprehensive understanding of the strategic environment in Iraq due in large part to the absence of communication channels among military, diplomatic, and intelligence organizations. Moreover, because of its exclusion in the war and postwar planning process, the diplomatic component of the limited war strategy was poorly coordinated with the military's strategic effort. Confirming the logic spelled out in chapter 2, this empowered stovepipe was incapable of producing sound strategic risk assessments. Not only were top policy makers not presented with a broad array of viable courses of action, but also at critical points, the evident trade-offs between military and diplomatic objectives were simply unrecognized.

In broad terms, democratic civil-military relations theory's expectation of this mixed outcome was confirmed. Specifically, the anticipated lack of military and diplomatic coordination was validated. According to Risa Brooks, political-military preference divergence is a key factor undermining close collaboration between civilian and military organizations.[2] The evidence presented in chapter 6, however, calls into question the argument that preference divergence played an exclusive role in undermining tight military-diplomatic coordination. Rather, coordination suffered in the Iraq War due primarily to the weakness of the National Security Council system, the component of the information institution that has the responsibility for facilitating overall interagency collaboration. Successful postwar reconstruction (as opposed postwar stability) required the full incorporation of America's diplomatic organizations in the strategic planning process. Factors other than civil-military relations, in other words, were at play in generating this case of mixed strategic performance. Finally, the theory's expectation of fluid information sharing was not met. Information from across the American national security apparatus was routinely prevented from influencing the strategic planning process. Ultimately, democratic civil-military relations theory correctly anticipates the outcome of the Iraq War, but its explanation for that outcome does not withstand scrutiny.

For its part, organizational culture theory's general expectation of a mixed outcome was confirmed, and the reason for this was that while the armed forces' prevailing conception of warfare remained military dominant, their relational norm had moved well toward its Clausewitzian counterpart. Under these conditions, information collection and analysis is likely to be moderate and fair—an outcome that is certainly confirmed by the evidence. Yet the theory incorrectly anticipated tight military-diplomatic coordination. Organizational culture theory's inability to explain the absence of coordination evinced in this case stems largely from the fact that senior civilian defense officials *did not* consider the military to be the most salient organization within the national security apparatus. To the contrary, Secretary of Defense Rumsfeld was determined to maintain strict control over the military's planning of the war. Poor coordination was a result of a divergence of preferences among *civilian* organizations, specifically the OSD and State Department. The military's organizational culture had little independent effect in determining American strategic performance in the Iraq War.

Causal Pathway 3: Military Isolated—Moderate Collection and
Fair Analysis of Information + Poor Military-Diplomatic
Coordination → Little Consolation (the Vietnam War)

In broad terms, the Vietnam War was a case of mixed strategic performance for the United States. While America was able to secure its diplomatic objective of preventing Chinese intervention in the war, it was incapable of defeating its primary opponent on the battlefield. As a result, America suffered extensive durational escalation of the war, at substantial costs in terms of lives, treasure, and international reputation. The evidence demonstrated, again broadly speaking, that this outcome resulted from moderate collection and fair analysis of information. The United States was able to reach a sophisticated and accurate understanding of Chinese intentions but was incapable of reaching a similar understanding of its primary military opponent, the National Liberation Front and People's Army of North Vietnam operating in South Vietnam. Additionally, the evidence showed that in some instances, military-diplomatic coordination functioned well (for example, with respect to its actions that could induce Chinese intervention) while in others the military behaved in ways that precluded coordination (for example, in its efforts to construct a viable and independent South Vietnam).

Only the information institution approach explains this case of strategic performance. The American information institution President Lyndon Johnson inherited was moderately truncated, wherein the army functioned in a manner that was largely isolated from top policy makers and other national security organizations. In this case, de facto strategic authority devolved down to MACV in Saigon due to the army's relative autonomy within the broader information institution. As a result, top policy makers were at a substantial information disadvantage vis-à-vis the army, and had little ability to ensure that American diplomatic and military missions worked in concert toward the broader political objectives of the war. At the same time, because their ability to receive a wealth of information pertaining to the interests and behavior of China, the United States was able to craft and implement a strategy that was well tailored to the broader strategic environment in which the war unfolded, and avoid horizontal escalation in the process.

In chapter 2, I noted that among the recognized benefits of process-tracing is its ability to uncover additional theoretically relevant observations, and this is precisely what occurred in this case. The evidence presented in chapter 4 shows that to a considerable extent, strategic direction of the air campaign over North Vietnam and the ground campaign in South Vietnam occurred in two nonintersecting information domains within the US government. As such, process-tracing enabled me to conduct fine-grained tests of the competing approaches in both of these campaigns. American strategic performance in the air campaign was particularly high. Although the United States was not able to secure its military objective, the reason for this was that American decision makers intentionally privileged the goal of avoiding Chinese intervention over that of coercing Hanoi through massive air bombardment. In other words, America faced a dilemma: as the tempo and destruction of the air campaign increased, so too did the probability of Chinese intervention. Top policy makers rationally chose to avoid the latter at the expense of the former. The air campaign benefited from high quality strategic decision making because the information flow pattern from which the strategy emerged was capable of generating sound strategic risk assessments. Numerous alternative courses of action were presented and thoroughly evaluated in light of new information made available by multiple organizational sources. Here again, the information institution approach receives strong confirmation: top policy makers received information from military and nonmilitary organizations alike, and these organizations widely shared information with each other as the air campaign was designed and executed. Neither organizational culture theory nor democratic civil-military relations theory receives much support in the case of the air campaign. The organizational culture of America's air force embodied a military dominant view of war and a Jominian relational norm, and as such, this approach anticipates both military and diplomatic failure in the air campaign. While democratic civil-military relations theory's expectation of fluid information flow is confirmed in the case of the air campaign, it incorrectly anticipates an absence of military-diplomatic coordination.

American strategic performance in the ground war, on the other hand, was very poor. Not only was the United States incapable of defeating its primary opponent, but also it was similarly unable to achieve its diplomatic objectives of creating and maintaining a legitimate, noncommunist South Vietnamese government. This outcome resulted from limited collection and dysfunctional analysis of information and an absence of military-diplomatic coordination. In the ground campaign too, the information institution approach receives strong confirmation. Because the army operated with near autonomy, this approach expects little information to be shared with top policy makers and other national security organizations, and military missions to undermine diplomacy—outcomes that clearly resulted. Because of MACV's unmatched influence in decision making in the ground campaign, sound strategic risk assessments were never conducted. In fact, accurate and timely information was prevented from reaching top officials in the

Pentagon, information that was necessary to systematically evaluate alternative—and potentially more productive—strategic approaches. Similarly, organizational culture theory receives strong support in the ground campaign. Following the culture of its parent organization, MACV held a military dominant conception of war and abided by a Jominian norm of civil-military relations. Under these conditions, organizational culture theory anticipates the double failure on the ground in South Vietnam. Democratic civil-military relations theory, on the other hand, cannot account for the systematic withholding (and obfuscation) of information by MACV, and thus cannot offer a complete explanation of the causal pathway that generated the double failure in the ground campaign in the Vietnam War.

Causal Pathway 4: Limited Collection and Dysfunctional Analysis of Information + Uncoordinated Military-Diplomatic Missions → Double Failure (the Korean War)

The Korean War is a case of extremely poor strategic performance for the United States. In terms of its military objectives, the United States failed to defeat its primary opponent, the North Korean Army, on the battlefield. And in terms of its diplomatic objectives, the United States was unable to prevent China's intervention into the war. As a result, the United States experienced first horizontal and then durational escalation of a war that was initially anticipated to last only a few short months. America found itself at limited war for three long years awaiting an outcome that would ultimately be determined by the death of Joseph Stalin.[3]

The evidence presented in chapter 3 demonstrates that this outcome resulted from the limited collection and dysfunctional analysis of information pertaining to the Korean Army and of the broader strategic environment. Moreover, the evidence shows that there was a substantial disconnect between America's military and diplomatic efforts in the war. Two of the three competing approaches offer an explanation of this causal pathway. The information institution approach expects double failure in limited war when the information institution is truncated, where top policy makers are beholden to a single organizational source of information, and when little information is shared among national security organizations. Organizational culture theory anticipates the causal pathway when the military's organizational culture entails a military dominant conception of warfare and when there is a prevailing Jominian norm of civil-military relations. On the other hand, democratic civil-military relations theory does not anticipate democratic states to experience double strategic failure in limited warfare because information sharing between civilian and the military should, at minimum, enable military success on the battlefield—an outcome clearly at odds with the empirical record.

Again, the information institution approach fares well in this case. The United States entered the war with a truncated information institution. President Truman and his top advisers received the vast majority of their information from a single dominant source, General Douglas MacArthur's command headquartered in Tokyo, while very little of the information MacArthur and his staff possessed was shared with the State Department, Central Intelligence Agency, and even the Joint Chiefs of Staff. As a result, information collection was limited and spotty, while the analysis of that information was dysfunctional. The United States knew very little of the actual strength of its primary opponent, North Korea, nor did it hold more than a caricatured view of China, the state that had the most to lose if the Korean Peninsula were unified under South Korean authority. Moreover, military and diplomatic coordination in the war was largely nonexistent. On multiple occasions, the American military undertook actions that violated the central political objectives of the war, and that undercut the diplomatic signals of restraint the United States attempted to convey to China. Finally, the quality of strategic risk assessments was particularly poor in this case. Top policy makers were incapable of evaluating the strengths and weaknesses of MacArthur's strategy against alternative courses of action due to his near absolute control over information in the Korean War.

Organizational culture theory similarly fares well in this case. Prior to and during the war, the organizational culture of the American army contained a military dominant conception of war and a Jominian norm of civil-military relations. The outcome of double failure was expected and confirmed, as was the theory's causal logic. To a considerable extent, the American army was culturally blind to the sophistication evinced in China's approach to the conflict, and was dead set against having diplomatic and intelligence priorities override its objective of wholesale unification of the peninsula by force.

ASSESSMENT OF DIRECT COMPETITORS

From the analysis above, three major conclusions can be reached regarding the sources of strategic performance in limited war. First, the information institution approach received substantial support in all of the cases examined in this book. Not only did the independent variable—information flow patterns among top policy makers and national security organizations—

correlate with the expected outcomes of each case, but the information institution approach's causal logic was also confirmed. The evidence demonstrates that the pattern of information flows among top policy makers and national security organizations affected the operation of the two information processing causal mechanisms (information collection and analysis and military-diplomatic coordination), which together strongly influenced the quality of the strategic risk assessments performed prior to and during each war. In sum, the information-processing capabilities of states directly affect their strategic performance in limited war, while state-level information institutions determine the extent of those information-processing capabilities.

Second, and at the other end of the spectrum, democratic civil-military relations theory received scant support from the evidence presented. Two patterns in the evidence stand out as particularly salient. First, despite the constancy of civilian domination of the military, the degree of information sharing among politicians and military officers varied widely. As such, we can conclude that information flow patterns are not a function of the domestic balance of power between civilian authorities and the military. Second, despite the prevalence of political-military preference divergence, the degree of military-diplomatic coordination varied widely as well. Preference divergence, while common, had no systematic effect on coordination.

Third, it should be noted that organizational culture theory received strong support in one case (double failure in Korea) and partial support in another (the ground campaign in Vietnam). As such, it would appear that under certain conditions, military organizational culture can indeed influence strategic performance. Yet the case of Vietnam poses a critical question: why was the strategic influence of the military's organizational culture felt only in the ground campaign and not in the air campaign? This variation is puzzling because in both campaigns, the cultural conception of war the American armed forces held was military dominant while the norm of civil-military relations was Jominian. As Douglass North suggests, the source of this type of variation lies in the institutional setting in which these organizations were positioned.[4] In the case of the air campaign, the air force was embedded in an information institutional context that structured the pattern of information exchange in a highly fluid fashion. So embedded, the air force's organizational culture succumbed to the incentivized pattern of behaviors the information institution determined. In this way, top policy makers were able to penetrate the organization's culture, rendering it incapable of exerting a direct causal effect on the level of strategic performance.

Conversely, in the case of the ground campaign, the army was embedded in an information institutional context that incentivized it to hoard and obfuscate the true nature of the information in its possession. Powerless to acquire information from additional sources, challenge MACV's analysis of the information they were receiving, and ensure tight military-diplomatic coordination on the ground in South Vietnam, top policy makers were incapable of overcoming the strong effects the culture of the American army exerted. In sum, the variation in organizational culture's influence on strategic performance in the Vietnam War serves as additional confirmation of the importance of information institutions.

The broad empirical support for the information institution approach suggests that when it comes to explaining strategic performance in war, we should be wary of any approach that does not incorporate all of the relevant state-level organizations and agencies that contribute to the design and execution of strategy. As I discussed in chapter 2, the information institution approach posits a very close causal connection between information institutions and the outcomes of limited war. As such, I argued that it was necessary to set the bar very high for empirical confirmation of the information institution approach. If a convincing argument could not be made that the outcomes of limited war were caused by the particular design of the information institution in each case, we should be ready to jettison this approach and privilege the alternative explanations drawn from the civil-military relations literature. Although the level of indeterminacy in the civil-military relations literature is higher than in the information institution approach, deference should be given to the extant approaches. Based on the evidence presented, however, the information institution approach consistently offered more compelling explanations for the outcomes of the four limited wars considered in this book.

THE RELEVANCE OF INFORMATION INSTITUTIONS: INFORMATION INSTITUTIONS VERSUS THE INDIRECT COMPETITOR

In chapter 2 I argued that in addition to testing an argument against its most important direct competitors, assessing the relevance of an argument against *indirect* competitors is also necessary. The most important indirect challenger to the information institution approach is rationalist bargaining theory. For rationalist bargaining theory, information is understood to be endogenous to the process of war fighting. The information institution approach, by contrast, sees information as an exogenous factor, one that independently affects strategic choice. To evaluate the relevance of the information institution approach, it is necessary to determine empirically whether information had an exogenous or endogenous affect on strategic performance.

In *How Wars End*, a recent and significant contribution to the study of war termination, Dan Reiter offers an elegant model of war aims variation that combines two factors rationalist approaches view as critical to the origins and termination of war: endogenous information and credible commitments. According to Reiter, the interaction of these factors produces incentives for states to modulate their war aims in ways that differ significantly from what the individual treatments of information and commitment concerns suggest. According to his model, one of the main drivers of conflict is the fear that the adversary will renege on a war-termination deal. As such, his model holds commitment fears constant at a high level. Given commitment fears, states engaging in combat interpret endogenous (or revealed) information from the battlefield in subtle but powerful ways. On the one hand, belligerents are likely to seek total victory (that is, they will raise or maintain their war aims at a high level) when: the costs of continued fighting are deemed acceptable, the dangers of a broken agreement grow, and/ or when there is a perceived hope in eventual victory. On the other hand, belligerents are likely to seek a limited victory (that is, they will lower or maintain their war aims at a lower level) when: the costs of continued fighting threaten to escalate significantly, the dangers of a broken agreement lessen, the chances of eventual victory approach zero, and/or when the belligerent is able to reduce the commitment problem through limited means (such as the capturing of strategically valuable territory).[5] Based on his extensive examination of numerous cases, Reiter concludes with three key observations: first, a high degree of uncertainty prevailed among belligerents pertaining to the balances of power and resolve *ex ante*; second, information revealed on the battlefield was "a relatively inefficient means of hastening war termination through information transmission"; and third, that "fears of adversarial noncompliance with war-ending agreements sometimes moot the connection between information and war-termination behavior."[6]

Reiter puts forth an important explanation of war aims variation, one that casts substantial doubt on the purported effects of domestic political factors in conditioning war termination.[7] Nevertheless, his model is open to both theoretical and empirical challenges. Theoretically, Reiter's model treats information solely as a by-product of combat outcomes. In other words, information is strictly endogenous to the conflict process; it is revealed in the process of strategic interaction. Considering information only in these terms reduces the analytical traction of the model to a significant extent. Specifically, Reiter's model provides little understanding as to how and why states adopt particular war aims and particular military strategies at the outset of a war. This omission is a problem due to the importance that information plays in all rationalist approaches: states seek out, learn from, and make strategic adjustments based on new information.[8] It thus stands to reason that just as revealed information exerts powerful pressures on war aims during wartime, so too does the information that states possess *before war commences*.[9]

Two implications follow from this observation. First, the initial strategies and war aims that states adopt serve as the benchmark from which future changes to war aims emerge. Explaining war aims variation must explicitly capture that benchmark. Second, and more importantly, states can vary in their capacities to design more or less appropriate strategies and war aims before war begins. While it is the case that uncertainty is a common problem facing all states, uncertainty is not uniformly distributed across states. The extent to which states can pierce the veil of prewar uncertainty will matter significantly to the appropriateness of their initial strategies, will affect the nature of information revealed during war, and thus will affect the variation in aims during wartime.

The evidence presented in chapters 3–6 calls into question Reiter's conclusions pertaining to the predominant role of endogenous information in causing strategic performance in these cases. In each of the cases examined, sufficient information was available *ex ante* that either did enable, or could have enabled, the United States to design and execute effective limited war strategies. In Korea, sufficient information (both military and diplomatic in nature) pertaining to China's intention to intervene was available prior to the PRC's First Phase Offensive. In the air campaign in the Vietnam War, the United States was able to accurately gauge China's intentions well before the PRC sent anything approximating a costly signal to the United States. In that war's ground campaign, the evidence presented showed clearly that while information pertaining to the strength and strategic approach of the National Liberation Front was widely available, MACV systematically skewed that information for its own (culturally determined) purposes. In the Persian Gulf War, the United States was able to amass and assess a wealth of information pertaining to Saddam's army and employ that information to great effect in Desert Storm. In the Iraq War, America was not short on information regarding either the Iraqi Army or the likely effects of a quick military campaign on postwar reconstruction. At issue in all of these cases was whether the available information was extracted and converted into strategy. As I have shown, the nature of America's information institutions affected how that information was employed. In short, the degree of strategic uncertainty confronting American policy makers was conditioned by the pattern of information flows among them and their national security organizations and not by the absence of prewar information per se.

The evidence presented here further suggests that the efficiency of information provided by combat on the strategic choices made during war was a direct function of information flow patterns among relevant state-level actors. In Korea, for example, little of the information available from the battlefield that indicated China's entry into the war had a discernible effect on how the war was prosecuted. Conversely, new evidence on the strength of the National Liberation Front in South Vietnam had a direct effect on how the air campaign was prosecuted. The difference in these two cases turned on how that information was collected, analyzed, and then employed by top policy makers. In Korea, it went largely unnoticed due to the truncated pattern of information flows; in Vietnam, it was noticed and acted upon to great effect due to the relatively robust pattern of information flows that governed strategic decision making in the air campaign.

With respect to the relative importance of credible commitments in terms of wartime strategy, Reiter assumes that all commitment fears are equally salient, that all such fears are predicated on equally legitimate concerns. Again, the Korean War demonstrates the potential problem with this assumption. As Reiter correctly notes, fears that North Korea would renege on any war termination deal short of absolute victory exerted a powerful effect on American strategic behavior. Yet there was a strategic option available that could have achieved America's aim of restoring the South Korean government and of avoiding Chinese intervention, *while simultaneously constructing a self-enforcing war-ending bargain.* Had the option of withdrawing American forces back to the "narrow neck" of the peninsula been subject to greater scrutiny, officials in Washington may well have decided to override MacArthur's preferences for outright unification. Such a move would have required the presence of US forces in Korea for a long period of time, to be sure. At the same time, given the relative ease of defending that position (as opposed to defending the length of the 38th parallel), the North Koreans and the Chinese would likely have averred from reigniting the war later on. Indeed, the evidence shows that Mao concluded that if the United

States were to have adopted this course, the war would have had to be put on hold for at least six months—sufficient time for the US and South Korean forces to establish a powerful defense in-depth of the southern portion of the peninsula. As it was, American policy makers' commitment fears were conditioned by a less than accurate understanding of China's intentions, an understanding that was in turn conditioned by the truncated information institution that guided American strategy in the war.[10]

Ultimately, the information institution approach passes the test of relevancy in the four cases of limited war discussed in this book. At the same time, this approach offers an alternative means of understanding how information affects strategic choice—namely, as an exogenous factor, and not one that is solely a by-product of combat. This is not to say, of course, that endogenous information has no effect on strategic choice in all cases. Rather, it is incumbent upon the investigator to model the effects of both types of information to see which is more relevant in any given case.

IMPLICATIONS FOR THEORY AND POLICY

The information institution approach outlined in this book has a number of implications for IR theory. Most critically, this book has shown that information flow patterns exert powerful institutional effects on actors within states, under the condition of a monopoly of policy authority (as is the case in waging war). Specifically, the evidence shows that different information flow patterns strongly affect the behavior of state-level organizations as well as the ability of top policy makers to understand the strategic environment and act purposefully in it. Robust information flows produced highly collaborative organizational behavior, mitigated many of the problems that individuals normally have when processing significant amounts of dynamic information, and led to higher levels of strategic performance. Truncated information flows, on the other hand, produced uncoordinated organizational behavior, exacerbated information processing dysfunctions, and led to lower levels of strategic performance.

The information institutional context provides an alternative theoretical lens for viewing and explaining how state-level organizations affect foreign policy.[11] In chapter 1, I argued that the utility of traditional organizational theory is limited because it examines organizational behavior without considering the institutional context in which those organizations are situated. The information institution approach reveals that under certain institutional conditions, traditional organizational theory can be usefully employed to explain foreign policy outcomes, but under other institutional conditions, its expectations concerning the behaviors of states are not met. In other words, the information institution approach can explain the worst instances of bureaucracies running amok as well as the best cases of bureaucratic responsiveness to civilian direction.

In response to traditional organization theory's myopia regarding the institutional context within states, a more recent variant of this school— hierarchical organizational theory—seeks to explain how state-level actors behave by conceiving of the state itself as a single organization with different functional divisions arranged according to particular forms. This approach explicitly considers the institutional context of relations among state-level actors, but in a way that is derivative of the organizational form of the state. The evidence presented in this book demonstrates that hierarchical organizational theory has the causal arrow between institutions and organizations backward. Specifically, in each of the cases considered above, the institutional pattern of behavior led directly to different modes of interorganizational behavior, and not the reverse. Indeed, the institutional pattern of information flows directly affected the level of governance costs (military-diplomatic coordination) and degree of departmentalism (the opportunism displayed by individual organizations) in ways that hierarchical organizational theory is incapable of modeling.[12] Taken together, the information institution approach demonstrates that state-level organizations and the institutional context in which they are embedded matter in explaining state behavior. The challenge for the investigator is to understand, first, how the institutional context can vary, and second, how that context affects organizational behaviors.

Additionally, the information institution approach has implications for theories of strategic choice in IR. Charles Glaser offers what is arguably the most sophisticated strategic choice theory to date. According to Glaser, three broad variables affect the strategic choices that states make when deciding to cooperate or compete with adversaries: state type (whether it is a greedy or security-seeking state), material factors (power, the offense-defense balance, and offense-defense differentiation), and informational factors (a state's belief about its adversary's motives and its beliefs about its adversary's beliefs about its motives). Each of these variables needs to be considered—on their own and in combination—in order to discover the strategy that a rational state ought to adopt in order to achieve its objectives. Two of these variables, power and information, merit closer consideration.[13]

With respect to relative power, Glaser makes a compelling case that a state's *potential* or *latent* power, not simply the actual military forces that have been deployed, must be incorporated in a theory of strategic choice. Focusing solely on the deployed military forces turns power into a consequence of state choice rather than a cause of it. Thus the relevant questions here are those related to the overall size of the military that should be built as well as those dealing with the type of military resources in which a state should invest. Both are germane to the fundamental issue at stake in strategic interaction: the type of military missions a state must be able to perform. Critically, Glaser's conception of state power is one of material extraction and conversion to relevant military assets. To fully explain rational strategic choice, scholars must then focus on states' institutional and domestic political assets that constrain or facilitate resource extraction and conversion. As Glaser notes, with a fuller conception of power, "the need for a theory of this input [power] to the strategic choice theory becomes more evident."[14]

Glaser's treatment of information is more problematic. Glaser convincingly argues that information regarding an adversary's motives and its beliefs about the adversary's beliefs about the state's motives is a crucial element affecting strategic choice. At the same time, he notes,

> A complication that arises with including this information variable is that a state's information about its adversary's motives might reflect prior interaction between the states, which could itself be influenced by the theory's other key variables [motives, power, and offense-defense variables]. At a given time, therefore, this information may not be independent of material variables and the state's own motives.

Glaser's solution to this problem boils down to recognizing and accepting this difficulty and then envisioning "a state's information as the information it has at the time of its decision."[15] While this approach is superior to the alternative of ignoring information variables altogether, it does not lessen (much less do away with) the problem of endogeneity, or that information may in fact be a by-product of power and motives, rather than an independent cause of strategic choice.

The information institution approach offers a vital correction to what is otherwise a promising theory of strategic choice. Fundamentally, the information institution approach is a theory of information extraction and conversion, one that examines a state's ability to acquire and use information as it makes strategic choices. By replacing state beliefs with the institutional capacity to extract and convert information (in a manner similar to that of raw materials), information variables become truly exogenous; no longer must information be seen as endogenous to strategic interaction, or epiphenomenal to power or motives.

Two implications follow from this observation, one specifically relevant to Glaser's argument, the other more generally to IR theory. First, the ability to mitigate uncertainty is just as important to explaining strategic choice as is the ability to generate military power. As Glaser notes, the extent of uncertainty regarding an adversary's motives and beliefs has a profound impact on strategic choice. Second, the ability of states to sufficiently lessen uncertainty through costly signaling or through transparency providing mechanisms (including international institutions), is questionable. On the one hand, uncertain security seeking states must hedge against the implications of being wrong about an adversary's type when they signal benign intentions. Moreover, under certain conditions practicing either restraint *or* engaging in competition can signal a determination to defend the status quo.[16] On the other hand, previous research demonstrates that increased information pertaining to states' capabilities, intentions, and decision-making processes does not only generate positive outcomes in instances of strategic interaction. According to Bernard Finel and Kristen Lord, increased transparency can directly harden preexisting preferences and complicate the signaling process.[17] In the end, states must interpret the signals being sent to them. In international environments saturated with information, it is up to the states to parse signals from noise. In both instances, uncertainty mitigation is a function of state-level institutional capacities.

The difference between exogenous and endogenous information turns on whether the relevant information is available prior to the interaction under investigation or whether it is a product of the interaction itself. I have argued that the information institution approach explains when and how states can effectively extract and convert information of either type. Given rationalist bargaining theory's emphasis on endogenous information, the major contribution of the information institution approach pertains to how exogenous information can be incorporated into theories of strategic choice. In the Persian Gulf War, for example, the United States was able to extract and convert a substantial amount of prewar information that was employed to great effect in the design and execution of the limited war strategy. Two potential objections to this analytical procedure may arise, however. First, on what grounds can I make the argument that prewar and wartime interactions are in fact distinct? The implication of this objection is that prewar diplomacy puts states along a path that informs how they engage in the limited war context, thus making it difficult to differentiate among various aspects of a given conflict. Second, even if prewar and wartime interactions are distinct, what explains failure of prewar coercive diplomacy, but wartime strategic success, when the state's information institution remains constant?

With respect to the first potential objection, prewar and wartime interactions can be conceptually distinguished along two criteria. The first, as Thomas Schelling discussed, pertains to the logic of the conflict that one side imposes on the other. In prewar coercive diplomacy, "It is the *threat* of damage, or of more damage to come, that can make someone yield or comply. It is *latent* violence that can influence someone's choice—violence that can be withheld or inflicted, or that a victim believes can be withheld or inflicted." By contrast, in times of war it is the actual application of violence with the intention of destroying the opponent's ability to defend itself that influences its choice.[18] In other words, when a state makes the choice to move the conflict from prewar coercive diplomacy to war, it is adopting a wholly new strategic course—one that is logically and conceptually distinct.[19] The second pertains to the stakes involved. Put simply, substantial and immediate material costs are at stake in wartime interactions, whereas in prewar contexts, the stakes (while not trivial) are substantially less. Capitulation to a coercer's demands short of war does, of course, entail costs. But those costs are may not be readily calculable, may be deferred or overcome, and do not necessarily preclude the target's ability to secure its objectives further down the road. Defeat in a war, especially against a far more powerful opponent, can call into question the existence of the state altogether. In sum, the differences between prewar and wartime interactions are substantial, entailing divergent logics and stakes. As such, and for the purposes of this study, it is particularly useful to conceive of prewar and wartime interactions as being conceptually distinct phenomena.

In addition to allowing us to differentiate between endogenous and exogenous information, the differences in logic and stakes between prewar and wartime interactions can also address the second potential objection. Despite the clarity of the threats issued to an opponent, and the military wherewithal to back up those threats if capitulation is not forthcoming, the credibility of the state engaging in coercive diplomacy may be doubted for a number of reasons. First, the target may discount a particular type of threat because the threat itself may be unfamiliar. This appears to have been Saddam Hussein's reaction to America's threatened use of air power prior to the Persian Gulf War.[20] Second, the target may be simultaneously facing threats from a third party, threats that may overwhelm those sent by the target. Prior to the Iraq War, Saddam viewed Iran as a threat of greater magnitude than that emanating from the United States.[21] Third, the target's own information institution may not be capable of discerning the credibility of the sender's threat. Again, prior to the Iraq War, it is clear from the available evidence that Saddam's years-long program of protecting himself and his regime from internal threats had the effect of preventing him from obtaining anything approximating an accurate understanding of the strategic environment, including an appreciation of the magnitude of the threat the United States posed and the sincerity of President Bush's declared intentions. Saddam was so secluded from accurate and timely information that it was not until the last days of major combat operations that he came to the realization that his regime had been, in fact, toppled.[22] In sum, the information institution approach allows scholars to understand when and how states will possess the capacities to effectively mitigate the problem of uncertainty, both prior to and during times of war.

Additionally, the information institution approach may be viewed as an important component of neoclassical realist theories of foreign policy.[23] Neoclassical realism holds that while material power conditions strongly influence state behavior, they do so only through the mediating effects of domestic-level factors. With respect to balancing, for example, Randall Schweller argues "that whether states balance against threats is not primarily determined by systemic factors but rather, like all national security decisions, by the domestic political process."[24] In particular, the state capacity to extract resources in the service of national security strategy is an issue that has received extensive consideration by neoclassical realists.[25] In a similar vein, the information institution approach may prove useful in explaining state capacity to extract and convert information as states navigate complex strategic environments. Just as embedded theories of resource extraction and conversion provide a more sophisticated understanding of state power, the information institution approach provides a compelling explanation for the variation in strategic sophistication.

At the same time, and notwithstanding the logical compatibility between information institutions and neoclassical realism, the findings presented in this book suggest that an uncritical acceptance of neoclassical realism's framework would be unwise. Put simply, material power considerations exerted no discernible effects on strategic performance in limited war.[26] This is perhaps the most surprising finding of my investigation. If realism is to be capable of offering compelling explanations of state behavior, then it should be able to speak to foreign policy outcomes under conditions of substantial power asymmetries, as was the case in all of the wars considered here. The evidence indicates that information institutions played a far greater role than that of a mediator of material power resources. To the contrary, information institutions played a direct role in determining the fortunes of the United States in limited war, and through strategic performance, American power was affected. In other words, my argument suggests that information played a substantial role in affecting power, rather than the reverse.

In terms of policy implications, the information institution approach suggests that while the problem of information in strategic decision making—to wit, the old saw pertaining to "drinking from a fire hose"—may never be eradicated, the ability of leaders to receive and act upon information of higher quality is certainly possible. To understand how requires that we view as distinct two aspects of the context of decision making: the pattern of information flows that connect leaders and their national security organizations, on the one hand, and the processes by which leaders make decisions, on the other. Information pathways, a product of individuals' creativity and design at one point in time, have profound effects on those same individuals at later points. Information institutions are, thus, not by-products of the decision-making process, but rather constitute the forum for decision making. As a result, presidents and their top advisers must give careful consideration at the start for how best to acquire information, deliberate effectively, and critically, how to maintain robust flows of information among organizations at lower levels in the hierarchy of government. In short, information institutional design should be at the forefront of administrative concern. Because of its importance, such considerations cannot be left to resolve themselves.[27]

There is a consensus in the vast literature on presidential decision making that the personal management style of top policy makers matters greatly in determining how information and advice flows within an administration.[28] Some presidents are "formalists" who prefer to have clear lines of administrative authority. Others prefer more "collegial" advisory systems that employ ad hoc task forces to tackle specific policy problems. Some presidents loathe witnessing disagreements among their top policy advisers either because they are uncomfortable in such situations, or because they feel such debates tend to stray from the pertinent topics at hand. Other leaders relish interpersonal confrontation because it allows them to probe the strengths and weaknesses of particular policy options.[29] These stylistic differences are real, and they certainly matter when it comes to designing decision-making processes in any administration.

Yet despite the manifest differences in styles across administrations, common features are evident in the decision-making systems of those presidents who were successful in national security policy. Specifically, successful administrations are those where presidents and top policy makers have

access to multiple sources of information, and where subordinate organizations widely share information at lower levels. Many different mechanisms
and configurations can produce these outcomes. I have argued that these
differences are not the most important causal factors in generating strategic success and failure in national security policy making, however. What
matters more is the range and quality of information that leaders receive,
factors that are determined by the broader information institution in which
leaders are embedded.

An issue not addressed in this book is that of the origins of information institutions. The findings presented above offer, at best, a first step in
understanding how presidents can simultaneously structure their access to
information in accordance with their personal preferences and ensure that
the broader information institution contains the features of a robust design.
A potentially productive avenue for future research would be the examination of this relationship directly. Investigations into the origins of information institutions along this line would likely advance our understanding of
how individual agency and institutional structures interact by examining
the conditions under which agents are more likely to influence structures,
and vice versa. For example, Schafer and Crichlow present evidence that
decision-making procedures among top policy makers can improve over
time.[30] Exploring the conditions under which similar improvements are
possible among top policy makers and organizations at much lower levels
in the state hierarchy would provide valuable insight into the origins of information institutions and the likelihood of their evolution.

The argument and findings in this book suggest that in order to maxi-
mize the chances of success in national security policy, legislatures must
not be viewed as either the "enemy" or "savior." Major pieces of legislation
pertaining to the structure of the national security apparatus have had beneficial effects on the strategic fortunes of the United States in wartime. For
example, the Central Intelligence Agency owes its existence to the National
Security Act of 1947, a piece of legislation that President Truman viewed
as an unwelcomed congressional intrusion into an area of exclusive presidential authority. But it wasn't until the Kennedy-era reforms of the early
1960s, however, that the CIA became more fully institutionalized in the
national security system.[31] Additionally, 1986 Goldwater-Nichols Act had a
profound impact on civilian control over the American military. In the face
of an entrenched uniformed opposition, Congress redesigned substantial
portions of the military establishment, the effect of which was to afford
the secretary of defense much greater power over the services individu-

ally, and in their joint capacities under the rubric of the Unified Combatant Commands. The impact of this landmark piece of legislation was to provide defense secretaries with greater access to better information from the military than had been the case previously.[32] Yet Goldwater-Nichols was not a panacea, as the variation in strategic performance in the Persian Gulf War and Iraq War suggests. What made the Persian Gulf War a success for the United States was the direct attention the first Bush administration paid early on to ensuring that information from across the national security apparatus (information from military and nonmilitary sources alike) was effectively managed under White House auspices. While a substantial amount of congressional attention has been given to the problems of "information sharing" and organizational capacities of the American intelligence community since 9/11, success in counterterrorism results from more than large budgets and "breaking down the walls" that prevent communication among organizations. Rather, the ability of presidents to design effective counterterror strategies comes when data are shared, vetted, and coordinated among agencies and organizations that still have distinct functions, overlapping jurisdictions, and which still succumb to bureaucratic inertia.[33] The information institutional context can certainly be affected by the actions of Congress. Yet information institutional design is ultimately a matter of presidential purview. With determination to ensure top policy makers access to multiple sources of information, and oversight mechanisms in place to facilitate information sharing across national security organizations, American national security strategy will be better served in the coming decades as new challenges and opportunities arise.

Notes

CHAPTER ONE

1. William C. Fuller Jr., *Strategy and Power in Russia, 1600-1914* (New York: Free Press, 1992), 260-64; Trevor Royle, *Crimea: The Great Crimean War, 1854-56* (New York: Palgrave Macmillan, 2004), 91-102.

2. A. J. P. Taylor, *The Struggle for Mastery in Europe, 1848-1918* (London: Oxford University Press, 1954), 201-28; Michael Howard, *The Franco-Prussian War: The German Invasion of France, 1870-1871* (New York: Routledge, 2001), 453-56.

3. Joseph E. Stiglitz and Linda J. Bilmes, *The Three Trillion Dollar War: The True Cost of the Iraq Conflict* (New York: W. W. Norton, 2008), 5-7, 133-34.

4. For a sampling of these works, see Michael C. Desch, *Power and Military Effectiveness: The Fallacy of Democratic Triumphalism* (Baltimore: Johns Hopkins University Press, 2008); Dan Reiter and Allan C. Stam, *Democracies at War* (Princeton, NJ: Princeton University Press, 2002); Stephen Biddle, *Military Power: Explaining Victory and Defeat in Modern Battle* (Princeton, NJ: Princeton University Press, 2004); John J. Mearsheimer, *Conventional Deterrence* (Ithaca, NY: Cornell University Press, 1983); and Eliot A. Cohen, *Supreme Command: Soldiers, Statesmen, and Leadership in Wartime* (New York: Free Press, 2002).

5. The vast majority IR scholarship understands the problem of information to be intractable, especially in situations of conflict. As such, scholars posit that other variables serve as proxies in the design and execution of foreign policy. For realism, uncertainty regarding others' intentions necessitates a focus on material power. Dale C. Copeland, "The Constructivist Challenge to Structural Realism: A Review Essay," *International Security* 25 (Fall 2000). For constructivism, states deal with complexity in international affairs by relying on collectively held ideas about the world. Jeffrey W. Legro, *Rethinking the World: Great Power Strategies and International Order* (Ithaca, NY: Cornell University Press, 2005). For liberalism, domestic regime type serves as a critical signal of intentions and thus conditions how a democratic state will behave toward it. John M. Owen, *Liberal Peace, Liberal War: American Politics and International Security* (Ithaca, NY: Cornell University Press, 2000).

6. Coordination among leaders and organizations is a prominent feature of organizational theory, discussed below. Barry R. Posen, *The Sources of Military Doctrine: France, Britain, and Germany between the World Wars* (Ithaca, NY: Cornell University Press, 1984), 24-29.

7. On international institutions, see John Duffield, "What Are International Institutions?" *International Studies Review* 9 (2007). On domestic political institutions, see Peter Trubowitz, *Politics and Strategy: Partisan Ambition and American Statecraft* (Princeton, NJ: Princeton University

Press, 2011); Helen V. Milner, *Interests, Institutions, and Information: Domestic Politics and International Relations* (Princeton, NJ: Princeton University Press, 1997).

8. This definition borrows from Doris A. Graber, *The Power of Communication: Managing Information in Public Organizations* (Washington, DC: CQ Press, 2003), 5.

9. Sun Tzu, *The Art of War*, trans. Roger T. Ames (New York: Ballantine Books, 1993), 113.

10. On the role of uncertainty in causing war, see James D. Fearon, "Rationalist Explanations for War," *International Organization* 49 (Summer 1995); Geoffrey Blainey, *The Causes of War* (New York: Free Press, 1973), 53-56. For a general assessment of bargaining theory, see Dan Reiter, "Exploring the Bargaining Model of War," *Perspectives on Politics* 1 (March 2003).

11. James D. Fearon, "Signaling Foreign Policy Interests: Tying Hands versus Sinking Costs," *Journal of Conflict Resolution* 41 (February 1997).

12. On information revelation during war, see Dan Reiter, *How Wars End* (Princeton, NJ: Princeton University Press, 2009), 14-18.

13. On the identification of (and an imperfect solution to) the problem of information endogeneity in affecting strategic choice, see Charles L. Glaser, *Rational Theory of International Politics: The Logic of Competition and Cooperation* (Princeton, NJ: Princeton University Press, 2010), 48-49.

14. Spencer D. Bakich, "Institutionalizing Supreme Command: Explaining Political-Military Integration in the Vietnam War, 1964-1968," *Small Wars and Insurgencies* 22 (October 2011): 699-701.

15. David A. Lake, "Two Cheers for Bargaining Theory: Assessing Rationalist Explanations of the Iraq War," *International Security* 35 (Winter 2010/11).

16. Glaser, *Rational Theory of International Politics*, 182.

17. Stephen Peter Rosen, *War and Human Nature* (Princeton, NJ: Princeton University Press, 2005); Yuen Foong Khong, *Analogies at War: Korea, Munich, Dien Bien Phu, and the Vietnam Decisions of 1965* (Princeton, NJ: Princeton University Press, 1992); Richard Ned Lebow, *Between Peace and War: The Nature of International Crises* (Baltimore: Johns Hopkins University Press, 1981); Robert Jervis, *Perception and Misperception in International Politics* (Princeton, NJ: Princeton University Press, 1976); and Irving Janis, *Victims of Groupthink: A Psychology Study of Foreign-Policy Decisions and Fiascoes* (Boston: Houghton Mifflin, 1972).

18. Richard C. Snyder, H. W. Bruck, and Burton Sapin, eds., *Foreign Policy Decision Making: An Approach to the Study of International Politics* (New York: Free Press of Glencoe, 1962).

19. Gregory M. Herek, Irving L. Janis, and Paul Huth, "Decision Making during International Crises: Is Quality of Process Related to Outcome?" *Journal of Conflict Resolution* 31 (June 1987).

20. Mark Schafer and Scott Crichlow, *Groupthink: High-Quality Decision Making in International Relations* (New York: Columbia University Press, 2010), 183-87.

21. William Stueck, *Rethinking the Korean War: A New Diplomatic and Strategic History* (Princeton, NJ: Princeton University Press, 2002), 114.

22. Bartholomew H. Sparrow, "Realism's Practitioner: Brent Scowcroft and the Making of the New World Order, 1989-1993," *Diplomatic History* 34 (January 2010): 152.

23. Milner, *Interests, Institutions, and Information*, 18.

24. Douglass C. North, *Institutions, Institutional Change, and Economic Performance* (New York: Cambridge University Press, 1990), 5.

25. Douglass C. North, "Epilogue: Economic Performance through Time," in *Empirical Studies in Institutional Change*, ed. Lee J. Alston, Thrainn Eggertsson, and Douglass C. North (New York: Cambridge University Press, 1996), 346.

26. Masahiko Aoki, *Toward a Comparative Institutional Analysis* (Cambridge, MA: MIT Press, 2001); Geoffrey M. Hodgson, *Economics and Institutions: A Manifesto for a Modern Institutional Economics* (Cambridge: Polity Press, 1988).

27. Graham Allison and Philip Zelikow, *Essence of Decision: Explaining the Cuban Missile Cri-*

sis, 2nd ed. (New York: Addison Wesley Longman, 1999); John D. Steinbruner, *The Cybernetic Theory of Decision: New Dimensions of Political Analysis* (Princeton, NJ: Princeton University Press, 1974).

28. David A. Welch, *Painful Choices: A Theory of Foreign Policy Change* (Princeton, NJ: Princeton University Press, 2005), 33.

29. David A. Welch, "The Organizational Process and Bureaucratic Politics Paradigms: Retrospect and Prospect," *International Security* 17 (Autumn 1992); Jonathan Bendor and Thomas H. Hammond, "Rethinking Allison's Models," *American Political Science Review* 86, no. 2 (1992); Robert J. Art, "Bureaucratic Politics and American Foreign Policy: A Critique," *Policy Sciences* 4 (1973); Stephen D. Krasner, "Are Bureaucracies Important? (Or Allison Wonderland)," *Foreign Policy* 7 (1972).

30. Arthur A. Stein, *Why Nations Cooperate: Circumstance and Choice in International Relations* (Ithaca, NY: Cornell University Press, 1990), 178-79.

31. Arthur L. Stinchcombe, *Information and Organizations* (Berkeley: University of California Press, 1990), 81.

32. Abdulkader H. Sinno, *Organizations at War in Afghanistan and Beyond* (Ithaca, NY: Cornell University Press, 2008), 11-13.

33. Alexander Cooley, *Logics of Hierarchy: The Organization of Empires, States, and Military Occupations* (Ithaca, NY: Cornell University Press, 2005), 4-6; Alfred D. Chandler Jr., *Strategy and Structure: Chapters in the History of the American Industrial Enterprise* (Cambridge, MA: MIT Press, 1969); Oliver Williamson, *The Economic Institutions of Capitalism* (New York: Free Press, 1985).

34. Cooley, *Logics of Hierarchy*, 5.

35. Ibid., 52.

36. See table 7.1 in chapter 7 for a summary of these findings.

37. Lisa L. Martin, and Beth A. Simmons, "Theories and Empirical Studies of International Institutions," *International Organization* 52 (1998): 729-57; John J. Mearsheimer, "The False Promise of International Institutions," *International Security* 19 (1994): 18.

38. Milner, *Interests, Institutions, and Information*, 18-23.

39. Chaim Kaufman, "Threat Inflation and the Failure of the Marketplace of Ideas: The Selling of the Iraq War," *International Security* 29 (Summer 2004): 5-48; Norman Ornstein and Thomas Mann, "When Congress Checks Out," *Foreign Affairs* 85 (November-December 2006): 67-82.

40. Krasner, "Are Bureaucracies Important?," 168-69.

41. As Legro and Moravcsik note, the distribution of information is one of the primary functions of institutions. Information flow patterns directly affect the distribution of information among relevant actors in a state's national security apparatus, including its leaders. Jeffrey W. Legro and Andrew Moravcsik, "Is Anybody Still a Realist?" *International Security* 24 (Autumn 1999): 46-47.

42. Milner, *Interests, Institutions, and Information*, 18.

43. Jeffrey W. Taliaferro, "Neoclassical Realism and Resource Extraction: State Building for Future War," in *Neoclassical Realism, the State, and Foreign Policy*, ed. Steven E. Lobell, Norrin M. Ripsman, and Jeffrey W. Taliaferro (New York: Cambridge University Press, 2009), 215.

44. For the theoretical foundations of "republican liberalism," see Andrew Moravcsik, "Taking Preferences Seriously: A Liberal Theory of International Politics," *International Organization* 51 (Autumn 1997): 530-33.

45. Owen, *Liberal Peace, Liberal War*, 27-29.

46. Trubowitz, *Politics and Strategy*, 26-28.

47. Randall L. Schweller, *Unanswered Threats: Political Constraints on the Balance of Power* (Princeton, NJ: Princeton University Press, 2006), 13-15.

48. Deborah D. Avant, *Political Institutions and Military Change: Lessons from Peripheral Wars* (Ithaca, NY: Cornell University Press, 1994).

49. For example, politically powerful militaries (i.e., pre–World War I Germany) can usurp an executive's monopoly of policy authority. Jack Snyder, "Civil-Military Relations and the Cult of the Offensive, 1914 and 1984," *International Security* 9 (Summer 1984): 115.

50. Milner, *Interests, Institutions, and Information*, 60–65.

51. This is especially the case for the United States. Andrew J. Polsky, *Elusive Victories: The American Presidency at War* (New York: Oxford University Press, 2012), 13.

52. Scott Wolford, Dan Reiter, and Clifford J. Carrubba, "Information, Commitment, and War," *Journal of Conflict Resolution* 55 (2011).

53. Glaser, *Rational Theory of International Politics*, 40–43, 182; John J. Mearsheimer, *The Tragedy of Great Power Politics* (New York: Norton 2001), 60–81.

54. On the timing of preventive wars, see Dale C. Copeland, *The Origins of Major War* (Ithaca, NY: Cornell University Press, 2000). The probability of victory increases when the initiating state has superior power and/or when the offense has the advantage. Stephen Van Evera, *Causes of War: Power and the Roots of Conflict* (Ithaca, NY: Cornell University Press, 1999), 160–66.

55. Patrick M. Morgan, *Deterrence Now* (New York: Cambridge University Press, 2003), 80–85.

56. On the relationship between decision making and foreign policy outcomes, see Schafer and Crichlow, *Groupthink*, 1–10.

57. Amy B. Zegart, *Spying Blind: The CIA, the FBI, and the Origins of 9/11* (Princeton, NJ: Princeton University Press, 2007), 43–49.

58. Ibid., chap. 2; *The 9/11 Commission Report*, authorized edition (New York: W. W. Norton, 2004); Richard K. Betts, *Enemies of Intelligence: Knowledge and Power in American National Security* (New York: Columbia University Press, 2007); and Richard H. Immerman, "Intelligence and Strategy: Historicizing Psychology, Policy, and Politics," *Diplomatic History* 32 (January 2008).

59. Elizabeth Kier, *Imagining War: French and British Military Doctrine between the Wars* (Princeton, NJ: Princeton University Press, 1997); John Nagl, *Learning to Eat Soup with a Knife: Counterinsurgency Lessons from Malaya and Vietnam* (Chicago: University of Chicago Press, 2002).

60. Jeffrey W. Legro, *Cooperation under Fire: Anglo-German Restraint during World War II* (Ithaca, NY: Cornell University Press, 1995), 26–28.

61. Risa A. Brooks, *Shaping Strategy: The Civil-Military Politics of Strategic Assessment* (Princeton, NJ: Princeton University Press, 2008), 7.

62. Leaders in democratic states are argued to receive more and better information from their militaries than are leaders of nondemocratic states. Reiter and Stam, *Democracies at War*, 23–24.

63. Joseph S. Nye Jr., *The Future of Power* (New York: Public Affairs, 2011), chap. 7.

64. Peter Feaver and William Inboden, "A Strategic Planning Cell on National Security at the White House," in *Avoiding Trivia: The Role of Strategic Planning in American Foreign Policy*, ed. Daniel Drezner (Washington, DC: Brookings Institution Press, 2009), 108–9.

CHAPTER TWO

1. Dale C. Copeland, *The Origins of Major War* (Ithaca, NY: Cornell University Press, 2000), 4.

2. Although the states involved may practice mutual restraint. Jeffrey W. Legro, *Cooperation under Fire: Anglo-German Restraint during World War II* (Ithaca, NY: Cornell University Press, 1995), 217–29.

3. The US Marine Corps defined small wars as "operations undertaken under executive authority, wherein military force is combined with diplomatic pressure in the internal or external affairs of another state whose government is unstable, inadequate, or unsatisfactory for the preservation of life and of such interests as are determined by the foreign policy of our Nation." US Marine Corps, FMFRP 12-15, "Small Wars Manual" (Washington, DC: US Government Printing Office, 1940), 1.

4. For the multitude of reasons why a state would want to avoid escalating a limited war, see Fred Charles Iklé, *Every War Must End*, rev. ed. (New York: Columbia University Press, 1991), 40–50.

5. This definition is similar to that offered in Robert Endicott Osgood, *Limited War: The Challenge to American Strategy* (Chicago: University of Chicago Press, 1966), 1–4.

6. Richard Smoke, *War: Controlling Escalation* (Cambridge, MA: Harvard University Press, 1977), 17. Original italics.

7. These thresholds tend to be tacit understandings between states. They can include geography, types of weapons, or "traditional conventions of war." Ibid., 15–16.

8. A sample of this literature includes William W. Kaufmann, "Limited Warfare," in *Military Policy and National Security*, ed. William W. Kaufman (Princeton, NJ: Princeton University Press, 1956); Morton H. Halperin, *Limited War in the Nuclear Age* (New York: Wiley, 1963); Osgood, *Limited War*; Osgood, *Limited War Revisited* (Boulder, CO: Westview Press, 1979); Thomas Schelling, *The Strategy of Conflict* (Cambridge, MA: Harvard University Press, 1980); Schelling *Arms and Influence* (New Haven, CT: Yale University Press, 1966); Herman Kahn, *On Escalation: Metaphors and Scenarios* (Baltimore: Penguin Books, 1968); and Barry R. Posen, *Inadvertent Escalation: Conventional War and Nuclear Risks* (Ithaca, NY: Cornell University Press, 1991).

9. Smoke, *War*, 8–18. Horizontal escalation concerns were to some extent embedded in America's "flexible response" approach to containment. See John Lewis Gaddis, *Strategies of Containment: A Critical Appraisal of Postwar American National Security Policy* (New York: Oxford University Press, 1982), 101, 206–32; Joshua M. Epstein, "Horizontal Escalation: Sour Notes on a Recurrent Theme," *International Security* 8 (Winter 1983/84). The idea of horizontal escalation is similar to that of the diffusion of war. Randolph Siverson and Harvey Starr, *The Diffusion of War: A Study of Opportunity and Willingness* (Ann Arbor: University of Michigan Press, 1991); Kelly M. Kadera, "Transmission, Barriers, and Constraints: A Dynamic Model of the Spread of War," *Journal of Conflict Resolution* 42 (June 1998).

10. Iklé, *Every War Must End*, 40–41. The incentives for continuing a losing war are discussed in H. E. Goemans, *War and Punishment: The Causes of War Termination and the First World War* (Princeton, NJ: Princeton University Press, 2000).

11. For works that focus exclusively on the military aspects of limited and small wars, see Stephen Peter Rosen, "Vietnam and the American Theory of Limited War," *International Security* 7 (Fall 1982); and Max Boot, *The Savage Wars of Peace: Small Wars and the Rise of American Power* (New York: Basic Books, 2003). Christopher M. Gacek, *The Logic of Force: The Dilemma of Limited War in American Foreign Policy* (New York: Columbia University Press, 1994), discusses the difficulty in limiting the use force to serve policy ends.

12. Robert Jervis, *System Effects: Complexity in Political and Social Life* (Princeton, NJ: Princeton University Press, 1997), 291.

13. General Omar N. Bradley, testimony before the Senate Committees on Armed Services and Foreign Relations, May 15, 1951. "Military Situation in the Far East, hearings," 82nd Congress, 1st sess., part 2, 732.

14. Terry L. Deibel, *Foreign Affairs Strategy: Logic for American Statecraft* (New York: Cambridge University Press, 2007), 8; B. H. Liddell Hart, *Strategy*, 2nd ed. (New York: Meridian, 1991), 322.

15. I avoid the term "grand strategy" because the vast majority of IR scholars reserve this term to describe strategy at the highest level of statecraft adopted during times of peace. Terminological disputes aside, the essence of strategy is the logical and comprehensive linkage between political objectives (ends) and military and nonmilitary resources (means) in a highly competitive environment. For the more expansive and familiar treatments of grand strategy, see Robert J. Art, *A Grand Strategy for America* (Ithaca, NY: Cornell University Press, 2003); and Barry R. Posen and Andrew L. Ross, "Competing Visions for U.S. Grand Strategy," *International Security* 21 (Winter 1996/97).

16. Charles A. Kupchan, "Getting In: The Initial Stage of Military Intervention," in *Foreign Military Intervention: The Dynamics of Protracted Conflict*, ed. Ariel E. Levite, Bruce W. Jentleson, and Larry Berman (New York: Columbia University Press, 1992), 249.

17. This is especially the case when precise signals need to be sent in complex strategic settings. See Alexander L. George and Richard Smoke, *Deterrence in American Foreign Policy: Theory and Practice* (New York: Columbia University Press, 1974), 561–65.

18. This problem is one of adopting war plans that fail to include an understanding of how the war might terminate. Iklé, *Every War Must End*, 2–8.

19. Robert Jervis, "The Impact of the Korean War on the Cold War," *Journal of Conflict Resolution* 24 (December 1980).

20. Anne E. Sartori, *Deterrence by Diplomacy* (Princeton, NJ: Princeton University Press, 2005), 43–72.

21. Stacie E. Goddard, "When Right Makes Might: How Prussia Overturned the European Balance of Power," *International Security* 33 (Winter 2008/9).

22. Francis Fukuyama, "Guidelines for Future Nation Builders," in *Nation Building: Beyond Afghanistan and Iraq*, ed. Francis Fukuyama (Baltimore: Johns Hopkins University Press, 2006), 232–34.

23. On the types of occupation strategies available to states, see David Edelstein, *Occupational Hazards: Success and Failure in Military Operations* (Ithaca, NY: Cornell University Press, 2008), 49–55. On nation building, see James Dobbins et al., *America's Role in Nation-Building: From Germany to Iraq* (Santa Monica, CA: Rand, 2003).

24. Osgood, *Limited War Revisited*, 11–14.

25. Ernest R. May, "Conclusions: Capabilities and Proclivities," in *Knowing One's Enemies: Intelligence Assessment before the Two World Wars*, ed. Ernest R. May (Princeton, NJ: Princeton University Press, 1986); and Thomas G. Mahnken, *Uncovering Ways of War: U.S. Intelligence and Foreign Military Innovation, 1918–1941* (Ithaca, NY: Cornell University Press, 2002).

26. Security dilemma theorists have captured these dynamics well. See Robert Jervis, *Perception and Misperception in International Politics* (Princeton, NJ: Princeton University Press, 1976), 96–107; Charles L. Glaser, *Rational Theory of International Politics: The Logic of Competition and Cooperation* (Princeton, NJ: Princeton University Press, 2010), 51–86.

27. See the discussion of national evaluative capabilities in affecting misperception in Charles L. Glaser, "The Political Consequences of Military Strategy: Expanding and Refining the Spiral and Deterrence Models," *World Politics* 44 (July 1992): 514–15.

28. I use the term "information institutions" as opposed to "networks" to highlight the role of institutional rigidities that accompany existing communication channels within and among relevant state-level actors. Further, state-level information institutions are seen as key elements of strategic choice theory. On "information structures" in strategic choice, see David A. Lake and Robert Powell, "International Relations: A Strategic-Choice Approach," in *Strategic Choice and International Relations*, ed. David A. Lake and Robert Powell (Princeton, NJ: Princeton University Press, 1999), 6–13. On information flows in bureaucracies, see Andrew Rudalevige, "The Structure of Leadership: Presidents, Hierarchies, and Information Flow," *Presidential Studies Quarterly* 35 (June 2005): 336; Terry M. Moe, "The Politics of Structural Choice: Toward a Theory of Public Bureaucracy," in *Organization Theory*, ed. Oliver E. Williamson (New York: Oxford University Press, 1995). On the links between organizations and informational needs, see Richard L. Daft and Robert H. Lengel, "Organizational Information Requirements, Media Richness, and Structural Design," *Management Science* 32 (May 1986); and Herbert A. Simon, *Administrative Behavior*, 4th ed. (New York: Free Press, 1997).

29. David A. Welch, *Painful Choices: A Theory of Foreign Policy Change* (Princeton, NJ: Princeton University Press, 2005), 32; Amy Zegart, *Flawed by Design: the Evolution of the CIA, JCS, and NSC* (Stanford, CA: Stanford University Press, 1999).

30. "Powerful shocks do cause [organizational] structural changes, but the new structural forms often stabilize and allow us to use them as an independent variable, at least for the duration of a significant cycle of strategic interaction." Abdulkader H. Sinno, *Organizations at War in Afghanistan and Beyond* (Ithaca, NY: Cornell University Press, 2008), 24.

31. The intentional manipulation of information institutions in firms is a far easier task than it is in the context of the state. Two potential reasons (among many) are the fact that formal restrictions (statutory, or otherwise) may exist pertaining to information dissemination, and that state bureaucracies wield authority and power that far outstrip that held by divisions in a firm. On the manipulation of communication channels in firms, see Rob Cross and Andrew Parker, *The Hidden Power of Social Networks: Understanding How Work* Really *Gets Done in Organizations* (Boston: Harvard Business School Press, 2004).

32. On the difference between environmental and task ambiguity, see Duncan J. Watts, *Six Degrees: The Science of a Connected Age* (New York: W. W. Norton, 2003), 268–69; William Lazonic, *Business Organization and the Myth of the Market Economy* (New York: Cambridge University Press, 1991), 199–200.

33. Gary J. Miller, *Managerial Dilemmas: The Political Economy of Hierarchy* (New York: Cambridge University Press, 1992), 33.

34. Samuel P. Huntington, *The Soldier and the State: The Theory and Politics of Civil-Military Relations* (Cambridge, MA: Harvard University Press, 1957), 11–16.

35. Jack Snyder, *Ideology of the Offensive: Military Decision Making and the Disasters of 1914* (Ithaca, NY: Cornell University Press, 1984), 26–30.

36. Arthur L. Stinchcombe, *Information and Organizations* (Berkeley: University of California Press, 1990), 78–81.

37. Doris A. Graber, *The Power of Communication: Managing Information in Public Organizations* (Washington, DC: CQ Press, 2003), 54, 76–79; Robert E. O'Conner and Larry D. Spence, "Communication Disturbances in a Welfare Bureaucracy: A Case for Self-Management," *Journal of Sociology and Social Welfare* 4 (1976).

38. Zegart, *Flawed by Design*, 37; Aaron L. Friedberg, *The Weary Titan: Britain and the Experience of Relative Decline, 1895–1905* (Princeton, NJ: Princeton University Press, 1988), 282.

39. Graber, *Power of Communication*, 25.

40. Graham Allison and Philip Zelikow, *Essence of Decision: Explaining the Cuban Missile Crisis*, 2nd ed. (New York: Longman, 1999), 298–99.

41. Simon, *Administrative Behavior*, 31–32.

42. Sinno, *Organizations at War in Afghanistan and Beyond*, 50.

43. The decision-making benefits of multiple sources of information have been recognized by political scientists and economists alike. David M. Edelstein, "Managing Uncertainty: Beliefs about Intentions and the Rise of Great Powers," *Security Studies* 12 (Autumn 2002): 11–12; Martin Van Creveld, *Command in War* (Cambridge, MA: Harvard University Press, 1985), 268–75; Stinchcombe, *Information and Organizations*, 9–17, chap. 4; Masahiko Aoki, *Information, Incentives, and Bargaining in the Japanese Economy* (New York: Cambridge University Press, 1998), 11–20; and Masahiko Aoki, "Horizontal vs. Vertical Information Structure of the Firm," *American Economic Review* 76 (December 1986).

44. Geoffrey M. Hodgson, *Economics and Institutions: A Manifesto for a Modern Institutional Economics* (Cambridge: Polity Press, 1988), 132–33.

45. Herbert A. Simon, "Applying Information Technology to Organizational Design," *Public Administration Review* 33 (1973): 270.

46. Stephen Peter Rosen, *War and Human Nature* (Princeton, NJ: Princeton University Press, 2005), chap. 2.

47. More decentralized organizations are better able to handle information overload problems than more centralized organizations. Sinno, *Organizations at War in Afghanistan and Beyond*, 84.

48. The theoretical foundations for this proposition (that lateral connections in hierarchies reduce the information overload problem) are discussed in Watts, *Six Degrees*, 277-84. For the argument that a small number of random connections reduce congestion in a system, see D. J. Watts, *Small Worlds: The Dynamics of Networks between Order and Randomness* (Princeton, NJ: Princeton University Press, 1999); D. J. Watts and S. H. Strogatz, "Collective Dynamics of 'Small-World' Networks," *Nature* 393 (1998). Random connectivity slights the realities (and purpose) of hierarchies. My argument relies on the notion that additional connections between/among independent units are beneficial, while accounting for the limitations of information processing in hierarchies.

49. Elinor Ostrom, *Understanding Institutional Diversity* (Princeton, NJ: Princeton University Press, 2005), 109.

50. Watts, *Six Degrees*, 273.

51. On the promise of, and difficulties in achieving coordination among subunits via lateral communications channels, see Laurence J. O'Toole Jr., "Interorganizational Communication: Opportunities and Challenges for Public Administration," in *Handbook of Administrative Communication*, ed. James L. Garnett and Alexander Kouzmin (New York: Marcel Dekker, 1997).

52. See the discussion of "institutionalizing distrust" in Richard Rose, "Organizing Issues in and Organizing Problems Out," in *The Managerial Presidency*, ed. James P. Pfiffner (Pacific Grove, CA: Brooks/Cole, 1991), 108. See also Thomas Hammond, "Structure, Strategy, and the Agenda of the Firm," in *Fundamental Issues in Strategy: A Research Agenda*, ed. Richard P. Rumelt, Dan E. Schendel, and David J. Teece (Boston: Harvard Business School Press, 1994), 152.

53. James G. March and Herbert A. Simon, *Organizations* (New York: Wiley, 1958); Anthony Downs, *Inside Bureaucracy* (Boston: Little, Brown, 1967). See also the discussion of the *ringi* system of consensual decision making in Japanese auto manufacturing in Lazonic, *Business Organization and the Myth of the Market Economy*, 39-40.

54. In this way, the information institution approach and political-psychological theories are complementary. Yet because the information institution approach also focuses on matters of organizational coordination (a focus absent in political-psychological theories), my argument offers a more comprehensive explanation of state behavior than is offered by individual-level theories.

55. Alexander L. George, *Presidential Decisionmaking in Foreign Policy: The Effective Use of Information and Advice* (Boulder, CO: Westview Press, 1980), 145-47.

56. Masahiko Aoki, *Toward a Comparative Institutional Analysis* (Cambridge, MA: MIT Press, 2001), 98.

57. On the relationship between group size and group behavior, see Mancur Olson, *The Logic of Collective Action: Public Goods and the Theory of Groups*, rev. ed. (Cambridge, MA: Harvard University Press, 1971), 40-41. Punishment can take many forms but generally boils down to restrictions on the organizations "essence," roles and missions, autonomy, and budgetary allocations. Morton H. Halperin and Priscilla A. Clapp, with Arnold Kanter, *Bureaucratic Politics and Foreign Policy*, 2nd ed. (Washington, DC: Brookings Institution Press, 2006), 25-61.

58. Mathew D. McCubbins and Thomas Schwartz, "Congressional Oversight Overlooked: Police Patrols versus Fire Alarms," *American Journal of Political Science* 28 (February 1984): 166-67. For applications of principal-agency theory to civil-military relations, see Peter D. Feaver, *Armed Servants: Agency, Oversight, and Civil-Military Relations* (Cambridge, MA: Harvard University Press, 2003); and Deborah D. Avant, *Political Institutions and Military Change: Lessons from Peripheral Wars* (Ithaca, NY: Cornell University Press, 1994).

59. I would like to thank one of this book's anonymous reviewers for the phrasing of this question.

60. Jeffrey W. Taliaferro, *Balancing Risks: Great Power Intervention in the Periphery* (Ithaca, NY: Cornell University Press, 2004), 30-51; Mark L. Haas, "Prospect Theory and the Cuban Missile Crisis," *International Studies Quarterly* 45 (June 2001); Robert Jervis, "Political Implications of Loss Aversion," *Political Psychology* 13 (June 1992).

61. This discussion is informed by two distinct aspects of strategic design: net assessments and strategic planning. On net assessments, see Paul Bracken, "Net Assessment: A Practical Guide," *Parameters* (Spring 2006); and Stephen Peter Rosen, "Net Assessment as an Analytical Concept," in *On Not Confusing Ourselves: Essays on National Security Strategy in Honor of Albert and Roberta Wohlstetter*, ed. A. W. Marshall, J. J. Martin, and Henry S. Rowen (Boulder, CO: Westview Press, 1991), 283-301. On strategic planning, see Aaron L. Friedberg, "Strengthening U.S. Strategic Planning," in *Avoiding Trivia: The Role of Strategic Planning in American Foreign Policy*, ed. Daniel W. Drezner (Washington, DC: Brookings Institution Press, 2009), 84-97; and Bruce W. Jentleson, "An Integrative Executive Branch Strategy for Policy Planning," in ibid., 69-83.

62. James G. March and Johan P. Olsen, *Rediscovering Institutions: The Organizational Basis of Politics* (New York: Free Press, 1989), 15. Emphasis added.

63. My use of the term "high quality assessment" is akin to Rudalevige's term "good advice." The relevant characteristics being that the information leaders receive is "useful" (fitting real-world problems), "comprehensive" (including all plausible options and likelihoods of success), and "diverse" (including winning and dissenting options, vetted by neutral people). Rudalevige, "The Structure of Leadership," 340.

64. That certain agencies can operate in isolation reflects the possibility that information institutions can vary across issue areas. Roger Porter, *Presidential Decision Making: The Economic Policy Board* (New York: Cambridge University Press, 1980); Charles Walcott and Karen Hult, *Governing the White House: From Hoover through LBJ* (Lawrence: University Press of Kansas, 1995).

65. Imre Lakatos, "Falsification and the Methodology of Scientific Research Programmes," in *Criticism and the Growth of Knowledge*, ed. Imre Lakatos and Alan Musgrave (Cambridge: Cambridge University Press, 1970).

66. Arthur A. Stein, *Why Nations Cooperate: Circumstances and Choice in International Relations* (Ithaca, NY: Cornell University Press), 183-84.

67. On the "salience" of competing arguments, see Copeland, *Origins of Major War*, 31.

68. Barry R. Posen, *The Sources of Military Doctrine: France, Britain, and Germany between the World Wars* (Ithaca, NY: Cornell University Press, 1984), 37.

69. Legro, *Cooperation under Fire*, 17-19.

70. Peter Feaver refers to this strand of civil-military relations scholarship as the "civilian supremacist" school. See his "The Right to Be Right: Civil-Military Relations and the Iraq Surge Decision," *International Security* 35 (Spring 2011): 93-97; and Eliot A. Cohen, *Supreme Command: Soldiers, Statesmen, and Leadership in Wartime* (New York: Free Press, 2002).

71. Spencer D. Bakich, "Institutionalizing Supreme Command: Explaining Political-Military Integration in the Vietnam War, 1964-1968," *Small Wars and Insurgencies* 22 (Winter 2011).

72. Legro, *Cooperation under Fire*, 19.

73. Ibid., 25-27. In times of peace, organizational culture tends to play an intervening role in the formation of national security policies, such as the military doctrinal choices. Elizabeth Kier, *Imagining War: French and British Military Doctrines between the Wars* (Princeton, NJ: Princeton University Press, 1997), 21.

74. Colin H. Kahl, "In the Crossfire or the Crosshairs? Norms, Civilian Casualties, and U.S. Conduct in Iraq," *International Security* 32 (Summer 2007).

75. See the discussion of the Soviet army's adherence to the big-battle paradigm in Robert M. Cassidy, *Counterinsurgency and the Global War on Terror* (Stanford, CA: Stanford University Press, 2008), 31-32.

76. Carl von Clausewitz, *On War*, trans. and ed. Michael Howard and Peter Paret (Princeton, NJ: Princeton University Press, 1984), 75-77. Examples of the military dominant culture include the armies captured by the "cult of the offensive" pre-World War I. Stephen Van Evera, "The Cult of the Offensive and the Origins of the First World War," *International Security* 9 (Summer 1984).

77. Clausewitz, *On War*, 78-89. An example of an army holding a balanced concept is the British Army before and during the Malayan War. John A. Nagl, *Learning to Eat Soup with a*

Knife: Counterinsurgency Lessons from Malaya and Vietnam (Chicago: University of Chicago Press, 2002), 51.

78. On the role of politics in wartime in the works of Antoine-Henry Jomini, see Michael I. Handel, *Masters of War: Classical Strategic Thought*, 2nd ed. (London: Frank Cass, 1996), 56–57. Examples of this culture can be found in the American army throughout much of its history. Cassidy, *Counterinsurgency and the Global War on Terror*, 103–14. On the American military's view of civilian violations of military autonomy, see Richard K. Betts, *Soldiers, Statesmen, and Cold War Crises* (New York: Columbia University Press, 1991), 12–15.

79. A possible example of this culture is that of the Israel Defense Forces. Rebecca L. Schiff, "Civil-Military Relations Reconsidered: A Theory of Concordance," *Armed Forces and Society* 22 (Fall 1995): 17–19.

80. "The military tends to favor policies that promote its organizational aims. Since these favored policies must be justified in strategic terms, strategic perceptions and analysis are likely to become skewed whenever organization interests are at odds with sound strategy." Snyder, *Ideology of the Offensive*, 18. On information asymmetries between politicians and military officers, see Feaver, *Armed Servants*, 68–69.

81. Risa A. Brooks, *Shaping Strategy: The Civil-Military Politics of Strategic Assessment* (Princeton, NJ: Princeton University Press, 2008), 53.

82. Dan Reiter and Allan C. Stam, *Democracies at War* (Princeton, NJ: Princeton University Press, 2002), 24.

83. Brooks, *Shaping Strategy*, 48–51.

84. Posen, *Sources of Military Doctrine*, 24–25.

85. Brooks, *Shaping Strategy*, 44, 50.

86. Ibid., 267.

87. Reiter and Stam, *Democracies at War*, 1–9.

88. Others have employed this conceptual disaggregation approach to reach a "finer-grained" understanding in causal relationships between variables. See Stephen Van Evera, *Causes of War: Power and the Roots of Conflict* (Ithaca, NY: Cornell University Press, 1999), 7–8.

89. The procedure of leveraging state-level variables to explain outcomes of strategic interaction is discussed in David Kinsella, "No Rest for the Democratic Peace," *American Political Science Review* 99 (August 2005): 453.

90. Dominic D. P. Johnson and Dominic Tierney, *Failing to Win: Perceptions of Victory and Defeat in International Politics* (Cambridge, MA: Harvard University Press, 2006), 24–34.

91. Jonathan Bendor and Thomas H. Hammond, "Rethinking Allison's Models," *American Political Science Review* 86 (June 1, 1992): 317.

92. Edmund F. McGarrell and Kip Schlegel, "The Implementation of Federally Funded Multi-jurisdictational Drug Task Forces: Organizational Structure and Interagency Relationships," *Journal of Criminal Justice* 21 (1993).

93. Graber, *Power of Communication*, 103–8. Individuals who are involved in interagency communications are referred to as liaisons, boundary spanners, or bridges.

94. See, for example, Cross and Parker, *Hidden Power of Social Networks*.

95. Legro, *Cooperation under Fire*, 30. Where there is consensus among scholars about the organizational culture of the American military in each case, I will code culture along those lines. Where no consensus exists, I will make an independent judgment based on this type of analysis.

96. Brooks, *Shaping Strategy*, 25.

97. It is important to clarify that this mechanism pertains to the processes of information management, and not to the quality of information per se. On the effects of uncertainty and ambiguity in different information institutional forms, see the section on strategic risk assessment above.

98. Alexander L. George and Andrew Bennett, *Case Studies and Theory Development in the Social Sciences* (Cambridge, MA: MIT Press, 2005), 235.

99. Andrew Bennett and Colin Elman, "Qualitative Research: Recent Developments in Case Study Methods," *Annual Review of Political Science* 9 (2006): 465–68.

100. For the multiple advantages of process-tracing, and how process-tracing relates to typological theory, see George and Bennett, *Case Studies and Theory Development*, 205–62.

101. Gary King, Robert O. Keohane, and Sidney Verba, *Designing Social Inquiry: Scientific Inference in Qualitative Research* (Princeton, NJ: Princeton University Press, 1994), 226–27.

102. Causal mechanisms "can be checked against the historical record, and the theory will be strengthened or weakened to the extent that they find empirical support." Sebastian Rosato, "The Flawed Logic of Democratic Peace," *American Political Science Review* 97 (November 2003): 585.

CHAPTER THREE

1. It was assumed that any attack by a Soviet client state would come only as a pretext to the initiation of global conflict. Because the administration believed that the Soviets had neither the interest nor the capabilities for such a war, reports of an impending invasion were dismissed. P. K. Rose, "Perceptions and Reality: Two Strategic Intelligence Mistakes in Korea, 1950," *Studies in Intelligence* (Fall/Winter 2001): 2–3; Central Intelligence Agency, "Intelligence Memorandum No. 301," June 30, 1950, in *Assessing the Soviet Threat: The Early Cold War Years*, ed. Woodrow J. Kuhns (Washington, DC: Central Intelligence Agency, 1997), 396.

2. John Lewis Gaddis, *Strategies of Containment: A Critical Appraisal of Postwar American National Security Policy* (New York: Oxford University Press, 1982), 35, 55–58; John Lewis Gaddis, "The Strategic Perspective: The Rise and Fall of the 'Defense Perimeter' Concept," in *Uncertain Years: Chinese-American Relations, 1947–1950*, ed. Dorothy Borg and Waldo H. Heinrichs (New York: Columbia University Press, 1980), 66–67. On China in NSC 68, see Gordon H. Chang, *Friends and Enemies: The United States, China, and the Soviet Union, 1948–1972* (Stanford, CA: Stanford University Press, 1990), 69–70.

3. Bruce Cumings, *The Origins of the Korean War*, vol. 2, *The Roaring of the Cataract, 1947–1950* (Princeton, NJ: Princeton University Press, 1990), 631–32.

4. Memorandum of NSC Consultants' Meeting, June 29, 1950, *Foreign Relations of the United States*, 1950, vol. 1 (Washington, DC: GPO, 1977), 327 (hereafter *FRUS*); "Draft Report by the NSC," July 1, 1950, ibid., 332; Rosemary Foot, *The Wrong War: American Policy and the Dimensions of the Korean War* (Ithaca, NY: Cornell University Press, 1985), 61.

5. For historical background on American policy regarding South Korea, see William Stueck, *Rethinking the Korean War: A New Diplomatic and Strategic History* (Princeton, NJ: Princeton University Press, 2002), chap. 2.

6. Harry S. Truman, *Memoirs*, vol. 2, *Years of Trial and Hope* (Garden City, NY: Doubleday, 1956), 333.

7. The lack of certainty regarding Soviet willingness to precipitate global conflict was a prominent feature of CIA reporting throughout June, July, and August. By September the CIA noted that while it had recently engaged in a "rapid advancement of a general war-readiness program," the Soviets were not in a position to successfully engage in "international military operations designed to defeat the US and its allies." See CIA, "Review of the World Situation, 7-50," Declassified Documents Reference System, Doc. #CK3100376174 (hereafter DDRS); CIA, "Review of the World Situation, 8-50," DDRS, Doc. #CK3100376181; and CIA, "Review of the World Situation, 9-50," DDRS, Doc. #CK3100376190.

8. Cumings, *Origins of the Korean War*, 2:643–51; Foot, *Wrong War*, 61.

9. "Memorandum of Conversation," June 26, 1950, *FRUS* 1950, vol. 7 (Washington, DC: GPO, 1976), 178–80.

10. Editorial Note, *FRUS* 1950, vol. 7, 238–39.

11. Gary R. Hess, *Presidential Decisions for War: Korea, Vietnam, and the Persian Gulf* (Baltimore: Johns Hopkins University Press, 2001), 28.

12. William Whitney Stueck Jr., *The Road to Confrontation: American Policy toward China and Korea, 1947-1950* (Chapel Hill: University of North Carolina Press, 1981), 181.

13. Acheson to Chinese Ambassador Koo, July 1, 1950, *FRUS 1950*, vol. 7, 276-77; Joint Chiefs of Staff to MacArthur, June 30, 1950, ibid., 269.

14. D. Clayton James, *Years of MacArthur*, vol. 3 (Boston: Houghton Mifflin, 1985), 446-51.

15. James F. Schnabel, *United States Army in the Korean War, Policy and Direction: The First Year* (Washington, DC: United States Army, 1972), 154.

16. The reluctance and doubt on the part of the chiefs concerning Inchon is significant to the extent that once MacArthur's plans were executed brilliantly, his superiors at the Pentagon were unwilling to question any further command decisions. James, *Years of MacArthur*, 464-85.

17. James F. Schnabel and Robert J. Watson, *History of the Joint Chiefs of Staff*, vol. 3, *1950-1951, The Korean War, Part One* (Washington, DC: Office of the Chairman of the Joint Chiefs of Staff, Office of Joint History, 1998), 201-18.

18. Only much later would it be realized that a majority of the senior North Korean officers and roughly one-third of their troops escaped the double envelopment between Inchon and the Naktong River and made their way back across the 38th parallel intact. D. Clayton James, *Refighting the Last War: Command and Crisis in Korea, 1950-1953* (New York: Free Press, 1993), 175.

19. Clay Blair, *The Forgotten War: America in Korea, 1950-1953* (Annapolis, MD: Naval Institute Press, 1987), 351-52, 363.

20. Shu Guang Zhang, *Deterrence and Strategic Culture: Chinese American Confrontations, 1949-1958* (Ithaca, NY: Cornell University Press, 1992), 100-101. According to Peng Dehuai, the Chinese commander at the time, "We employed the tactics of purposely showing ourselves to be weak, increasing the arrogance of the enemy, letting him run amuck, and luring him deep into our areas." Quoted in Eliot A. Cohen and John Gooch, *Military Misfortunes: The Anatomy of Failure in War* (New York: Free Press, 1990), 178.

21. For a succinct summary of the First Phase Offensive, see Roy E. Appleman, *Disaster in Korea: The Chinese Confront MacArthur* (College Station: Texas A&M University Press, 1989), 19-22.

22. Patrick Roe, *The Dragon Strikes: China and the Korean War, June-December 1950* (Novato, CA: Presidio, 2000), 252-56.

23. Halting, or withdrawing, to the narrow neck was America's last chance to avoid "the worst damage of the Chinese attack." Alexander L. George and Richard Smoke, *Deterrence in American Foreign Policy: Theory and Practice* (New York: Columbia University Press, 1974), 223. China would have called off the offensive for at least six months time, during which time further US/UN forces could have been deployed to deter future attacks. Shu Guang Zhang, *Mao's Military Romanticism: China and the Korean War, 1950-1953* (Lawrence: University Press of Kansas, 1995), 86-92.

24. Blair, *Forgotten War*, 391.

25. Eliot A. Cohen, "'Only Half the Battle': American Intelligence and the Chinese Intervention in Korea, 1950," *Intelligence and National Security* 5 (January 1990): 138-39.

26. Blair, *Forgotten War*, 400-401.

27. Memorandum of Conversation, November 17, 1950, *FRUS 1950*, vol. 7, 1175.

28. Roe, *Dragon Strikes*, 268.

29. Blair, *Forgotten War*, 422-23.

30. This was made clear in NIE-2/1, "Chinese Communist Intervention in Korea," November 24, 1950. DDRS, Doc. #CK3100353110.

31. Rosemary Foot, *A Substitute for Victory: The Politics of Peacemaking at the Korean Armistice Talks* (Ithaca, NY: Cornell University Press, 1990), 26-27.

32. For the CPV order of battle at the time, see Zhang, *Mao's Military Romanticism*, 264. For total figure, see Roe, *Dragon Strikes*, 268.

33. This behavior followed the pattern established by ICAPS's predecessor, the Central Planning Staff under the first DCI, Sydney Souers. Arthur B. Darling, *The Central Intelligence Agency: An Instrument of Government, to 1950* (University Park: Pennsylvania State University Press, 1990), 138-39.

34. Ibid., 205-17.

35. Rhodri Jeffreys-Jones, *The CIA and American Democracy*, 2nd ed. (New Haven, CT: Yale University Press, 1989), 58.

36. Anne Karalekas, "The Central Intelligence Group and the Central Intelligence Agency, 1946-1952," in *The Central Intelligence Agency: History and Documents*, ed. William M. Leary (Tuscaloosa: University of Alabama Press, 1984), 24.

37. Michael Warner, *Central Intelligence: Origin and Evolution* (Washington, DC: Central Intelligence Agency, 2001), 1-2. "In those days the military did not know everything the State Department knew, and the diplomats did not have access to all the Army and Navy knew. The Army and the Navy, in fact, had only a very informal arrangement to keep each other informed as to their plans." Truman, *Memoirs*, 2:55-56.

38. Karalekas, "The Central Intelligence Group and the Central Intelligence Agency," 25. Nor did the military provide communications and signals intelligence to the ORE. Matthew M. Aid, "US HUMINT and COMINT in the Korean War: From the Approach of War to the Chinese Intervention," *Intelligence and National Security* 14 (1999); Ray S. Cline, *The CIA under Reagan, Bush, and Casey* (Washington, DC: Acropolis Books, 1981), 130; Christopher Andrew, *For the President's Eyes Only: Secret Intelligence and the American Presidency from Washington to Bush* (New York: HarperCollins, 1995), 166; Woodrow J. Kuhns, preface to Kuhns, *Assessing the Soviet Threat*, 7.

39. R. Jack Smith to Theodore Babbitt, "Contents of the CIA Daily Summary," September 21, 1950, in *The CIA under Harry Truman*, ed. Michael Warner (Washington, DC: Central Intelligence Agency, 1994), 337.

40. Karalekas, "The Central Intelligence Group and the Central Intelligence Agency," 26. The majority of ORE's information came from the State Department. George S. Jackson and Martin P. Claussen, *Organizational History of the Central Intelligence Agency, 1950-1953*, vol. 8 (Washington, DC: Central Intelligence Agency, 1957), 2.

41. Amy B. Zegart, *Flawed by Design: The Evolution of the CIA, JCS, and NSC* (Stanford, CA: Stanford University Press, 1999), 190.

42. From R. Jack Smith, *The Unknown CIA* (Washington, DC: Pergamon-Brassey's, 1989), 34.

43. Cline, *CIA under Reagan, Bush, and Casey*, 114.

44. On the origins of the ISG, see National Security Council Resolution, January 13, 1948, *FRUS 1945-1950, Emergence of the Intelligence Establishment*, Doc. #336, http://history.state .gov/historicaldocuments/frus1945-50Intel/d336.

45. Report from the Intelligence Survey Group to the National Security Council, ibid., Doc. #358, http://history.state.gov/historicaldocuments/frus1945-50Intel/d358.

46. See list of participants at the two Blair House meetings in *FRUS 1950*, vol. 7, 157, 178.

47. Karalekas, "The Central Intelligence Group and the Central Intelligence Agency," 29.

48. Alexander L. George, *Presidential Decisionmaking in Foreign Policy: The Effective Use of Information and Advice* (Boulder, CO: Westview Press, 1980), 151-52.

49. James S. Lay and Robert H. Johnson, *Organizational History of the National Security Council during the Truman and Eisenhower Administrations* (Washington, DC: Central Intelligence Agency, 1960), 3, 14-22.

50. Even here, though, information sharing among the departments was poor. Melvyn P. Leffler, *A Preponderance of Power: National Security, the Truman Administration, and the Cold War* (Stanford, CA: Stanford University Press, 1992), 358.

51. Doris M. Condit, *History of the Office of the Secretary of Defense*, vol. 2, *The Test of War, 1950-1953* (Washington, DC: Office of the Secretary of Defense, 1988), 15; Dean Acheson, *Present*

at the Creation: My Years in the State Department (New York: W. W. Norton, 1969), 373-74; David Rothkopf, *Running the World: The Inside Story of the National Security Council and the Architects of American Power* (New York: Public Affairs, 2005), 59.

52. John Prados, *Keepers of the Keys: A History of the National Security Council from Truman to Bush* (New York: William Morrow, 1991), 34, 40-47.

53. Stephen E. Ambrose, *Ike's Spies: Eisenhower and the Espionage Establishment* (Garden City, NY: Doubleday, 1981), 170. See also James, *Refighting the Last War*, 43; and Thomas F. Troy, *Donovan and the CIA: A History of the Establishment of the Central Intelligence Agency* (Frederick, MD: University Publications of America, 1981), 280, 283.

54. Roe, *Dragon Strikes*, 98.

55. Schnabel, *United States Army in the Korean War, Policy and Direction*, 103. For the implications on these command decisions on waging coalition war, see James, *Years of MacArthur*, 440.

56. James, *Refighting the Last War*, 42-43.

57. Michael E. Bigelow, "Disaster along the Ch'ongch'on: Intelligence Breakdown in Korea," *Military Intelligence* (July–September 1992): 12.

58. Thomas J. Christensen, *Useful Adversaries: Grand Strategy, Domestic Mobilization, and Sino-American Conflict, 1947-1958* (Princeton, NJ: Princeton University Press, 1997), 97. The effects of the absence of direct state-to-state contacts between the United States and China should not be overblown. While the United States and China did maintain ambassadorial contacts in Warsaw during the Vietnam War, these exchanges produced very little in the way of usable information about each side's intentions. James G. Hershberg and Chen Jian, "Reading and Warning the Likely Enemy: China's Signals to the United States about Vietnam in 1965," *International History Review* 27 (March 2005).

59. Condit, *History of the Office of the Secretary of Defense*, 2:516.

60. Intelligence Survey Group report, *FRUS 1945-50, Emergence of the Intelligence Establishment*, Doc. #358, http://history.state.gov/historicaldocuments/frus1945-50Intel/d358.

61. Ambassador in the Soviet Union Kirk to the Secretary of State, July 6, 1950, *FRUS 1950*, vol. 7, 312.

62. For the entire exchange, see Kennan to Acheson, August 14, 1950, *FRUS 1950*, vol. 7, 574-76; Webb to Johnson, August 14, 1950, ibid., 576-77; Johnson to Acheson, August 21, 1950, ibid., 613-14; Memorandum by Director of the Executive Secretariat (McWilliams), August 28, 1950, ibid., 614n1.

63. On the PRC's domestic social and economic challenges that weighed against the preference for intervention, see Allen S. Whiting, *China Crosses the Yalu: The Decision to Enter the Korean War* (Stanford, CA: Stanford University Press, 1969), 15-22; William Stueck, *The Korean War: An International History* (Princeton, NJ: Princeton University Press, 1997), 45-46.

64. Memorandum of Conversation, June 25, 1950, *FRUS 1950*, vol. 7, 157-65.

65. Kirk to Acheson, June 25, 1950, *FRUS 1950*, vol. 7, 139. See also CIA, Daily Summary Excerpt, June 26, 1950, ibid., 391; and comments by Charles Bohlen on June 30 in a meeting with his DOS colleagues in *FRUS 1950*, vol. 7, 258.

66. By June 1950, the PRC was seen as being nearly wholly subordinate to the Kremlin in terms of its ability to conduct foreign policy. CIA, "Review of the World Situation, 6-50," June 14, 1950, 6, DDRS, Doc. #CK3100376164. This report did indicate that Soviet control was not complete, and "transformation of the entire country into a full-fledged Soviet Satellite probably will be a long and involved process."

67. Intelligence Estimate Prepared by the Estimates Group, June 25, 1950, *FRUS 1950*, vol. 7, 148-54.

68. Specifically, the combined effect of the interposition of the Seventh Fleet in the Taiwan Strait and the American crossing of the 38th parallel was viewed by the PRC to be a clear indication that the United States was intent on waging, at minimum, a protracted campaign against the

new regime in Beijing. Sergei N Goncharov, John W. Lewis, Xue Litai, *Uncertain Partners: Stalin, Mao, and the Korean War* (Stanford, CA: Stanford University Press, 1995), 157; Foot, *Wrong War*, 65–66; Christensen, *Useful Adversaries*, 162–63. As the United States advanced toward the Chinese border, the PRC feared that the industrial heartland of Manchuria was subject to immediate US military harassment. On the importance of Manchuria to the PRC's security, see Chen Jian, *China's Road to the Korean War: The Making of the Sino-American Confrontation* (New York: Columbia University Press, 1995), 106–13.

69. CIA, "Intelligence Memorandum 302, Consequences of the Korean Incident," July 8, 1950, in Kuhns, *Assessing the Soviet Threat*, 409–13. Specific elements of this logic can be found in CIA, "Review of the World Situation," June 14, 1950, DDRS, Doc. #CK3100376164; CIA, "Intelligence Memorandum 301 Estimate of Soviet Intentions and Capabilities for Military Aggression," June 30, 1950, in Kuhns, *Assessing the Soviet Threat*, 396–402; CIA, "Daily Summary Views of Hong Kong Residents on Korean Problem," July 6, 1950, in ibid., 403–4 (see especially CIA comment); CIA, "Weekly Summary, The Korean Situation: Soviet Intentions and Capabilities," July 7, 1950, in ibid., 406–8. It should be noted that the CIA did consider in a separate memo the potential downside to Soviet employment of Chinese troops in Korea. Significantly, these potential disadvantages were not considered to be of sufficient magnitude to cast doubt on the analysis in Intelligence Memorandum 302. See CIA, Weekly Summary, Communist China's Role," July 14, 1950, in ibid., 419–21.

70. CIA, "Review of the World Situation," July 19, 1950, 3, DDRS, Doc. #CK3100376174; CIA, "Weekly Summary, Soviet/Satellite Intentions," July 28, 1950, in Kuhns, *Assessing the Soviet Threat*, 425–27; CIA, "Review of the World Situation," August 16, 1950, 4, DDRS, Doc. #CK3100376181.

71. Memorandum Prepared in the Central Intelligence Agency, August 18, 1950, *FRUS 1950*, vol. 7, 600–603. Importantly, the CIA argued that the most likely method of Chinese involvement would be the deployment of troops at the 38th parallel in defense of North Korea—although the Soviets might use Chinese troops at any stage in the fighting.

72. CIA, Review of the World Situation, September 20, 1950, 4, DDRS, Doc. #CK310037619.

73. The consistency of the CIA's reporting ended on October 12 with the publication of ORE 58-50, wherein the CIA speculated that Chinese and Soviet intervention was not likely during 1950. An explanation for this change in estimates can only be speculative. Nevertheless, two possible reasons are (1) the replacement of Roscoe Hillenkoetter by Walter B. Smith as DCI, and (2) the crossing of the parallel by the United States in the absence of early intervention by either Communist power might have prompted the CIA to change its foundational assumptions pertaining to Chinese intentions. CIA, "ORE 58-50: Critical Situations in the Far East," October 12, 1950, in Kuhns, *Assessing the Soviet Threat*, 450–51.

74. Allison to Rusk, July 1, 1950, *FRUS 1950*, vol. 7, 272, and Allison to Rusk, July 15, 1950, ibid., 393–95.

75. Cumings, *Origins of the Korean War*, 2:709–10.

76. Draft Memorandum Prepared by the Policy Planning Staff, July 22, 1950, *FRUS 1950*, vol. 7, 449–54. The PPS did not completely rule out the possibility of crossing the 38th parallel, however. The lone contingency was "in the unlikely event that there is a complete disintegration of North Korean forces together with a failure of the Kremlin and Communist China to take any action whatever to exert influence in North Korea, U.S. forces, acting in pursuance of an additional Security Council resolution, might move into North Korea in order to assist in the establishment of a united and independent Korea."

77. Allison to Nitze, July 24, 1950, *FRUS 1950*, vol. 7, 458–61.

78. Draft Memorandum Prepared by the Policy Planning Staff, July 25, 1950, *FRUS 1950*, vol. 7, 469–73.

79. NSC 76, "U.S. Courses of Action in the Event Soviet Forces Enter Korean Hostilities," July 21, 1950, DDRS, Doc. #CK3100353827; and NSC 76/1 "U.S. Courses of Action in the Event Soviet Forces Enter Korean Hostilities," July 25, 1950, DDRS, Doc. #CK3100353831. By "war plans" the JCS were referring to the war plans in the event of global conflict with the Soviet Union. The general strategy envisioned a strategic offensive in the west, and a strategic defensive in the east. Condit, *History of the Office of the Secretary of Defense*, 2:294-302, 520.

80. Memorandum of Conversation, August 25, 1950, *FRUS 1950*, vol. 7, 646-48.

81. "U.S. Course of Action as to Korea," August 30, 1950, *FRUS 1950*, vol. 7, 660-63.

82. NSC 81/1, "United States Courses of Action with Respect to Korea," September 9, 1950, *FRUS 1950*, vol. 7, 712-21. Emphasis added.

83. Although the JCS were not opposed to unification in the absence of Soviet intervention. Draft Memorandum Prepared in the Department of Defense, July 31, 1950, *FRUS 1950*, vol. 7, 506-7. See also Stueck, *The Road to Confrontation*, 206.

84. McConaughy to Jessup, August 25, 1950, *FRUS 1950*, vol. 7, 649.

85. Consul General at Hong Kong (Wilkinson) to Acheson, September 5, 1950, *FRUS 1950*, vol. 7, 698; Wilkinson to Acheson, September 12, 1950, ibid., 724-25. See also Stueck, *The Korean War*, 90-91.

86. Memorandum of Conversation, September 27, 1950, *FRUS 1950*, vol. 7, 793-94; Acheson to Webb, September 28, 1950, ibid., 797-98.

87. Ambassador in the Netherlands (Chapin) to Acheson, October 3, 1950, *FRUS 1950*, vol. 7, 858.

88. Whiting, *China Crosses the Yalu*, 86.

89. Quoted in Zhang, *Mao's Military Romanticism*, 77.

90. P. K. Rose, "Perceptions and Reality: Two Strategic Intelligence Mistakes in Korea, 1950," *Studies in Intelligence* 45 (Fall/Winter 2001): 62.

91. Wilkinson to Acheson, October 2, 1950, *FRUS 1950*, vol. 7, 852.

92. Quoted in Chen, *China's Road to the Korean War*, 180. See also Chapin to Acheson, October 3, 1950, *FRUS 1950*, vol. 7, 858.

93. Matthew M. Aid, *The Secret Sentry: The Untold History of the National Security Agency* (New York: Bloomsbury Press, 2009), 30.

94. Acting Secretary of State to Certain Diplomatic and Consular Offices, October 5, 1950, *FRUS 1950*, vol. 7, 877.

95. Aid, *Secret Sentry*, 29-30.

96. Cohen, "Only Half the Battle," 137-38. On September 15, the CIA estimated that the total Military District strength in Manchuria stood at 505,000. CIA, "Situation Summary," September 15, 1950, DDRS, Doc. #CK3100382292.

97. CIA, "Situation Summary" September 8, 1950, DDRS, Doc. #CK3100382287.

98. Zhang, *Deterrence and Strategic Culture*, 87-88.

99. Webb to Acheson, September 26, 1950, *FRUS 1950*, vol. 7, 781-82; Acheson to Webb, September 26, 1950, ibid., 785-86; Marshall to MacArthur, September 29, 1950, ibid., 826; Schnabel and Watson, *History of the Joint Chiefs of Staff*, 3:277.

100. "United States Policy toward Formosa: Statement by President Truman," January 16, 1950, *Department of State Bulletin* 22 (January-March 1950), 79; "United States Policy toward Formosa: Extemporaneous Remarks by Secretary Acheson," January 16, 1950, *Department of State Bulletin*, ibid., 81.

101. Blair, *Forgotten War*, 400-401.

102. Quoted in James, *The Years of MacArthur*, 507-8.

103. Quoted in Blair, *Forgotten War*, 391, 395.

104. For a sophisticated assessment of the FEC-G2's intelligence failure, see Roe, *Dragon Strikes*, chap. 10. The FEC's information monopoly is reflected in the CIA's reporting during this

period. CIA, "Daily Summary, Reports on Chinese Involvement in Korea," October 28, 1950, in Kuhns, *Assessing the Soviet Threat*, 457. Emphasis added. Oddly, in its "Daily Korean Summary" reports on November 1, 3, 4, and 7 (i.e., during the First Phase Offensive), the CIA included *no* reference to Chinese forces in Korea. These reports can be found in a single file containing 179 Daily Summaries beginning on June 26, 1950, DDRS, Doc. #CK3100420671. See also CIA, "Weekly Summary, Chinese Communist Plans: Korean Intervention," November 3, 1950, in Kuhns, *Assessing the Soviet Threat*, 462; and CIA, "NIE-2, Chinese Communist Intervention in Korea," November 8, 1950, DDRS, Doc. #CK3100398564.

105. Commander in Chief U.S. Pacific Fleet, "Korean War, U.S. Pacific Fleet Operations, Interim Evaluation Report No. 1, Period 25 June to 15 October 1950," 1500, DDRS, Doc. #CK3100346776.

106. On the PLA's tactical efficiency, see Robert L. Smith to Secretary of State, January 19, 1949, DDRS, Doc. #CK2349348096. On the PLA's operational effectiveness, see the report issued by John Melby, Political Officer, Embassy, Congquing/Nanjing, 1945-48 reprinted in *China Confidential: American Diplomats and Sino-American Relations, 1945-1996*, ed. Nancy Bernkopf Tucker (New York: Columbia University Press, 2001), 48.

107. DOD, "Prospects for an Early Successful Chinese Communist Attack on Taiwan," July 26, 1950. DDRS, Doc. #CK2349047045.

108. Blair, *Forgotten War*, 400-401.

109. Quoted in ibid., 402. See also Omar Bradley, *A General's Life* (New York: Simon and Schuster, 1983), 587, 594.

110. Stueck, *Rethinking the Korean War*, 114; Dean G. Acheson, *The Korean War* (New York: W. W. Norton, 1969), 68.

111. NSC 81/2, "United States Courses of Action with Respect to Korea," November 14, 1950, DDRS, Doc. #CK3100353850. Emphasis added.

112. As will be discussed in the conclusion of this book, the devolution of strategic authority is a key condition for military organizational culture to dominate the design and execution of limited war strategies.

113. Eric J. Labs, "Beyond Victory: Offensive Realism and the Expansion of War Aims," *Security Studies* 6 (1997): 37.

114. Christopher M. Gacek, *The Logic of Force: The Dilemma of Limited War in American Foreign Policy* (New York: Columbia University Press, 1994), 37; Cumings, *Origins of the Korean War*, 2:161.

115. Christopher P. Twomey, *The Military Lens: Doctrinal Difference and Deterrence Failure in Sino-American Relations* (Ithaca, NY: Cornell University Press, 2010), 56-57.

116. Richard K. Betts, *Soldiers, Statesmen, and Cold War Crises* (New York: Columbia University Press, 1991), 154.

117. Robert M. Cassidy, *Counterinsurgency and the Global War on Terror: Military Culture and Irregular War* (Stanford, CA: Stanford University Press, 2008), 111-13.

CHAPTER FOUR

1. John Lewis Gaddis, *Strategies of Containment: A Critical Appraisal of Postwar American National Security Policy* (New York: Oxford University Press, 1983), 238; Mark Moyar, *Triumph Forsaken: The Vietnam War, 1954-1965* (New York: Cambridge University Press, 2006), 290; Gordon H. Chang, *Friends and Enemies: The United States, China, and the Soviet Union, 1948-1972* (Stanford, CA: Stanford University Press, 1990), 256.

2. National Security Action Memorandum No. 288, March 17, 1964, *Foreign Relations of the United States, 1964-68*, vol. 1 (Washington, DC: GPO, 1992), 172-73 (hereafter *FRUS*). No other document superseded NSAM 288 as the statement of American war aims. Leslie H. Gelb with

Richard K. Betts, *The Irony of Vietnam: The System Worked* (Washington, DC: Brookings Institution, 1979), 187. On the necessity of avoiding Chinese intervention, see Memorandum of a Meeting, September 9, 1964, *FRUS, 1964-168*, vol. 1, 749-55.

3. Jeffrey Record, *The Wrong War: Why We Lost in Vietnam* (Annapolis, MD: Naval Institute Press, 1998), 55.

4. Mark Clodfelter, *The Limits of Air Power: The American Bombing of North Vietnam* (New York: Free Press, 1989), 66.

5. David Kaiser, *American Tragedy: Kennedy, Johnson, and the Origins of the Vietnam War* (Cambridge, MA: Harvard University Press, 2000), 330-36; Fredrik Logevall, *Choosing War: The Lost Chance for Peace and the Escalation of War in Vietnam* (Berkeley: University of California Press, 1999), 197-205.

6. Clodfelter, *Limits of Air Power*, 78-79; George Kahin, *Intervention: How America Became Involved in Vietnam* (New York: Anchor, 1987), 307.

7. Brian VanDeMark, *Into the Quagmire: Lyndon Johnson and the Escalation of the Vietnam War* (New York: Oxford University Press, 1995), 108-13.

8. Doris Kearns Goodwin, *Lyndon Johnson and the American Dream* (New York: St. Martin's Griffin, 1991), 264-65.

9. H. R. McMaster, *Dereliction of Duty: Lyndon Johnson, Robert McNamara, the Joint Chiefs of Staff, and the Lies That Led to Vietnam* (New York: HarperCollins, 1997), 93-94.

10. Joint War Games Agency, JCS, "Final Report: SIGMA II-64," October 5, 1964, D-16, Declassified Documents Reference System, Doc. #CK3100220846 (hereafter DDRS); Robert D. Schulzinger, "The Johnson Administration, China, and the Vietnam War," in *Re-Examining the Cold War: U.S.-China Diplomacy, 1954-1973*, ed. Robert S. Ross and Jiang Changbin (Cambridge, MA: Harvard University Press, 2001), 245.

11. Chen Jian, *Mao's China and the Cold War* (Chapel Hill: University of North Carolina Press, 2001), 207-12; Xiaoming Zhang, "The Vietnam War, 1964-1969: A Chinese Perspective," *Journal of Military History* 60 (October 1996): 734. On the relationship between the PRC and DRV prior to 1964, see Qiang Zhai, *China and the Vietnam Wars, 1950-1975* (Chapel Hill: University of North Carolina Press, 2000), 117-29; Yang Kuisong, "Changes in Mao Zedong's Attitude toward the Indochina War, 1949-1973," Cold War International History Project Working Paper #34, trans. Qiang Zhai (Washington, DC: Woodrow Wilson International Center for Scholars, February 2002), 27-29.

12. See Allen S. Whiting, *The Chinese Calculus of Deterrence: India and Indochina* (Ann Arbor: University of Michigan Press, 1975), 173; and Frank E. Rogers, "Sino-American Relations and the Vietnam War, 1964-66," *China Quarterly* 66 (June 1976): 296.

13. Qiang Zhai, "Beijing and the Vietnam Conflict, 1964-1965: New Chinese Evidence," *CWIHP Bulletin* 6-7 (Washington, DC: Woodrow Wilson International Center for Scholars, Winter 1995/96), 237; Zhai, *China and the Vietnam Wars*, 140-41.

14. Chen, *Mao's China*, 212-13.

15. Zhang, "The Vietnam War," 740-41.

16. Chen, *Mao's China*, 213.

17. Whiting, *Chinese Calculus of Deterrence*, 175.

18. The Third Front initiative should be seen as "an expression of serious intent to wage a war, if necessary, with the United States. The Third Front is powerful evidence of the seriousness of Beijing's warnings to the United States. These were not minor moves to signal messages to Washington. They were serious efforts to prepare China for a major war with America." John W. Garver, "The Chinese Threat in the Vietnam War," *Parameters* 23 (Spring 1992): 79-81.

19. Chen, *Mao's China*, 215.

20. From the President's Special Assistant for National Security Affairs (Bundy) to the President, September 8, 1964, *FRUS, 1964-68*, vol. 1, 746-49; National Security Action Memorandum No. 314, September 10, 1964, ibid., 758-60.

21. Quoted in Clodfelter, *Limits of Air Power*, 57.

22. Qiang Zhai, "Reassessing China's Role in the Vietnam War: Some Mysteries Explored," in *China and the United States: A New Cold War History*, ed. Xiaobing Li and Hongshan Li (Lanham, MD: University Press of America, 1998), 103; Robert K. Brigham, "Three Alternative U.S. Strategies in Vietnam: A Reexamination Based on New Chinese and Vietnamese Sources," in *Argument without End: In Search of Answers to the Vietnam Tragedy*, ed. Robert S. McNamara et al. (New York: Public Affairs, 1999), 410.

23. Chen, *Mao's China*, 217-18. See also James G. Hershberg and Chen Jian, "Reading and Warning the Likely Enemy: China's Signals to the United States about Vietnam in 1965," *International History Review* 27 (March 2005): 69-73.

24. Zhai, *China and the Vietnam Wars*, 133-35.

25. On the PRC's material and manpower support from 1965 to 1969, see Chen Jian, "China's Involvement in the Vietnam War, 1964-69," *China Quarterly* 142 (June 1995): 371-80.

26. Zhai, *China and the Vietnam Wars*, 135, 138; Whiting, *Chinese Calculus of Deterrence*, 186; Allen S. Whiting, "Forecasting Chinese Foreign Policy: IR Theory vs. the Fortune Cookie," in *Chinese Foreign Policy: Theory and Practice*, ed. Thomas W. Robinson and David Shambaugh (New York: Oxford University Press, 1994), 515; and Allen Whiting, "China's Role in the Vietnam War," in *The American War in Vietnam*, ed. Jayne Werner and David Hunt (Ithaca, NY: Southeast Asia Program, Cornell University, 1993), 75.

27. National Security Action Memorandum No. 328, April 6, 1965, *FRUS*, 1964-68, vol. 2 (Washington, DC: GPO, 1996), 537-39.

28. Kaiser, *American Tragedy*, 478.

29. Andrew F. Krepinevich, *The Army and Vietnam* (Baltimore: Johns Hopkins University Press, 1986), 140. On the stages of a protracted armed struggle, see Mao Zedong, *Selected Writings of Mao Tse-tung* (Beijing: Foreign Language Press, 1967), 210-19.

30. Stanley Karnow, *Vietnam: A History* (New York: Viking Press, 1983), 463. Thomas L. Hughes to Dean Rusk, Department of State, "Giap's Third Phase in Prospect in South Vietnam?" July 23, 1965, DDRS, Doc. #CK3100420168.

31. John A. Nagl, *Learning to Eat Soup with a Knife: Counterinsurgency Lessons from Malaya and Vietnam* (Chicago: University of Chicago Press, 2002), 155.

32. Krepinevich, *Army and Vietnam*, 167.

33. Quoted in Carter Malkasian, "Toward a Better Understanding of Attrition: The Korean and Vietnam Wars," *Journal of Military History* 68 (2004): 932.

34. William C. Westmoreland, *A Soldier Reports* (New York: De Capo, 1989), 145.

35. John J. Tolson III, *Airmobility, 1961-1971* (Washington, DC: GPO, 1973), 117.

36. Krepinevich, *Army and Vietnam*, 202.

37. Herbert Y. Schandler, "U.S. Military Victory in Vietnam: A Dangerous Illusion?" in *Argument without End: In Search of Answers to the Vietnam Tragedy*, ed. Robert S. McNamara et al. (New York: Public Affairs, 1999), 360.

38. Michael A. Hennessy, *Strategy in Vietnam: The Marines and Revolutionary Warfare in I Corps, 1965-1972* (Westport, CT: Praeger, 1997), 80.

39. Krepinevich, *Army and Vietnam*, 240.

40. George C. Herring, *America's Longest War: The United States and Vietnam, 1950-1975*, 2nd ed. (New York: Knopf, 1986), 206-7.

41. Robert D. Schulzinger, *A Time for War: The United States and Vietnam, 1941-1975* (New York: Oxford University Press, 1997), 163-267.

42. Amy Zegart, *Flawed by Design: The Evolution of the CIA, JCS, and CIA* (Stanford, CA: Stanford University Press, 1999), 82; John Prados, *Keepers of the Keys: A History of the National Security Council from Truman to Bush* (New York: William Morrow, 1991), 61-85; James S. Lay and Robert H. Johnson, *Organizational History of the National Security Council during the Truman and Eisenhower Administrations* (Washington, DC: Central Intelligence Agency, 1960), 25-49; Anna Kasten

Nelson, "The 'Top of Policy Hill': President Eisenhower and the National Security Council," *Diplomatic History* 7 (October 1983).

43. Bromley K. Smith, *Organizational History of the National Security Council during the Kennedy and Johnson Administrations* (Washington, DC: National Security Council, 1988), 9; Prados, *Keepers of the Keys*, 99.

44. Andrew Preston, "The Little State Department: McGeorge Bundy and the National Security Council Staff, 1961-1965," *Political Studies Quarterly* 31 (December 2001): 645.

45. Prados, *Keepers of the Keys*, 102.

46. Quoted in I. M. Destler, Leslie H. Gelb, and Anthony Lake, *Our Own Worst Enemy: The Unmaking of American Foreign Policy* (New York: Simon and Schuster, 1984), 190-91.

47. Stephen Hess with James P. Pfiffner, *Organizing the Presidency*, 3rd ed. (Washington, DC: Brookings Institution, 2002), 71; Preston, "The Little State Department," 646.

48. Smith, *Organizational History of the National Security Council*, 37-38.

49. Preston, "The Little State Department," 650. An important element of this process was the ability for the staff to monitor compliance by the bureaucracy with decisions made at higher levels. National Security Action Memoranda (NSAMs) were drawn up and circulated by Bundy and contained specific delineations of approved national security policies. Jeffrey T. Richelson, "Presidential Directives and National Security Policy" (Washington, DC: National Security Archive, 2004), http://nsarchive.chadwyck.com/collections/content/PR/essayx.jsp, last accessed February 20, 2013. Moreover, staff members were charged with the responsibilities of policy advice and of policy implementation. "[Staff] assignments . . . do not distinguish between 'planning' and 'operation,' and resistance to this distinction is fundamental to our whole concept of work." Memorandum for President Kennedy, June 22, 1961, *FRUS*, 1961-63, vol. 8 (Washington, DC: GPO, 1996), 106-7. See also Carnes Lord, *The Presidency and the Management of National Security* (New York: Free Press, 1988), 71.

50. Zegart, *Flawed by Design*, 84-85.

51. Smith, *Organizational History of the National Security Council*, 21-22.

52. Destler, Gelb, and Lake, *Our Own Worst Enemy*, 194-97.

53. Quoted in David C. Humphrey, "Tuesday Lunch at the White House: A Preliminary Assessment," *Diplomatic History* 8 (Winter 1984): 82.

54. Among the most critical scholars are Irving Janis, *Groupthink*, 2nd ed. (Boston: Houghton Mifflin, 1983), 99-101, 111-25; and John P. Burke and Fred I. Greenstein, *How Presidents Test Reality: Decisions on Vietnam, 1954 and 1965* (New York: Russell Sage Foundation, 1989), 183-85.

55. David M. Barrett, *Uncertain Warriors: Lyndon Johnson and His Vietnam Advisers* (Lawrence: University Press of Kansas, 1993), 167-71; David M. Barrett, "The Mythology Surrounding Lyndon Johnson, His Advisers, and the 1965 Decision to Escalate the Vietnam War," *Political Science Quarterly* 103 (Winter 1988/89): 657-63.

56. According to Walt Rostow, "Clashing, exploratory, or even frivolous views could be expressed with little bureaucratic caution and with confidence no scars would remain." Prados, *Keepers of the Keys*, 150.

57. "The air war against North Vietnam was directly under the control of the Department of Defense and was therefore influenced by the PPBS." Gregory Palmer, *The McNamara Strategy and the Vietnam War: Program Budgeting in the Pentagon, 1960-1968* (Westport, CT: Greenwood Press, 1978), 104, 120-21.

58. Michael K. Bohn, *Nerve Center: Inside the White House Situation Room* (Washington, DC: Brassey's, 2003), 138-39.

59. David M. Barrett, "Doing 'Tuesday Lunch' at Lyndon Johnson's White House: New Archival Evidence on Vietnam Decisionmaking," *PS: Political Science and Politics* 24 (December 1991): 678.

60. Christopher Andrew, *For the President's Eyes Only: Secret Intelligence and the American Presidency from Washington to Bush* (New York: HarperCollins, 1995), 272-74.

61. Anne Karalekas, "History of the Central Intelligence Agency," in *The Central Intelligence Agency: History and Documents*, ed. William M. Leary (Tuscaloosa: University of Alabama Press, 1984), 87–88. Philip Taubman, *Secret Empire: Eisenhower, the CIA, and the Hidden Story of America's Space Espionage* (New York: Simon and Schuster, 2003), 345–47.

62. Karalekas, "History of the Central Intelligence Agency," 92–93.

63. Terms of Reference for the Senior United States Military Commander in Vietnam, January 12, 1962, *FRUS*, 1961–63, vol. 2 (Washington, DC: GPO, 1990), 35–36. While the terms of reference do indicate that the commander, MACV, was "nominally subordinate to the Ambassador, he was in fact autonomous." Austin Long, "Doctrine of Eternal Recurrence—The U.S. Military and Counterinsurgency Doctrine, 1960-1970 and 2003-2006," *RAND Counterinsurgency Study*, Paper 6 (Santa Monica, CA: Rand, 2008), 9.

64. The air and ground wars were essentially separate wars with their own sets of objectives and conducted by distinct command authorities. Record, *Wrong War*, 64, 101.

65. Roger Hilsman, *To Move a Nation: The Politics of Foreign Policy in the Administration of John F. Kennedy* (Garden City, NY: Doubleday, 1967), 415.

66. Lawrence Freedman, *Kennedy's Wars: Berlin, Cuba, Laos, and Vietnam* (New York: Oxford University Press, 2000), 289–91.

67. National Security Action Memorandum No. 124, January 18, 1962, *FRUS* 1961–63, vol. 2, 48–50.

68. Michael McClintock, *Instruments of Statecraft: U.S. Guerrilla Warfare, Counter-Insurgency, and Counter-Terrorism, 1940-1990* (New York: Pantheon Books, 1992), 166.

69. National Security Action Memorandum No. 182, August 24, 1962, DDRS, Doc. #CK3100431347; Charles Maechling, "Camelot, Robert Kennedy, and Counter-Insurgency: A Memoir," *Virginia Quarterly Review* 75 (Summer 1999), http://www.vqronline.org/articles/1999/summer/maechling-camelot-robert-kennedy/, last accessed February 18, 2013.

70. Douglas S. Blaufarb, *The Counterinsurgency Era: U.S. Doctrine and Performance, 1950 to the Present* (New York: Free Press, 1977), 85.

71. Two of the leading American experts in the field of counterinsurgency, Roger Hilsman and Edward Lansdale, were not among the SGCI's principals. On their views of the American approach in Vietnam, see Gerald J. Protheroe, "Limiting America's Engagement: Roger Hilsman's Vietnam War, 1961-1963," *Diplomacy and Statecraft* 19 (June 2008): 283; and James McAllister, "The Lost Revolution: Edward Lansdale and the American Defeat in Vietnam, 1964-1968," *Small Wars and Insurgencies* 14 (Summer 2003): 6-9.

72. Krepinevich, *Army and Vietnam*, 34.

73. Blaufarb, *Counterinsurgency Era*, 119–120.

74. Robert Asprey, *War in the Shadows: The Guerrilla in History* (New York: William Morrow, 1994), 611.

75. Hoang Ngoc Lung, *Strategy and Tactics* (Washington, DC: US Army Center for Military History, 1980), 38–39; Record, *Wrong War*, 52.

76. Clodfelter, *Limits of Air Power*, 111.

77. Arthur L. Stinchcombe, *Information and Organizations* (Berkeley: University of California Press, 1990), 78–81.

78. Quoted in Barrett, *Uncertain Warriors*, 224n57. See also Eliot A. Cohen, *Supreme Command: Soldiers, Statesmen, and Leadership in Wartime* (New York: Free Press, 2002), 182.

79. Schulzinger, "The Johnson Administration, China, and the Vietnam War," 242.

80. Telegram from the Embassy in Vietnam to the Department of State, August 9, 1964, *FRUS*, 1964–68, vol. 1, 654–56; Telegram from the Embassy in Vietnam to the Department of State, August 10, 1964, ibid., 662; Telegram from the Embassy in Vietnam to the Department of State, August 18, 1964, ibid., 690.

81. Memorandum from the President's Special Assistant for National Security Affairs (Bundy) to the President, August 13, 1964, *FRUS*, 1964–68, vol. 1, 678.

82. Memorandum from the President's Special Assistant for National Security Affairs (Bundy) to the President, September 8, 1964, *FRUS*, 1964-68, vol. 1, 746-49. The consensus "Courses of Action" memo was drafted by William Bundy after McNaughton submitted a similar memo, "Plan for Action in South Vietnam." In that memo, McNaughton recommended different types of military actions that could be taken that would provoke a military response by the DRV. Included were, "mining of harbors . . . air strikes against North Vietnam moving from southern to northern targets, from targets associated with infiltration . . . to targets of military then industrial importance. . . . *The possibility that such actions would escalate further, perhaps bringing China into the war, would have to be faced.*" Quoted in Daniel Ellsberg, *Secrets: A Memoir of Vietnam and the Pentagon Papers* (New York: Viking, 2002), 54.

83. CIA, "The Situation in South Vietnam," August 20, 1964, 18, DDRS, Doc. #CK3100390402.

84. Memorandum of a Meeting, White House, September 9, 1964, *FRUS*, 1964-68, vol. 1, 749-55; National Security Action Memorandum No. 314, September 10, 1964, ibid., 758-60.

85. Memorandum of a Meeting, White House, September 9, 1964, *FRUS*, 1964-68, vol. 1, 749-50.

86. From the Joint Chiefs of Staff to the Secretary of Defense (McNamara), August 14, 1964, *FRUS*, 1964-68, vol. 1, 681. Emphasis added.

87. On the differences between punishment and denial, see Robert A. Pape, *Bombing to Win: Air Power and Coercion in War* (Ithaca, NY: Cornell University Press, 1996), 13-15.

88. The senior participants of the game were: McGeorge and William Bundy, McCone, McNaughton, Vance, and the JCS. McNamara, Rusk, Ball, and Rostow either participated as observers and/or were briefed on the outcomes of the game. McMaster, *Dereliction of Duty*, 156.

89. This range of institutional perspective allowed for "a further expected benefit [of SIGMA II] . . . the exchange of ideas between individuals and agencies during preparation and play." Joint War Games Agency, JCS, "Final Report," B-6-10, D-10, Tab G.

90. The red team consisted of both the PRC and DRV, except for the highest policy makers, which were the control team; the blue team consisted of the United States and South Vietnam, except for the highest policy makers, which, again, were the control team.

91. Joint War Games Agency, JCS, "Final Report," G-8, D-15. See also McMaster, *Dereliction of Duty*, 157n7.

92. Joint War Games Agency, JCS, "Final Report," D-12.

93. Joint War Games Agency, JCS, "Final Report," D-16; Schulzinger, "The Johnson Administration, China, and the Vietnam War," 245.

94. From the Chairman of the Policy Planning Council (Rostow) to the Secretary of State, September 19, 1964, *FRUS*, 1964-68, vol. 1, 783. A further indication of the significance of SIGMA II is that senior participants referred to the exercise either in retrospect or in memoranda drafted after the game. See, for example, McNamara's use of the game to assess the likely effects of bombing the ninety-four targets list in Robert S. McNamara with Brian VanDeMark, *In Retrospect: The Tragedy and Lessons of Vietnam* (New York: Times Books, 1995), 153. George Ball references SIGMA II in his famous October 5 memo, as does William Bundy in his response to Ball. See George W. Ball, "Top Secret: The Prophecy the President Rejected," *Atlantic* 230 (July 1972): 39; and Kaiser, *American Tragedy*, 352.

95. Editorial Note, *FRUS*, 1964-68, vol. 1, 886-88.

96. United States Department of Defense, OSD/ISA, "China as a Nuclear Power (Some Thoughts Prior to the Chinese Test)," October 7, 1964, Digital National Security Archive, Doc. #CH00020 (hereafter DNSA), http://gateway.proquest.com/openurl?url_ver=Z39.88-2004&res _dat=xri:dnsa&rft_dat=xri:dnsa:article:CCH00020, last accessed February 19, 2013; Kaiser, *American Tragedy*, 354.

97. Kaiser, *American Tragedy*, 351, 356-57.

98. Michael Forrestal was now Rusk's special assistant for Southeast Asia.

99. Editorial Note, *FRUS*, 1964–68, vol. 1, 887; Kaiser, *American Tragedy*, 357–58.

100. Kaiser, *American Tragedy*, 357–58.

101. Ibid., 359.

102. Ibid., 359–60.

103. Ibid., 360–61.

104. NSC Working Group on Vietnam, CIA-DIA-INR Panel, "Probable Communist Reactions to US Options B and C," November 16, 1964, 6–7, DDRS Doc. #CK3100080649.

105. Ibid., 3–5.

106. Memorandum for the Record of a Meeting, White House, November 19, 1964, *FRUS*, 1964–68, vol. 1, 914–16.

107. The desire for an explicit acknowledgment of the use of nuclear weapons by the joint chiefs was consonant with the Air Force's extant doctrine on waging both limited and general wars. See Clodfelter, *Limits of Air Power*, 26–37.

108. JCSM-982-64, "Courses of Action in Southeast Asia," November 23, 1964, 2–5, 7–11, DDRS, Doc. #CK3100134323.

109. Option B entailed the same military risk as the highest level of pressure under C and C', but at a much faster tempo. NSC Working Group on Vietnam, CIA-DIA-INR Panel, "Probable Communist Reactions to Option C or C-Prime Measures," November 23, 1964, DDRS, Doc. #CK3100080677.

110. NSC Working Group on Vietnam, "Intelligence Assessment: The Situation in Vietnam," November 24, 1964, 12, DDRS, Doc. #CK3100066450.

111. Ibid., 14–15.

112. Memorandum of the Meeting of the Executive Committee, November 24, 1964, *FRUS*, 1964–68, vol. 1, 943–45.

113. Memorandum of the Meeting of the Executive Committee, November 27, 1964, *FRUS*, 1964–68, vol. 1, 959–60.

114. Kaiser, *American Tragedy*, 373–74.

115. From the President to the Secretary of State, the Secretary of Defense (McNamara), and the Director of Central Intelligence (McCone), December 7, 1964, *FRUS*, 1964–68, vol. 1, 984.

116. LBJ delayed implementing phase II of the strategy because from December 1964 to February 1965 the GVN neared collapse. VanDeMark, *Into the Quagmire*, 42–46.

117. John A. McCone, "Memorandum for the President: Communist Reactions to U.S. Air Attacks on North Vietnam," March 13, 1965, DDRS, Doc. #CK3100194296.

118. CIA, "Monthly Report: The Situation in South Vietnam," April 2, 1965, DDRS, Doc. #CK3100409382.

119. For McCone's meetings with Rusk and McNamara, see Memorandum for the Record, March 18, 1965, *FRUS*, 1964–68, vol. 2, 457–58; Memorandum for the Record, March 18, 1965, ibid., 458–60.

120. John A. McCone, "Memorandum for the President," March 13, 1965, DDRS, Doc. #CK3100194296.

121. Paper Prepared by the Assistant Secretary of Defense for International Security Affairs (McNaughton), March 10, 1965, *FRUS*, 1964–68, vol. 2, 427–32.

122. Memorandum from the Joint Chiefs of Staff to Secretary of Defense McNamara, March 15, 1965, *FRUS*, 1964–68, vol. 2, 441.

123. Memorandum from the Joint Chiefs of Staff to Secretary of Defense McNamara, March 20, 1965, *FRUS*, 1964–68, vol. 2, 466–67.

124. CIA, "Intelligence Memorandum: Chinese Communist Arms in Viet Cong Hands Increasing," March 1, 1965, DDRS, Doc. #CK3100436827.

125. Telegram from American Consul General Hong Kong Rice to Secretary of State Rusk,

March 30, 1965, DDRS, Doc. #CK3100361000. For further reporting on the PRC's support of the NLF call for foreign troops, see Telegram from Rice to Rusk, March 25, 1965, DDRS, Doc. #CK3100360997; CIA, "Monthly Report: The Situation in South Vietnam," April 2, 1965, 15, DDRS, Doc. #CK3100409382.

126. NIE 13-3-65, "Communist China's Military Establishment," March 10, 1965, DDRS, Doc. #CK3100130661; CIA, "Memorandum: The Situation in Vietnam," March 20, 1965, DDRS, Doc. #CK3100169293; CIA, "Memorandum: The Situation in Vietnam," March 11, 1965, DDRS, Doc. #CK3100361709.

127. CIA, "Memorandum: The Situation in Vietnam," March 20, 1965, DDRS, Doc. #CK3100169293. This frequency and intensity of Chinese threats to the United States and statements supporting the DRV and NLF prompted the CIA to issue a special report on April 9 titled "Selected Significant Communist Statements on Intervention in Vietnam." DDRS, Doc. #CK3100169320. CIA/ONE, "Communist Differences over Political Settlement in Indochina," March 5, 1965, DDRS, Doc. #CK3100185887; CIA, "Memorandum: The Situation in Vietnam," March 13, 1965, DDRS, Doc. #CK3100361713; DOS/INR, "Soviet Aid to North Vietnam," March 25, 1965, DDRS, Doc. #CK3100187597.

128. See CIA, "Monthly Report: The Situation in South Vietnam," April 2, 1965, 1-8, DDRS, Doc. #CK3100409382.

129. Memorandum by the President's Special Assistant for National Security Affairs (Bundy), April 1, 1965, FRUS, 1964-68, vol. 2, 506-10.

130. National Security Action Memorandum No. 328, April 6, 1965, FRUS, 1964-68, vol. 2, 537-39.

131. Memorandum for the Record, April 21, 1965, FRUS, 1964-68, vol. 2, 578-81.

132. Intelligence Memorandum, April 21, 1965, FRUS, 1964-68, vol. 2, 594-95. This conclusion found support in CIA, SNIE 10-5-65, "Communist Reactions to Certain US Actions," April 28, 1965, DNSA, Doc. #SE00401, http://gateway.proquest.com/openurl?url_ver=Z39.88-2004&res _dat=xri:dnsa&rft_dat=xri:dnsa:article:CSE00401, last accessed February 19, 2013; and Special State-Defense Study Group, "Communist China (Short Range Report)," April 30, 1965, DDRS, Doc. #CK3100119641.

133. Memorandum for the Record, April 22, 1965, FRUS, 1964-68, vol. 2, 598.

134. According to the documentary record, it is apparent that the PRC's message did not make its way to top American officials until early June. From the President's Special Assistant for National Security Affairs (Bundy) to President Johnson, June 4, 1965, FRUS, 1964-88, vol. 30 (Washington, DC: GPO, 1998), 173-74.

135. Kaiser, American Tragedy, 444-46.

136. For an extended discussion of this delay, see Spencer D. Bakich, "Information, Diplomacy, and Strategy: Balancing Avoidance in Limited Warfare" (PhD diss., University of Virginia, 2006), 313-20.

137. Edward G. Lansdale, "Viet Nam: Do We Understand Revolution?" Foreign Affairs 43 (October 1964): 84-85.

138. McAllister, "The Lost Revolution," 11-12.

139. Nagl, Learning to Eat Soup with a Knife, 158.

140. Pentagon Papers, Part IV, C-8, "Re-Emphasis on Pacification, 1965-1967," 74, http://media.nara.gov/research/pentagon-papers/Pentagon-Papers-Part-IV-C-8.pdf, last accessed February 19, 2013.

141. Long, "Doctrine of Eternal Recurrence," 10-12.

142. "Memorandum from the Joint Chiefs of Staff to Secretary of Defense McNamara," August 24, 1966, FRUS, 1964-68, vol. 4 (Washington, DC: GPO, 1998), 591-92.

143. Krepinevich, Army and Vietnam, 180-82.

144. Peter M. Dunn, "The American Army: The Vietnam War, 1965-1973," in Armed Forces

and Modern Counter-Insurgency, ed. Ian Beckett and John Pimlott (New York: St. Marin's Press, 1985), 99.

145. Patrick J. McGarvey, "DIA: Intelligence to Please," *Washington Monthly* 11 (July 1970): 72. See also Richard M. Pious, *Why Presidents Fail* (New York: Rowman and Littlefield, 2008), 59.

146. "Management Concept for Pacification Discussed by Robert Komer and Secretary McNamara," September 1, 1966, DDRS, Doc. #CK3100271356.

147. This tendency reflected the "dogma" within the American military that "military policy must be left to military men alone." Robert M. Cassidy, *Counterinsurgency and the Global War on Terror: Military Culture and Irregular Warfare* (Stanford, CA: Stanford University Press, 2008), 110.

148. Memorandum from the President's Special Assistant (Rostow) to President Johnson, August 29, 1966, *FRUS*, 1964-68, vol. 4, 603-6. For additional commentary, see Memorandum from the President's Special Consultant (Taylor) to President Johnson, August 30, 1966, ibid., 607-8.

149. By this time McNamara was convinced that a full-scale pacification effort was essential to producing results. McNamara's "view is that what is needed now is not a Washington exercise to review Westmoreland's message, but a reorganization of the military and civil resources in South Vietnam to produce concrete working plans, region by region, for pacification. In turn, this requires clear-cut chains of command and assignments of responsibility on our side and the Vietnamese side." Memorandum from the President's Special Assistant (Rostow) to President Johnson, August 31, 1966, *FRUS*, 1964-68, vol. 4, 613-14. See also Draft Memorandum from Secretary of Defense McNamara to President Johnson, September 22, 1966, ibid., 659-60; Memorandum from the President's Special Assistant (Komer) to Secretary of Defense McNamara, September 29, 1966, ibid., 672-77.

150. The JCS were fully convinced that the United States was making substantial progress in the war, that Rolling Thunder operations should not be limited beyond what was necessary to avoid civilian deaths, that force levels be bolstered rather than stabilized, and that they considered the proposal to install a civilian "pacification czar" ill-considered. Memorandum from the Joint Chiefs of Staff to Secretary of Defense McNamara, October 14, 1966, *FRUS*, 1964-68, vol. 4, 738-42.

151. For example, see discussion of the report prepared by Under Secretary of State Katzenbach's office critical of the conventional strategy in early 1967. Pentagon Papers, Part IV, c-6, "U.S. Ground Strategy and Force Deployments, 1965-1967," 13-21, http://media.nara.gov /research/pentagon-papers/Pentagon-Papers-Part-IV-C-6-b.pdf, last accessed February 19, 2013.

152. Krepinevich, *Army and Vietnam*, 183.

153. Pentagon Papers, Part IV, c-6, "U.S. Ground Strategy and Force Deployments, 1965-1967," 83, http://media.nara.gov/research/pentagon-papers/Pentagon-Papers-Part-IV-C-6-b.pdf, last accessed February 19, 2013. Emphasis in original.

154. As the Pentagon Papers note, "Little if anything new was revealed in the discussion but it serves to indicate the President's concern with the opportunity costs associated with the large force increase. The discussion also reveals the kind of estimates about the duration of the war which were reaching the President." Ibid., 85.

155. Krepinevich, *Army and Vietnam*, 186-88.

156. For example, see "Southeast Asia: Analysis Report," OASD (SA) Sea Programs Division, July 1967, DDRS, Doc. #CK3100448402.

157. Krepinevich, *Army and Vietnam*, 189.

158. McGarvey, "DIA: Intelligence to Please," 72-73.

159. Nagl, *Learning to Eat Soup with a Knife*, 167-68.

160. Krepinevich, *Army and Vietnam*, 5-6; Long, "Doctrine of Eternal Recurrence," 12-17.

161. Alexander L. George, "The Role of Force in Diplomacy: A Continuing Dilemma for U.S. Foreign Policy," in *Managing Global Chaos*, ed. Chester Crocker, Fen Hampson, and Pamela Aall (Washington, DC: United States Institute of Peace, 1996), 212.

162. Clodfelter, *Limits of Air Power*, 3.

163. Robert F. Futrell, "The Influence of the Air Power Concept on Air Force Planning, 1945–1962," in *Military Planning in the Twentieth Century: Proceedings of the Eleventh Military History Symposium*, ed. Lieutenant Colonel Harry R. Borowski (Washington, DC: Office of Air Force History, 1986), 269; Kaiser, *American Tragedy*, 14–15.

164. Quoted in Clodfelter, *Limits of Air Power*, 30–31.

165. Philip E. Tetlock and Aaron Belkin, "Counterfactual Thought Experiments in World Politics: Logical, Methodological, and Psychological Perspectives," in *Counterfactual Thought Experiments in World Politics: Logical, Methodological, and Psychological Perspectives*, ed. Philip E. Tetlock and Aaron Belkin (Princeton, NJ: Princeton University Press, 1996), 17–18.

166. Jeffrey Record, *Beating Goliath: Why Insurgencies Win* (Washington, DC: Potomac Books, 2007), 12–15.

CHAPTER FIVE

1. National Security Directive 45, "U.S. Policy in Response to the Iraqi Invasion of Kuwait," August 20, 1990, http://bushlibrary.tamu.edu/research/pdfs/nsd/nsd45.pdf, last accessed February 21, 2013.

2. Christian Alfonsi, *Circle in the Sand: Why We Went Back to Iraq* (New York: Doubleday, 2006), 63.

3. Lawrence Freedman and Efraim Karsh, *The Gulf Conflict, 1990–1991: Diplomacy and War in the New World Order* (Princeton, NJ: Princeton University Press, 1993), xxix–xxxii.

4. George H. W. Bush, "Address before a Joint Session of the Congress on the Persian Gulf Crisis and the Federal Budget Deficit," September 11, 1990, http://bushlibrary.tamu.edu/research/public_papers.php?id=2217&year=1990&month=9, last accessed February 21, 2013.

5. Richard N. Haass, *War of Necessity, War of Choice: A Memoir of Two Iraq Wars* (New York: Simon and Schuster, 2009), 76.

6. Alfonsi, *Circle in the Sand*, 60–61.

7. Ibid., 101–7, 140–41.

8. George Bush and Brent Scowcroft, *A World Transformed* (New York: Alfred A. Knopf, 1998), 322.

9. Interview with Secretary of State James Baker, the Gulf War Oral History, *Frontline*, http://www.pbs.org/wgbh/pages/frontline/gulf/oral/baker/1.html, last accessed February 21, 2013.

10. Christopher Maynard, *Out of the Shadow: George H. W. Bush and the End of the Cold War* (College Station: Texas A&M University Press, 2008), 78.

11. Haass, *War of Necessity, War of Choice*, 71–72.

12. James A. Baker III with Thomas M. DeFrank, *The Politics of Diplomacy: Revolution, War, and Peace, 1989–1992* (New York: Putnam, 1995), 277–78.

13. Steve A. Yetiv, *Explaining Foreign Policy: U.S. Decision-Making and the Persian Gulf War* (Baltimore: Johns Hopkins University Press, 2004), 64–77.

14. Alfonsi, *Circle in the Sand*, 72.

15. Baker, *Politics of Diplomacy*, 277–78.

16. In addition to the content of the coalition, American diplomacy also included successful efforts by the allies to share in the burden of funding the war as well as obtaining American domestic support (both in Congress and among the American people). The meeting between Baker and Aziz, the "extra mile for peace," which outraged the Saudis on January 9, was done largely for domestic political purposes. Haass, *War of Necessity, War of Choice*, 103–4. On burden sharing in

the Gulf War generally, see Andrew Bennett, Joseph Lepgold, and Danny Unger, eds., *Friends in Need: Burden Sharing in the Persian Gulf War* (London: Macmillan, 1997).

17. Dilip Hiro, *Desert Shield to Desert Storm: The Second Gulf War* (New York: Routledge, 1992), 435.

18. Bob Woodward, *The Commanders* (New York: Touchstone, 1991), 239-49, 263-73.

19. Alfonsi, *Circle in the Sand*, 123-25.

20. Freedman and Karsh, *Gulf Conflict, 1990-1991*, 168-70.

21. Rick Atkinson, *Crusade: The Untold Story of the Persian Gulf War* (New York: Houghton Mifflin, 1993), 24, 144-45.

22. Jeremy Pressman, *Warring Friends: Alliance Restraint in International Politics* (Ithaca, NY: Cornell University Press, 2008), 109-14.

23. Hiro, *Desert Shield to Desert Storm*, 435-36.

24. Alexander Thompson, *Channels of Power: The UN Security Council and U.S. Statecraft in Iraq* (Ithaca, NY: Cornell University Press, 2009), 51-52.

25. NSD 54 also stated that the United States desired the maximum participation of its coalition partners and that the United States would discourage Israel from participating in military action. National Security Directive 54, "Responding to Iraqi Aggression in the Gulf," January 15, 1991, http://bushlibrary.tamu.edu/research/pdfs/nsd/nsd54.pdf, last accessed February 21, 2013.

26. United States Department of Defense, *Conduct of the Persian Gulf War: Final Report to Congress* (Washington, DC: United States Department of Defense, 1992), 119-23.

27. Michael R. Gordon and General Bernard E. Trainor, *The Generals' War: The Inside Story of the Conflict in the Gulf* (Boston: Little, Brown, 1995), 71-72, 228-37; Atkinson, *Crusade*, chap. 3.

28. Haass, *War of Necessity, War of Choice*, 131. On the specific motivations of leaders in Washington, see Alfonsi, *Circle in the Sand*, 173-76.

29. For assessments of the cause of the lopsided nature of the outcome, see Daryl G. Press, "The Myth of Air Power in the Persian Gulf War and the Future of Warfare," *International Security* 26 (Fall 2001); and Stephen Biddle, *Military Power: Explaining Victory and Defeat in Modern Battle* (Princeton, NJ: Princeton University Press, 2004), 146-50.

30. National Security Directive 1, "Organization of the National Security Council System," January 30, 1989, http://bushlibrary.tamu.edu/research/pdfs/nsd/nsd1.pdf, last accessed February 21, 2013.

31. National Security Directive 1a, "Supplement to National Security Directive 1 (Crisis Management)," October 25, 1989, http://bushlibrary.tamu.edu/research/pdfs/nsd/nsd1a.pdf, last accessed February 21, 2013.

32. Remarks by Dennis Ross, in "Oral History Roundtables: The Bush Administration National Security Council," in *The National Security Council Project*, moderators Ivo H. Daalder and I. M. Destler (Washington, DC: Brookings Institution, April 29, 1999), 11 (hereafter The Bush Administration National Security Council).

33. David J. Rothkopf, *Running the World: The Inside Story of the National Security Council and the Architects of American Power* (New York: Public Affairs, 2005), 262.

34. Alfonsi, *Circle in the Sand*, 79.

35. See remarks by Philip Zelikow, "The Bush Administration National Security Council," 5. See also David Lauter, "Brent Scowcroft," in *Fateful Decisions: Inside the National Security Council*, ed. Karl F. Inderfurth and Loch K. Johnson (New York: Oxford University Press, 2004), 205.

36. Quoted in Yetiv, *Explaining Foreign Policy*, 107.

37. Ivo H. Daalder and I. M. Destler, *In the Shadow of the Oval Office: Profiles of the National Security Advisers and the Presidents They Served—From JFK to George W. Bush* (New York: Simon and Schuster, 2009), 180.

38. For example, Scowcroft was unwilling to speak to Powell about matters of military planning without first securing Cheney's approval. Interview with National Security Advisor Brent

Scowcroft, the Gulf War Oral History, *Frontline*, http://www.pbs.org/wgbh/pages/frontline /gulf/oral/scowcroft/1.html, last accessed February 21, 2013.

39. Daalder and Destler, *In the Shadow of the Oval Office*, 181-82; Rothkopf, *Running the World*, 263.

40. Gary R. Hess, *Presidential Decisions for War: Korea, Vietnam, the Persian Gulf, and Iraq*, 2nd ed. (Baltimore: Johns Hopkins University Press, 2009), 202.

41. Haass, *War of Necessity, War of Choice*, 82-83.

42. Michael K. Bohn, *Nerve Center: Inside the White House Situation Room* (Washington, DC: Potomac Books, 2004), 46-47.

43. Daalder and Destler, *In the Shadow of the Oval Office*, 190-92.

44. Ibid., 169. See also John Prados, *Keeper of the Keys: A History of the National Security Council from Truman to Bush* (New York: William Morrow, 1991), 537-38.

45. Remarks by Roger Porter, "The Bush Administration National Security Council," 36.

46. Bush and Scowcroft, *A World Transformed*, 31.

47. Rothkopf, *Running the World*, 267.

48. "Important Figures in the NSC," National Security Council Project, Brookings Institution, http://www.brookings.edu/~/media/Projects/nsc/KeyPeople.PDF, last accessed February 21, 2013.

49. See remarks by Zelikow, "The Bush Administration National Security Council," 9-10.

50. See remarks by Kimmitt, "The Bush Administration National Security Council," 32.

51. Quoted in Daalder and Destler, *In the Shadow of the Oval Office*, 190.

52. Yetiv, *Explaining Foreign Policy*, 131-32.

53. Daalder and Destler, *In the Shadow of the Oval Office*, 186; Remarks by Haass, "The Bush Administration National Security Council," 33.

54. Bush and Scowcroft, *A World Transformed*, 30.

55. Quoted in Rothkopf, *Running the World*, 297-98.

56. See remarks by Zelikow, "The Bush Administration National Security Council," 32.

57. Interview with Robert M. Gates, George H. W. Bush Oral History, Miller Center of Public Affairs, University of Virginia, July 23-24, 2000, http://millercenter.org/president/bush/oral history/robert-gates, last accessed February 21, 2013.

58. Michael R. Beschloss and Strobe Talbot, *At the Highest Levels: The Inside Story of the End of the Cold War* (Boston: Little, Brown, 1993), 72-74.

59. Alfonsi, *Circle in the Sand*, 52. In fact, Pickering would attend key meetings on military matters during the crisis. U.S News & World Report, *Triumph without Victory: The Unreported History of the Persian Gulf War* (New York: Random House, 1992), 49.

60. Alfonsi, *Circle in the Sand*, 47.

61. Woodward, *The Commanders*, 240.

62. Andrew J. Bacevich, "Elusive Bargain: The Pattern of U.S. Civil-Military Relations since World War II," in *The Long War: A New History of U.S. National Security Policy since World War II*, ed. Andrew J. Bacevich (New York: Columbia University Press, 2007), 246-47; Eliot A. Cohen, *Supreme Command: Soldiers, Statesmen, and Leadership in Wartime* (New York: Free Press, 2002), 188-99.

63. Dale R. Herspring, *The Pentagon and the Presidency: Civil-Military Relations from FDR to George W. Bush* (Lawrence: University Press of Kansas, 2005), 329-30.

64. Colin L. Powell with Joseph E. Persico, *My American Journey* (New York: Random House, 1995), 435-26.

65. Gordon and Trainor, *Generals' War*, 142-47.

66. Herspring, *The Pentagon and the Presidency*, 310.

67. Bush and Scowcroft, *A World Transformed*, 24.

68. Atkinson, *Crusade*, 73.

69. Christopher Andrew, *For the President's Eyes Only: Secret Intelligence and the American Presidency from Washington to Bush* (New York: HarperCollins, 1995), 504–5.

70. Tim Weiner, *Legacy of Ashes: The History of the CIA* (New York: Doubleday, 2007), 427–28.

71. Alfonsi, *Circle in the Sand*, 74–75.

72. Andrew, *For the President's Eyes Only*, 520, 526.

73. Bohn, *Nerve Center*, 46, 111, 114, 168–69.

74. "NSC/DC Meetings—George H. W. Bush Administration (1989–1993)," George H. W. Bush Presidential Library, http://bushlibrary.tamu.edu/research/pdfs/nsc_and_dc_meetings_1989-1992 -declassified.pdf, last accessed February 21, 2013.

75. Woodward, *The Commanders*, 223–24.

76. U.S. News & World Report, *Triumph without Victory: The Unreported History of the Persian Gulf War* (New York: Times Books, 1992), 36–39.

77. Woodward, *The Commanders*, 225–29.

78. Bush and Scowcroft, *A World Transformed*, 317–18.

79. Daalder and Destler, *In the Shadow of the Oval Office*, 196.

80. Haass, *War of Necessity, War of Choice*, 62.

81. Alfonsi, *Circle in the Sand*, 62–68.

82. Thompson, *Channels of Power*, 50.

83. Norman Schwarzkopf with Peter Petre, *It Doesn't Take a Hero* (New York: Bantam Books, 1992), 348–50; Woodward, *The Commanders*, 228, 253–54.

84. Powell, *My American Journey*, 465.

85. Bush and Scowcroft, *A World Transformed*, 333.

86. Webster conceded the point in the next NSC meeting held on August 6. Alfonsi, *Circle in the Sand*, 74–75.

87. Ibid., 75–76. On Baker's motivations, see Baker, *Politics of Diplomacy*, 281–83. On Bush's concern that Baker was too interested in bringing the Soviets into the crisis, see Bush and Scowcroft, *A World Transformed*, 338.

88. Alfonsi, *Circle in the Sand*, 91.

89. Powell, *My American Journey*, 469–71; Woodward, *The Commanders*, 284.

90. Haass, *War of Necessity, War of Choice*, 79–80.

91. Freedman and Karsh, *Gulf Conflict, 1990–1991*, 147–49; Bush and Scowcroft, *A World Transformed*, 352; Baker, *Politics of Diplomacy*, 285–86.

92. CIA, "Background Paper Iraq: Saddam's Political Options," August 12, 1990, http://www .foia.cia.gov/sites/default/files/document_conversions/89801/DOC_0000266050.pdf, last accessed February 21, 2013.

93. Alfonsi, *Circle in the Sand*, 102–7.

94. Powell, *My American Journey*, 470.

95. Interviews with Gates and Haass reported in Alfonsi, *Circle in the Sand*, 144–45.

96. Interview with National Security Council Director for Near East and South Asian Affairs Richard Haass, the Gulf War Oral History, *Frontline*, http://www.pbs.org/wgbh/pages/frontline /gulf/oral/haass/1.html, last accessed February 21, 2013.

97. Schwarzkopf, *It Doesn't Take a Hero*, 401.

98. Interview with Chairman of the Joint Chiefs of Staff Colin Powell, the Gulf War Oral History, *Frontline*, http://www.pbs.org/wgbh/pages/frontline/gulf/oral/powell/1.html, last accessed February 21, 2013.

99. Woodward, *The Commanders*, 41–42, 298–302; Powell, *My American Journey*, 478–80.

100. General Buster Glosson, *War with Iraq: Critical Lessons* (Charlotte, NC: Glosson Family Foundation, 2003), chap. 2.

101. Gordon and Trainor, *Generals' War*, 126–27.

102. Powell, *My American Journey*, 484.

103. Gordon and Trainor, *Generals' War*, 133–34.

104. Ibid., 135–39.

105. Interview with Deputy National Security Advisor Robert Gates, the Gulf War Oral History, *Frontline* 3, http://www.pbs.org/wgbh/pages/frontline/gulf/oral/gates/1.html, last accessed February 21, 201.

106. Bush and Scowcroft, *A World Transformed*, 381.

107. Schwarzkopf, *It Doesn't Take a Hero*, 419–20; Powell, *My American Journey*, 485.

108. Gordon and Trainor, *Generals' War*, 140–41.

109. Bush and Scowcroft, *A World Transformed*, 374.

110. Alfonsi, *Circle in the Sand*, 121–25.

111. Haass, *War of Necessity, War of Choice*, 94.

112. Bush and Scowcroft, *A World Transformed*, 392.

113. For Powell's presentation at this meeting, see Interview with Chairman of the Joint Chiefs of Staff Colin Powell, the Gulf War Oral History, *Frontline*, http://www.pbs.org/wgbh/pages/frontline/gulf/oral/powell/1.html, last accessed February 21, 2013.

114. Bush and Scowcroft, *A World Transformed*, 393–95.

115. The ambiguity in phrasing was intentional, a means of achieving Soviet support for the resolution. Interview with Secretary of State James Baker, the Gulf War Oral History, *Frontline*, http://www.pbs.org/wgbh/pages/frontline/gulf/oral/baker/1.html, last accessed February 21, 2013.

116. Haass, *War of Necessity, War of Choice*, 97–103. On American diplomatic efforts, see Baker, *Politics of Diplomacy*, 305–28.

117. This was precisely Cheney's intention. Interview with Secretary of Defense Richard Cheney, the Gulf War Oral History, *Frontline*, http://www.pbs.org/wgbh/pages/frontline/gulf/oral/cheney/1.html, last accessed February 21, 2013.

118. Henry S. Rowen, "Inchon in the Desert: My Rejected Plan," *National Interest* 40 (Summer 1995).

119. Gordon and Trainor, *Generals' War*, 144–45.

120. Ibid., 146–49.

121. Schwarzkopf, *It Doesn't Take a Hero*, 428.

122. Gordon and Trainor, *Generals' War*, 152.

123. Interview with David Jeremiah, George H. W. Bush Oral History, Miller Center of Public Affairs, University of Virginia, November 15, 2010, http://millercenter.org/president/bush/oral history/david-jeremiah, last accessed February 21, 2013.

124. Schwarzkopf, *It Doesn't Take a Hero*, 460.

125. Woodward, *The Commanders*, 330, 347.

126. Alfonsi, *Circle in the Sand*, 141–42; Bush and Scowcroft, *A World Transformed*, 425.

127. Freedman and Karsh, *Gulf Conflict, 1990–1991*, 253–61.

128. Haass, *War of Necessity, War of Choice*, 117–18 Cf. Interview with Secretary of Defense Richard Cheney, the Gulf War Oral History, *Frontline*, http://www.pbs.org/wgbh/pages/frontline/gulf/oral/cheney/1.html, last accessed February 21, 2013.

129. Baker, *Politics of Diplomacy*, 385–90.

130. The suggestion to approach the Israeli problem diplomatically came from Haass. Interview with National Security Council Director for Near East and South Asian Affairs Richard Haass, the Gulf War Oral History, *Frontline*, http://www.pbs.org/wgbh/pages/frontline/gulf/oral/haass/1.html, last accessed February 21, 2013.

131. Haass, *War of Necessity, War of Choice*, 119–20.

132. Freedman and Karsh, *Gulf Conflict, 1990–1991*, 339.

133. U.S. News & World Report, *Triumph without Victory*, 123, 243; Interview with Chairman of the Joint Chiefs of Staff Colin Powell, the Gulf War Oral History, *Frontline*, http://www.pbs.org/wgbh/pages/frontline/gulf/oral/powell/1.html, last accessed February 21, 2013.

134. CIA, "Seizing the Day: Iran's Response to the Persian Gulf Crisis," November 1, 1990, http://www.foia.cia.gov/sites/default/files/document_conversions/89801/DOC_0000266045.pdf, last accessed February 21, 2013; and Memo prepared for Deputy Director of Central Intelligence, "Three Scenarios to End the Gulf Crisis," December 19, 1990, http://www.foia.cia.gov/sites/default/files/document_conversions/89801/DOC_0000695242.pdf, last accessed February 21, 2013.

135. Alfonsi, *Circle in the Sand*, 155-57.

136. Interview with National Security Council Director for Near East and South Asian Affairs Richard Haass, the Gulf War Oral History, *Frontline*, http://www.pbs.org/wgbh/pages/frontline/gulf/oral/haass/1.html, last accessed February 21, 2013.

137. Alfonsi, *Circle in the Sand*, 161-63; Daalder and Destler, *In the Shadow of the Oval Office*, 200-201.

138. Baker, *Politics of Diplomacy*, 392.

139. CIA, "Iraq-Kuwait Situation Report #502," January 24, 1991, http://www.foia.cia.gov/sites/default/files/document_conversions/89801/DOC_0000132185.pdf, last accessed February 21, 2013.

140. Hess, *Presidential Decisions for War*, 205-9; Baker, *Politics of Diplomacy*, 402-8.

141. Interview with Deputy National Security Advisor Robert Gates, the Gulf War Oral History, *Frontline*, http://www.pbs.org/wgbh/pages/frontline/gulf/oral/gates/1.html, last accessed February 21, 2013.

142. Michael C. Desch, *Civilian Control of the Military: The Changing Security Environment* (Baltimore: Johns Hopkins University Press, 1999), 31.

143. Interview with National Security Advisor Brent Scowcroft, the Gulf War Oral History, *Frontline*, http://www.pbs.org/wgbh/pages/frontline/gulf/oral/scowcroft/1.html, last accessed February 21, 2013.

144. Haass, *War of Necessity, War of Choice*, 130-33.

145. Schwarzkopf, *It Doesn't Take a Hero*, 339-440.

146. Risa A. Brooks, *Shaping Strategy: The Civil-Military Politics of Strategic Assessment* (Princeton, NJ: Princeton University Press, 2008), 44, 50.

147. Powell, *My American Journey*, 465-66.

148. Colin S. Gray, "The American Way of War: Critique and Implications," in *Rethinking the Principles of War*, ed. Anthony D. Mc Ivor (Annapolis, MD: Naval Institute Press, 2005), 27-33; Robert M. Cassidy, *Counterinsurgency and the Global War on Terror: Military Culture and Irregular War* (Stanford, CA: Stanford University Press, 2008), 117-18; Robert M. Cassidy, "Prophets or Praetorians? The Uptonian Paradox and the Powell Corollary," *Parameters* 33 (Autumn 2003).

149. For stronger states with a military dominant concept of war, attrition is attractive because of the perceived reduction in strategic uncertainty. Colin S. Gray, *Modern Strategy* (New York: Oxford University Press, 1999), 95.

150. John J. Mearsheimer, *Conventional Deterrence* (Ithaca, NY: Cornell University Press, 1983), 33-35.

151. Cassidy, *Counterinsurgency and the Global War on Terror*, 114.

152. Cohen, *Supreme Command*, 186-87.

153. Michael I. Handel, *Masters of War: Classical Strategic Thought*, 2nd rev. ed. (London: Frank Cass, 1996), 185-204.

CHAPTER SIX

1. Russell A. Burgos, "Origins of Regime Change: 'Ideapolitik' on the Long Road to Baghdad, 1993-2000," *Security Studies* 17 (April 2008); Benjamin A. Gilman, H.R. 4655, "Iraq Liberation Act of 1998," 105th Congress, October 5, 1998, http://thomas.loc.gov/cgi-bin/bdquery/z?d105:H.R.4655, last accessed, February 21, 2013.

2. Douglas J. Feith, *War and Decision: Inside the Pentagon at the Dawn of the War on Terrorism* (New York: Harper, 2008), 214–16; Bob Woodward, *Plan of Attack* (New York: Simon and Schuster, 2004), 26.

3. James Mann, *Rise of the Vulcans: The History of Bush's War Cabinet* (New York: Viking, 2004), 315–31. The literature on the 2002 NSS is extensive. For a sampling, see G. John Ikenberry, "America's Imperial Ambition," *Foreign Affairs* (September/October 2002); Robert Jervis, "Understanding the Bush Doctrine," *Political Science Quarterly* 118 (Fall 2003); Jeffrey Record, *Dark Victory: America's Second War against Iraq* (Annapolis, MD: Naval Institute Press, 2004), 30–44; and John Lewis Gaddis, *Surprise, Security, and the American Experience* (Cambridge, MA: Harvard University Press, 2004), 69–114.

4. According to Melvyn Leffler, few top administration officials devote any attention to the 2002 NSS in their memoirs. Rice, on the other hand, insists that the overriding objective of the NSS was to establish a strong ideological foundation, "akin to NSC 68," for America's overriding political goal of creating a "balance of power in favor of freedom." Melvyn P. Leffler, "The Foreign Policies of the George W. Bush Administration: Memoirs, History, Legacy," *Diplomatic History* 37 (2013): 14–15; Condoleezza Rice, *No Higher Honor: A Memoir of My Years in Washington* (New York: Crown, 2011), 152–56. The scant attention devoted to the NSS by most of the former top administration officials in their memoirs should not be interpreted as evidence of the document's irrelevance. As Alan Stolberg argues, national security strategy documents serve three vital functions: (1) to ensure that government departments understand clearly the intentions of senior leadership in national security affairs, (2) to inform legislatures of the resources required for the execution of the executive branch's strategy, and (3) to communicate to international and domestic audiences which threats the state considers most salient and how the state will go about addressing those threats. Alan G. Stolberg, *How Nation-States Craft National Security Strategy Documents* (Carlisle, PA: Strategic Studies Institute, U.S. Army War College, 2012), 2–3. In short, the 2002 NSS is essential to understanding why America went to war against Iraq.

5. White House, "The National Security Strategy of the United States of America," September 2002, 1–3, 13–14, http://georgewbush-whitehouse.archives.gov/nsc/nss/2002/, last accessed February 21, 2013.

6. The NSS contains both preventive and preemptive logics: "Our immediate focus will be those terrorist organizations of global reach and any terrorist or state sponsor of terrorism *which attempts to gain* or use weapons of mass destruction (WMD) *or their precursors.*" Ibid., 6. Emphasis added.

7. Ibid., 9. Emphasis added.

8. Woodward, *Plan of Attack*, 24–51.

9. "Virtually every memoir makes clear that officials in the Bush administration did believe that Saddam had WMD (specifically biological and/or chemical weapons) or would soon acquire them or seek to develop them." Leffler, "The Foreign Policies of the George W. Bush Administration," 13.

10. See discussion of NSC paper, "Iraq: Goals, Objectives, Strategy," signed by Bush in late August 2002, in Feith, *War and Decision*, 283–89. On American threat sensitivity, see Ron Suskind, *The One Percent Doctrine: Deep Inside America's Pursuit of Its Enemies since 9/11* (New York: Simon and Schuster, 2006), 62.

11. Feith, *War and Decision*, 222–24.

12. Richard N. Haass, *War of Necessity, War of Choice: A Memoir of Two Iraq Wars* (New York: Simon and Schuster, 2009), 235. Peter W. Galbraith, *The End of Iraq: How American Incompetence Created a War without End* (New York: Simon and Schuster, 2006), 9–10.

13. John M. Owen IV, *The Clash of Ideas in World Politics: Transnational Networks, States, and Regime Change, 1510–2010* (Princeton, NJ: Princeton University Press, 2010), 236–37. As Dick Cheney notes, "A question that came up early and often in our discussions of a government to fol-

low Saddam was whether we were committed to establishing a democracy in Iraq. I believed we had no alternative." Dick Cheney with Liz Cheney, *In My Time: A Personal and Political Memoir* (New York: Simon and Schuster, 2011), 387. In addition to overthrowing Saddam's regime in Iraq, the United States initiated a project called the Greater Middle East Initiative, which sought to make the promotion of freedom in the region the primary objective of its foreign policy. Fred Kaplan, *Daydream Believers: How a Few Grand Ideas Wrecked American Power* (Hoboken, NJ: Wiley, 2008), 134-36.

14. Bob Woodward, *State of Denial: Bush at War, Part III* (New York: Simon and Schuster, 2006), 83-85.

15. Thom Shanker and Eric Schmitt, "Rumsfeld Says Iraq Is Collapsing, Lists 8 Objectives of War," *New York Times*, March 22, 2003, A1. Two additional war aims were noted by Rumsfeld: the collection of intelligence related to terrorist networks and to the global network of illicit WMD activity.

16. Bradley Graham, *By His Own Rules: the Ambitions, Successes, and Ultimate Failures of Donald Rumsfeld* (New York: Public Affairs, 2009), 327.

17. The exact timing of the rise of the Sunni insurgency is difficult to pinpoint. While the outbreak of violence in the area known as the "Sunni Triangle" occurred in late April 2003, outside observers could only ascertain the dimensions of the insurgency later in August. Ahmed S. Hashim, *Insurgency and Counter-Insurgency in Iraq* (Ithaca, NY: Cornell University Press, 2006), 23; Ali A. Allawi, *The Occupation of Iraq: Winning the War, Losing the Peace* (New Haven, CT: Yale University Press, 2007), 170.

18. Woodward, *Plan of Attack*, 85-95, 130-33.

19. Tommy Franks, *American Soldier* (New York: Regan Books, 2004), 328-97; Michael R. Gordon and Bernard E. Trainor, *Cobra II: The Inside Story of the Invasion and Occupation of Iraq* (New York: Pantheon, 2006), 24-54.

20. On the political incentives to lower the number of troops, see Isaiah Wilson, "America's Anabasis," in *War in Iraq: Planning and Execution*, ed. Thomas G. Mahnken and Thomas A. Keaney (New York: Routledge, 2007), 14-15. On the incentive to deploy quietly, see Woodward, *Plan of Attack*, 57-58, 136. On specific deployments to the theater, see Gregory Fontenot, E. J. Degen, and David Tohn, *On Point: The United States Army in Operation Iraqi Freedom* (Fort Leavenworth, KS: Combat Studies Institute Press, 2004), 29-84.

21. Woodward, *Plan of Attack*, 41-42.

22. Ivo H. Daalder and I. M. Destler, *In the Shadow of the Oval Office: Profiles of the National Security Advisers and the President They Served—From JFK to George W. Bush* (New York: Simon and Schuster, 2009), 279-80; Haass, *War of Necessity, War of Choice*, 215-16. Feith contends that for Bush, war became inevitable only after Iraq submitted its WMD declaration to the UN in December 2002. Feith, *War and Decision*, 347.

23. Alexander Thompson, *Channels of Power: The UN Security Council and U.S. Statecraft in Iraq* (Ithaca, NY: Cornell University Press, 2009), 161-62; Woodward, *Plan of Attack*, 296, 341.

24. Thompson, *Channels of Power*, 140-54; Woodward, *Plan of Attack*, 343-45.

25. Nora Bensahel et al., *After Saddam: Prewar Planning and the Occupation of Iraq* (Santa Monica, CA: Rand, 2008), 9.

26. Larry Diamond, *Squandered Victory: The American Occupation and the Bungled Effort to Bring Democracy to Iraq* (New York: Owl Books, 2005), 27.

27. Feith, *War and Decision*, 316-17; Woodward, *State of Denial*, 91-92.

28. George Packer, *The Assassins Gate: America In Iraq* (New York: Farrar, Straus and Giroux, 2005), 120.

29. Gordon and Trainor, *Cobra II*, provides an excellent summary of major combat operations throughout. See also John Keegan, *The Iraq War* (London: Hutchinson, 2004).

30. Figure includes American and British commitment (116,000 and 46,000 respectively).

Geraint Hughes, "The Insurgencies in Iraq, 2003-2009: Origins, Development, and Prospects," *Defence Studies* 10 (March–June 2010): 158.

31. American SOF and conventional forces were deployed in the west as well to capture suspected WMD sites and search for SCUD missile launchers.

32. Richard B. Andres, "The Afghan Model in Northern Iraq," in *War in Iraq: Planning and Execution*, ed. Thomas G. Mahnken and Thomas A. Keaney (New York: Routledge, 2007), 58-59.

33. Gordon and Trainor, *Cobra II*, 61-63.

34. Thomas Ricks, *Fiasco: The American Military Adventure in Iraq* (New York: Penguin Press, 2006), 125-27.

35. Kevin M. Woods et al., "Iraqi Military Effectiveness," in *War in Iraq: Planning and Execution*, ed. Thomas G. Mahnken and Thomas A. Keaney (New York: Routledge, 2007), 45-46.

36. Stephen Biddle, "Speed Kills? Reassessing the Role of Speed, Precision, and Situation Awareness in the Fall of Saddam," *Journal of Strategic Studies* 30 (February 2007).

37. Woodward, *Plan of Attack*, 401; Matthew M. Aid, *The Secret Sentry: The Untold History of the National Security Agency* (New York: Bloomsbury Press, 2009), 246-63.

38. Toby Dodge, "The Causes of U.S. Failure in Iraq," *Survival* 49 (Spring 2007): 88.

39. James DeFronzo, *The Iraq War: Origins and Consequences* (Boulder, CO: Westview Press, 2010), 159.

40. Michael Eisenstadt and Jeffrey White, "Assessing Iraq's Sunni Arab Insurgency," *Military Review* 86 (May–June 2006): 33-34; Ahmed Hashim, "The Iraqi Insurgency, 2003-2006," in *War in Iraq: Planning and Execution*, ed. Thomas G. Mahnken and Thomas A. Keaney (New York: Routledge, 2007), 148-50.

41. Nir Rosen, *In the Belly of the Green Bird: The Triumph of the Martyrs in Iraq* (New York: Free Press, 2006), 42-48.

42. Hughes, "The Insurgencies in Iraq," 159.

43. L. Paul Bremer III, *My Year in Iraq: The Struggle to Build a Future of Hope* (New York: Simon and Schuster, 2006), 36-59.

44. Allawi, *Occupation of Iraq*, 147-59; Hashim, *Insurgency and Counterinsurgency in Iraq*, 281.

45. Diamond, *Squandered Victory*, 39. In their defense of the CPA, even Bremer and his coauthors concede that this decision swelled the ranks of the burgeoning insurgency. L. Paul Bremer, James Dobbins, and David Gompert, "Early Days in Iraq: Decisions of the CPA," *Survival* 50 (August–September 2008): 26-27.

46. Allawi, *Occupation of Iraq*, 159; Hughes, "The Insurgencies in Iraq," 159.

47. Carter Malkasian, "Counterinsurgency in Iraq: May 2003-January 2007," in *Counterinsurgency in Modern Warfare*, ed. Daniel Marton and Carter Malkasian (Oxford: Osprey Publishing, 2008), 201-5.

48. Galbraith, *End of Iraq*, 175; Brian Burton and John Nagl, "Learning as We Go: The U.S. Army Adapts to Counterinsurgency in Iraq, July 2004-December 2006," *Small Wars and Insurgencies* 19 (September 2008).

49. Daniel Byman, "An Autopsy of the Iraq Debacle: Policy Failure or a Bridge Too Far?" *Security Studies* 14 (2008): 602. Byman argues that even under the best circumstances, the United States would face tremendous hurdles in Iraq. Nevertheless, Byman concludes that the United States could have achieved victory if it had been able to avoid the outbreak of the Sunni insurgency.

50. Dale R. Herspring, *The Pentagon and the President: Civil-Military Relations from FDR to George W. Bush* (Lawrence: University Press of Kansas, 2005), 378.

51. John P. Burke, *Becoming President: The Bush Transition, 2000-2003* (Boulder, CO: Lynne Rienner, 2004), 107-21.

52. The White House, National Security Presidential Directive 1, "Organization of the National Security Council System," February 13, 2001, http://www.fas.org/irp/offdocs/nspd/nspd-1

.htm, last accessed February 21, 2013. Donald R. Drechsler, "Reconstructing the Interagency Process after Iraq," *Journal of Strategic Studies* 28 (February 2005): 4–5.

53. Daalder and Destler, *In the Shadow of the Oval Office*, 278.

54. Feith, *War and Decision*, 143–44, 249–50. See also Packer, *Assassins Gate*, 110.

55. John P. Burke, "From Success to Failure? Iraq and the Organization of George W. Bush's Decision Making," in *The Polarized Presidency of George W. Bush*, ed. George C. Edwards III and Desmond S. King (New York: Oxford University Press, 2007), 173–212.

56. Scott McClellan, *What Happened: Inside the Bush White House and Washington's Culture of Deception* (New York: Public Affairs, 2008), 85.

57. Mann, *Rise of the Vulcans*, 252–53.

58. Barton Gellman, *Angler: The Cheney Vice Presidency* (New York: Penguin Press, 2008), 44.

59. Woodward, *Plan of Attack*, 48–50; David Rothkopf, *Running the World: The Inside Story of the National Security Council and the Architects of American Power* (New York: Public Affairs, 2004), 423.

60. Rothkopf, *Running the World*, 408; Haass, *War of Necessity, War of Choice*, 183.

61. Ricks, *Fiasco*, 89.

62. Herspring, *The Pentagon and the President*, 383; Woodward, *State of Denial*, 71–72.

63. Daalder and Destler, *In the Shadow of the Oval Office*, 274.

64. Graham, *By His Own Rules*, 265, 344.

65. George W. Bush, *Decision Points* (New York: Crown, 2010), 234–35.

66. Woodward, *Plan of Attack*, 44. By securing the president's attention, Rumsfeld was able to obtain access to information from other institutional sources that served military operations effectively. Most notably, the National Security Agency and the CIA shared vital information with CENTCOM both before and during the war. On the CIA in particular, see George Tenet, *At the Center of the Storm: The CIA during America's Time of Crisis* (New York: Harper Perennial, 2007), 386–87.

67. Dale R. Herspring, *Rumsfeld's Wars: The Arrogance of Power* (Lawrence: University Press of Kansas, 2008), 92.

68. Bensahel et al., *After Saddam*, 11, 50. TFIV was disbanded at the end of March 2003.

69. Woodward, *State of Denial*, 105–19; Drechsler, "Reconstructing the Interagency Process after Iraq," 19–20.

70. Bremer, Dobbins, and Gompert, "Early Days in Iraq," 21.

71. Bremer, *My Year in Iraq*, 4.

72. James Dobbins et al., *Occupying Iraq: A History of the Coalition Provisional Authority*, (Santa Monica, CA: Rand, 2009), 14–18. Coordination between CJTF-7 and CPA began to improve in September 2003. Andrew Rathmell, "Planning Post-Conflict Reconstruction in Iraq: What Can We Learn?" *International Affairs* 81 (2005): 1028.

73. Graham, *By His Own Rules*, 215–16.

74. Herspring, *Rumsfeld's Wars*, 113.

75. Woodward, *State of Denial*, 74.

76. Steven Metz, *Decisionmaking in Operation Iraqi Freedom: Removing Saddam Hussein by Force* (Carlisle, PA: Strategic Studies Institute, U.S. Army War College, 2010), 18–19.

77. Suskind, *One Percent Doctrine*, 168–71; Woodward, *State of Denial*, 77–79.

78. On the CIA's exclusion at the highest level, see Tenet, *At the Center of the Storm*, 308–9; Paul R. Pillar, "Intelligence, Policy, and the War in Iraq," *Foreign Affairs* (March/April 2006). On the relationship between CIA and DOD in war and postwar planning, see Feith, *War and Decision*, 360–75.

79. Michael Heazle, "Policy Lessons from Iraq on Managing Uncertainty in Intelligence Assessment: Why the Strategic/Tactical Distinction Matters," *Intelligence and National Security* 25 (June 2010); Michael Fitzgerald and Richard Ned Lebow, "Iraq: The Mother of All Intelligence Failures," *Intelligence and National Security* 21 (October 2006).

80. Daalder and Destler, *In the Shadow of the Oval Office*, 254–55.

81. James P. Pfiffner, "The Contemporary Presidency: Decision Making in the Bush White House," *Presidential Studies Quarterly* 39 (June 2009): 380.

82. Haass, *War of Necessity, War of Choice*, 214–15.

83. Drechsler, "Reconstructing the Interagency Process after Iraq," 9.

84. Rothkopf, *Running the World*, 407–8; Haass, *War of Necessity, War of Choice*, 228.

85. Daalder and Destler, *In the Shadow of the Oval Office*, 277.

86. Feith, *War and Decision*, 250.

87. Woodward, *Plan of Attack*, 104, 176–77.

88. Bensahel et al., *After Saddam*, 21–23.

89. Woodward, *Plan of Attack*, 321–22.

90. Bensahel et al., *After Saddam*, 21–23.

91. Ibid., 5–19.

92. James Fallows, *Blind into Baghdad: America's War in Iraq* (New York: Viking, 2006), 61. Rumsfeld is reported to have threatened to fire anyone who talked about the need for a postwar plan. Herspring, *Rumsfeld's Wars*, 108.

93. Feith accuses DOS and CIA officials of exerting undue influence over Franks, at the expense of his office. Feith, *War and Decision*, 382.

94. CENTCOM believed that postwar reconstruction was the responsibility of Feith's policy office. Woodward, *Plan of Attack*, 90–91. Feith counters that CENTCOM knew that these responsibilities belonged to it. Feith, *War and Decision*, 317–18.

95. Ibid., 386–87.

96. Rumsfeld implied that Cheney made this decision. Woodward, *State of Denial*, 126–29.

97. Ibid., 144–45.

98. Feith, *War and Decision*, 299–317.

99. Woodward, *Plan of Attack*, 283–84.

100. Graham, *By His Own Rules*, 388–89.

101. Woodward, *Plan of Attack*, 30–44.

102. Ibid., 96–106.

103. Gordon and Trainor, *Cobra II*, 88.

104. Woodward, *Plan of Attack*, 116–38, 145–53.

105. Gordon and Trainor, *Cobra II*, 75–94.

106. Ibid., 96–98; Ricks, *Fiasco*, 71.

107. Donald Rumsfeld, *Known and Unknown: A Memoir* (New York: Sentinel, 2011), 437–38; Herspring, *Rumsfeld's Wars*, 128.

108. Bensahel et al., *After Saddam*, 9–10.

109. Herspring, *Rumsfeld's Wars*, 128.

110. Gordon and Trainor, *Cobra II*, 141–42.

111. Woodward, *Plan of Attack*, 148.

112. Graham, *By His Own Rules*, 355–56.

113. Woodward, *Plan of Attack*, 401.

114. Fontenot, Degen, and Tohn, *On Point*, 422–23.

115. Future of Iraq Project, Transitional Justice Working Group, "The Road to Re-Establishing Rule of Law and Restoring Civil Society," National Security Archive, http://www.gwu.edu/~nsarchiv/NSAEBB/NSAEBB198/FOI%20Transitional%20Justice.pdf, last accessed February 21, 2013.

116. Future of Iraq Project, Defense Policy and Institutions Working Group, "A New Iraq: Democracy and the Role of the Army," 3–5, National Security Archive, http://www.gwu.edu/~nsarchiv/NSAEBB/NSAEBB198/FOI%20Defense%20Policy%20and%20Institutions.pdf, last accessed February 21, 2013.

117. Fallows, *Blind into Baghdad*, 57–58.

118. Rumsfeld, *Known and Unknown*, 486.

119. Haass, *War of Necessity, War of Choice*, 226–28.

120. Fallows, *Blind into Baghdad*, 61.

121. CIA, "The Postwar Occupations of Germany and Japan: Implications for Iraq," August 7, 2002, National Security Archive, http://www.google.com/url?sa=t&rct=j&q=&esrc=s&source=web&cd=1&ved=0CDIQFjAA&url=http%3A%2F%2Fwww.gwu.edu%2F~nsarchiv%2FNSAEBB%2FNSAEBB328%2FII-Doc17.pdf&ei=4qEnUZeRCIXW0gHguIDIDw&usg=AFQjCNFuqgTkmlwbiFaLMvYWZDb1L015uA&bvm=bv.42768644,d.dmQ&cad=rja, last accessed February 22, 2013.

122. United States Senate, Select Committee on Intelligence, 110th Congress, "Report on Prewar Intelligence Assessments about Postwar Iraq," May 2007, 100–101, http://www.intelligence.senate.gov/11076.pdf, last accessed February 22, 2013.

123. Ibid., 55–57.

124. Richard Kerr et al., "Intelligence Collection and Analysis on Iraq: Issues for the US Intelligence Community," in *Intelligence and National Security Policymaking on Iraq*, ed. James P. Pfiffner and Mark Phythian (College Station: Texas A&M University Press, 2008), 152–53.

125. Graham, *By His Own Rules*, 354–59.

126. Conrad C. Crane and W. Andrew Terrill, *Reconstructing Iraq: Insights, Challenges, and Missions for Military Forces in a Post-Conflict Scenario* (Carlisle, PA: U.S. Army War College, 2003), 32.

127. Ricks, *Fiasco*, 96–98.

128. In his memoir, Bush notes that he did "seek advice from scholars, Iraqi dissidents in exile, and others outside the administration." The lone individual Bush singles out as being particularly persuasive is Elie Wiesel, who said to the president, "you have a moral obligation to act against evil." Bush, *Decision Points*, 247–48.

129. Woodward, *Plan of Attack*, 259.

130. Donald P. Wright et al., *On Point II: Transition to the New Campaign: The United States Army in Operation IRAQI FREEDOM May 2003–January 2005* (Fort Leavenworth, KS: US Army Combined Arms Center, 2008), 66.

131. Rice, *No Higher Honor*, 189–90.

132. Bensahel et al., *After Saddam*, 22–23; Rathmell, "Planning Post-Conflict Reconstruction in Iraq," 1021.

133. Feith, *War and Decision*, 229–73.

134. Bensahel et al., *After Saddam*, 26–28.

135. Ibid., 31.

136. Future of Iraq Project, Transparency and Anti-Corruption Measures Working Group, National Security Archive, http://www.gwu.edu/~nsarchiv/NSAEBB/NSAEBB198/FOI%20Transparency.pdf, last accessed February 21, 2013.

137. Future of Iraq Project, Democratic Principles Working Group, "The Transition to Democracy in Iraq," National Security Archive, http://www.gwu.edu/~nsarchiv/NSAEBB/NSAEBB198/FOI%20Democratic%20Principles.pdf, last accessed February 21, 2013.

138. Future of Iraq Project, Defense Policy and Institutions Working Group, "A New Iraq: Democracy and the Role of the Army," National Security Archive, http://www.gwu.edu/~nsarchiv/NSAEBB/NSAEBB198/FOI%20Defense%20Policy%20and%20Institutions.pdf, last accessed February 21, 2013.

139. Future of Iraq Project, Economy and Infrastructure Working Group, National Security Archive, http://www.gwu.edu/~nsarchiv/NSAEBB/NSAEBB198/FOI%20Economy%20and%20Infrastructure.pdf, last accessed February 21, 2013.

140. Feith, *War and Decision*, 376.

141. Bensahel et al., *After Saddam*, 35. On USAID's relationship with the NGO community, see Fallows, *Blind into Baghdad*, 67–71.

142. Feith, *War and Decision*, 316–17, 347.

143. Haass, *War of Necessity, War of Choice*, 218.

144. Bensahel et al., *After Saddam*, 53–69.

145. Daalder and Destler, *In the Shadow of the Oval Office*, 284.

146. Gordon and Trainor, *Cobra II*, 475–76.

147. Woodward, *Plan of Attack*, 339–43.

148. James P. Pfiffner, "US Blunders in Iraq: De-Baathification and Disbanding the Army," *Intelligence and National Security* 25 (February 2010): 76–79.

149. Tenet, *At the Center of the Storm*, 426.

150. Quoted in Ricks, *Fiasco*, 159.

151. Dobbins et al., *Occupying Iraq*, 112–19.

152. Woodward, *Plan of Attack*, 339–343.

153. Michael R. Gordon, "Fateful Choice on Iraq Army Bypassed Debate," *New York Times*, March 17, 2008, http://www.nytimes.com/2008/03/17/world/middleeast/17bremer.html?page wanted=all&_r=0, last accessed February 21, 2013.

154. Dobbins et al., *Occupying Iraq*, 53.

155. Pfiffner, "US Blunders in Iraq," 81.

156. Dobbins et al., *Occupying Iraq*, 55–56.

157. Pfiffner, "US Blunders in Iraq," 82.

158. Ibid., 82.

159. Gordon, "Fateful Choice on Iraq Army Bypassed Debate."

160. Dobbins et al., *Occupying Iraq*, 57–58.

161. Pfiffner, "US Blunders in Iraq," 83.

162. Anthony H. Cordesman, *Iraq's Insurgency and the Road to Civil Conflict*, vol. 1 (Westport, CT: Praeger Security International, 2008), 47–50.

163. Rumsfeld's "Parade of Horribles" memo on what could go wrong in the war is a case in point. Rumsfeld, *Known and Unknown*, 387; Feith, *War and Decision*, 332–35.

164. Risa A. Brooks, *Shaping Strategy: The Civil-Military Politics of Strategic Assessment* (Princeton, NJ: Princeton University Press, 2008), 241–42.

165. In other words, the information institution contains emergent properties that separate it conceptually from the individuals embedded therein. Robert Jervis, *System Effects: Complexity in Political and Social Life* (Princeton, NJ: Princeton University Press, 1997), 5–6.

166. Quoted in Jeffrey Record, *Beating Goliath: Why Insurgencies Win* (Washington, DC: Potomac Books, 2007), 104. See also Colin S. Gray, "The American Way of War: Critique and Implications," in *Rethinking the Principles of War*, ed. Anthony D. Mc Ivor (Annapolis, MD: Naval Institute Press, 2005), 27–33; Thomas G. Mahnken, "The American Way of War in the Twenty-First Century," in *Democracies and Small Wars*, ed. Efram Inbar (Portland, OR: Frank Cass, 2003).

167. Steven Metz, *Iraq and the Evolution of American Strategy* (Washington, DC: Potomac Books, 2008), 33.

168. Dana Priest, *The Mission: Waging War and Keeping Peace with America's Military* (New York: Norton, 2003), 56.

169. Quoted in Ricks, *Fiasco*, 79.

170. Rumsfeld, *Known and Unknown*, 485.

171. On the military-diplomatic demands required of senior American military commanders, see Wesley K. Clark, *Waging Modern War* (New York: Public Affairs, 2002), 417–61.

172. On the numerous responsibilities of CENTCOM commanders between the Persian Gulf and Iraq wars, see Priest, *The Mission*, 61–77.

173. Drechsler, "Reconstructing the Interagency Process after Iraq," 4–5.

CHAPTER SEVEN

1. Elinor Ostrom, *Understanding Institutional Diversity* (Princeton, NJ: Princeton University Press, 2005), 119. Emphasis added.

2. Risa A. Brooks, *Shaping Strategy: The Civil-Military Politics of Strategic Assessment* (Princeton, NJ: Princeton University Press, 2008), 23–27.

3. Gideon Rose, *How Wars End: Why We Always Fight the Last Battle; a History of American Intervention from World War I to Afghanistan* (New York: Simon and Schuster, 2010), 134–35.

4. Douglass C. North, "Epilogue: Economic Performance through Time," in *Empirical Studies in Institutional Analysis*, ed. Lee J. Alston, Thrainn Eggertsson, and Douglass C. North (New York: Cambridge University Press, 1996), 346.

5. Dan Reiter, *How Wars End* (Princeton, NJ: Princeton University Press, 2009), 5.

6. Ibid., 220–21.

7. Cf. Hein Goemans, *War and Punishment: The Causes of War Termination and the First World War* (Princeton, NJ: Princeton University Press, 2000).

8. These assumptions, of course, are common among all rationalist approaches. David A. Lake, "Two Cheers for Bargaining Theory: Assessing Rationalist Explanations of the Iraq War," *International Security* 35 (Winter 2010/11).

9. Uncertainty plays an important role in the initiation of war in rationalist approaches. James D. Fearon, "Rationalist Explanations of War," *International Organization* 49 (1995); Dan Reiter, "Exploring the Bargaining Model of War," *Perspectives on Politics* 1 (March 2003): 27–43.

10. I thank Angelina Peck for bringing this to my attention.

11. Graham Allison and Philip Zelikow, *Essence of Decision: Explaining the Cuban Missile Crisis*, 2nd ed. (New York: Addison Wesley Longman, 1999); David A. Welch, *Painful Choices: A Theory of Foreign Policy Change* (Princeton, NJ: Princeton University Press, 2005), 33.

12. Alexander Cooley, *Logics of Hierarchy: The Organization of Empires, States, and Military Occupations* (Ithaca, NY: Cornell University Press, 2005), 45–46.

13. Charles L. Glaser, *Rational Theory of International Politics: The Logic of Competition and Cooperation* (Princeton, NJ: Princeton University Press, 2010).

14. Ibid., 40–43, 182.

15. Ibid., 48–49.

16. Ibid., 102, 106–7.

17. Bernard I. Finel and Kristin M. Lord, "The Surprising Logic of Transparency," *International Studies Quarterly* 43 (June 1999): 320.

18. Thomas C. Schelling, *Arms and Influence* (New Haven, CT: Yale University Press, 1966), 1–4.

19. For a recent treatment of the distinction between the strategic logic of coercive diplomacy and the strategic logic of war, see Thomas J. Christensen, *Worse Than a Monolith: Alliance Politics and Problems of Coercive Diplomacy in Asia* (Princeton, NJ: Princeton University Press, 2011), 2–8.

20. Janice Gross Stein, "Deterrence and Compellence in the Gulf, 1990–91: A Failed or Impossible Task?" *International Security* 17 (Autumn 1992): 174.

21. Michael R. Gordon and Bernard E. Trainor, *Cobra II: The Inside Story of the Invasion and Occupation of Iraq* (New York: Pantheon, 2006), 55; Glenn Kessler, "Saddam Hussein Said WMD Talk Helped Him Look Strong to Iran," *Washington Post*, July 2, 2009, http://articles.washingtonpost.com/2009-07-02/news/36847839_1_interviews-saddam-hussein-weapons-of-mass-destruction, last accessed February 22, 2013.

22. Kevin Woods, James Lacey, and Williamson Murray, "Saddam's Delusions: The View from the Inside," *Foreign Affairs* (May/June 2006): 21–26.

23. On neoclassical realism as a theory of foreign policy, see Jeffrey W. Taliaferro, "Security Seeking under Anarchy: Defensive Realism Revisited," *International Security* 25 (Winter 2000–2001).

24. Randall L. Schweller, "Unanswered Threats: A Neoclassical Realist Theory of Underbalancing," *International Security* 29 (Fall 2004): 166.

25. Jeffrey W. Taliaferro, "Neoclassical Realism and Resource Extraction: State Building for

Future War," in *Neoclassical Realism, the State, and Foreign Policy*, ed. Steven E. Lobell, Norrin M. Rispman, and Jeffrey W. Taliaferro (New York: Cambridge University Press, 2009); Jennifer Sterling-Folker, "Realist Environment, Liberal Process, and Domestic-Level Variables," *International Studies Quarterly* 41 (March 1997); Thomas J. Christensen, *Useful Adversaries: Grand Strategy, Domestic Mobilization, and Sino-American Conflict, 1947-1958* (Princeton, NJ: Princeton University Press, 1996).

26. That is, apart from America's ability to project power at global distance—a function of both absolute and relative power.

27. The necessity of institutionalizing strategic planning for American national security policy has been recognized and in some instances acted upon to great effect. Aaron L. Friedberg, "Strengthening U.S. Strategic Planning," *Washington Quarterly* 31 (Winter 2007/8); Peter Feaver and William Inboden, "A Strategic Planning Cell on National Security at the White House," in *Avoiding Trivia: The Role of Strategic Planning in American Foreign Policy*, ed. Daniel Drezner (Washington, DC: Brookings Institution Press, 2009), 108-9.

28. Mark Schafer and Scott Crichlow, *Groupthink: High-Quality Decision Making in International Relations* (New York: Columbia University Press, 2010), 185-87; Gregory M. Herek, Irving L. Janis, and Paul Huth, "Decision Making during International Crises: Is Quality of Process Related to Outcome?" *Journal of Conflict Resolution* 31 (June 1987).

29. On the different forms of advisory systems, see Alexander L. George, *Presidential Decisionmaking in Foreign Policy: The Effective Use of Information and Advice* (Boulder, CO: Westview Press, 1980).

30. Schafer and Crichlow, *Groupthink*, 243.

31. Amy B. Zegart, *Flawed by Design: The Evolution of the CIA, JCS, and NSC* (Stanford, CA: Stanford University Press, 1999), chap. 3.

32. James R. Locher III, *Victory on the Potomac: The Goldwater-Nichols Act Unifies the Pentagon* (College Station: Texas A&M University Press, 2002), 437-50.

33. Matthew M. Aid, ed., "Intel Wars: The Lessons for U.S. Intelligence from Today's Battlefields," National Security Archive Electronic Briefing Book No. 370 (February 13, 2012), http://www.gwu.edu/~nsarchiv/NSAEBB/NSAEBB370/index.htm, last accessed February 22, 2013.

Bibliography

PRIMARY DOCUMENTS COLLECTIONS

Brookings Institution. "The Bush Administration National Security Council," Oral History Round-tables, the National Security Council Project. http://www.brookings.edu/about/projects/archive/nsc/19990429.

Central Intelligence Agency. Freedom of Information Act Reading Room. http://www.foia.cia.gov/.

Declassified Documents Reference System, Gale Digital Collections. http://gdc.gale.com/products/declassified-documents-reference-system/.

Federation of American Scientists. Intelligence Resource Program. http://www.fas.org/irp/offdocs/direct.htm.

Frontline, PBS. "The Gulf War: An Oral History." http://www.pbs.org/wgbh/pages/frontline/gulf/oral/.

George H. W. Bush Presidential Library and Museum, Texas A&M University. http://bushlibrary.tamu.edu/research/research.php.

Kuhns, Woodrow J., ed. *Assessing the Soviet Threat: The Early Cold War Years*. Washington, DC: Central Intelligence Agency, 1997.

Miller Center of Public Affairs, University of Virginia. George H. W. Bush Oral Histories, Presidential Oral History Project. http://millercenter.org/president/bush/oralhistory.

National Archive and Records Administration. Pentagon Papers. http://www.archives.gov/research/pentagon-papers/.

National Security Archive, George Washington University. http://www.gwu.edu/~nsarchiv/.

US Department of State. Foreign Relations of the United States: 1945–50, Emergence of the Intelligence Establishment. Washington, DC: GPO, 1996.

US Department of State. Foreign Relations of the United States: 1950, vol. 1. Washington, DC: GPO, 1977.

US Department of State. Foreign Relations of the United States: 1950, vol. 7. Washington, DC: GPO, 1976.

US Department of State. Foreign Relations of the United States: 1961–63, vol. 8. Washington, DC: GPO, 1996.

US Department of State. Foreign Relations of the United States: 1964–68, vol. 1. Washington, DC: GPO, 1992.

US Department of State. Foreign Relations of the United States: 1964–68, vol. 2. Washington, DC: GPO, 1996.

US Department of State. Foreign Relations of the United States: 1964–68, vol. 4. Washington, DC: GPO, 1998.

US Department of State. Foreign Relations of the United States: 1964-68, vol. 30. Washington, DC: GPO, 1998.

US Select Committee on Intelligence, United States Senate. http://intelligence.senate.gov/.

White House, President George W. Bush. http://georgewbush-whitehouse.archives.gov/.

SECONDARY SOURCE MATERIAL

Acheson, Dean. *The Korean War.* New York: W. W. Norton, 1969.

———. *Present at the Creation: My Years in the State Department.* New York: W. W. Norton, 1969.

———. "United States Policy toward Formosa: Extemporaneous Remarks by Secretary Acheson." *Department of State Bulletin* 22 (March 1950).

Aid, Matthew M. *The Secret Sentry: The Untold History of the National Security Agency.* New York: Bloomsbury Press, 2009.

———. "US HUMINT and COMINT in the Korean War: From the Approach of War to the Chinese Intervention." *Intelligence and National Security* 14, no. 4 (1999): 17-63.

Alfonsi, Christian. *Circle in the Sand: Why We Went Back to Iraq.* New York: Doubleday, 2006.

Allawi, Ali A. *The Occupation of Iraq: Winning the War, Losing the Peace.* New Haven, CT: Yale University Press, 2007.

Allison, Graham T, and Philip Zelikow. *Essence of Decision: Explaining the Cuban Missile Crisis.* 2nd ed. New York: Longman, 1999.

Ambrose, Stephen E. *Ike's Spies: Eisenhower and the Espionage Establishment.* Garden City, NY: Doubleday, 1981.

Andres, Richard B. "The Afghan Model in Northern Iraq." In *War in Iraq: Planning and Execution,* edited by Thomas G Mahnken and Thomas A Keaney. New York: Routledge, 2007.

Andrew, Christopher M. *For the President's Eyes Only: Secret Intelligence and the American Presidency from Washington to Bush.* New York: HarperCollins, 1995.

Aoki, Masahiko. "Horizontal vs. Vertical Information Structure of the Firm." *American Economic Review* 76, no. 5 (1986): 971-83.

———. *Information, Incentives, and Bargaining in the Japanese Economy.* Cambridge: Cambridge University Press, 1988.

———. *Toward a Comparative Institutional Analysis.* Cambridge, MA: MIT Press, 2001.

Appleman, Roy E. *Disaster in Korea: The Chinese Confront MacArthur.* College Station: Texas A&M University Press, 1989.

Art, Robert J. "Bureaucratic Politics and American Foreign Policy: A Critique." *Policy Sciences* 4 (December 1973): 467-90.

———. *A Grand Strategy for America.* Ithaca, NY: Cornell University Press, 2004.

Asprey, Robert B. *War in the Shadows: Guerillas in History.* New York: William Morrow, 1994.

Atkinson, Rick. *Crusade: The Untold Story of the Persian Gulf War.* Boston: Houghton Mifflin, 1993.

Avant, Deborah D. *Political Institutions and Military Change: Lessons from Peripheral Wars.* Ithaca, NY: Cornell University Press, 1994.

Bacevich, Andrew J. "Elusive Bargain: The Pattern of U.S. Civil-Military Relations since World War II." In *The Long War: A New History of U.S. National Security Policy since World War II,* edited by Andrew J. Bacevich. New York: Columbia University Press, 2007.

Baker, James Addison. *The Politics of Diplomacy: Revolution, War, and Peace, 1989-1992.* New York: Putnam, 1995.

Bakich, Spencer D. "Information, Diplomacy, and Strategy: Balancing Avoidance in Limited Warfare." PhD diss., University of Virginia, 2006.

———. "Institutionalizing Supreme Command: Explaining Political-Military Integration in the Vietnam War, 1964-1968." *Small Wars and Insurgencies* 22 (2011): 688-711.

Ball, George W. "Top Secret: The Prophecy the President Rejected." *The Atlantic* 230 (July 1972).

Barrett, David M. "Doing 'Tuesday Lunch' at Lyndon Johnson's White House: New Archival Evidence on Vietnam Decisionmaking." *PS: Political Science and Politics* 24 (December 1991): 676-79.

———. "The Mythology Surrounding Lyndon Johnson, His Advisers, and the 1965 Decision to Escalate the Vietnam War." *Political Science Quarterly* 103 (December 1988): 637-63.

———. *Uncertain Warriors: Lyndon Johnson and His Vietnam Advisors.* Lawrence: University Press of Kansas, 1993.

Bendor, Jonathan, and Thomas H. Hammond. "Rethinking Allison's Models." *American Political Science Review* 86 (June 1, 1992): 301-22.

Bennett, Andrew, and Colin Elman. "Qualitative Research: Recent Developments in Case Study Methods." *Annual Review of Political Science* 9 (2006): 455-76.

Bennett, Andrew, Joseph Lepgold, and Danny Unger, eds. *Friends in Need: Burden Sharing in the Persian Gulf War.* New York: St. Martin's Press, 1997.

Bensahel, Nora, et al. *After Saddam: Prewar Planning and the Occupation of Iraq.* Santa Monica, CA: Rand, 2008.

Beschloss, Michael R, and Strobe Talbott. *At the Highest Levels: The Inside Story of the End of the Cold War.* Boston: Little, Brown, 1993.

Betts, Richard K. *Enemies of Intelligence: Knowledge and Power in American National Security.* New York: Columbia University Press, 2007.

———. *Soldiers, Statesmen, and Cold War Crises.* New York: Columbia University Press, 1991.

Biddle, Stephen. *Military Power: Explaining Victory and Defeat in Modern Battle.* Princeton, NJ: Princeton University Press, 2004.

———. "Speed Kills? Reassessing the Role of Speed, Precision, and Situation Awareness in the Fall of Saddam." *Journal of Strategic Studies* 30 (February 1, 2007): 3-46.

Bigelow, Michael E. "Disaster along the Ch'ongch'on: Intelligence Breakdown in Korea." *Military Intelligence* (September 1992).

Blainey, Geoffrey. *The Causes of War.* London: Macmillan, 1973.

Blair, Clay. *The Forgotten War: America in Korea, 1950-1953.* Annapolis, MD: Naval Institute Press, 1987.

Blaufarb, Douglas S. *The Counterinsurgency Era: U.S. Doctrine and Performance, 1950 to the Present.* New York: Free Press, 1977.

Bohn, Michael K. *Nerve Center: Inside the White House Situation Room.* Washington, DC: Brassey's, 2003.

Boot, Max. *The Savage Wars of Peace: Small Wars and the Rise of American Power.* New York: Basic Books, 2003.

Bracken, Paul. "Net Assessment: A Practical Guide." *Parameters* 36 (Spring 2006): 90-100.

Bradley, General Omar N. *Military Situation in the Far East.* 82nd Congress. Washington, DC, 1951.

Bradley, Omar Nelson. *A General's Life.* New York: Simon and Schuster, 1983.

Bremer, L. Paul. *My Year in Iraq: The Struggle to Build a Future of Hope.* New York: Simon and Schuster, 2006.

Bremer, L. Paul, James Dobbins, and David Gompert. "Early Days in Iraq: Decisions of the CPA." *Survival* 50 (2008): 21-56.

Brigham, Robert K. "Three Alternative U.S. Strategies in Vietnam: A Reexamination Based on New Chinese and Vietnamese Sources." In *Argument without End: In Search of Answers to the Vietnam Tragedy*, edited by Robert S. McNamara, James G. Blight, and Robert K. Brigham. New York: Public Affairs, 1999.

Brooks, Risa. *Shaping Strategy: The Civil-Military Politics of Strategic Assessment.* Princeton, NJ: Princeton University Press, 2008.

Burgos, Russell. "Origins of Regime Change: Ideapolitik on the Long Road to Baghdad, 1993–2000." *Security Studies* 17 (April 2008): 221–56.

Burke, John P. *Becoming President: The Bush Transition, 2000–2003*. Boulder, CO: Lynne Rienner, 2004.

———. "From Success to Failure? Iraq and the Organization of George W. Bush's Decision Making." In *The Polarized Presidency of George W. Bush*, edited by George C. Edwards III and Desmond King. New York: Oxford University Press, 2007.

Burke, John P., and Fred I. Greenstein. *How Presidents Test Reality: Decisions on Vietnam, 1954 and 1965*. New York: Russell Sage Foundation, 1989.

Burton, Brian, and John Nagl. "Learning as We Go: The US Army Adapts to Counterinsurgency in Iraq, July 2004–December 2006." *Small Wars and Insurgencies* 19 (2008).

Bush, George, and Brent Scowcroft. *A World Transformed*. New York: Knopf, 1998.

Bush, George W. *Decision Points*. New York: Crown, 2010.

Byman, Daniel. "An Autopsy of the Iraq Debacle: Policy Failure or Bridge Too Far?" *Security Studies* 17, no. 4 (2008): 599–643.

Cassidy, Robert. *Counterinsurgency and the Global War on Terror: Military Culture and Irregular War*. Stanford, CA: Stanford University Press, 2008.

———. "Prophets or Praetorians? The Uptonian Paradox and the Powell Corollary." *Parameters* 33 (Autumn 2003): 130–43.

Chandler, Alfred D. *Strategy and Structure: Chapters in the History of the Industrial Enterprise*. Cambridge, MA: MIT Press, 1969.

Chang, Gordon H. *Friends and Enemies: The United States, China, and the Soviet Union, 1948–1972*. Stanford, CA: Stanford University Press, 1990.

Chen Jian. "China's Involvement in the Vietnam War, 1964–69." *China Quarterly* 142 (June 1995): 356–87.

———. *China's Road to the Korean War*. New York: Columbia University Press, 1996.

———. *Mao's China and the Cold War*. Chapel Hill: University of North Carolina Press, 2001.

Cheney, Dick, with Liz Cheney. *In My Time: A Personal and Political Memoir*. New York: Simon and Schuster, 2011.

Christensen, Thomas J. *Useful Adversaries: Grand Strategy, Domestic Mobilization, and Sino-American Conflict, 1947–1958*. Princeton, NJ: Princeton University Press, 1996.

———. *Worse Than a Monolith: Alliance Politics and Problems of Coercive Diplomacy in Asia*. Princeton, NJ: Princeton University Press, 2011.

Clark, Wesley K. *Waging Modern War: Bosnia, Kosovo, and the Future of Combat*. New York: Public Affairs, 2002.

Clausewitz, Carl von. *On War*. Edited and translated by Michael Howard and Peter Paret. Princeton, NJ: Princeton University Press, 1984.

Cline, Ray S. *The CIA under Reagan, Bush, and Casey: The Evolution of the Agency from Roosevelt to Reagan*. Washington, DC: Acropolis Books, 1981.

Clodfelter, Mark. *The Limits of Air Power: The American Bombing of North Vietnam*. New York: Free Press, 1989.

Cohen, Eliot A. "'Only Half the Battle': American Intelligence and the Chinese Intervention in Korea, 1950." *Intelligence and National Security* 5 (1990): 129–49.

———. *Supreme Command: Soldiers, Statesmen, and Leadership in Wartime*. New York: Free Press, 2002.

Cohen, Eliot A., and John Gooch. *Military Misfortunes: The Anatomy of Failure in War*. New York: Free Press, 1990.

Condit, Doris M. *History of the Office of the Secretary of Defense*. Vol. 2, *The Test of War, 1950–1953*. Washington, DC: Office of the Secretary of Defense, 1988.

Cooley, Alexander. *Logics of Hierarchy: The Organization of Empires, States, and Military Occupations*. Ithaca, NY: Cornell University Press, 2005.

Copeland, Dale C. *The Origins of Major War*. Cornell Studies in Security Affairs. Ithaca, NY: Cornell University Press, 2000.

―――. "The Constructivist Challenge to Structural Realism: A Review Essay." *International Security* 25 (Autumn 2000): 187–212.

Cordesman, Anthony H. *Iraq's Insurgency and the Road to Civil Conflict*. Vol. 1. Westport, CT: Praeger, 2008.

Crane, Conrad C., and W. Andrew Terrill. *Reconstructing Iraq: Insights, Challenges, and Missions for Military Forces in a Post-Conflict Scenario*. Carlisle, PA: U.S. Army War College, 2003.

Cross, Robert L. *The Hidden Power of Social Networks: Understanding How Work Really Gets Done in Organizations*. Boston: Harvard Business School Press, 2004.

Cumings, Bruce. *The Origins of the Korean War*. Vol. 2, *The Roaring of the Cataract, 1947–1950*. Princeton, NJ: Princeton University Press, 1990.

Daalder, Ivo H., and I. M. Destler. *In the Shadow of the Oval Office: Profiles of the National Security Advisors and the Presidents They Served; From JFK to George W. Bush*. New York: Simon and Schuster, 2009.

Daft, Richard L., and Robert H. Lengel. "Organizational Information Requirements, Media Richness, and Structural Design." *Management Science* 32 (May 1, 1986): 554–71.

Darling, Arthur B. *The Central Intelligence Agency: An Instrument of Government, to 1950*. University Park: Pennsylvania State University Press, 1990.

DeFronzo, James. *The Iraq War: Origins and Consequences*. Boulder, CO: Westview Press, 2010.

Deibel, Terry L. *Foreign Affairs Strategy: Logic for American Statecraft*. New York: Cambridge University Press, 2007.

Desch, Michael C. *Civilian Control of the Military: The Changing Security Environment*. Baltimore: Johns Hopkins University Press, 1999.

―――. *Power and Military Effectiveness: The Fallacy of Democratic Triumphalism*. Baltimore: Johns Hopkins University Press, 2008.

Destler, I. M., Leslie H. Gelb, and Anthony Lake. *Our Own Worst Enemy: The Unmaking of American Foreign Policy*. New York: Simon and Schuster, 1984.

Diamond, Larry Jay. *Squandered Victory: The American Occupation and the Bungled Effort to Bring Democracy to Iraq*. New York: Times Books, 2005.

Dobbins, James, Seth G. Jones, Benjamin Runkle, and Siddharth Mohandas. *Occupying Iraq: A History of the Coalition Provisional Authority*. Santa Monica, CA: Rand, 2009.

Dobbins, James, et al., eds. *America's Role in Nation-Building: From Germany to Iraq*. Santa Monica, CA: Rand, 2003.

Dodge, Toby. "The Causes of US Failure in Iraq." *Survival* 49 (2007).

Drechsler, Donald R. "Reconstructing the Interagency Process after Iraq." *Journal of Strategic Studies* 28 (2005).

Duffield, John. "What Are International Institutions?" *International Studies Review* 9 (May 1, 2007): 1–22.

Dunn, Peter M. "The American Army: The Vietnam War, 1965–1973." In *Armed Forces and Modern Counter-Insurgency*, edited by I. F. W Beckett and John Pimlott. New York: St. Martin's Press, 1985.

Edelstein, David M. "Managing Uncertainty: Beliefs about Intentions and the Rise of Great Powers." *Security Studies* 12, no. 1 (2002): 1–40.

―――. *Occupational Hazards: Success and Failure in Military Occupation*. Ithaca, NY: Cornell University Press, 2008

Eisenstadt, Michael, and Jeffrey White. "Assessing Iraq's Sunni Arab Insurgency." *Military Review* 86 (May 2006): 33–51.

Ellsberg, Daniel. *Secrets: A Memoir of Vietnam and the Pentagon Papers*. New York: Viking Press, 2002.

Epstein, Joshua M. "Horizontal Escalation: Sour Notes of a Recurrent Theme." *International Security* 8 (1983): 19–31.

Fallows, James M. *Blind into Baghdad: America's War in Iraq*. New York: Vintage Books, 2006.

Fearon, James D. "Rationalist Explanations for War." *International Organization* 49 (Summer 1995): 379-414.

———. "Signaling Foreign Policy Interests: Tying Hands versus Sinking Costs." *Journal of Conflict Resolution* 41 (February 1, 1997): 68-90.

Feaver, Peter D. *Armed Servants: Agency, Oversight, and Civil-Military Relations*. Cambridge, MA: Harvard University Press, 2003.

———. "The Right to Be Right: Civil-Military Relations and the Iraq Surge Decision." *International Security* 35 (April 24, 2011): 87-125.

Feaver, Peter, and William Inboden. "A Strategic Planning Cell on National Security at the White House." In *Avoiding Trivia: The Role of Strategic Planning in American Foreign Policy*, edited by Daniel W. Drezner. Washington, DC: Brookings Institution Press, 2009.

Feith, Douglas J. *War and Decision: Inside the Pentagon at the Dawn of the War on Terrorism*. New York: Harper, 2008.

Finel, Bernard I., and Kristin M. Lord. "The Surprising Logic of Transparency." *International Studies Quarterly* 43 (1999): 325-39.

Fitzgerald, Michael, and Richard Ned Lebow. "Iraq: The Mother of All Intelligence Failures." *Intelligence and National Security* 21 (2006): 884-909.

Fontenot, Gregory, E. J Degen, and David Tohn. *On Point: The United States Army in Operation Iraqi Freedom*. Annapolis, MD: Naval Institute Press, 2005.

Foot, Rosemary. *Substitute for Victory: The Politics of Peacemaking at the Korean Armistice Talks*. Ithaca, NY: Cornell University Press, 1990.

———. *The Wrong War: American Policy and the Dimensions of the Korean Conflict, 1950-1953*. Ithaca, NY: Cornell University Press, 1985.

Franks, Tommy. *American Soldier*. New York: Regan Books, 2004.

Freedman, Lawrence. *Kennedy's Wars: Berlin, Cuba, Laos, and Vietnam*. New York: Oxford University Press, 2000.

Freedman, Lawrence, and Efraim Karsh. *The Gulf Conflict, 1990-1991: Diplomacy and War in the New World Order*. Princeton, NJ: Princeton University Press, 1993.

Friedberg, Aaron L. *The Weary Titan: Britain and the Experience of Relative Decline, 1895-1905*. Princeton, NJ: Princeton University Press, 1988.

Friedberg, Peter. "Strengthening U.S. Strategic Planning." In *Avoiding Trivia: The Role of Strategic Planning in American Foreign Policy*, edited by Daniel W. Drezner. Washington, DC: Brookings Institution Press, 2009.

Fukuyama, Francis. "Guidelines for Future Nation Builders." In *Nation-Building: Beyond Afghanistan and Iraq*, edited by Francis Fukuyama. Baltimore: Johns Hopkins University Press, 2006.

Fuller, William C. *Strategy and Power in Russia, 1600-1914*. New York: Free Press, 1992.

Futrell, Robert F. "The Influence of the Air Power Concept on Air Force Planning, 1945-1962." In *Military Planning in the Twentieth Century*, edited by Lieutenant Colonel Harry R. Borowski. Washington, DC: Office of Air Force History, US Air Force, 1986.

Gacek, Christopher M. *The Logic of Force: The Dilemma of Limited War in American Foreign Policy*. New York: Columbia University Press, 1994.

Gaddis, John Lewis. "The Strategic Perspective: The Rise and Fall of the 'Defense Perimeter' Concept." In *Uncertain Years: Chinese-American Relations, 1947-1950*, edited by Dorothy Borg and Waldo H. Heinrichs. New York: Columbia University Press, 1980.

———. *Strategies of Containment: A Critical Appraisal of Postwar American National Security Policy*. New York: Oxford University Press, 1982.

———. *Surprise, Security, and the American Experience*. Cambridge, MA: Harvard University Press, 2004.

Galbraith, Peter. *The End of Iraq: How American Incompetence Created a War without End*. New York: Simon and Schuster, 2007.

Garver, John W. "The Chinese Threat in the Vietnam War." *Parameters* 23 (Spring 1992): 73–85.

Gelb, Leslie H., and Richard K. Betts. *The Irony of Vietnam: The System Worked*. Washington, DC: Brookings Institution, 1979.

Gellman, Barton. *Angler: The Cheney Vice Presidency*. New York: Penguin Press, 2008.

George, Alexander L. *Presidential Decisionmaking in Foreign Policy: The Effective Use of Information and Advice*. Boulder, CO: Westview Press, 1980.

———. "The Role of Force in Diplomacy: A Continuing Dilemma for U.S. Foreign Policy." In *Managing Global Chaos: Sources of and Responses to International Conflict*, edited by Chester A Crocker, Fen Osler Hampson, and Pamela R. Aall. Washington, DC: United States Institute of Peace Press, 1996.

George, Alexander L., and Andrew Bennett. *Case Studies and Theory Development in the Social Sciences*. Cambridge, MA: MIT Press, 2005.

George, Alexander L., and Richard Smoke. *Deterrence in American Foreign Policy: Theory and Practice*. New York: Columbia University Press, 1974.

Glaser, Charles L. "Political Consequences of Military Strategy: Expanding and Refining the Spiral and Deterrence Models." *World Politics* 44 (July 1, 1992): 497–538.

———. *Rational Theory of International Politics: The Logic of Competition and Cooperation*. Princeton, NJ: Princeton University Press, 2010.

Glosson, General Buster. *War with Iraq: Critical Lessons*. Charlotte, NC: Glosson Family Foundation, 2003.

Goddard, Stacie E. "When Right Makes Might: How Prussia Overturned the European Balance of Power." *International Security* 33 (2008): 110–42.

Goemans, H. E. *War and Punishment: The Causes of War Termination and the First World War*. Princeton, NJ: Princeton University Press, 2000.

Goncharov, Sergei, John Lewis, and Litai Xue. *Uncertain Partners: Stalin, Mao, and the Korean War*. Stanford, CA: Stanford University Press, 1995.

Goodwin, Doris Kearns. *Lyndon Johnson and the American Dream*. New York: St. Martin's Press, 1991.

Gordon, Michael R. "Fateful Choice on Iraq Army Bypassed Debate." *New York Times*, March 17, 2008.

Gordon, Michael R., and Bernard E. Trainor. *Cobra II: The Inside Story of the Invasion and Occupation of Iraq*. New York: Pantheon Books, 2006.

———. *The Generals' War: The Inside Story of the Conflict in the Gulf*. Boston: Little, Brown, 1995.

Graber, Doris A. *The Power of Communication: Managing Information in Public Organizations*. Washington, DC: Congressional Quarterly, 2003.

Graham, Bradley. *By His Own Rules: The Ambitions, Successes, and Ultimate Failures of Donald Rumsfeld*. New York: Public Affairs, 2009.

Gray, Colin S. *Modern Strategy*. New York: Oxford University Press, 1999.

———. "The American War of War: Critique and Implications." In *Rethinking the Principles of War*, edited by Anthony D. Mc Ivor. Annapolis, MD: Naval Institute Press, 2005.

Haas, Mark L. "Prospect Theory and the Cuban Missile Crisis." *International Studies Quarterly* 45 (June 1, 2001): 241–70.

Haass, Richard. *War of Necessity: War of Choice*. New York: Simon and Schuster, 2009.

Halperin, Morton H. *Limited War in the Nuclear Age*. New York: Wiley, 1963.

Halperin, Morton H., and Priscilla Clapp. *Bureaucratic Politics and Foreign Policy*. 2nd ed. Washington, DC: Brookings Institution Press, 2006.

Hammond, Thomas. "Structure, Strategy, and the Agenda of the Firm." In *Fundamental Issues in*

Strategy: A Research Agenda, edited by Richard P. Rumelt, Dan Schendel, and David J. Teece. Boston: Harvard Business School Press, 1994.

Handel, Michael I. *Masters of War: Classical Strategic Thought*. 2nd rev. and expanded ed. London: Frank Cass, 1996.

Hashim, Ahmed. *Insurgency and Counter-Insurgency in Iraq*. Ithaca, NY: Cornell University Press, 2006.

———. "The Iraqi Insurgency, 2003-2006." In *War in Iraq: Planning and Execution*, edited by Thomas G. Mahnken and Thomas A. Keaney. New York: Routledge, 2007.

Heazle, Michael. "Policy Lessons from Iraq on Managing Uncertainty in Intelligence Assessment: Why the Strategic/Tactical Distinction Matters." *Intelligence and National Security* 25 (June 1, 2010): 290-308.

Hennessy, Michael A. *Strategy in Vietnam: The Marines and Revolutionary Warfare in I Corps, 1965-1972*. Westport, CT: Praeger, 1997.

Herek, Gregory M., Irving L. Janis, and Paul Huth. "Decision Making during International Crises: Is Quality of Process Related to Outcome?" *Journal of Conflict Resolution* 31 (June 1, 1987): 203-26.

Herring, George C. *America's Longest War: The United States and Vietnam, 1950-1975*. 2nd ed. New York: Knopf, 1986.

Hershberg, James G., and Chen Jian. "Reading and Warning the Likely Enemy: China's Signals to the United States about Vietnam in 1965." *International History Review* 27 (March 2005): 47-84.

Herspring, Dale R. *The Pentagon and the Presidency: Civil-Military Relations from FDR To George W. Bush*. Lawrence: University Press of Kansas, 2005.

———. *Rumsfeld's Wars: The Arrogance of Power*. Lawrence: University Press of Kansas, 2008.

Hess, Gary R. *Presidential Decisions for War: Korea, Vietnam, and the Persian Gulf*. Baltimore: Johns Hopkins University Press, 2001.

———. *Presidential Decisions for War: Korea, Vietnam, the Persian Gulf, and Iraq*. 2nd ed. Baltimore: Johns Hopkins University Press, 2009.

Hess, Stephen. *Organizing the Presidency*. 3rd ed. Washington, DC: Brookings Institution, 2002.

Hilsman, Roger. *To Move a Nation: The Politics of Foreign Policy in the Administration of John F. Kennedy*. Garden City, NY: Doubleday, 1967.

Hiro, Dilip. *Desert Shield to Desert Storm: The Second Gulf War*. New York: Routledge, 1992.

Hoang Ngoc Lung. *Strategy and Tactics*. Washington, DC: U.S. Army Center for Military History, 1980.

Hodgson, Geoffrey Martin. *Economics and Institutions: A Manifesto for a Modern Institutional Economics*. Oxford: Polity Press, 1988.

Howard, Michael. *The Franco-Prussian War: The German Invasion of France, 1870-1871*. New York: Routledge, 2001.

Hughes, Geraint. "The Insurgencies in Iraq, 2003-2009: Origins, Developments, and Prospects." *Defence Studies* 10 (March 1, 2010): 152-76.

Humphrey, David C. "Tuesday Lunch at the Johnson White House: A Preliminary Assessment." *Diplomatic History* 8 (1984): 81-102.

Huntington, Samuel P. *The Soldier and the State: The Theory and Politics of Civil-Military Relations*. Cambridge, MA: Harvard University Press, 1957.

Ikenberry, G. John. "America's Imperial Ambition." *Foreign Affairs* 81 (2002): 44-60.

Iklé, Fred Charles. *Every War Must End*. 2nd rev. ed. New York: Columbia University Press, 2005.

Immerman, Richard H. "Intelligence and Strategy: Historicizing Psychology, Policy, and Politics." *Diplomatic History* 32 (January 1, 2008): 1-23.

Jackson, George S., and Martin P. Claussen. *Organizational History of the Central Intelligence Agency, 1950-1953*. Vol. 8. Washington, DC: Central Intelligence Agency, 1957.

James, D. Clayton. *Refighting the Last War: Command and Crisis in Korea, 1950–1953*. New York: Free Press, 1993.

———. *The Years of MacArthur: Triumph and Disaster, 1945–1964*. Vol. 3. Boston: Houghton Mifflin, 1985.

Janis, Irving L. *Groupthink: Psychological Studies of Policy Decisions and Fiascoes*. 2nd ed., rev. Boston: Houghton Mifflin, 1983.

———. *Victims of Groupthink: A Psychological Study of Foreign-Policy Decisions and Fiascoes*. Boston: Houghton Mifflin, 1972.

Jeffreys-Jones, Rhodri. *The CIA and American Democracy*. 2nd ed. New Haven, CT: Yale University Press, 1989.

Jentleson, Bruce W. "An Integrative Executive Branch Strategy for Policy Planning." In *Avoiding Trivia: The Role of Strategic Planning in American Foreign Policy*, edited by Daniel W. Drezner. Washington, DC: Brookings Institution Press, 2009.

Jervis, Robert. "The Impact of the Korean War on the Cold War." *Journal of Conflict Resolution* 24 (December 1, 1980): 563–92.

———. *Perception and Misperception in International Politics*. Princeton, NJ: Princeton University Press, 1976.

———. "Political Implications of Loss Aversion." *Political Psychology* 13, no. 2 (1992): 187–204.

———. *System Effects: Complexity in Political and Social Life*. Princeton, NJ: Princeton University Press, 1997.

———. "Understanding the Bush Doctrine." *Political Science Quarterly* 118 (October 1, 2003): 365–88.

Johnson, Dominic D. P., and Dominic Tierney. *Failing to Win: Perceptions of Victory and Defeat in International Politics*. Cambridge, MA: Harvard University Press, 2006.

Kadera, Kelly M. "Transmission, Barriers, and Constraints: A Dynamic Model of the Spread of War." *Journal of Conflict Resolution* 42 (June 1, 1998): 367–87.

Kahin, George McTurnan. *Intervention: How America Became Involved in Vietnam*. Garden City, NY: Anchor Press/Doubleday, 1987.

Kahl, Colin H. "In the Crossfire or the Crosshairs? Norms, Civilian Casualties, and U.S. Conduct in Iraq." *International Security* 32 (2007): 7–46.

Kaiser, David E. *American Tragedy: Kennedy, Johnson, and the Origins of the Vietnam War*. Cambridge, MA: Harvard University Press, 2000.

Kaplan, Fred M. *Daydream Believers: How a Few Grand Ideas Wrecked American Power*. Hoboken, NJ: John Wiley and Sons, 2008.

Karalekas, Anne. "The Central Intelligence Group and the Central Intelligence Agency, 1946–1952." In *The Central Intelligence Agency, History and Documents*, edited by William M. Leary. Tuscaloosa: University of Alabama Press, 1984.

———. "History of the Central Intelligence Agency." In *The Central Intelligence Agency, History and Documents*, edited by William M. Leary. Tuscaloosa: University of Alabama Press, 1984.

Karnow, Stanley. *Vietnam: A History*. New York: Penguin Books, 1984.

Kaufmann, Chaim. "Threat Inflation and the Failure of the Marketplace of Ideas: The Selling of the Iraq War." *International Security* 29 (Summer 2004): 5–48.

Kaufmann, William W. "Limited War." In *Military Policy and National Security*, edited by William W. Kaufmann. Princeton, NJ: Princeton University Press, 1956.

Keegan, John. *The Iraq War*. New York: Vintage Books, 2005.

Kerr, Richard, Thomas Wolfe, Rebecca Donegan, and Aris Pappas. "Intelligence Collection and Analysis on Iraq: Issues for the US Intelligence Community." In *Intelligence and National Security Policymaking on Iraq: British and American Perspectives*, edited by James P. Pfiffner and Mark Phythian. College Station: Texas A&M University Press, 2008.

Kessler, Glenn. "Saddam Hussein Said WMD Talk Helped Him Look Strong to Iran." *Washington Post*, July 2, 2009.

Khan, Herman. *On Escalation: Metaphors and Scenarios*. Baltimore: Penguin Books, 1968.

Khong, Yuen Foong. *Analogies at War: Korea, Munich, Dien Bien Phu, and the Vietnam Decisions of 1965*. Princeton, NJ: Princeton University Press, 1992.

Kier, Elizabeth. *Imagining War: French and British Military Doctrine between the Wars*. Princeton, NJ: Princeton University Press, 1997.

King, Gary, Robert O. Keohane, and Sidney Verba. *Designing Social Inquiry: Scientific Inference in Qualitative Research*. Princeton, NJ: Princeton University Press, 1994.

Kinsella, David. "No Rest for the Democratic Peace." *American Political Science Review* 99 (August 2005): 453–57.

Krasner, Stephen D. "Are Bureaucracies Important? (Or Allison Wonderland)." *Foreign Policy* 7 (July 1, 1972): 159–79.

Krepinevich, Andrew F. *The Army and Vietnam*. Baltimore: Johns Hopkins University Press, 1986.

Kupchan, Charles A. "Getting In: The Initial Stage of Military Intervention." In *Foreign Military Intervention: The Dynamics of Protracted Conflict*, edited by Ariel Levite, Bruce W. Jentleson, and Larry Berman. New York: Columbia University Press, 1992.

Labs, Eric J. "Beyond Victory: Offensive Realism and the Expansion of War Aims." *Security Studies* 6 (1997).

Lakatos, Imre. "Falsification and the Methodology of Scientific Research Programmes." In *Criticism and the Growth of Knowledge*, edited by Imre Lakatos and Alan Musgrave. Cambridge: Cambridge University Press, 1970.

Lake, David A. "Two Cheers for Bargaining Theory: Assessing Rationalist Explanations of the Iraq War." *International Security* 35 (2010): 7–52.

Lake, David A., and Robert Powell. "International Relations: A Strategic-Choice Approach." In *Strategic Choice and International Relations*, edited by David A. Lake and Robert Powell. Princeton, NJ: Princeton University Press, 1999.

Lansdale, Edward G. "Viet Nam: Do We Understand Revolution?" *Foreign Affairs* 43 (October 1964): 75–86.

Lauter, David. "Brent Scowcroft." In *Fateful Decisions: Inside the National Security Council*, edited by Karl Inderfurth and Loch K Johnson. New York: Oxford University Press, 2004.

Lay, James S., and Robert H. Johnson. *Organizational History of the National Security Council during the Truman and Eisenhower Administrations*. Washington, DC: Central Intelligence Agency, 1960.

Lazonick, William. *Business Organization and the Myth of the Market Economy*. Cambridge: Cambridge University Press, 1991.

Lebow, Richard Ned. *Between Peace and War: The Nature of International Crisis*. Baltimore: Johns Hopkins University Press, 1981.

Leffler, Melvyn P. "The Foreign Policies of the George W. Bush Administration: Memoirs, History, Legacy." *Diplomatic History* 37 (February 2013): 190–216.

———. *A Preponderance of Power: National Security, the Truman Administration, and the Cold War*. Stanford, CA: Stanford University Press, 1992.

Legro, Jeffrey. *Cooperation under Fire: Anglo-German Restraint during World War II*. Ithaca, NY: Cornell University Press, 1995.

———. *Rethinking the World: Great Power Strategies and International Order*. Ithaca, NY: Cornell University Press, 2005.

Legro, Jeffrey W., and Andrew Moravcsik. "Is Anybody Still a Realist?" *International Security* 24 (Autumn 1999): 5–55.

Liddell Hart, Basil Henry. *Strategy*. 2nd rev. ed. New York: Meridian, 1991.

Locher, James R., III. *Victory on the Potomac: The Goldwater-Nichols Act Unifies the Pentagon*. College Station: Texas A&M University Press, 2004.

Logevall, Fredrik. *Choosing War: The Lost Chance for Peace and the Escalation of War in Vietnam.* Berkeley: University of California Press, 1999.

Long, Austin. *Doctrine of Eternal Recurrence: The U.S. Military and Counterinsurgency Doctrine, 1960–1970 and 2003–2006.* Santa Monica, CA: Rand, 2008.

Lord, Carnes. *The Presidency and the Management of National Security.* New York: Free Press, 1988.

Maechling, Charles. "Camelot, Robert Kennedy, and Counter-Insurgency: A Memoir." *Virginia Quarterly Review* (Summer 1999): 438–58.

Mahnken, Thomas G. "The American Way of War in the Twenty-First Century." In *Democracies and Small Wars,* edited by Efraim Inbar. Portland, OR: Frank Cass, 2003.

———. *Uncovering Ways of War: U.S. Intelligence and Foreign Military Innovation, 1918–1941.* Ithaca, NY: Cornell University Press, 2002.

Malkasian, Carter. "Counterinsurgency in Iraq." In *Counterinsurgency in Modern Warfare,* edited by Daniel Marston and Carter Malkasian. Oxford: Osprey, 2008.

———. "Toward a Better Understanding of Attrition: The Korean and Vietnam Wars." *Journal of Military History* 68 (July 2004): 911–42.

Mann, Jim. *Rise of the Vulcans: The History of Bush's War Cabinet.* New York: Penguin Books, 2004.

Mao Zedong. *Selected Writings of Mao Tse-tung.* Beijing: Foreign Language Press, 1986.

March, James G., and Johan P. Olsen. *Rediscovering Institutions: The Organizational Basis of Politics.* New York: Free Press, 1989.

March, James G., and Herbert A. Simon. *Organizations.* New York: Wiley, 1958.

Martin, Lisa L., and Beth A. Simmons. "Theories and Empirical Studies of International Institutions." *International Organization* 52 (Autumn 1998): 729–57.

May, Ernest R. "Conclusions: Capabilities and Proclivities." In *Knowing One's Enemies: Intelligence Assessment before the Two World Wars,* edited by Ernest R. May. Princeton, NJ: Princeton University Press, 1984.

Maynard, Christopher. *Out of the Shadow: George H. W. Bush and the End of the Cold War.* College Station: Texas A&M University Press, 2008.

McAllister, James. "The Lost Revolution: Edward Lansdale and the American Defeat in Vietnam, 1964–1968." *Small Wars and Insurgencies* 14 (2003).

McClellan, Scott. *What Happened: Inside the Bush White House and Washington's Culture of Deception.* New York: Public Affairs, 2008.

McClintock, Michael. *Instruments of Statecraft: U.S. Guerilla Warfare, Counter-Insurgency, Counter-Terrorism, 1940–1990.* New York: Pantheon Books, 1992.

McCubbins, Mathew D., and Thomas Schwartz. "Congressional Oversight Overlooked: Police Patrols versus Fire Alarms." *American Journal of Political Science* 28 (February 1, 1984): 165–79.

McGarrell, Edmund F., and Kip Schlegel. "The Implementation of Federally Funded Multijurisdictional Drug Task Forces: Organizational Structure and Interagency Relationships." *Journal of Criminal Justice* 21 (1993): 231–44.

McGarvey, Patrick J. "DIA: Intelligence to Please." *Washington Monthly* 11 (July 1970).

McMaster, H. R. *Dereliction of Duty: Lyndon Johnson, Robert McNamara, the Joint Chiefs of Staff, and the Lies That Led to Vietnam.* New York: HarperCollins, 1997.

McNamara, Robert S. *In Retrospect: The Tragedy and Lessons of Vietnam.* New York: Times Books, 1995.

Mearsheimer, John J. *Conventional Deterrence.* Ithaca, NY: Cornell University Press, 1983.

———. "The False Promise of International Institutions." *International Security* 19, no. 3 (1995/94): 5–49. doi:10.2307/2539078.

———. *The Tragedy of Great Power Politics.* New York: Norton, 2001.

Metz, Steven. *Decisionmaking in Operation Iraqi Freedom: Removing Saddam Hussein by Force.* Carlisle, PA: Strategic Studies Institute, U.S. Army War College, 2010.

————. *Iraq and the Evolution of American Strategy*. Washington, DC: Potomac Books, 2008.

Miller, Gary J. *Managerial Dilemmas: The Political Economy of Hierarchy*. New York: Cambridge University Press, 1992.

Milner, Helen V. *Interests, Institutions, and Information: Domestic Politics and International Relations*. Princeton, NJ: Princeton University Press, 1997.

Moe, Terry M. "The Politics of Structural Choice: Toward a Theory of Public Bureaucracy." In *Organizational Theory: From Chester Barnard to the Present and Beyond*, edited by Oliver E. Williamson. Expanded ed. New York: Oxford University Press, 1995.

Moravcsik, Andrew. "Taking Preferences Seriously: A Liberal Theory of International Politics." *International Organization* 51 (Autumn 1997): 513-53.

Morgan, Patrick M. *Deterrence Now*. Cambridge Studies in International Relations 89. New York: Cambridge University Press, 2003.

Moyar, Mark. *Triumph Forsaken: The Vietnam War, 1954-1965*. New York: Cambridge University Press, 2006.

Nagl, John A. *Learning to Eat Soup with a Knife: Counterinsurgency Lessons from Malaya and Vietnam*. Chicago: University of Chicago Press, 2005.

National Commission on Terrorist Attacks upon the United States. *The 9/11 Commission Report: Final Report of the National Commission on Terrorist Attacks upon the United States*. Authorized ed. New York: Norton, 2004.

Nelson, Anna Kasten. "The 'Top of Policy Hill': President Eisenhower and the National Security Council." *Diplomatic History* 7 (October 1983): 307-26.

North, Douglass C. "Epilogue: Economic Performance through Time." In *Empirical Studies in Institutional Change*, edited by Lee J. Alston, Thrainn Eggertsson, and Douglass C. North. New York: Cambridge University Press, 1996.

————. *Institutions, Institutional Change, and Economic Performance*. New York: Cambridge University Press, 1990.

Nye, Joseph S. *The Future of Power*. New York: Public Affairs, 2011.

O'Conner, Robert E., and Larry D. Spence. "Communication Disturbance in a Welfare Bureaucracy: A Case for Self-Management." *Journal of Sociology and Social Welfare* 4 (1976).

O'Toole, Laurence J., Jr. "Interorganizational Communication: Opportunities and Challenges for Public Administration." In *Handbook of Administrative Communication*, edited by James L. Garnett and Alexander Kouzmin. New York: Marcel Dekker, 1997.

Olson, Mancur. *The Logic of Collective Action: Public Goods and the Theory of Groups*. Cambridge, MA: Harvard University Press, 1971.

Ornstein, Norman J., and Thomas E. Mann. "When Congress Checks Out." *Foreign Affairs* 85 (2006).

Osgood, Robert Endicott. *Limited War: The Challenge to American Strategy*. Chicago: University of Chicago Press, 1957.

————. *Limited War Revisited*. A Westview Special Study. Boulder, CO: Westview Press, 1979.

Ostrom, Elinor. *Understanding Institutional Diversity*. Princeton, NJ: Princeton University Press, 2005.

Owen, John M. *The Clash of Ideas in World Politics: Transnational Networks, States, and Regime Change, 1510-2010*. Princeton, NJ: Princeton University Press, 2010.

————. *Liberal Peace, Liberal War: American Politics and International Security*. Ithaca, NY: Cornell University Press, 1997.

Packer, George. *The Assassins' Gate: America in Iraq*. New York: Farrar, Straus and Giroux, 2005.

Palmer, Gregory. *The McNamara Strategy and the Vietnam War: Program Budgeting in the Pentagon, 1960-1968*. New York: Greenwood Press, 1978.

Pape, Robert A. *Bombing to Win: Air Power and Coercion in War*. Ithaca, NY: Cornell University Press, 1996.

Pfiffner, James P. "The Contemporary Presidency: Decision Making in the Bush White House." *Presidential Studies Quarterly* 39 (June 2009): 363-84.

———. "US Blunders in Iraq: De-Baathification and Disbanding the Army." *Intelligence and National Security* 25 (February 2010): 76-85.

Pillar, Paul R. "Intelligence, Policy, and the War in Iraq." *Foreign Affairs* 85 (March 2006): 15-27.

Pious, Richard M. *Why Presidents Fail*. Lanham, MD: Rowman and Littlefield, 2008.

Polsky, Andrew Joseph. *Elusive Victories: The American Presidency at War*. New York: Oxford University Press, 2012.

Porter, Roger B. *Presidential Decision Making: The Economic Policy Board*. New York: Cambridge University Press, 1980.

Posen, Barry R. *Inadvertent Escalation: Conventional War and Nuclear Risks*. Ithaca, NY: Cornell University Press, 1991.

———. *The Sources of Military Doctrine: France, Britain, and Germany between the World Wars*. Ithaca, NY: Cornell University Press, 1984.

Posen, Barry R., and Andrew L. Ross. "Competing Visions for U.S. Grand Strategy." *International Security* 21 (Winter 1996/97): 5-53.

Powell, Colin L. *My American Journey*. Rev. ed. New York: Ballantine Books, 2003.

Prados, John. *Keepers of the Keys: A History of the National Security Council from Truman to Bush*. New York: Morrow, 1991.

Press, Daryl G. "The Myth of Air Power in the Persian Gulf War and the Future of Warfare." *International Security* 26 (Autumn 2001): 5-44.

Pressman, Jeremy. *Warring Friends: Alliance Restraint in International Politics*. Ithaca, NY: Cornell University Press, 2008.

Preston, Andrew. "The Little State Department: McGeorge Bundy and the National Security Council Staff, 1961-65." *Presidential Studies Quarterly* 31 (December 2001): 635-59.

Priest, Dana. *The Mission: Waging War and Keeping Peace with America's Military*. New York: W. W. Norton, 2003.

Protheroe, Gerald J. "Limiting America's Engagement: Roger Hilsman's Vietnam War, 1961-1963." *Diplomacy and Statecraft* 19 (2008): 263-88.

Qiang Zhai. "Beijing and the Vietnam Conflict, 1964-1965." In *CWIHP Bulletin*. Vols. 6-7. Washington, DC: Woodrow Wilson International Center for Scholars, 1995.

———. *China and the Vietnam Wars, 1950-1975*. Chapel Hill: University of North Carolina Press, 2000.

———. "Reassessing China's Role in the Vietnam War: Some Mysteries Explored." In *China and the United States: A New Cold War History*, edited by Xiaobing Li and Hongshan Li. Lanham, MD: University Press of America, 1998.

Rathmell, Andrew. "Planning Post-Conflict Reconstruction in Iraq: What Can We Learn?" *International Affairs* 81 (October 2005): 1013-38.

Record, Jeffrey. *Beating Goliath: Why Insurgencies Win*. Washington, DC: Potomac Books, 2007.

———. *Dark Victory: America's Second War against Iraq*. Annapolis, MD: Naval Institute Press, 2004.

———. *The Wrong War: Why We Lost in Vietnam*. Annapolis, MD: Naval Institute Press, 1998.

Reiter, Dan. "Exploring the Bargaining Model of War." *Perspectives on Politics* 1 (2003): 27-43.

———. *How Wars End*. Princeton, NJ: Princeton University Press, 2009.

Reiter, Dan, and Allan C. Stam. *Democracies at War*. Princeton, NJ: Princeton University Press, 2002.

Rice, Condoleezza. *No Higher Honor: A Memoir of My Years in Washington*. New York: Crown, 2011.

Richelson, Jeffrey T. "Presidential Directives and National Security Policy." *National Security Archive*. http://nsarchive.chadwyck.com/collections/content/PR/essayx.jsp.

Ricks, Thomas E. *Fiasco: The American Military Adventure in Iraq.* New York: Penguin Press, 2006.

Roe, Patrick. *The Dragon Strikes: China and the Korean War, June–December 1950.* Novato, CA: Presidio Press, 2000.

Rogers, Frank E. "Sino-American Relations and the Vietnam War, 1964–66." *China Quarterly* 66 (June 1976): 293–314.

Rosato, Sebastian. "The Flawed Logic of Democratic Peace Theory." *American Political Science Review* 97 (November 2003): 585–602.

Rose, Gideon. *How Wars End: Why We Always Fight the Last Battle; a History of American Intervention from World War I to Afghanistan.* New York: Simon and Schuster, 2010.

Rose, P. K. "Perceptions and Reality: Two Strategic Intelligence Mistakes in Korea, 1950." *Studies in Intelligence* (Fall/Winter 2001).

Rose, Richard. "Organizing Issues In and Organizing Problems Out." In *The Managerial Presidency*, edited by James P. Pfiffner. Pacific Grove, CA: Brooks/Cole 1991.

Rosen, Nir. *In the Belly of the Green Bird: The Triumph of the Martyrs in Iraq.* New York: Simon and Schuster, 2006.

Rosen, Stephen Peter. "Net Assessment as an Analytical Concept." In *On Not Confusing Ourselves: Essays on National Security Strategy in Honor of Albert and Roberta Wohlstetter*, edited by Andrew W. Marshall, J. J. Martin, and Henry S. Rowen. Boulder, CO: Westview Press, 1991.

———. "Vietnam and the American Theory of Limited War." *International Security* 7 (October 1, 1982): 83–113.

———. *War and Human Nature.* Princeton, NJ: Princeton University Press, 2005.

Rothkopf, David J. *Running the World: The Inside Story of the National Security Council and the Architects of American Power.* New York: Public Affairs, 2005.

Rowen, Henry S. "Inchon in the Desert: My Rejected Plan." *National Interest* 40 (Summer 1995).

Royle, Trevor. *Crimea: The Great Crimean War, 1854–1856.* New York: St. Martin's Press, 2004.

Rudalevige, Andrew. "The Structure of Leadership: Presidents, Hierarchies, and Information Flow." *Presidential Studies Quarterly* 35 (2005): 333–60.

Rumsfeld, Donald. *Known and Unknown: A Memoir.* New York: Sentinel, 2011.

Sartori, Anne E. *Deterrence by Diplomacy.* Princeton, NJ: Princeton University Press, 2005.

Schafer, Mark, and Scott Crichlow. *Groupthink versus High-Quality Decision Making in International Relations.* New York: Columbia University Press, 2010.

Schandler, Herbert Y. "U.S. Military Victory in Vietnam: A Dangerous Illusion?" In *Argument without End: In Search of Answers to the Vietnam Tragedy*, edited by Robert S. McNamara, James G. Blight, and Robert K. Brigham. New York: Public Affairs, 1999.

Schelling, Thomas C. *Arms and Influence.* New Haven, CT: Yale University Press, 1966.

Schiff, Rebecca L. "Civil-Military Relations Reconsidered: A Theory of Concordance." *Armed Forces and Society* 22 (October 1, 1995): 7–24.

Schnabel, James F. *United States Army in the Korean War, Policy and Direction: The First Year.* Washington, DC: United States Army, 1972.

Schnabel, James F., and Robert J. Watson. *The History of the Joint Chiefs of Staff: The Joint Chiefs of Staff and National Policy.* Vol. 3, *1950–1951, The Korean War, Part One.* Washington, DC: Office of the Chairman of the Joint Chiefs of Staff, Office of Joint History, 1998.

Schulzinger, Robert. "The Johnson Administration, China, and the Vietnam War." In *Re-Examining the Cold War: U.S.-China Diplomacy, 1954–1973*, edited by Robert S. Ross and Changbin Jiang. Harvard East Asian Monographs 203. Cambridge, MA: Harvard University Asia Center, 2001.

———. *A Time for War: The United States and Vietnam, 1941–1975.* New York: Oxford University Press, 1997.

Schwarzkopf, H. Norman. *It Doesn't Take a Hero: The Autobiography of General H. Norman Schwarzkopf.* New York: Bantam Books, 1992.

Schweller, Randall L. "Unanswered Threats: A Neoclassical Realist Theory of Underbalancing." *International Security* 29 (October 2004): 159-201.

———. *Unanswered Threats: Political Constraints on the Balance of Power*. Princeton, NJ: Princeton University Press, 2006.

Shanker, Thom, and Eric Schmitt. "Rumsfeld Says Iraq Is Collapsing, Lists 8 Objectives of War." *New York Times*, March 22, 2003.

Simon, Herbert A. *Administrative Behavior: A Study of Decision-Making Processes in Administrative Organizations*. 4th ed. New York: Free Press, 1997.

———. "Applying Information Technology to Organization Design." *Public Administration Review* 33, no. 3 (1973): 268-78. doi:10.2307/974804.

Sinno, Abdulkader H. *Organizations at War in Afghanistan and Beyond*. Ithaca, NY: Cornell University Press, 2008.

Siverson, Randolph M. *The Diffusion of War: A Study of Opportunity and Willingness*. Ann Arbor: University of Michigan Press, 1991.

Smith, Bromley K. *Organizational History of the National Security Council during the Kennedy and Johnson Administrations*. Washington, DC: National Security Council, 1988.

Smith, Russell Jack. *The Unknown CIA: My Three Decades with the Agency*. Washington, DC: Pergamon-Brassey's, 1989.

Smoke, Richard. *War: Controlling Escalation*. Cambridge, MA: Harvard University Press, 1977.

Snyder, Jack L. "Civil-Military Relations and the Cult of the Offensive, 1914 and 1984." *International Security* 9 (July 1, 1984): 108-46.

———. *The Ideology of the Offensive: Military Decision Making and the Disasters of 1914*. Ithaca, NY: Cornell University Press, 1984.

Snyder, Richard C., H. W. Bruck, and Burton Sapin, eds. *Foreign Policy Decision-Making: An Approach to the Study of International Politics*. New York: Free Press of Glencoe, 1962.

Sparrow, Bartholomew H. "Realism's Practitioner: Brent Scowcroft and the Making of the New World Order, 1989-1993." *Diplomatic History* 34 (2010): 141-75.

Stein, Arthur A. *Why Nations Cooperate: Circumstance and Choice in International Relations*. Ithaca, NY: Cornell University Press, 1990.

Stein, Janice Gross. "Deterrence and Compellence in the Gulf, 1990-91: A Failed or Impossible Task?" *International Security* 17 (October 1992): 147-79.

Steinbruner, John D. *The Cybernetic Theory of Decision: New Dimensions of Political Analysis*. Princeton, NJ: Princeton University Press, 1974.

Sterling-Folker, Jennifer. "Realist Environment, Liberal Process, and Domestic-Level Variables." *International Studies Quarterly* 41 (1997): 1-26.

Stiglitz, Joseph E. *The Three Trillion Dollar War: The True Cost of the Iraq Conflict*. New York: W. W. Norton, 2008.

Stinchcombe, Arthur L. *Information and Organizations*. Berkeley: University of California Press, 1990.

Stolberg, Alan G. *How Nation-States Craft National Security Strategy Documents*. Carlisle, PA: Strategic Studies Institute, U.S. Army War College, 2012.

Stueck, William W. *The Korean War: An International History*. Princeton, NJ: Princeton University Press, 1997.

———. *Rethinking the Korean War: A New Diplomatic and Strategic History*. Princeton, NJ: Princeton University Press, 2002.

———. *The Road to Confrontation: American Policy toward China and Korea*. Chapel Hill: University of North Carolina Press, 1981.

Sun Tzu. *The Art of War*. Translated by Roger T. Ames. New York: Ballantine Books, 1993.

Suskind, Ron. *The One Percent Doctrine: Deep Inside America's Pursuit of Its Enemies since 9/11*. New York: Simon and Schuster, 2007.

Taliaferro, Jeffrey W. *Balancing Risks: Great Power Intervention in the Periphery*. Ithaca, NY: Cornell University Press, 2004.

———. "Neoclassical Realism and Resource Extraction: State Building for Future War." In *Neoclassical Realism, the State, and Foreign Policy*, edited by Steven E. Lobell, Norrin M. Ripsman, and Jeffrey W. Taliaferro. Cambridge: Cambridge University Press, 2009.

———. "Security Seeking under Anarchy: Defensive Realism Revisited." *International Security* 25 (Winter 2000/2001): 128–61.

Taubman, Philip. *Secret Empire: Eisenhower, the CIA, and the Hidden Story of America's Space Espionage*. New York: Simon and Schuster, 2003.

Taylor, A. J. P. *The Struggle for Mastery in Europe, 1848–1918*. Oxford: Clarendon Press, 1954.

Tenet, George. *At the Center of the Storm: The CIA during America's Time of Crisis*. New York: Harper Perennial, 2007.

Tetlock, Philip E., and Aaron Belkin. "Counterfactual Thought Experiments in World Politics: Logical, Methodological, and Psychological Perspectives." In *Counterfactual Thought Experiments in World Politics*, edited by Philip E. Tetlock and Aaron Belkin. Princeton, NJ: Princeton University Press, 1996.

Thompson, Alexander. *Channels of Power: The UN Security Council and U.S. Statecraft in Iraq*. Ithaca, NY: Cornell University Press, 2009.

Tolson, John J. *Airmobility, 1961–1971*. Washington, DC: GPO, 1973.

Troy, Thomas F. *Donovan and the CIA: A History of the Establishment of the Central Intelligence Agency*. Frederick, MD: University Publications of America, 1981.

Trubowitz, Peter. *Politics and Strategy: Partisan Ambition and American Statecraft*. Princeton, NJ: Princeton University Press, 2011.

Truman, Harry S. *Memoirs*. Vol. 1, *Years of Trial and Hope*. Garden City, NY: Doubleday, 1956.

———. "United States Policy toward Formosa: Statement by President Truman." *Department of State Bulletin* 22 (March 1950).

Tucker, Nancy Bernkopf, ed. *China Confidential: American Diplomats and Sino-American Relations, 1945–1996*. New York: Columbia University Press, 2001.

Twomey, Christopher P. *The Military Lens: Doctrinal Difference and Deterrence Failure in Sino-American Relations*. Ithaca, NY: Cornell University Press, 2010.

US Department of Defense. *Conduct of the Persian Gulf War: Final Report to Congress*. Washington, DC: Department of Defense, 1992.

US Marine Corps. *FMFRP 12–15, Small Wars Manual*. Washington, DC: GPO, 1940.

U.S. News & World Report. *Triumph without Victory: The Unreported History of the Persian Gulf War*. New York: Times Books, 1992.

Van Creveld, Martin. *Command in War*. Cambridge, MA: Harvard University Press, 1985.

VanDeMark, Brian. *Into the Quagmire: Lyndon Johnson and the Escalation of the Vietnam War*. New York: Oxford University Press, 1991.

Van Evera, Stephen. *Causes of War: Power and the Roots of Conflict*. Ithaca, NY: Cornell University Press, 1999.

———. "The Cult of the Offensive and the Origins of the First World War." *International Security* 9 (Summer 1984): 58–107.

Walcott, Charles Eliot, and Karen Marie Hult. *Governing the White House: From Hoover through LBJ*. Studies in Government and Public Policy. Lawrence: University Press of Kansas, 1995.

Warner, Michael. *Central Intelligence: Origin and Evolution*. Washington, DC: Central Intelligence Agency, 2001.

Watts, Duncan J. *Six Degrees: The Science of a Connected Age*. New York: W. W. Norton, 2003.

———. *Small Worlds: The Dynamics of Networks between Order and Randomness*. Princeton, NJ: Princeton University Press, 1999.

Watts, Duncan J., and Steven H. Strogatz. "Collective Dynamics of 'Small-World' Networks." *Nature* 393 (June 4, 1998).

Weiner, Tim. *Legacy of Ashes: The History of the CIA*. New York: Doubleday, 2007.

Welch, David A. "The Organizational Process and Bureaucratic Politics Paradigms: Retrospect and Prospect." *International Security* 17 (October 1, 1992): 112-46.

———. *Painful Choices: A Theory of Foreign Policy Change*. Princeton, NJ: Princeton University Press, 2005.

Westmoreland, William C. *A Soldier Reports*. New York: Da Capo Press, 1989.

Whiting, Allen S. *China Crosses the Yalu: The Decision to Enter the Korean War*. Stanford, CA: Stanford University Press, 1969.

———. "China's Role in the Vietnam War." In *The American War in Vietnam*, edited by Jayne Werner and David Hunt. Ithaca, NY: Cornell University Press, 1993.

———. *The Chinese Calculus of Deterrence: India and Indochina*. Ann Arbor: University of Michigan Press, 1975.

———. "Forecasting Chinese Foreign Policy: IR Theory vs. the Fortune Cookie." In *Chinese Foreign Policy: Theory and Practice*, edited by Thomas W. Robinson and David L. Shambaugh. New York: Oxford University Press, 1994.

Williamson, Oliver E. *The Economic Institutions of Capitalism: Firms, Markets, Relational Contracting*. New York: Free Press, 1985.

Wilson, Isaiah. "America's Anabasis." In *War in Iraq: Planning and Execution*, edited by Thomas G. Mahnken and Thomas A. Keaney. New York: Routledge, 2007.

Wolford, Scott, Dan Reiter, and Clifford J. Carrubba. "Information, Commitment, and War." *Journal of Conflict Resolution* 55 (August 1, 2011): 556-79.

Woods, Kevin M. "Iraqi Military Effectiveness." In *War in Iraq: Planning and Execution*, edited by Thomas G. Mahnken and Thomas A. Keaney. New York: Routledge, 2007.

Woods, Kevin, James Lacey, and Williamson Murray. "Saddam's Delusions: The View from the Inside." *Foreign Affairs* 85 (May 2006): 2-26.

Woodward, Bob. *The Commanders*. New York: Simon and Schuster, 1991.

———. *Plan of Attack*. New York: Simon and Schuster, 2004.

———. *State of Denial*. New York: Simon and Schuster, 2006.

Wright, Donald P., and Timothy R. Reese. *On Point II: Transition to the New Campaign: The United States Army in Operation Iraqi Freedom, May 2003-January 2005*. Fort Leavenworth, KS: Combat Studies Institute Press, 2008.

Xiaoming Zhang. "The Vietnam War, 1964-1969: A Chinese Perspective." *Journal of Military History* 60 (October 1996): 731-62.

Yang Kuisong. *Changes in Mao Zedong's Attitude toward the Indochina War, 1949-1973*. Translated by Qiang Zhai. Cold War International History Project Working Paper No. 34. Washington, DC: Woodrow Wilson International Center for Scholars, February 2002.

Yetiv, Steven A. *Explaining Foreign Policy: U.S. Decision-Making and the Persian Gulf War*. Baltimore: Johns Hopkins University Press, 2004.

Zegart, Amy B. *Flawed by Design: The Evolution of the CIA, JCS, and NSC*. Stanford, CA: Stanford University Press, 1999.

———. *Spying Blind: The CIA, the FBI, and the Origins of 9/11*. Princeton, NJ: Princeton University Press, 2007.

Zhang, Shu Guang. *Deterrence and Strategic Culture: Chinese-American Confrontations, 1949-1958*. Ithaca, NY: Cornell University Press, 1993.

———. *Mao's Military Romanticism: China and the Korean War, 1950-1953*. Lawrence: University Press of Kansas, 1995.

Index

National Security Action Memorandum
(NSAM) 288, 150, 277n2
National Security Council: ineffectiveness
of (Korean War), 64-65, 68-69, 72-73,
73-74, 79, 83, 91; ineffectiveness of (Iraq
War), 196-98, 199-200, 202, 203, 204-9,
219, 221, 228; positions of (Iraq War), 224,
223; reforms under Kennedy of, 109-11;
system of (Persian Gulf War), 152-56, 161,
162, 163-65, 180
National Security Directive (NSD) 1, 152-53, 156
National Security Directive (NSD) 45, 145, 150
National Security Directive (NSD) 54, 151,
176, 287n25
national security organizations. *See* organizations; *and specific organizations*
National Security Presidential Directive
(NSPD) 1, 196-97, 205
National Security Presidential Directive
(NSPD) 24, 201, 202, 208, 220-21, 222
National Security Strategy of the United States
of America, 188-91, 292n4, 292n6
neoliberal institutionalism, 11
new world order, 146, 181
9/11, 188-89, 190, 200, 203-4, 259
Nixon, Richard M., 196, 184
North, Douglass, 8, 246
North Korea: initial defeat of, 60; invasion
of, 61; 1950 invasion and, 57. *See also*
Korean War
NSC 68, 58, 69
NSC 81/1, 74, 78, 79, 82-84
NSC 81/2, 91
NSC Staff: and Iraq War, 198-200, 202, 205,
208, 219; and Korean War, 69, 83, 84; and
Persian Gulf War, 155; and Vietnam War,
109-10
NSC working group on Vietnam, 120-26
nuclear weapons: consideration of, during
Persian Gulf War, 147, 149, 151, 152,
167-68, 173, 175, 179, 203; consideration
of, during Vietnam War, 121-22, 123, 124,
141; and Iraq War, 188-92, 203, 221,
292n6, 292n9, 293n15, 293n22, 294n31

Office of Intelligence Research (OIR), 76
Office of Northeast Asian Affairs. *See* Allison,
John
Office of Reconstruction and Humanitarian
Assistance (ORHA): creation of, 192, 221,
227, 228; disbanding of, 202, 222; issues

of, 208, 219, 222, 227, 228; role, 202,
221-22, 208, 225
Office of Reports and Estimates (V), 65-67,
73. *See also* Central Intelligence Agency
Office of Research and Reports (ORR), 113
Office of Special Operations (OSO), 66
Office of Special Plans (OSP), 220, 223. *See
also* Feith, Douglas
Office of Strategic Services (OSS), 69
Office of Systems Analysis (OSA), 135-36
Office of the Secretary of Defense: and Iraq
War, 199, 206-7, 208, 215, 217, 220,
227-28, 229-30, 232, 242; and Persian
Gulf War, 173; and Vietnam War, 112-13,
119, 121, 134-37. *See also* Department of
State; Rumsfeld, Donald
Olsen, Johan, 37
operational measures for causal variables, 52-53
Operation CHROMITE, 60
Operation Desert Shield, 148, 165-66
Operation Desert Storm, 148, 151, 231, 249
Operation Scorpion, 174, 184
organizational culture theory: assessment of,
246-47; explanatory limitations of, 16;
and Iraq War, 16, 229, 231-33, 240-41;
and Korean War, 16, 94-96, 244-45; main
argument of, 16, 42-43; and Persian Gulf
War, 16, 144-45, 183-85, 238-39; and
propositions on strategic outcomes, 43-46;
and Vietnam War, 16, 140-41, 242-44
organizational theory (hierarchical): and addressing traditional limitations, 10; explanatory limitations of, 10-11; and hierarchical
structures, 10; and Korean War, 11; main
argument of, 10; and Persian Gulf War, 11
organizational theory (traditional): biased information and, 31; explanatory limitations
of, 9, 11, 42; main argument of, 8-9, 42.
See also Allison, Graham
organizations: coordination between, 3, 4, 9,
34; definition of, 8; divisions within, 10;
as implementers of strategy, 4; institutional setting of, 8, 11; versus institutions,
7-11; leaders and, 9, 11, 13-14, 17, 35; and
strategic outcomes, 11; and strategy design,
8, 12, 15-16, 31
Ostrom, Elinor, 33, 234
Owen, John M., 190, 261

Pace, Peter, 225
Panikkar, K. M., 84-86